The SOUND and the SILENCE

Tony Foster

NIMBUS
PUBLISHING LTD

Nimbus Publishing Limited
PO Box 9301, Station A
Halifax, NS B3K 5N5
(902) 455-4286

Design: Arthur B. Carter, Halifax
Printed and bound in Canada

Canadian Cataloguing in Publication Data
Foster, Tony, 1932-
The sound and the silence
Includes bibliographical references.
ISBN 1-55109-151-8
1. Bell, Alexander Graham, 1847-1922—Marriage. 2. Bell,
Mabel Gardiner Hubbard, 1859-1923. 3. Inventors—United States—
Biography. I. Title.
TK6143.B4F67 1996   621.385'092   C96-950056-4

He was always trying to re-create sound for her
and she was always trying to understand that sound....
She couldn't remember sound. And she wrote once
that she imagined it was something like the sound
of humming of the bees....

> Lilian Grosvenor Jones, one of Bell's
> granddaughters, to Joan Marshall for the
> Canadian Broadcasting Corporation.

In the last century six discoveries altered forever
the course of human destiny: nuclear fission, the
microchip, television, the radio, the telephone and
development of the airplane. This is a true story of
the man who was responsible for two of them ...
and the woman he loved.

FOREWORD

Alexander Graham Bell was born in 1847, in the tenth year of twenty-eight-year-old Queen Victoria's reign. The world's population stood at two billion. Canada was still a colony and part of the richest and most far-flung empire the world has ever seen. The United States of America had existed for only seven decades. James Polk, its eleventh president, was in the White House. The nation was less than fourteen years away from a tragic civil war that would cost a half million lives and either wound or maim over three times that number of its citizens. By the time Bell died in 1922, he had lived through the reigns of three British monarchs, eighteen American presidents, the Crimean War, the American Civil War, the Boer War, the First World War and a variety of lesser conflicts taking place about the world. He had seen the invention of electric lights, street cars, motor cars, high speed internal combustion engines, the development of radio communication, commercial aircraft, phonograph recording and the telephone—which he invented. It would be inaccurate to state that Bell was a twentieth-century man caught in the nineteenth century. He was a man of all centuries—curious, compassionate, artistic and loving. But above all else he was brilliant.

Before the invention of Morse's telegraph and Bell's telephone, people communicated by writing letters. Mail delivery within cities was prompt, sometimes within hours of mailing. Many cities had two deliveries a day. As a result, it was possible in London, Boston or New York to mail a letter in the early morning, have it delivered before noon and receive a reply in the late afternoon. People spent hours writing letters, notes, memos and personal diaries. These written records have become the principal source of information for all historical biographers. For the most part the telephone has replaced this medium of communication. It is ironic that Bell, the man most responsible for the slow demise of the personal written word, should have felt compelled to amass such a record of his own life in writing. The Bell Museum in Baddeck, Nova Scotia, and the Library of Congress in the United States, hold over five hundred volumes of handwritten notes dictated or written by Mabel and Alexander Graham Bell. Those volumes and personal letters between members of the Bell family form the basis of this book.

Feature film and television versions of any book are rarely satisfactory experiences either for the viewers or the writer. Due to time constraints, the need to condense a story's dramatic highlights into a screenplay results invariably in omitting huge sections of the book from which it was adapted. Like a diner hurrying from the table after a splendid hors d'oeuvre, the viewer is left with a sense of having missed the main course. For those who have or will see the television mini-series, this book should correct those omissions; for those who may never have an opportunity to view "The Sound and the Silence" television production, the full story upon which the series is based can be found between the covers of this book.

ACKNOWLEDGMENTS

In the late summer of 1984 I visited Beinn Bhreagh on a lovely sunny afternoon to meet and interview the five surviving Bell grandchildren, all in their seventies and early eighties. We sat in the main reception room before a huge fireplace and for nearly three hours with incredible patience and generosity of spirit, Dr. Mabel Grosvenor, Dr. Alexander Graham Bell (Sandy) Fairchild, Mrs. Gertrude Cayley, Mrs. Barbara Muller and Mrs. Carol Myers talked of their childhood memories at Beinn Bhreagh and Washington, and about their grandfather and grandmother. It was one of the most fascinating interviews I have ever conducted. The tape of this interview is on deposit with the Bell Museum in Baddeck.

My profound thanks to the Bell grandchildren, to Mrs. Lilias Toward Q.C. who started me on this project because of her book "Mabel Bell, Alexander's Silent Partner." Thanks also to Peter Wickwire Foster, my son, and to my other tireless researcher and daughter Emily Jane Wickwire Foster, for their invaluable help, hard work and travel. And above all to Janet Rosenstock and Dennis Adair, without whose guidance, editing, careful perusing and rewriting of the text, this book would not have been possible.

AUTHOR'S NOTE

This book is non-fiction in novelized form. It is based on the television presentation, "The Sound and the Silence," but goes beyond the actual script and scenes, and the written chapters do not necessarily coincide with the film.

Many of the scenes and descriptions in this book are a product of the author's imagination in the same way the sets of a television production are the product of the director's imagination. Other scenes are based on partial descriptions given in letters, journals, pictures and other research documents.

By the same token, dialogue is partially invented or partially based on the aforementioned materials. Where dialogue is quoted or paraphrased from actual letters or journals, it is duly footnoted. In all cases, an attempt has been made to remain true to the language of the period and to the characters as they are seen through their letters and journals, to the primary events in their lives, and to the events as they are historically recorded for posterity.

Part I

CHAPTER ONE

St. Andrews, Scotland, 1790

Alexander Bell was born in St. Andrews, County Fife, Scotland on 3 March 1790, nearly a hundred years before the invention of the telephone by his grandson, Alexander Graham Bell. The east coast town would achieve international fame two centuries later for its golf course. The elder Bell came from a family of shoemakers. As was expected within the layered strata of pre-Victorian society, he began his apprenticeship at the age of fourteen after a rudimentary education.

"In those days the ability to read, write and do your sums was considered a perfectly adequate education for the lower classes and my grandfather might have spent the rest of his life making shoes for a living had he not met and married my grandmother, in 1814," Alexander Graham Bell reflected in his later years.

"In my grandfather's eyes, the seventeen-year-old Elizabeth Coville was much too beautiful for her own good. She had the pick of any man above her social class in the town, most with considerably more to offer her than he did."

Nevertheless, Elizabeth fixed her calculating gaze on the tall and very handsome twenty-three-year-old shoemaker. She arranged a propitious moment and Alexander proposed. Elizabeth accepted—on condition. If she married him they must move to the city where there were more opportunities. Blinded by her charms, Alexander promised her everything she wanted, even agreeing to abandon his profession and try his luck as an actor on the Edinburgh stage. They were married soon after and left town.

Showbiz held the same titillating fascination for the public then, as now. Yet even for the most gifted actors it was, and remains, a precarious occupation. With his deep voice and handsome features Alexander had no difficulty finding a job. On stage his commanding presence, dramatically dark piercing eyes, unusual height—over six feet—and jet black hair provided the illusion of a man of substance.

In January of 1818, after only a year in the profession, James Dibdin's *Annuals of the Edinburgh Stage* commented that the role in *Rob Roy* of: "Andrew Fairservice, spoken by Mr. Bell in the Scotch dialect was indeed very amusing." But after a couple of years with a second-rate theatrical company performing in underpaid minor roles, Alexander discovered himself typecast as the burly Scot cuckold who, by the end of the first act, emerges as the butt of a joke and, in the last act, loses the heroine to the leading man. He also realized that the income of a part-time actor was not enough to support a wife and their two sons, David Charles, born in 1818, and Alexander Melville, born a year later, plus the third child that Elizabeth was expecting. As his acting career shrivelled away, he was forced to take what he called the "responsible and honourable position of prompter."[1] He decided to move back to St. Andrews. At home, they would be among supportive relatives while Alexander tried to find more practical employment. Over Elizabeth's violent objections, they fled the city, owing several months rent and a variety of other creditors. Returning home bankrupt and a failure was a bitter pill for Elizabeth to swallow.

To make matters worse, Alexander's father refused to take him back into the family business, telling him that his hands were too soft and his skills too dated to be of value. Every other avenue for employment that Alexander tried either required experience that he did not have, or paid too little to support his family. The weeks passed with no prospects. His father coldly suggested they go back to Edinburgh. Frustrated, Alexander decided to try something unconventional. The Edinburgh stage had forced him to perfect his diction and pronunciation, and had vastly increased his vocabulary. He would put those assets to work.

He cleaned his best suit, polished his shoes and decided to go out knocking on the doors of wealthy citizens, presenting himself as a "Professor of Phonetics." Did parents want their children to grow up with a regional accent? Certainly not. Regional accents placed aspiring merchants and landowners at a distinct social, cultural and political disadvantage. Success in life came from proper pronunciation and enunciation. An Edinburgh accent had become the recognized "lingua franca" of Scotland. Alexander could teach children to speak in a proper Edinburgh accent. The parents bought the story and "Professor" Alexander Bell was on his way to becoming a teacher.

His students, like most children, were natural mimics. Within a few weeks, he had them speaking properly accented Scottish Edinburgh English. Although he had bluffed his way into the profession, any initial misgivings he had were dispelled. To his delight, he discovered that he had a natural ability to teach, and teaching was a far more respectable profession than acting. Filled with self-confidence, he arranged a series of public lectures and recitals on the subject of elocution in the Town Hall and in the process became a regional celebrity. The astonished parents lost no time in bragging about Professor Bell's unusual teaching abilities. The principal of the local grammar school asked him to join the teaching staff as a boarding English Master. His future appeared limitless. But, by 1826, the market had been saturated. Learning proper enunciation was not a high priority for the townspeople. He decided to shift his operational base to the much larger town of Dundee. Fortunately, his reputation followed him. He had no difficulty in re-establishing himself. His mornings were spent teaching elocution, his evenings on house calls for special tutoring sessions. He was a superb instructor, capable of producing impressive results—and his list of clients grew, so that by his second year in Dundee, Alexander had become modestly prosperous.

~~

Unfortunately, his elocution business took up so much of his time that he failed to notice that his wife had begun an affair with William Murry, rector of Dundee Academy. By the time Alexander discovered the affair, everyone in town knew about the scandal.

Shortly after Christmas 1829, he completed writing a book on speech and needed a publisher. He asked Elizabeth to visit an Edinburgh publishing firm that had expressed an interest in the book. Elizabeth took the opportunity to arrange a rendezvous in the city with her lover. On their second day in Edinburgh, a friend of Alexander's saw the couple entering a third-class hotel where they had registered as Mr. and Mrs. Gordon MacDonald. Alexander was informed of Elizabeth's duplicity and confronted his wife upon her return. She offered him a convoluted explanation then hastily wrote to Murry in order to ensure their stories would coincide. She sent her letter with the guard of the Edinburgh coach in the hope of connecting with the returning Murry. The letter never reached him but wound up in the clenched fist of Alexander Bell. His wife's final desperate letter to Murry concluded with the solemn promise, "I shall never betray you." [2] Bell was crushed; while Elizabeth, in a moment of panic, realizing that she had been discovered, pleaded with her servant girl to help her commit suicide. The girl refused and Elizabeth survived only to see her marriage end in divorce court. During the proceedings she testified that Alexander was the father of their servant's unborn child. Bell never admitted to the claim and, in the end, the chief magistrate decided that "Mr. Bell's private character has been irreproachable." [3] In all, the divorce cost Alexander £800, a sizable sum for the time.

"The irreparable damage to my grandfather's reputation and name in the Dundee community was more than enough to extinguish his fledgling elocution business. He sued William Murry for compensation. However, a legal technicality forced him eventually to settle for £300."

The year 1833 had not been good. Alexander's reputation in Scotland had been badly tarnished, his business lay in ruins and his wife was gone. He decided to move to London, taking his sickly son, Alexander "Sandy" Melville Bell, and his oldest son, David, with him. Elizabeth returned to Gauldry, Scotland, with their eleven-year-old daughter. Five years after his parents divorced David wrote his mother: "You will be anxious to know if I have given up the stage, most likely I will once again tempt the angry main. Of my ultimate success either as a teacher or an actor I have no doubt. My fears so far as the stage is concerned, arise from its uncertainty and bad name." [4] Like his father,

David had become a teacher of English and elocution in a small Durhamshire academy. He commented on how his consumptive brother Melville's health had improved since visiting her. "At least his good looks obtained him several compliments. He had much need of some fresh air after his long confinement."[5]

⁓

In London, Bell found at last a publisher for his book *The Practical Elocutionist*. The book used comma-like symbols to indicate where one should pause and breathe—an innovative idea for teaching public speakers. In 1836, he published another short work called *Stammering and other Impediments of Speech*. His next work in 1837 was a publication of the New Testament complete with notations on proper elocution. By the following year, he had regained his position of respect to the extent that he was now referred to as the celebrated "professor of elocution." During his travels around London, he met his second wife—the widow of a local publisher. This marriage was a happy one and it endured until she died, twenty years later.

Meanwhile, his son Melville—who was now working as an apprentice draper's assistant—had fallen ill. The dust and fine debris in the shop had caused his health to deteriorate. Alexander quickly made arrangements with a family and friends in St. John's, Newfoundland, to take him in. The air in the colonies was much cleaner than the air in London.

The move probably saved his son's life, and for the rest of his days Melville believed that the brisk Canadian air contained a variety of magical healing properties that were absent in the grimy soot-encrusted cities of England. In Newfoundland, Melville rose each day with the sun to row in the harbour. He called it the "finest exercise in the world."[6] As his health improved he began taking an active role in the community; energetically promoting the cause for shorter working hours, setting up Shakespeare study groups, mounting small-scale productions and giving lessons in elocution, using the methods learned from his father. Melville was gratified by the success of these lessons. The sense of achievement at being able to liberate stammerers from their affliction and enable them to develop a properly articulated voice were his greatest rewards. By the time he returned to London in

1842, Melville had developed an intense interest in his father's work. Alexander, realizing for the first time his son's potential as a teacher, offered him a share of the business. They became a team. Each day that Melville taught students his appetite for information grew, and he soon discovered how little material existed on the subject of speech and elocution. He decided to research the subject for himself. Meanwhile, his brother David had married and had two children. He was now a teacher of speech and a respected member of the community. Taking a cue from David, Melville turned his attention to finding a wife. "I intend to get married as soon as I can meet with a young lady to please me."[7]

In 1843, he met Eliza Grace Symonds in Edinburgh. Recalling the incident years later, Melville Bell wrote to his grandchildren that: "It was not exactly a case of love at first sight but it was a case of struck at first sight. I found the lady very pretty, slim, and delicate looking and with the sweetest expression I think I ever saw. But she was deaf, and could only hear with the help of an ear-tube. My sympathy was deeply excited. But she was so cheerful under her affliction that sympathy soon turned to admiration." Eliza, was thirty-four, nearly ten years older than Melville and lived with her widowed mother. She seemed destined to be a spinster. A portrait of Melville during this period shows a handsome young man with the family's dark eyes and wavy jet-black hair. Eliza, a competent miniature painter, was probably the artist responsible for the portrait. Melville spoke to Eliza about his hope for a future in the research of speech and speech problems. He decided to stay in Edinburgh and rent several empty rooms in the same building as Eliza. They were married six months later on 19 July 1844. Soon after the honeymoon, they found a house for a good price in the respected neighbourhood of Charlotte Square. Eliza managed the house while Melville's earnings continued to grow. It was a happy marriage based on mutual respect. Later in life Melville summed up their relationship: "She was so kind, so gentle, so loving that during the fifty-two years of our companionship, I never saw a frown on her sweet face."[8] Their first two sons were born in the Charlotte Square house; Melville James in 1845, nicknamed "Melly," and Alexander, on 3 March 1847. As his fortunes grew and his family expanded, Melville moved to much grander accommodations at 13

Hope Street. The new house had a splendid view of the square and St. George's Church. Here, their last child, Edward Charles Bell, was born in 1848.

A miniature painting of Alexander by his mother, completed when he was ten depicts a serious little boy with dark, thoughtful eyes, a shock of black hair and a determined jaw. Like all children, Aleck, as they called him, had an insatiable curiosity about things in general. He saw everything as a mystery waiting to be solved—a trait that would remain with him throughout life. His first memory was of being lost in a wheat-field on Ferny Hill, near Edinburgh. The wheat tops were far above his head, making it impossible to tell which way was out. "I crept into the middle of the field and sat very quietly for a long time listening intently to see if I could hear the wheat grow. Unable to find my way out, I cried myself to sleep." After a frantic search, he awoke to hear his father calling him and was carried back to the safety of his mother's arms. He had all the usual childhood ills, including scarlet fever and its accompanying delirium. Lying in a large four-poster, he became transfixed by the figure of a cloaked female at the end of his bed. In the darkened room, he could barely make out her shadowy features except for the staring eyes. His curiosity overcame his fear of the ghost-like image, and he crept to the end of the bed to touch her cloak. The cloak and cap turned out to be empty and hung lifeless upon the bed post. Satisfied, he crawled back under the covers only to see that the cloak had once again come alive. In a desperate attempt to free himself of the ghost, he pulled it down. Years later he recalled that: "This did not better matters, however, for now I saw the ghostly figure lying near me on the bed staring at me with shadowy eyes. I could stand the strain no longer and, thoroughly alarmed, I screamed for help."[9]

Aleck's fascination with the written and spoken word began early. When a friend of the family came to visit, the four-year-old Aleck crept into the guest's room and discovered several sheets of writing paper and an inkwell on the writing desk. He decided to try writing a letter. He put the scribbles in an envelope with an appropriate scrawl for an address. A further search produced a stamp. He went to one of the servants and asked politely if she would post his letter. The girl laughed. Later, Aleck was called into his father's study. He recalled that "up to this moment I had no conception that I had done anything wrong: but, when I entered my father's presence a guilty feeling came over me, and I hid my letter behind my back. My father wanted to know what I had in my hand so I showed him the letter. He laughed, and asked me where I got the stamp. Then I knew that something was wrong, and stammered that my mother had given it to me."[10] The senior Bell asked his son to bring his mother to the study. Instead, he ran upstairs to the guest room and hid in a small corner between the wardrobe and the wall. A search was organised to find him. Aleck sat silently as the searchers hunted about the guest room. They opened the wardrobe and checked the drawer below it. Nothing. He held his breath until they left the room. He remained hidden past supper and well into the evening—too afraid to move or reply to his father's anxious shouts and promises to forego any retribution. Melville decided to search the house one more time before calling the police. Both parents were worried that he might run away. Once more they came to search the wardrobe. This time they looked behind it and found the terrified boy. Still unwilling to come out, the entire wardrobe had to be moved aside. Aleck was then hauled down to Melville's study for a thrashing.

⁓

Eliza saw to it that the family attended church on a regular basis. Even though Melville remained a religious sceptic throughout most of his life, he did attend the Sunday services in order to copy down the sermon in his stylized shorthand. During the services the boys helped their deaf mother find the bible and hymn selections so that she could follow along. After the service Melville read his shorthand copy of the sermon to Eliza at home, shouting into her ear trumpet. Aleck turned out to be the most pious of the three boys, "at least until I reached years of discretion," he recalled later. Although Eliza's artistic abilities seemed to have bypassed her three sons, Aleck did inherit her ear for music and played the piano with considerable natural talent. He could play some selections the first time he saw the music. By resting her hearing tube upon the piano, Eliza could distinguish the notes remarkably well. Mother and son filled the house with Scottish melodies.

"After teaching me as much as she knew, my mother hired Monsieur Auguste Benoit Bertini, an accomplished pianist, to complete my musical education. My playing was not driven by any personal artistic necessity to express myself, but rather for pleasure and the knowledge that it was something I knew I could do well."

After Bertini died, any dreams Aleck might have had of becoming a professional musician were abandoned when he was ten.

In 1857—a year after the Crimean War ended—Aleck and his younger brother Edward were sent to the James Maclaren's Hamilton Place Academy. Their primary education had consisted of home lessons taught by Eliza. The time had arrived to begin the formal part of their education. James Maclaren was already well-known as a teacher. He had an unusual knack at holding the students interest in education. His results were swift.

"My imagination brimmed with new ideas and a thirst to learn more about the world around me. I decided to change my name. Alexander Bell was not nearly substantial enough to suit me. So I chose the surname of one of my father's former pupils, who had come to board at our house, Alexander Graham. It had a fine strong sound to it."

Aleck let it be known that from then on he was Alexander Graham Bell. Alexander Melville Bell voiced no objections, and at his son's eleventh birthday party toasted his new name.

⁓

When Aleck was eleven, John Herdman, a local miller, sent his son Ben to Melville Bell hoping to cure the boy's stammer. Ben and Aleck hit it off immediately and became avid partners in a variety of boyhood mischief. Their favourite place for adventure was a large flour mill owned by Ben's father. To the senior Herdman there was nothing more annoying than children who argued—except possibly children who were happy. Aleck and Ben were a nuisance for him—always hanging around the mill. Herdman called them into his office for a talk. He told them he would no longer allow them the use of the mill as a rumpus room and suggested that they try and find something useful to do with their time.

"I took him at his word and asked impudently what he considered to be useful. Mr. Herdman thought for a moment: If you could only take the husks off this wheat you would be of some help."[12]

Ben and Aleck left the office determined to solve the puzzle. Armed with a sample of wheat, the boys began experimenting to see what method of abrasion would remove wheat husks effectively. The result was a series of paddles with protruding nails that could be used to brush off the husks. By placing the paddles on an existing rotating machine, they were able to clean the wheat. Herdman was elated by the ingenious invention and put the paddles to good use. Thereafter, the boys had permission to roam the mill whenever they pleased.

Meanwhile, Melville's business had prospered to such a degree that he decided to buy a two-storey stucco house—named Milton Cottage—on the outskirts of the city. The cottage had a flowering garden enclosed by an ivy-covered brick wall and Melville relished the fresh country air.

Melville's sons also found inspiration in the garden, as Aleck recalled. "The back grounds were outlined by blue-grey gravel walking paths and rainbows of English flowers that perfumed the air. An old abandoned pulpit sat in the centre of the garden, beckoning to the passerby to come and speak to the surrounding countryside. Edward and I delivered many speeches and opinions from the open air pulpit."

At the age of eleven Aleck began writing poetry. His thoughts of a *A Summer Day* were typical.

The sun was shining beautifully when, on a summer's day,
Into my little garden home it sent its golden ray:
And everything looked then, alive, the air with voices sang,
Quite like the ancient poet's lyre those little warblers sang.
The little flowers e'en looked bright and lift their heads to
*   ascent*
The breeze, that rocks their tiny bed and waves their stems,
*   now bent.*[11]

His fascination with science prompted him to found the "The Society for the Promotion of Fine Arts among Boys." The members became "professors of some sort," so that someone could be in charge of everything. Brother Edward became professor of drawing and Aleck took the chair responsible for anatomy. In time his keen interest in the way things worked led to a large collection of skeletons which he would arrange in scientific order from largest to smallest. For big animals, he kept only the skulls. His collections also included several plants and various birds' eggs. One of his experiments involved taking a thrush's egg and placing it in the nest of another species. Unfortunately, when the thrush hatched—being larger than the other birds—it pushed the others out of the nest. After this disappointment, his interest moved on to the study of the innards of birds, mice and cats.

A dead suckling-pig was donated by a local friend. The event called for a special meeting in the attic of the Bell house for a demonstration of the Professor of Anatomy's skills. Bell recalled. "It was a great moment when I started to thrust my knife into the abdomen of the subject for dissection. But, unfortunately, there happened to be some air in the creature, so that the knife thrust was followed by a rushing sound of what resembled a groan and we thought the creature alive. We tumbled over one another in our eagerness to get downstairs. Each boy fled to his home and none returned to hear the lecture. Even the lecturer himself was too frightened to revisit the lecture hall. My father was obliged to go upstairs to investigate, and he took charge of the corpse. I never saw it again."[13]

Aleck and Edward finished their year at the Hamilton Place Academy and proceeded to the Royal High School. While at high school the brothers became closer—even sharing the same group of friends. Melly, who was several years ahead of his brothers, saw them only occasionally. The older boys regarded the younger Bells as Melly's "little brothers with whom it was a condescension to play."[14] As part of their moral upbringing, the boys' mother had warned them about the wickedness of fist-fights—turning the other cheek was the Christian thing to do. However, once classmates found this out they began taunting the Bell brothers in the hope of a confrontation. When one boy slapped Aleck's face, he turned the other cheek. The young ruffian promptly slapped the other. This time Aleck cast his Christian teachings aside and lit into the boy—giving better than he'd got. A ring of schoolboys formed around the pair. They shouted out enthusiastic cheers and sideline directions. Eventually, a schoolmaster appeared on the scene and put an end to the entertainment. As the crowd thinned, Aleck and the boy blended in, leaving the bewildered teacher searching for the culprits. Aleck felt bad for having gone against his mother's wishes. Still, he continued to fight whenever it became necessary to protect either himself or Edward.

"School held no real interest for me and I was generally marked as a below average student. I much preferred nature studies. Unfortunately, there were no such courses offered in the school's curriculum."[15] Guided by his father, he kept a private collection of plants, rocks and animal skeletons. In the process, he was becoming a self-taught amateur botanist and zoologist. Reading interested him, particularly stories of fantasy or tales of the animal kingdom. Poetry classes were the only creative outlet that held his interest at school. His low marks in nearly every other subject reflected this bias. On the other hand, his brother Melly did well at school and collected a number of academic prizes. Of the three brothers, Melly certainly held the most promise of excelling at what he chose to do in life. Aleck found lecture halls stuffy places and much preferred the outdoors for his classroom. His various report cards reflected his indifference to organized education. After one particularly scathing report, his father exploded.

"Alexander Graham Bell!" his father bellowed as he strode across the threshold and slammed shut the heavy door of their house on Charlotte Square.

"Aleck! Come to my study at once! At once!"

Aleck stood before his father in the study. Strangely he felt no fear, only a strong desire to be elsewhere—perhaps to be building something, or trying to reconstruct the bones he had found....

"Without distinction! A son of mine without distinction!"

Melville Bell unfolded the school report dramatically and shouted even more dramatically. His father's voice was stunning, almost mesmerizing.

"I'm sorry, father." Aleck's eyes strayed to a drawing of the vocal organs on his father's slate. The slate was lying on the edge of the desk in front of him. Without thinking he put his finger in his mouth to feel his tongue move. His father's diagrams fascinated him.

"Sorry is not useful! Sorry is not acceptable!" his father ranted.

Melville Bell's dark eyes were like little stones when he was angry. However, his father never stayed angry long and Aleck had no doubt that he would soon forget the school report and return to his normal demeanour.

Aleck tried to focus his attention on the tall, imposing figure of his father. He noticed that when his father shouted, his throat vibrated and the vein on the side of his head seemed to throb with blood.

Suddenly, his father had grasped his wrist and pulled his hand out of his mouth. "Pay attention! Stop your infernal daydreaming. You *will* mind your p's and q's."

"What are they? I mean what does that mean, exactly?" he looked up.

"What?" his father demanded, as he let go of his wrist.

"P's and q's. What does that mean—to mind them?"

Melville turned thoughtful. "You know, when you're learning to print. P and q look alike in small letters. Many children print 'p' when they should print 'q,' or 'q' when they should print 'p'."

Aleck struggled to maintain a straight face. His father was always distracted by the opportunity to answer a question and, in truth, it was an honest question. He really hadn't understood the expression, though when he thought about it, it was simple enough.

Melville caught himself. "Don't try to distract me, Aleck. You need good form, hard work, self-control, that's what you need."

Aleck picked up the plaster hand on his father's desk and spelled out 'p.'

"Aleck!" his father shouted, pulling him close. "Listen to me! You're a bright boy. You have a good head on your shoulders. But you don't apply yourself. No, not at all. We think it will be best if you go to London to continue your studies."

Aleck looked into his father's eyes. He didn't know how to react. Going to London was his father's sentence—a punishment—but his imagination had raced at the thought. However, his enthusiasm was brief—he didn't want to leave his mother.

"London," he repeated.

"I've written to your grandfather. You'll begin a proper education at the end of the term. You will remain in London till you matriculate."

"Yes, father." And with that, he left the study.

Aleck hated the thought of leaving his mother. She was his rock and they depended upon each other. When Aleck spoke directly into her ear trumpet she could feel the vibrations. She could understand him and it was with him she most often communicated. He didn't want to be separated from her because he knew how much she counted on him. He found her in the drawing room at work on a miniature. He handed her the ear trumpet.

"I'm to go to London," he told her sadly.

"For goodness sake, Aleck, it's not a punishment, it's an opportunity! Your grandfather is a great man and a great teacher. He knows all of Shakespeare's plays off by heart."

"I want to stay here. I'm the only one you can hear."

She smiled and hugged him. "Don't be silly. I'll be perfectly fine."

But he knew she was putting on a brave face, he knew she would miss him as much as he would miss her.

A few days later there was a last conversation with his father.

"There are no limitations in this life, Aleck," his father said, as the two of them walked on the narrow cliff path above the ocean.

Melville was intense, focused. That was the difference between them. His father could hone in on a single problem and concentrate on it until he found the solution. His own mind danced from one idea to another.

"Every hardship can be overcome." His father stroked his beard, then turned to him. "What is the fundamental question?"

"To be or not to be," he replied clearly. This was a conversation they'd had before, and he knew both the question and the answer well.

Then, suddenly, his father covered Aleck's eyes with his hands and propelled him forward up the hill and out onto the rocks. He took his hands away. The view was breathtaking. Before them lay the shimmering North Sea, and in the distance, the dark jagged mountains that curved around the bay.

"It's all yours, Aleck. The world and all that's in it."

"The world and all that's in it." The phrase stuck in his mind and he thought of it again and again.

It was a sad goodbye at the Edinburgh train station for everyone but the fifteen-year-old Aleck. Dressed in his best clothes, he was impatient to be away, his thoughts already filled with the endless possibilities and opportunities that awaited him in London. As the train pulled out, his parents and brothers waved goodbye. It would be the last they would see of him for the next eighteen months. At their next meeting, Aleck would be a mature young man.

Since grandfather Alexander Bell's second marriage in 1838, life had been treating him generously. He had become well known for his elocution and lectures. His original London elocution business had provided sufficient income to maintain a seven-room house on Bond Street. The London lectures included *Morning Shakespearian Readings, Parliament and the Social Order, National Education* and even one called *Humbug*. He had obtained a teaching position at the Red Lion Square School where he lectured on English Literature and gave lessons in elocution. Cavendish College also employed him part-time for the "Instruction of Ladies in Languages, Arts, and Sciences." In 1846, he published his first literary work, *The Tongue*. While the book was not a commercial success, it did describe accurately the modern age decline in proper speech and elocution. It also included a complete historical description of the importance of speech in the past. He tried another literary piece in 1847, this time a five-act play called *The Bride*. In its opening pages, a valet describes how he, single-handedly, transformed a family from a low common status to one of high society merely by improving their speech. A copy of the book was given to the elder Bell's brother, David. The play was read by David's son, Chichester, who passed the work on to his good friend, George Bernard Shaw. *The Bride* may very well have been the inspiration for Shaw's *Pygmalion,* which was later turned into the popular twentieth-century musical comedy, *My Fair Lady*. In the opening of *Pygmalion* there is a reference to "the illustrious Alexander Melville Bell."[16]

Two years later, Bell tried to secure a teaching position at King's College in London. He was refused and, as a result, began making arrangements to give up his Bond Street home and leave London.

Melville came to the rescue. He provided his father with a small loan so that he could move to Harrington Square, a new residential area in the city. Bell wrote to Melville that the house was "new, elegantly ornamented and, certainly, most delightfully situated." Harrington Square was near Regents Park. The new house contained eleven rooms and enough land in the back for a garden. It was one of a row of homes separated by thin, brick partitions and faced a small park. The front was done in the latest style of brick and stone. The yearly cost of his new residence came to one hundred pounds, a hefty sum at the time. But Alexander handled the payments easily by renting out rooms in the four-storey building.

Then, in March 1860, his second wife died. Bell, then in his seventies, felt very much alone and yearned for family companionship. So, after two years of hearing about young Aleck's less than illustrious academic performance in Edinburgh, he proposed to bring him to London where he could monitor Aleck's thirst for the things that interested him. Thus, it was decided in the fall of 1862, that Melville would send his free-spirited son to stay with his grandfather in London.

Aleck arrived at Victoria Station on an overcast day after an all-night train ride. He emerged bleary-eyed from a third-class coach onto the crowded platform, lugging his suitcase. He soon spotted his grandfather's tall, imposing figure and white mane of carefully combed hair. He waved and hurried to embrace him. The elder Bell beamed at his grandson. "Well now, young Alexander, you look to be sound of wind, limb, and piddle."

"Yes grandfather, I am."

"Welcome to London!" his grandfather thundered. "You've come to the right place! London, my boy, is the focus of the world! The centre of geopolitics, international finance, literature and the theatre. Here, you will not only learn, but you will want to learn."

During the cab ride to Harrington Square, Aleck took in London's charms. The city appeared as dirty as Edinburgh, only more crowded. Thick black coal smoke curled heavenward from thousands of chimneys. As he looked about, he had no trouble believing what he had heard about the river Thames—it being filled with human excrement, garbage and the occasional body sliding out to sea. It served as the city's cesspool and provided it with its drinking water. The average life expectancy for those living in the city and its surroundings was forty-one years for men and forty-five for women. Most doctors were charlatans; most surgeons no better than butchers. People of all classes still died of typhoid fever on a daily basis. Queen Victoria, Empress of India and her dominions beyond, was in the twenty-fifth year of her reign. Aleck recalled in later years that: "this period of my life, as I look back at it, was the turning point of my whole career. It converted me from a boy somewhat prematurely into a man."[17]

After arriving in London, the first thing to change in his life were his clothes. Alexander shuddered at his grandson's dress. Clothes appropriate for Edinburgh simply would not do in fashion-conscious London. Aleck tried to explain that his parents had encouraged the brothers to dress as they pleased. Asking a young man to dress up on Sundays was bad enough, but every day? Nevertheless, Alexander insisted that Aleck "should never appear outside or in the public streets unless dressed as a gentleman."[18] A man, his grandfather explained patiently, is first judged by his outward appearance. "You are what people believe you to be; a young gentleman or a young ruffian. Your dress is everything." It was the old actor in him talking.

His grandfather's tailor was instructed to transform Aleck and in due course equipped him with a jacket that he described later as something that "resembled the swallow-tail coat of today with the tail cut off."[19] A pair of kid gloves, a small cane with a built-in twirl and a tall silk hat perched on top of his wavy black hair completed the outfit. Quite naturally, he felt wildly self-conscious about his new appearance. His grandfather insisted on daily outings to the Harrington Square gardens where they walked for an hour. Aleck was convinced that everyone was smirking at his strange appearance. They would see him as a young teenager trying to put on airs, pretending to be something he wasn't. To his immense relief he never met anyone his own age—male or female—on any these outings. Finally it dawned on him that no one was the least interested in his appearance.

One day, as he approached the house after his walk, a burly drayman—twice his age and size—climbed down from a delivery wagon and paused on the sidewalk to touch his cap respectfully as Aleck passed. Aleck nodded gravely, as if the man's action had been no more than he was entitled to receive. His grandfather had been right. In class-conscious Victorian society, the drayman had perceived him to be a young gentleman of substance and reacted accordingly. He marvelled at the ease of this deception. Certainly he didn't feel like a gentleman, and as for substance—his grandfather had put him on a weekly allowance of two shillings. When compared to the frugal Bell household in Edinburgh, the allowance constituted wealth beyond his wildest dreams. Still, he was practical enough to realize that it hardly made him a gentleman of substance. Nevertheless, from that point on, he paid particular attention to his personal grooming.

The old man began to understand very quickly that his grandson's education could not be force fed. Aleck was bored by the daily lessons his grandfather so carefully prepared prior to his arrival. He decided that Aleck needed a variety of mental stimulation to pique his interest. During his time in London, Alexander had attracted an eclectic assortment of intellectual friends and acquaintances whom he met and entertained on a regular basis. Some would drop by the house unannounced for a chat and a glass of port. Others came to ask his opinion or to offer their own. It was a stimulating period in world history. New advances in medicine, engineering, machinery, mining, law and global exploration were happening every month. Alexander knew many of those on the fringe and a few in the centre of these developments. He encouraged Aleck to join the discussions whenever visitors dropped by. The subjects discussed were well beyond his grandson's grasp but, as he had anticipated, sparked his curiosity. He began asking questions, shyly and self-consciously at first, then with more assurance once he realized that the visitors enjoyed the opportunity to tell him about their particular areas of expertise. Aleck began to acquire the rudiments of a basic university education from the best minds in England without ever having to leave the house.

Fairy tales were replaced by the magical world of language, philosophy and the literature of Homer, Milton and Shakespeare. His grandfather taught him elocution and diction using passages from the plays he studied. They went to the theater where Aleck studied the actors' movements closely. He memorized whole sections from *Hamlet, Macbeth, Julius Caesar* and recited them in the best Drury Lane fashion to his grandfather's friends. Although Aleck had the talent and desire needed to be a first-class performer, Alexander steered his grandson away from the profession quickly with a few depressing stories about his own frustrating stage career. "Emulate, lad, but don't imitate." His grandson was destined for much bigger things than the uncertain future of an impoverished actor. Aleck listened and, with the old man's help, devised a personal educational plan which would provide him with enough knowledge to attend college. The two got along so well that, in the fall of 1862, Alexander asked that his grandson be allowed to remain in London for the rest of the year. Reluctantly, Melville and Eliza agreed.

Aleck was experiencing a new degree of freedom and independence in London. His two shillings a week permitted him to do as he pleased. He also liked that his grandfather treated him as an adult. But there were drawbacks. His new companions were all much older and as a consequence he began to seem older. He was beginning to adopt the mannerisms of someone twice his age.

The year passed quickly. Finally the day arrived for his father to come to London to bring him home. Instead of a boy, Melville found himself speaking to a self-assured young man with opinions of his own. Although he said nothing, he was taken aback by the transformation. Before returning to Edinburgh, Melville took Aleck along on a visit he had arranged with Sir Charles Wheatstone, a professor of experimental philosophy and respected physicist at King's College. Phonetics were among Wheatstone's special interests. After studying the eighteenth-century notes of Baron De Kempelin, Wheatstone had constructed a speaking machine very similar to the Baron's model of nearly a hundred years earlier. Sir Charles set up his machine, delighted to share the success of his discovery with another student of phonetic art. The professor turned two cranks. Aleck and Melville watched in fascination as the machine uttered a few mechanical-sounding words and, with great manipulations by Wheatstone, an intelligible sentence. As they were leaving, Wheatstone presented them a copy of Baron De Kempelin's written work *Le Mecanisme de la Parole* (*The Mechanics of the Power of Speech*).

Back in Edinburgh, Aleck's new independence put him again at odds with his father. As before, his never-ending curiosity and inability to concentrate on one idea at a time, clashed with Melville's vision of what he should be. He wanted to continue his eclectic pursuit of knowledge while his father seemed to expect him to chose a single field of endeavour. "I had to concentrate on one subject," Melville told him repeatedly.

But he couldn't do as his father had done. Melville was obsessed with phonetics. He had devoted years of his life to what he called Visible Speech—trying to invent a universal alphabet that would represent every sound. His theory assumed that if each sound was given a symbol, they could be learned. Once learned, it would be possible to pronounce any word in any language. It was a system that could revolutionize education, especially the education of the deaf.

Aleck knew he was being groomed to follow in his father's footsteps. And, although he was interested in speech, in the science of sound and even in Visible Speech, did he simply want to carry on for his father? He didn't think so.

Melville began translating DeKempelin's book as a guide for Aleck and Melly. He also asked the boys to try and create a mechanism similar to Mr. Wheatstone's talking machine. The boys decided to divide the work; Melly took responsibility for the lungs and throat while Aleck worked on creating a tongue and mouth. Still, they had no idea how or where the vocal chords and larynx were situated in the human body. They decided to examine Henry Gray's drawings for the human anatomy but found them confusing. Finding human parts to dissect and study was out of the question. Eventually, they decided to sacrifice a pet cat to science. They consulted a medical student friend of Melly's for the most humane method of execution. He agreed to help and assured them his method would be both modern and painless.

Aleck wrote: "The execution took place in our greenhouse at Milton Cottage. My brother Melville and I, with tears in our eyes, held the cat, while the medical student poured down its throat a fluid warranted, he said, to produce a speedy and painless death. We were quite unprepared for the result; for the liquid turned out to be pure nitric acid."[20] The poor cat screeched and ran in circles about the green house. Aleck and Melly stood horrified watching the pathetic animal suffer a long painful death. The medical student laughed at their distress. He found the whole episode hilarious.

A vivid image of the suffering cat remained with the brothers for some time. They decided that from now on they would get their dissecting material from the family butcher—who promptly provided them with a lamb's throat. Work on their speaking machine resumed. After careful examination of the throat assembly, Melly managed to construct an artificial larynx made of tin and rubber. Aleck borrowed a human skull from a local apothecary. He made rubber gutta percha[21] moulds of the roof of the skull's mouth and teeth. A gutta percha lower jaw was then connected to the skull with wires. The result of their work was a reasonable representation of the organs necessary for speech. Everything could be moved or manipulated. On their first trial, Melly, providing the lung power, blew into the apparatus while Aleck manipulated the mouth and tongue. The resulting sound came as an audible "ah." After a few minor adjustments, it imitated the sound of a baby.

They carried the assembly to the stairwell and set it up. Melly took a deep breath and blew. A mournful "Mama! Mama!" could be heard on every floor. A door from one of the upstairs apartments opened and a voice shouted: "Gracious, what's the matter with that baby?" As the neighbour descended the staircase the boys slipped away, stifling their laughter and leaving the mystery unsolved.

"We work well together," Aleck said aloud, thinking of Melly. It was true. They enjoyed making their mechanical voice machine together.

In London, Aleck's grandfather had provided him with a small weekly allowance. At home in Edinburgh, such luxuries ceased. His grandfather also saw him as a mature young man and treated him like an adult. His parents did not. They treated him like a little boy. When he discussed his unhappiness with Melly, he found Melly felt the same way.

"I'm stifled and treated like a child," he had fumed at his father to no avail.

It was then that Aleck decided to run away to sea. He packed his bag and set a day and time to board one of the vessels at the Leith Docks. But, at the last moment, he changed his mind.

His next option was the help wanted section of the newspaper. After several days of checking through Edinburgh's two major papers, he found a job that both he and Melly were qualified for. It was a teaching job at Weston House in the Northern town of Elgin.

They applied, using their father as a reference. "Life works in strange ways," Aleck muttered.

As it turned out, the headmaster of Weston House, James Skinner, had been a former student of their father. Skinner had contacted Melville immediately with an enthusiastic offer to employ them.

"Melly! Aleck! Come to my study at once!"

Their father's summons echoed through the house and the two boys obeyed immediately, wondering what they had done.

In his study, their father paced before the fireplace. He was clearly agitated. Their mother sat in a big chair, her eyes moving first from them, then back to their father.

"I have received a letter from one James Skinner, the Headmaster of Weston House in the town of Elgin."

Aleck and his brother exchanged quick, furtive glances.

"It is clear that you have applied for a teaching position there. Is this correct?"

They nodded.

"And you did this without consulting with your mother or with me? You did this without discussing the matter openly?"

"The time has come for us to make our own decisions in life," Aleck said clearly and politely. "We're both mature young men and we're ready to leave home and start earning a living."

His father seemed surprised—even hurt.

Suddenly Aleck understood. His father could not face losing them both at the same time.

The boys stood silently. Finally, their father cleared his throat and muttered, "I suppose a compromise is in order."

"What sort of compromise?" Melly asked.

Melville frowned and pulled on his beard. "You Melly will receive a weekly allowance and go to Edinburgh University for a year as a student of Greek and Latin. Aleck will go to Elgin and try his hand as a teacher. You will switch positions next year."

They looked at each other, then back at their father, then nodded their agreement.

Their father stared at the floor. "I'm sorry not to have realized how you felt, how much you have matured."

They accepted the apology.

Aleck arrived in the small fishing town of Elgin for the 1863–64 school year and reported to Mr. Skinner. Aleck would be teaching both music and elocution. His salary was ten pounds, including room and board. At sixteen, he was younger than some of his students. However, his height and maturity served him well. He had no trouble controlling his class.

In his spare time, Aleck read constantly and studied Latin and Greek until his head ached. He also used this time to explore the town and surrounding area. One of his favourite spots was the Lady Mound—a grassy hill rising up from the west end. It was said that for hundreds of years church officials had ordered Elgin's deflowered virgins to carry a basket of earth to the top of the hill—one for every child born out of wedlock. Since then, the hill had risen to over one hundred feet and was close to two thousand feet in circumference. When it was warm and the grass dry, he would stretch out on the top of the hill and stare at the sky. Looking up at its vastness seemed to clear his mind and relax him. Here, in misty Elgin, the ground was seldom dry. Cold winds swept in from the North Sea throughout the year, and the spring was always late. Sometimes he would sit on a rock and contemplate the scenery. The peace and quiet soothed his head. Lately, he had been having a lot of headaches. They always came when his mind was at its busiest. At night he had trouble shutting down his brain so he could get to sleep. Hundreds of thoughts kept rushing through his head in the darkness. By morning, after a sleepless night, he would have a splitting headache. A visit to the Lady Mound always soothed the pain.

His dark eyes gazed up and fastened on the circling gulls. There weren't as many here as on the coast. The more adventurous breed moved inland to flock at the river's edge or gather by a country pond. These creatures, with their magical gliding abilities, loud demanding squawks and darting intelligent eyes, were most adaptable. They were equally at home atop the mast of the sailing vessels in Portsmouth Harbour or perched on the iron shoulder of Lord Nelson high above Nelson's column in London's Trafalgar Square. Their flight fascinated him. They seemed to ride the wind so effortlessly. What secret did they possess?

In the middle of term, Melly came up to see what the school was like. Aleck took him to the top of the Lady Mound.

"I don't know what to do with myself," Melly confessed sitting on the rock.

"Nor do I," Aleck replied.

"Do you like teaching, little brother? Would you consider making it a career?"

"I think so. But, however nice Elgin is, it doesn't offer enough scope for me to make any kind of intelligent decision. I'd have to teach somewhere else before I would know for sure."

"I'm sure you're right. I don't know, sometimes I want to teach, sometimes I want to be an academic."

He had laughed, "Sometimes I want to be a researcher—perhaps even an inventor."

"An inventor! What a grand idea. Well, I confess, I wouldn't mind being a writer."

"The trouble is, I can't decide," he admitted honestly.

Melly shrugged, "Nor I."

They both laughed. How strange. They had lived their whole lives together and not until that moment did they realize how much they had in common.

Years later, Aleck recalled: "Later that day, if someone had asked me I would have to admit that I felt like a teacher. I had succeeded! As young as I was, I had managed my classroom well, my students had learned and I knew they respected me."

On the first day of March 1864, he sent a birthday sonnet to his father. At the top of the verse he drew a bell with the inscription "Many Happy Returns of the Day."

Dear Guide! Nought can thy tender care repay;
Each seeming harsh reproof was, now I see, an act of love...

Each absence makes me prize my home the more.
Return shall find me—worthier than before.

Melville couldn't have received a better birthday present. He was, as always, engrossed in his search to perfect Visible Speech. He wrote to his son: "For a hundred years researchers have been seeking the elusive universal alphabet—but I don't need to tell you this! What is new, Aleck, what is exciting, is that I think I'm extremely close to success. I'm quite certain that I've found a formula that works! How glad I am that you will soon be home! I need you to learn my system so that I may illustrate it to the scientific world."

Going home at the end of the school year would be different this time. This time he would be treated as an adult—with a mind of his own.

"At the end of the school year at Elgin there were a series of gruelling public examinations for my students. Fortunately, all of them did very well. I was enormously proud of them, and myself."

Aleck took the train home. He had missed his family.

CHAPTER TWO

New York City, January 1863

Gardiner Greene Hubbard's forefathers arrived in Massachusetts from England in 1635. Five generations later, Hubbards fought against England at Bunker Hill and Yorktown. By 1822, the year that Gardiner was born, they had become one of the wealthiest and most respected families in Massachusetts. His father was a state supreme court justice. His maternal grandfather, Gardiner Greene, had arrived from Ireland with a bundle of money, which he managed to parlay into one of the largest fortunes in Boston. The grandeur of his Pemberton Hill estate was considered excessive even by Bostonian standards. His grandson and namesake, Gardiner, grew up believing that nothing was impossible to achieve provided there was a will to succeed. And, of course, the money to back it.

Gardiner graduated from Dartmouth College in Hanover, New Hampshire. His grades were not brilliant although he was recorded as being "an enthusiastic student with an inquisitive mind and a good sense of opportunity." Whether this referred to a potential business acumen or his pursuit of the young ladies of Hanover was open to conjecture. Gardiner had grown into a slim, friendly looking young man of medium height who seemed much taller than he actually was. He had a high forehead and an intense penetrating gaze that tended to unsettle people. His gifts of an ironic sense of humour and an unusual ability with words made him a natural for the legal profession. He apprenticed with a respectable Boston law firm and was admitted into the practice the following year.

Mid-nineteenth-century American attorneys were a mixed bag of political opportunists, scoundrels and a few skilled jurists. In 1842, each state and territory had its own regulations regarding lawyers. In Kansas, an applicant need only demonstrate an "ability to read and write and be of good Christian character" to hang out his shingle. Massachusetts and New York had the most stringent controls. Few women entered the profession because law was considered a vocation unsuitable for females. Women married early—usually in their teens—and raised large broods of children. After their child-bearing years, few women had the education to take up a profession. Often, they were too worn out to care.

Gardiner mastered the rudiments of the profession quickly. But, unlike his eminent father who enjoyed interpreting legal precedence and jurisprudence, he wanted action. A man of principle, Gardiner wouldn't champion a cause he thought unjust simply for the sake of financial, social or political gain. As a result, The firm's partners—distressed by the strength of Gardiner's convictions—decided to use him only in cases where the moral considerations involved bore no relation to the legal outcome. Real estate, probate, appeals, company incorporations, tax and patent law became Gardiner's fields of expertise, of which he enjoyed patent law the most. He found tremendous personal satisfaction in helping an inventor turn an idea into reality and insuring that his client's brilliance received fair compensation. Of course, most patent requests crossing his desk were from crackpots. But, instead of taking their money, Gardiner would suggest gently that they rethink their proposals and try again. He learned to recognize the difference between pipe dreams and practical commercial ideas. Nearly all of his clients were older men. To disguise his youth, Gardiner allowed his beard to grow in the hope that his elders would take him more seriously.

On a business trip to New York City, he met the angelic looking Gertrude McCurdy, daughter of a prominent city family. Gertrude, a woman of principle, held a number of radical beliefs about a woman's place in Victorian society. Gardiner thought her ideas inspiring and found he shared many of her philosophies towards life. They challenged each other—passionately agreeing at times and fiercely arguing at others. It wasn't long before Gardiner fell in love and proposed to Gertrude. She accepted and they were married in October 1846.

With financial help from their parents, they bought a spacious newly renovated house in the quiet town of Cambridge, Massachusetts. Lush lawns and tall elms surrounded the Brattle Street house. Gertrude organized a garden. They had the dining room redone in crimson velvet wallpaper. Matching damask curtains with gilt valances were hung in the large comfortable drawing room. Solid mahogany carved banisters encircled the stairwell up to the third floor. The gas fixtures in each of the main rooms were a sparkling crystal. Out front a hard-packed dirt road led down Brattle Street to the train station with regular connections to Boston and New York.

Like most upper-middle class Americans, Gardiner and Gertrude employed domestic staff. A properly run household required at the very least a housekeeper, a cook, someone to clean the ovens and wash the dishes, two maids, a coachman and a stable boy who attended to the horses, harness, sleighs and carriages. A gardener kept the lawns trimmed, the flower beds planted and weeded. Later, as families expanded, nursemaids and tutors were engaged. It was not unusual for a family of eight or ten to have an equal number of servants living on the top floors of their expansive three-storey homes. In 1845, servants received wages of twenty-five cents a day, including room and board.

Their first baby, a boy, was born a year later and died soon after. It was an age of appalling infant mortality. One in four babies died before the age of two. It was not unusual for a mother to see one-fourth of her children die before the age of twenty. Gardiner named their next baby Gertrude over his wife's objections. She saw no sense in having two Gertrudes in the same house. How would they know which Gertrude he meant when he shouted their name? They settled it by Gardiner agreeing, thereafter, to call the baby Gertrude and his wife Mrs. Hubbard.

It was the dawn of an age of American inventiveness. Every week, two or three new mechanical or electrical inventions came across

Gardiner's desk. In 1850, he wrote a long letter to physicist Joseph Henry—the inventor of the electromagnetic telegraph—asking his advice about a client's patent for a telegraphic recording apparatus. Henry didn't think it would work and Gardiner didn't invest. Nevertheless, his conviction never wavered that high-speed communication and transportation were the keys to America's future prosperity.

The time it took him to commute between Cambridge and his Boston office annoyed him. New York had street railway lines. Why didn't someone build a line connecting Cambridge and Boston? Gardiner decided to build it himself and formed the Cambridge Horse Railway Company. It took a year to lay the tracks by which time Boston City Council—which had scoffed at the idea—announced plans for street lines of their own and began laying track. A race developed. Which company would be the first to open for business? Cambridge had tracks but no tramcars. Boston had tramcars but its tracks were still under construction. Gardiner hurried off to New York. In Brooklyn, he found four well-used red and yellow tramcars still wearing their Greenwood Cemetery destination signs. He bought them on the spot and shipped them home. A week later, the Cambridge Horse Railway Company opened for business—two months ahead of its Boston competitors.

His next challenge was the town of Cambridge itself. Its freshwater supply and drainage system were a health hazard by any standard. A new water supply was needed. If the municipal council refused, they would be exposing the residents of Cambridge to typhoid. What would the Boston newspapers say if the facts were known, Gardiner warned. The council could only imagine. Hurriedly, construction for the new water supply began.

Gardiner was developing a reputation as a troublemaker, a stubborn man to be handled with kid gloves. Next, he badgered the town's officials until they agreed to his formation of the Cambridge Gas Light Company. A month later, after a particularly disastrous fire, he was back at council again, demanding new reels for the Cambridge Fire Department. It was said around Boston that if you needed something done in a hurry Gardiner Hubbard was your man. Gardiner was a man with flair; he was a promoter and he was honest. He was also a father again. His second daughter, Mabel, was born on 25 November 1857.

Gertrude Hubbard considered herself a progressive parent. She believed that every child—boy or girl—should be given the opportunity for a proper education. Mabel, like her older sister Gertrude, and her younger sisters Berta and Grace, was introduced to books as soon as she learned to speak. Mrs. Hubbard read with dramatic flair and could produce a variety of different voices to suit the characters in each story. Her daughters acquired substantial vocabularies early. They also developed an enthusiastic appreciation for a good story—especially those told by their mother. When Mabel was old enough to travel, her parents introduced her to the world beyond their comfortable Cambridge home. On one exciting trip to New York, Gardiner took the family to see P. T. Barnum's famous sideshow. General Tom Thumb, Barnum's twenty-one-inch dwarf, and his equally diminutive wife, Lavinia Warren, made a deep impression on Mabel.

One of Mabel's presents for her fifth birthday was the promise of a trip to New York to visit her grandparents. Thanksgiving, Christmas and the New Year came and went. Mabel could hardly contain her excitement. Early in January, on the night before their departure, Mabel was wide awake and chattering with her mother in anticipation of the big event. Yet by morning, when she appeared for breakfast in a bright new dress, she looked tired and complained of a sore throat and upset tummy. Gertrude scolded her for having stayed awake until the wee hours of the morning. She could sleep on the train.

But Mabel didn't sleep on the train. She became cranky and withdrawn, fussing and squirming throughout the journey and complaining continuously about her throat and a headache. Gertrude checked her throat again. It appeared no different than it had in Cambridge. She felt Mabel's forehead for signs of fever. She was warm but certainly not fevered. "It's because you were up all night," she told Mabel sternly.

After negotiating the maze of tracks on the outskirts of New York, the train came to a jolting halt in Grand Central Station.

"This way!" Gertrude Hubbard bustled down the aisle and then stopped, turning slightly when she reached the open door at the end of the car. Four steep metal steps led down to the platform.

Mabel's eyes focused on the very end of the car where the coaches joined. Even though she didn't feel well, the train ride had been fascinating, and the place between the cars, which was covered by heavy dark material reminded her of a huge accordion. Earlier, when walking through the moving train, she had passed through the accordion at the ends of each car. As she opened the door, a gust of cold air had fanned her face. She had stepped gingerly onto the swaying metal floor and paused for a moment before pushing through the next heavy door. It was all designed so that passengers could walk through the train even when it was going around curves, her mother had explained. Still, the moving floor was frightening; so was the shuddering of the train as she moved from car to car. What if the train came apart just as she and her mother stepped on the moving metal? Mabel imagined them being sucked down between the cars. As she left the train, she studied the accordion design and remembered one more time how frightened she had been on their journey to the dining car.

"Come along, darling," her mother urged. "Let the conductor assist you. The steps are very steep."

Mabel—her legs feeling wobbly—blinked into the conductor's weathered face as he reached out and grasped her round the waist, lifting her as if she were a feather all the way to the cement platform.

"There you go, missy." He sat her down and then looked up and smiled at her mother who handed him some coins.

"Best wrap your scarf tightly," her mother suggested. "Goodness, it's so damp in here! And it was so hot on that coach! The change is enough to make a body feel ill."

Hundreds of passengers milled about. The trains in the station looked huge and cold. To Mabel, they looked like steel dragons, constantly hissing and spouting off vapours.

"Baggage boy!" The conductor's command caused Mabel to jump and edge closer to her mother.

"Better take my hand," her mother suggested.

Mabel took the gloved hand. She looked up at her mother who looked wonderfully elegant in her long dark coat with the high fur collar, her big muff and satin trimmed hat. She supposed that she too looked quite smart in her new coat and soft white fur cap. But—however she looked—she felt terrible. Her throat was sore, so sore she could hardly swallow. Worse yet, she felt hot and cold at the same time. And now that she was standing, she felt dizzy too. She blinked, trying to focus her eyes. There were so many people and so much to see. But they all seemed to be walking on air. In fact, she could hardly feel the platform beneath her feet.

Just then Mabel heard a band playing the "Battle Hymn of the Republic" and the crowd on the platform parted as a troop of Union soldiers marched by.

"So young," her mother whispered softly.

"Ma'am?" the baggage boy looked at her mother questioningly.

Her mother smiled and indicated their suitcases standing in a row on the platform. The scruffily dressed lad picked up the cases, loaded them quickly onto a baggage cart and headed off to the station. Mabel and her mother walked slowly behind.

The ceiling of the station was like that in a conservatory. It had a dome made of opaque glass and a huge clock hung from its centre. It was the biggest clock Mabel had ever seen.

"Gertrude! Over here! Gertrude!"

Mabel and her mother stopped. They looked around, seeking the familiar voice that called out from the crowd. Then before Mabel knew what had happened, she was swept into her grandfather's arms.

"There's my little princess! Gertrude are you all right?" Grandmother McCurdy asked, "It's so difficult travelling these days. I know it's not far from Cambridge, but even a few hours can be trying.

"I'm fine, but I think Mabel is a bit overtired."

Mabel let her grandfather hold her. She didn't feel like walking or standing up. She longed to snuggle under a hundred woolly blankets and go to sleep.

"There, there. Is my little princess tired?"

Mabel looked into her grandfather's face and, without answering, nuzzled against him.

"She's been complaining since this morning. Of course, she hardly got any sleep last night. She's so excited! She's been looking forward to this trip ever since we promised it to her for her birthday."

"This way," Mabel's grandfather directed. He continued to carry Mabel as he hurried her mother and grandmother along. The baggage boy followed, pushing the luggage cart.

In moments they were in front of a large, brass-trimmed carriage. Mabel's grandfather set her down inside on a soft leather seat. He then helped her mother and grandmother and climbed in after, pulling the door closed behind him.

Mabel wrapped her arms around herself. "I'm cold," she said, her teeth chattering. She was shivering uncontrollably even though her cheeks were red hot.

Her grandmother's face blurred before her. She felt a cool hand on her brow.

"This child is burning up!"

Her grandmother's hand felt her forehead, then her mother's hand moved across her face.

"Oh, dear heaven! She has a terribly high fever!" her mother said in alarm.

Mabel was only vaguely aware of her grandfather opening the speaking trap and calling to the driver: "Proceed at a gallop, my good man! At a gallop!"

⌒

"I come from dear old Boston, the land of the bean and the cod, where the Lowells speak only to Cabots, and the Cabots speak only with God." It was a children's rhyme that Mabel's mother always recited to her—ending it with: "Your father's people aren't Lowells or Cabots, but they're just as rooted in the New England soil."

Mabel wasn't certain what her mother meant, but from what followed, she figured it must have something to do with her father's family and their prominent position. "The Hubbards," Mabel was told, "came to Massachusetts over two hundred years ago." She couldn't imagine two hundred years of time; although she was quite certain that no one alive now lived in Massachusetts two hundred years ago.

Her mother always went on to say that the Hubbards fought at Bunker Hill with the British. Did that mean *with* the British as in against, or did it mean *with* as in side by side?

After all, she sometimes argued with her sister and her mother would say, "Don't fight with your sister. And then again, sometimes mama would say, "go out and play with your sister." That word, *with*, confused her, especially when mama was talking about the British—whoever they were. And there was another word Mabel didn't understand. It was "Brahmin." "Yes, the Hubbards are proper Boston Brahmins," her mother would say. "Just as Brahmin as the Lowells."

Mabel thought back to her last trip to the city. She thought about P. T. Barnum's American Museum, a huge building with bright mural advertisements out front. She thought for a moment of General Tom Thumb. He and his tiny wife were her size but, as her mother explained, were much older. She hoped she would feel better soon. Perhaps General Tom Thumb was still in town—perhaps they could go to Barnum's again.

Mabel's thoughts returned to her family. She thought of her house in Cambridge and of the paintings of her relatives—living and dead—that hung along the upstairs hall of their house. Their faces filled her dreams. She tried to say "Daddy," but she couldn't make her lips move. She just seemed lost in the long hall, lost among all the paintings of her family; people unknown, but still somehow familiar.

Suddenly, Mabel forced her eyes open. She wasn't in the upstairs hall at all! She was in a big bed and her grandparents, her mother and a strange man were standing at the end of the bed looking at her, their faces solemn and serious. Was this a dream? She could see their lips moving but everything was silent. Absolutely silent. It suddenly occurred to her that she might be dead.

She pulled her arm out from under the covers and reached for the glass of water on the table next to the bed. Accidentally, she knocked the glass with her hand and it fell to the floor. Mabel saw the glass shatter, but it made no sound. No sound at all. All the grown-ups were looking now, talking and pointing. But as much as their lips moved, they said nothing she could hear. A dream! It must all be a terrible dream. When she woke up—really woke up—it would be all right. Either she would be in heaven with the angels, or she would be able to hear.

Her mother moved to the side of the bed and touched her shoulder. Mabel looked at her mother's hand—she could feel it and she could see her mother's lips moving.

In a gesture of frustration, Mabel covered her ears with her hands. Everyone's lips stopped moving. She uncovered them and looked at her mother, then her grandparents. She tried to speak but couldn't. She became painfully aware of the look of panic on everyone's face. I'm not dead, she thought. Dead people can't feel or see. She took a deep breath and watched as everyone talked at once—except her mother who wept quietly by her side. The world, and everything in it, had suddenly become absolutely silent, as silent as a snowflake falling to the ground.

Outside, a bitter cold wind whipped snow pellets against the bedroom window, causing the panes to shudder.

Inside, a slow-burning fire crackled in the bedroom hearth. It was a pleasant room, large and bright, with two big windows facing the road. There was an easy chair, a writing desk and a large dresser. The furniture was of rich maple design and a colourful handmade quilt covered the large four-poster bed.

Gertrude, dressed in a simple woolen dress and crisp white apron, looked out the window at the swirling snow. She stared hard at each curling flake, praying that she could summon her strength once again. It was difficult ... so difficult.

Mabel was lying in bed, her eyes following every move, fastening on peoples' lips as they talked. She was growing stronger by the day, but as she grew stronger, Gertrude grew more upset. Poor child. Struck deaf and dumb! Never a word from her. A few days before, Gardiner had swept his daughter into his arms, dancing her around the room singing wildly. He was looking for a response— any response. But there was nothing. Had her poor baby suffered permanent brain damage from the fever? Gertrude's eyes filled with tears and she shuddered. It was too horrible to contemplate. How could they rear a mentally disabled deaf child? What would they do?

"A decision has to be made." That was what her father had told her the previous evening during dinner. "If she's been brain damaged, there is no use taking her home to Boston. She'll only be pitied there. She will be a constant reminder of your loss."

For a long time no one spoke. Gardiner was uncharacteristically quiet. Her mother wiped the tears from her face and blew her nose delicately. Gertrude was terrified. Mabel was her baby—to be separated, she couldn't bear it!

"Perhaps," her father had suggested, "she needs to be in an institution where she can receive proper care."

"No," Gertrude had murmured. That was exactly what they shouldn't do! How could they abandon her?

"Surely there is some alternative." Her mother was also distraught at the thought of institutionalizing Mabel.

"We must find an alternative," she had said firmly. But there seemed to be no other option. Mabel could be institutionalized and helped, or she could spend her life hidden away from ridicule.

As a result of their deliberations, Gardiner was, that very day, looking into various institutions. "We must do the right thing," he had said. She had not argued.

Gertrude forced herself away from the window. She turned and looked at her small daughter propped up by three giant down-filled pillows. Mabel was such a beautiful child, her small face framed by dark curls. Her huge dark eyes followed Gertrude everywhere. She seemed to be trying to understand her new world of silence.

Gertrude turned away and continued straightening the bedroom. She opened the top drawer of the desk. It was filled with postcards. She picked a few up and fingered through them. Perhaps Mabel would enjoy looking at them.

She brought a few over to the bed and sat down. Mabel took them eagerly in her small hands and began to look through them. Suddenly, she stopped and pulled one out.

Gertrude leaned over, Mabel was holding a postcard of Tom Thumb and his wife. Before her illness, Mabel talked endlessly about the little couple—would she remember them?

Mabel pointed to Tom Thumb's wife. "Little lady," she said quite clearly.

Gertrude's mouth opened with astonishment. She caught her breath and pointed to the little woman. Again Mabel said, "Little Lady."

Gertrude burst into tears and reached for her daughter, hugging her tightly. She rocked her in her arms for a long time, then got up and began pointing at objects in the room.

"Rug," Mabel managed, then, "dresser," and, "mirror."

Gertrude ran around the room, and Mabel responded. It was a game, a wonderful game. Her mother could hear her, even if she couldn't hear her mother.

Gertrude came back to the bed and again held Mabel close. "Your hearing is gone, but thank God in Heaven, your intelligence and memory are intact."

She looked into her daughter's small face. "You can speak. It's a start. We can build on it!"

True, her daughter's voice was flat and lacked the rise and fall of common speech. But she could speak! Naturally, she would have to learn how to say the words she didn't already know.

But, no matter what lay ahead, there would be no need for institutional care. Instead, Mabel would grow up to be a whole person with a brain that worked and an intellect waiting only to be rekindled.

She did not yet know how deaf children learned but she vowed to find out. She looked into Mabel's face again, and kissed her on the cheek. "You're going to be educated as any young woman should be; you're going to learn to speak normally; and you're going to have a normal life, that I promise you."

"Mrs. Hubbard!" Her husband's voice boomed from the downstairs hall.

Gertrude waved to Mabel and hurried downstairs. "I've wonderful news to tell you!" she sang out as she descended the winding staircase. "Mabel can talk! She can actually speak! And there isn't anything wrong with her mind!"

Gardiner smiled broadly as she ran into his arms. "Take us home to Cambridge," Gertrude pleaded. "Take us both home so we can begin learning."

Gardiner Hubbard was, as always, immaculately dressed, his beard perfectly groomed and his posture excellent. He believed that the way a man carried himself affected his entire outlook on life. Thus, whenever he walked, he moved briskly with his head held high, his back straight and his stomach sucked in. He was not a man to feel self-conscious, although, at this moment, as he walked through the gray halls of the Hartford School for Deaf Mutes, he felt strangely affected.

"As you no doubt know, Mr. Hubbard, for centuries the deaf were treated as deformed outcasts. They were shunned even by the church. Being deaf and dumb came to mean stupid and ignorant—a hopeless plight. The poor things could only make strange gargling noises and wave their hands when trying to communicate with the rest of the world—a world that they could never take part in," the principal explained sadly.

"But things have changed," Gardiner ventured.

"They have changed, but progress is slow. It began in the six-teenth century when a Spanish educator, Pedro de Ponce, discovered that the deaf could learn. He managed to teach a number of his deaf pupils to read and write and to even speak a few words."

The principal had a great handlebar moustache and he twirled it thoughtfully as they stopped in the doorway of a classroom. There were five students in the class whom the teacher, who sat at the front, communicated with in sign language. Her pupils looked at her, seri-ous and silent—there was no sound of laughter, no children playing, no humour. For Gardiner, the school seemed awfully depressing.

"Two hundred years later, in Paris, Abbé de L'Epée determined that deaf children could be educated. He opened the first school for the deaf and devised a uniform alphabet using hand signs so that deaf people could communicate amongst themselves and with others."

"But only those who also know how to sign." Gardiner corrected. "That's terribly limiting, surely deaf children should be able to communicate with everyone."

"We don't think that's practical. We believe that being able to communicate with each other and with those who have learned to sign, is better than no communication at all." he said, a little defensive.

There was a pause. The principal went on, "In any case, our school has been in operation since 1817. It began when the Reverend Gallaudet was sent to Paris to study. He returned a year later fluent in sign language, accompanied by Laurent Clerc, a gifted teacher from the Paris school of Abbé Sicard—the successor to L'Epée's original school."

"What about lip reading?" Gardiner asked.

The principal shrugged. "We find that sign language is the most practical way to educate deaf people."

Gardiner didn't answer.

"And how old is your daughter?" the principal asked.

"Five. She lost her hearing as the result of a fever."

"Ah, yes. Tragic. Of course, you know Mr. Hubbard, that your daughter cannot be enrolled here until she is eleven."

"Eleven!" Gardiner stared at the man, aware he had shattered the silence of the school with his emphatic response. His face reddened in embarrassment. The principal quickly closed the door to the classroom and they moved back into the hall.

"Eleven," the principal advised firmly. "Hartford rules. Mr. Hubbard, I understand your dilemma, but our experience has shown us that deaf children under the age of eleven are simply too immature to learn sign language."

"If I wait six years to enrol Mabel she will forget what little speech and vocabulary she has now." Gardiner could feel his indignation growing by the second.

The principal shook his head sympathetically. "I suppose there are a few cases where earlier education has helped ... but I certainly couldn't recommend that you give oral training until the student, in this case your daughter, has mastered signing."

"I can't wait that long." Gardiner looked the principal in the eye, then asked, "You won't reconsider?"

"I can't. Rules are rules."

Gardiner did not argue. It was no doubt a good school. He had been told by some that it was the best school for the deaf in the United States. Still, he didn't like it. He didn't like the serious atmosphere, the silence, or the absence of play and of laughter. This wasn't what he wanted for Mabel. Yet he was uncertain and left the school with a heavy heart, wondering if Mabel could ever be properly educated.

⁓

Gardiner stood in front of the fireplace in the study, his eyes on the flickering flames. The study was a warm, friendly room. Its walls were lined with books and it smelled of leather and fine pipe tobacco.

Gertrude sat in the chair listening to him. Not wanting to reveal the emotion in his face, Gardiner spoke with his back turned. He had just finished telling her what had happened at the school and how defeated he felt.

"Everything worth having is worth working for," Gertrude offered at last.

"I'm not really sure what you mean, Mrs. Hubbard."

"Gardiner, you're a man of action. If you don't like the way things are, then change it." Gertrude was determined. "Mabel will talk, she will learn to read, and she will learn to communicate."

"You're right, my dear. Something has to be done and I'll be the one to do it. The way deaf children are educated will change or, by heavens, my name isn't Gardiner Hubbard!"

Gertrude smiled. "That's the spirit."

"And, for the time being, we're going to ignore conventional wisdom, Mrs. Hubbard. We will force Mabel to speak and treat her as if she can hear. There will be no more pointing. Any objections she has will be ignored."

Gertrude nodded thoughtfully, "At times it may break our hearts to see her struggling."

"But we must be strong. And we must instruct the servants to be strong too."

"You're right, Gardiner. If we force her to talk now, she will at least retain the small vocabulary she already has acquired."

"I'll meet with the household staff and advise them of our decision. You talk with her sisters."

"Tell them it won't be easy," Gertrude advised.

Gertrude and Mabel were returning home from a walk. Gertrude inhaled a deep lungful of air. There was no doubt about it, spring had come to Cambridge. Already, she could feel the warm breeze and see the blossoms sprouting in the garden. The trees were bright green with buds and her imported tulips, crocuses and daffodils had burst forth in an array of colours.

Gertrude watched as Mabel skipped up the walkway, pausing to watch the gardener as he busily put the flower beds in order and planted the shrubs in the ground.

Quite a bit of time had passed since they had made their decision to treat Mabel normally and she was improving. Yet, it had been a daily struggle. In the beginning, she had pointed imperiously at food when she wanted it passed to her at the table. Under the new rules, if she wanted bread, she had to ask for it. Her hoarse howls of outrage, her tears and her tantrums were studiously ignored by everyone. It broke Gertrude's heart—especially when she passed Mabel's room at night and found her sobbing into her pillow. And then if she tried to hold her daughter, Mabel would reject her angrily. Gertrude shook her head. Would it ever end? Were they doing the right thing?

Gertrude watched her daughter as she bent to pick a newly planted flower. She walked quickly to her and pulled her back, but Mabel struggled. Then suddenly she looked at her mother, smiled and said quite clearly, "Mabel wants a flower."

The gardiener was astonished and so was she. Quickly, he snipped her a blossom and presented it to her. Mabel smiled again, "Thank you," she said.

Gertrude felt tears flood her eyes. Finally, Mabel understood the rules! She understood that if she tried to speak, she would be rewarded. She felt as if her heart were bursting with joy when only moments before she had doubted. She bent down and hugged her daughter tightly. This time she was not rebuffed. "We have so much to do," she whispered, even though she knew Mabel could not hear her.

CHAPTER THREE

Edinburgh, June 1864

Melville Bell had spent most of his life in search of the universal alphabet—an alphabet that could be adapted around the world by applying a symbol to every sound. For years, he had written and rewritten various possibilities for the alphabet. Still, success had remained elusive.

Then, late one evening in 1864, all the pieces fell into place. Bell was elated and by the end of April 1864, he had composed his final draft of the sound symbols for the definitive universal alphabet. With the proper combination of his symbols, any language could be read and spoken without the speaker knowing the language. The possibilities seemed endless.

"It's a splendid day! A superb day!" Aleck called out fervently as he ran ahead of his older brother Melly and his younger brother Ted. Spring had arrived early in Edinburgh. The air was clearer, the sky was bluer, the sun was brighter. As a warm breeze blew from the south, the new leaves shuddered with gratitude as they struggled to cover the trees made barren by winter winds.

"Let's have that package, Aleck!" Melly called out. He lifted his arms to catch it. Aleck, laughing, hurled it through the air as they happily practised a game of running catch.

Melly caught the package in a magnificent flying leap then posed to send the package flying back when both boys stopped abruptly.

Ted had fallen behind and stood now, stark still, coughing violently.

"Are you all right?" Melly asked, walking quickly back to where Ted had stopped.

Aleck ran to reach them. Ted had been coughing a lot lately, he thought. Their mother said he was weakened from growing so quickly but that explanation didn't satisfy him and it didn't satisfy Melly. As for their father, he had been so busy travelling about he didn't seem to notice.

Melly had his arm around Ted's shoulders.

Ted was panting, coughing and wheezing. He couldn't seem to catch his breath, his face had turned a greyish white. "We better get you home," Aleck said, touching his brother's shoulder. "You've just had too much summer all at once."

"Mother," Ted inhaled, forcing his words, still struggling to suck air into his lungs, "Mother says I'm growing too fast."

"And you are," Melly confirmed. "Soon you'll be as tall as Aleck and I."

"C'mon. We'll walk slowly now."

Aleck watched, feeling helpless. Every step up the hill toward the house seemed too much for Ted. He gasped and wheezed. It seemed an interminable journey. Finally they reached the front door and Aleck pushed it open.

"Only the stairs now," Aleck said, realizing they were perhaps the most challenging obstacle yet. Ted didn't say anything, he just grasped the banister and winced, pushing himself up the stairs, making himself take every upward step. When they had made it to the top, Ted fell weakly across his bed, panting and coughing.

"Help him into bed," Aleck whispered. "I'll go and find mother."

"Mother?" Aleck peered into the kitchen.

Eliza was standing at the counter grinding meat; she seemed to be studying the meat grinder with great intensity. He reached out and tapped her shoulder.

Her head turned quickly. "Aleck, I usually know when you're near."

He leaned over her and spoke directly into her ear, "Today I surprised you."

She nodded.

"Mother, Melly and I brought Ted home. He seems very ill. He's short of breath and wheezing badly. He could hardly make it up the stairs."

"I'll go and see to him." Eliza, looking very concerned, quickly wiped her hands in her apron and headed upstairs.

"I think a doctor should be summoned." Aleck called after her, a thousand thoughts racing through his mind.

⁓

Aleck watched his father carefully. Melville's eyes followed his wife's footsteps above him on the second floor. His father then turned his head slightly as he heard her footsteps descending the stairs.

"You should have started without me," she said, slipping into her chair at the dining table. "No use letting good hot food get cold."

"It didn't hurt us one bit to wait," Melville replied.

"I just took Ted a tray, and I wanted to be sure he ate a bit."

His father smiled, "The boy will be just fine, Eliza. What he needs is a fine spring, a warm summer and a lot of bed rest."

His mother nodded. However, she didn't look as convinced that Ted would recover easily.

Melville grasped the bowl of potatoes helped himself to an ample serving and passed on the bowl. "By the way," he said conversationally, then choked back the words, "I've finished the final draft of the sound symbols for the definitive universal alphabet," he concluded in a near whisper.

Eliza leaned forward, and Aleck leaned to her ear. He repeated his father's words. "Good, good," she said.

"I had it or thought I had it, almost a month ago. Now I do have it. Late last night it came to me, the last obstacle just disappeared." He hesitated and glanced up at the ceiling, troubled by his youngest son's illness. His eyes blinked back the tears, which belied his confidence in Ted's recovery.

"And are we to remain in suspense?" Melly asked, passing on the potatoes and receiving the platter of meat.

"No, certainly not." Melville said, stifling his emotions. "You see, all this time I had been proceeding on the theory that there were three classes of vowels—and it almost worked, I was almost there.

Then I discovered that there is a fourth class of vowels and their sound, my lads, falls somewhere between that of a vowel and a consonant!"

"Brilliant," Aleck said.

"And elusive! Like catching a shadow and now that I've caught it everything else has fallen into place." Melville was absorbed now by his lifelong passion.

Aleck repeated Melville's words to his mother. She clapped her hands in glee.

"Of course I still have to test it. Aleck and Melly, how would you like to be my students?"

"We two?" Melly said, raising his dark brow.

"Indeed! I will have to have two students who can illustrate their knowledge to the doubting men of academia."

"When do we start?"

"Tonight! Right after this delicious dinner. Yes, if Visible Speech can be learned by students of average intelligence in a reasonable time—well, the implications of my discovery are limitless!"

Eliza nodded. A little guiltily, her eyes came to rest on Aleck, her middle son. He was, without question the one closest to her. It was he who took special care to talk to her, he who had befriended stuttering children and deaf children—children his other playmates had no time for. Aleck was different. He really wanted to help those afflicted with speech and hearing difficulties. She loved him for caring and felt a deep pride in being his mother.

Aleck could not remember when he encountered his first deaf child, but he was certain he had been quite young. Parents of deaf children, some with great hopes, others in desperation, brought them to his father who, by now, had a widespread reputation as a teacher of speech.

Over the years, he had come to realize that speech, not hearing, was the biggest problem for the deaf. Because they could not hear, they could not speak. Deaf people were ridiculed and mistreated—called "deaf and dumb." Some languished in asylums, some in jails. The more fortunate were tutored and taught. If they did learn to speak, their speech was laboured and difficult to understand. It was unnatural because it lacked inflection, because the sounds they made were not made correctly. Melville Bell had devoted his life to this aspect of speech. He built models illustrating how sounds were made. Now he had completed his lifelong dream of creating Visible Speech. In his system, each phonetic symbol indicated a definite position of the organs of speech, such as the lips, tongue and soft palate. The symbols could be used by the deaf to imitate the sounds of speech in the regular way. As he learned the system, Aleck understood his father's enthusiasm. He also began to share his father's conviction— that the system would revolutionize how the deaf learned.

He and Melly had been studying their father's symbols for four weeks now and both had nearly mastered them. In just one more week they would go to the university and there, following their father's lecture, they would serve to illustrate how the system worked to a roomful of sceptical academics.

But that was next week. Tonight, Aleck intended to entertain Ted.

"We're going to make him laugh," he told Melly. Carefully, he lifted his sheet-covered model off the table. "If this doesn't do it, nothing will."

"Or, it might scare him to death," Melly suggested, laughing.

They walked down the dimly-lit hall. Ted's room was at the end of the corridor. It was a small room with a bed, some bookcases and a desk. Both bookcases and desk were overflowing. Ted lay in the centre of the bed, propped up by a mountain of pillows.

"We're coming in," Aleck called out. "And we've a guest."

Ted looked up, forcing a smile. "Good heavens, what is it?"

Aleck and Melly put down their secret guest. It was mounted on their mother's dressing stand. "Are you ready?" Aleck asked playfully.

Ted nodded, the curiosity showing on his pale face.

Aleck whipped off the sheet.

Ted gasped.

Aleck looked fondly at his creation. It was the plaster skull he'd made before going to Elgin. Now it had teeth and jaws, rubber cheeks and lips, tin lungs and a tin throat. "It's our speaking machine. Look, Ted, see there. The palate is rubber stuffed with cotton and the tongue has wooden sections underneath so when I move this..." He pulled the lever, "See, see? Each section moves as if it's alive!"

Ted winced in mock disgust. "It's revolting. Even worse than before."

Melly laughed loudly, "I think she's beautiful."

"She?" Ted queried.

Melly shrugged. "Talks like a she."

"She talks?" Ted questioned. Aleck could hear the amazement in his brother's voice. He might think the creation revolting, but he was curious about it.

Melly blew into the tin tube and Aleck manipulated the lips, palate and tongue. The sound that sprang forth was unintelligible gibberish, a sort of quacking sound.

A smile crept into Ted's expression. "That's not talking."

Aleck and Melly both looked around, startled as their mother and father edged into the small room.

"You're sitting up," Eliza said softly to her youngest son.

Melville in the meantime was going over the unusual contraption. "Well done, boys. Very well done. I see you've made some improvements to your original model."

Aleck smiled at his older brother and they both smiled at Ted who, for the first time in many days, looked alert and interested. It's important to keep him that way, Aleck thought.

"Are you ready for our public demonstration?" Melville asked.

"Of this?" Melly said, looking at their speaking machine.

Melville shook his head in mock irritation. "No, not this. I mean are you ready to illustrate my system for all the doubting Thomases at the university?"

"Indeed we are," Melly answered.

Aleck nodded, though his mind was still very much on his younger brother.

⁓

The lecture hall held several hundred. Its pew-like seats formed a semicircle, making it look like an indoor Roman amphitheatre. Further down, there were individual desks and in the very centre, called the pit, there was a chalkboard mounted on an easel and a podium for the lecturer. It was a solemn room, a room well suited to its academic use. The furniture was of a highly polished dark wood and the seats were covered in dark green velvet. To one side, there was a small antechamber. It was here that Aleck and Melly waited for their moment in the sun.

"Papa's in fine form," Aleck whispered.

Melville Bell stood just behind the podium, illustrating a point. His father was, by nature, a flamboyant man—a man who never spoke without gesturing. Right now, he was waving his arms and pacing back and forth behind the podium. The notes laid out before him were not used as his entire lecture was committed to memory.

"From those who have scientifically studied sight, have come such wondrous achievements as the microscope and the telescope. What triumph could we experience through scientific study of speech? Perhaps an acoustical magnifying aid of some sort? Or perhaps a machine which hears sounds unavailable to the human ear."

Aleck studied his reflection in a bronze plaque hanging on the wall of the small anteroom. "I wonder," he murmured. Then he pinched his own vocal cavity and tried to hum, "Coming through the Rye."

"What are you doing, Aleck?"

Melly had turned and looked slightly annoyed.

"Have you ever noticed that the pitch changes if you constrict the vocal cavity?"

"No, but I'm sure it does. Pay attention, Aleck."

In the lecture hall, his father continued. "To understand the faculty of speech we must first study the nature of the sounds we make when we speak. To that end, man has for centuries sought a universal alphabet. A system of symbols which articulates the positions of the vocal organs so that anyone who understands them could pronounce correctly, at sight, any language written in these symbols."

"They're hooked," Melly said.

"Oh, I hear a few murmurs of doubt," Aleck said, with a wink. "Won't last long, of course."

"Gentlemen, I give you the most glorious discovery! A system which will establish precise expression between the diverse peoples and cultures of this world. I call it Visible Speech!"

Melville stepped from behind the podium and uncovered the chalkboard.

A noise rippled through the assembled academics. The slate was entirely covered with the symbolic alphabet. "A curved line means a consonant, a straight line means a vowel, a line within a curve means a vocal consonant and so on. But why explain when I can easily demonstrate?"

"It's almost our turn," Melly whispered.

Aleck ran his hand through his thick dark hair. "Ready for my debut," he said with a dramatic bow.

Melville pulled the cloth off a second, empty chalkboard. "Would someone be kind enough to volunteer a word, any word, any language."

"Impossibilit!" a French professor sitting near the front muttered.

Melville wrote the word in Visible Speech.

Another man stood and shouted out. In a matter of minutes, Melville had written ten words from ten different languages on the chalkboard.

He stood up and looked toward the entrance of the little ante-room. "Mr. Melville James Bell and Mr. Alexander Graham Bell. They have studied the system for five weeks."

There was polite applause.

Both boys followed their father to the centre of the room. Melville picked up his pointer and selected one of the words on the chalkboard.

Melly cleared his throat—then, grinning ever so slightly, "The Eatonian pronunciation of the Latin ... Familia."

A low murmuring was heard throughout the room.

Encouraged, Melville pointed to another word.

Aleck looked at it. "It might be Japanese. 'Carina?'"

"Bravo!" a man said, jumping to his feet.

Again Melville pointed, although it was easy for Aleck to see that his father was having a hard time controlling his emotions.

"I don't know the language ... but it's pronounced 'wadulisi'."

Melville grinned. "Tribal Indian—Cherokee, I believe—for maple sugar."

And again he pointed. Aleck studied the symbols. Was his father trying to trick him? The symbols on the chalkboard represented not a word, but a yawn.

Aleck yawned.

The audience broke into tremendous applause, the whole assembly was now on their feet.

"Astounding," an elderly man with a moustache muttered. "I did indeed offer a yawn. But I'm wide awake now."

Again there was applause and Melly and Aleck stepped aside. It was their father's moment of glory. "One day, we'll make our own discovery," Melly said, pinching Aleck's arm.

"Let's go home," Aleck suggested. "Let's go and give Ted and Mama the good news."

⁓

The weather had turned brisk and windy, a sure sign that fall had arrived in Edinburgh. It had been a good year for the Bells and they were now looking forward to the future.

When Melville Bell tapped his crystal drinking glass, everyone looked up. The dinner dishes were not yet cleared from the long table. A few potatoes remained in the serving bowl, and the leg of roast mutton still had enough meat for tomorrow's stew.

Melville slowly withdrew a folded paper from inside his vest pocket. He looked at his sons.

Ted, now mostly recovered from his illness, was at the table. Although he still needed to rest a great deal, the warm summer sun had done him good. Melville too looked fit, and Aleck, still subject to violent headaches when overworked, nonetheless seemed happy, healthy and filled with enthusiasm.

Eliza, seeing that Melville was going to read from the piece of paper, leaned forward and turned her ear toward Aleck.

"I've received a letter from your grandfather in London," Melville said.

Aleck repeated the words to his mother.

"He writes: 'Your invention will certainly be esteemed as one of the wonders of this wonderful age.'[1] Melville smiled broadly and listened as Aleck repeated the words to Eliza. She looked wonderfully pleased, and clapped her hands in approval. The boys might not understand, Melville thought, but Eliza understood. She knew well how important his father's approval was to Melville.

"On the basis of this letter," Melville said, looking at his sons. "I have decided we should take Edward and Aleck to London. We're going to set up your grandfather's Harrington Square House as the Headquarters and Information Centre for Visible Speech in the United Kingdom."

"And me?" Melly asked.

"You will remain here and study. Next term, Aleck will return to study and you will come to London."

"Fair enough," Melly replied.

Aleck dared not look at his older brother. In spite of their independence—an independence they had fought for—their father still treated them like children at times. Melly was probably dying to be on his own, as was Aleck.

"I've not given you much warning," Melville went on. "But it's not as if we were going to a strange house. No, everything is ready for us. All we need to do is pack our bags and leave."

Aleck leaned back in his chair. He liked London and couldn't wait to spend time with his grandfather again.

⁓

It was early morning and Melville Bell was sitting at the breakfast table eating a meal of kippers, fruit and bread. During his second cup of tea, he unfolded his newspaper and perused its contents. After it was fully scanned, he began to read in earnest, starting with the Letters to the Editor.

It was a ritual Melville had observed all of his adult life. Though he read to himself, strange sounds could often be heard from behind the pages of *The London Morning Star*. Sometimes it was an "mmmm" of thoughtfulness, sometimes a "hrumpf!" indicating disapproval, and now and again an, "ah" escaped, suggesting full agreement. These sounds were seldom augmented by comment, and when they were, all others present knew that the topic was important.

"Humph!" Aleck, Ted, and Eliza all looked toward the newspaper enshrouding Melville. "We'll just have to change that!" he uttered, then he put down the paper and looked at his family. They stared curiously.

"Alexander J. Ellis," he announced.

"The famous phoneticist?" Aleck asked, raising his dark, expressive brow.

"One and the same. This letter deals with Visible Speech of which he's read an account. He says he has serious doubts that my thirty-four symbols can possibly represent all the speech sounds."

"Small wonder he doubts it," Aleck said with a grin. "The closest he ever got in his own attempt was a set of over ninety symbols."

Melville nodded at his son. "Besides, his system of symbols were just that, symbols. There was no attempt to instruct on how the sounds were to be made."

"I think we should invite Dr. Ellis here. We should give a private demonstration."

"He would be a most important convert," Melville said slowly as he touched his beard thoughtfully. "Yes, we should do just that."

"And when he is convinced, as he surely will be, we'll seek his support."

"God knows we need money," Melville muttered. "Visible Speech needs to be printed and distributed."

"Write him now," Ted urged.

Melville nodded and stood up from the table without finishing his morning paper. "Right now," he said firmly. "We will bring this tiger into our den."

⁓

"He's here!" Ted called out. "He's just getting out of his carriage."

"And what does he look like?" Aleck responded playfully.

"Oh, like a man of serious purpose. He has a case with him and an armful of books."

"Ah, the better to challenge us."

"I daresay."

The sound of the door knocker instantly restored the house to a silence.

Ted and Melville waited in Alexander's study while the charwoman went to the door. Grandfather Alexander peered into Aleck's bedroom. "He's here, lad." His gaze took in the self-satisfied expression on his grandson's face. "You look well prepared and rather like the traditional Cheshire cat."

Aleck smiled. "I'm ready, willing and able to prove the value of father's method of Visible Speech."

Alexander grinned and patted Aleck's shoulder. Then he winked. "Well, no need to be deadly serious. Give Mr. Ellis a few laughs."

Aleck nodded. They proceeded to the study where Ted and Melville and Mr. Ellis were now waiting. Aleck felt confident. As he descended the stairs, he could not stop himself from humming his favourite highland tune, "A Highland Laddie." Mr. Alexander J. Ellis was dressed formally in a black suit, a proper tall hat, and a shirt as starched and stiff as his personality. He wore his glasses like a badge of intellectual honour, and he was unsmiling as he put down his cumbersome case and opened it.

"I've brought with me a collection of recently published articles in obscure languages so that this demonstration can be as difficult, and as a result, as conclusive as possible. Indeed, only one of the languages uses the Roman alphabet."

He unpacked a selection of the documents and then looked to Melville and Aleck. "Is that satisfactory?"

"Quite," Melville replied.

"Here, make yourself comfortable in this chair. The light is good, and you can read from whatever language you wish." Melville directed their guest to a green velvet chair.

Mr. Ellis handed them the documents to examine. "There's ancient Sumerian, Hittite and two Mongolian dialects. Of course, you don't speak any of them."

Aleck smiled, "I don't have to know the language to speak the sounds."

Ellis raised his brow. "That is precisely the claim about which I am sceptical."

"Aleck will leave the room," Melville suggested. "You read aloud in the languages and I'll take down what you read in the symbols of Visible Speech. When Aleck returns, he will take the symbols I have recorded and read exactly what you read to me."

"Impossible," Ellis muttered, even as he agreed.

Aleck left. He had to wait outside on the front steps so that Mr. Ellis could see he was outside the house and could not possibly hear or memorize the stanzas being recited.

After a short time, he looked up from his thoughts. His father was tapping on the window glass and beckoning him to return.

"Here you are," Melville said, handing his son several neatly written pages covered with the symbols of Visible Speech. Without hesitating, Aleck began.

Midway through the first page, Mr. Alexander Ellis made a noise of surprise, then a sound of undeniable admiration. When Aleck had finished, he rose to his feet. "You've echoed my very words!" he stamped his foot for emphasis. "I shall have to write the *Morning Star* this very day! I shall have to say your accent, tone, drawl, quantity— all were reproduced with remarkable fidelity, with an accuracy for which I was totally unprepared!"[2]

Melville Bell's greatest sceptic had been converted.

CHAPTER FOUR

Cambridge, Massachusetts, Spring 1865

"A veritable gaggle of girls." Gardiner Hubbard's face filled with pride as he peered into the ornately decorated white wicker bassinet where Marion, his tiny daughter lay sleeping. It was the same bassinet in which his other daughters, Gertrude, Mabel, Berta and Grace had once slept. Its wicker base was covered with white eyelet and ribbons. Before the birth of each daughter, they recovered the bassinet and new satin ribbons were sewn on. "Yes, I am the proud father of a gaggle of girls."

"If you wake her, I will be annoyed," Gertrude said from the big four-poster bed.

Gardiner turned and smiled. She looked radiant, although a little tired, which was natural. After all little Marion was only three days old.

"I shan't wake her," he lowered his voice. "Babies are so fascinating, so tiny. Look at those little hands."

"And always hungry," Gertrude added. Then, a little wistfully, "The bassinet looks almost new. Do you like it?"

"Very pretty, though I've never understood why they can't go directly into a crib."

"Babies like small cozy places. She'd be lost in a big crib."

"I suppose she would."

"Gardiner, are you sorry we have another girl?"

For a moment he studied her face. He realized that she had asked the question in all seriousness.

"Of course not!" he replied emphatically. "I love my girls … all of them! But most of all I love their mother."

Gertrude smiled with satisfaction. Their first baby had been a boy, but he had died shortly after birth. She knew that losing his only son had hurt Gardiner as much as it had her. She pushed the thought from her mind and changed the subject. "Mabel seems very excited about her new sister."

Gardiner chuckled. "Excited is hardly the word. She calls her 'baby Marion' and calls Berta and Grace, 'the children.'[1] I wonder how she thinks of herself."

"As one of the children, I imagine. She's such a bright thing, Gardiner."

"Every child would be if they had a mother like you, my sweet. You've done more for Mabel than anyone." He could not begin to calculate his wife's contribution towards the education of their daughters, especially in Mabel's case. She had a wonderfully expressive way of reading to the children and could imitate different accents and voices, bringing each story to life. But in Mabel's case she'd had to handle things differently.

In order to understand the meanings of new words, reference always had to be made to Mabel's pre-deaf vocabulary. Mabel would point to an object for a name. If she knew the components of the word—as in the case of a teapot—it was easy enough, but if she did not, the word had to be spelled out on paper and its pronunciation connected to words she knew already. Since she knew how to say *pussycat,* she knew the sound of 'p.' She knew how to say *hot,* so she could be taught to replace the 'h' with the sound of 'p' and thus could learn the word, *pot.* As Mabel had learned to speak, she had also learned to read and write.

"Since getting pregnant I haven't spent as much time with Mabel as I should have done. I'm feeling a little guilty."

"Isn't that why we hired Mrs. Conklin."

Gertrude frowned. "Mrs. Conklin is a pleasant enough woman, but she doesn't have much interest or talent for teaching. I want our girls to be taught together. Mrs. Conklin simply lacks the patience to deal with Mabel's slower progress."

"Even so, her vocabulary has grown enormously."

"But she's very difficult to understand unless you're used to her. She needs something special—someone special."

"Should I dismiss Mrs. Conklin?"

"I hate dismissing anyone."

"Perhaps there's a solution, a painless dismissal if you like."

"And how would you handle that?"

"We are a larger family now. There are house repairs that need to be made. I'd like to renovate, re-shingle the roof and build an extension. It will be necessary for all of us to escape the confusion during construction."

"Escape? To where?"

"The White Mountains of Maine. How does that sound for the summer?"

"Oh, Gardiner! That would be wonderful."

"I'm negotiating arrangements with a Dr. Nathanial P. True. He has a large home with several rooms we could rent. It will be good for you, my dear—good for all of my girls. Do I have your permission to pursue the plan?"

Gertrude nodded. "But what about Mrs. Conklin?"

He shrugged. "I'll tell her that we're leaving for an extended period and her services are no longer required." He could see that she agreed. "And moreover, I may know of a temporary replacement for her. Dr. True has a daughter freshly graduated from teacher's college. She will be with him for the summer. We might be able to engage her as a tutor over the summer."

"Oh, Gardiner, that sounds ideal."

He leaned over and kissed her cheek. "I think we'll have a fine summer."

⁓

The village of Bethal lay nestled in the White Mountains of Maine, ten miles east of the Vermont border. In the winter it became an isolated winter fairyland, in summer it was warm and delightful. The air was fresh and sweet, and the fields that surrounded the town were a sea of wildflowers.

Gertrude stood in her bedroom. A suitcase lay open on the big four-poster bed. She moved slowly from dresser to case, folding and packing their clothes. With each item she packed, she felt a twinge of regret at leaving this beautiful place. What a summer they'd had here! Mabel had made astonishing progress. Mary, Dr. True's daughter, had turned out to be far more than a mere tutor. The girl was worth her weight in gold.

"Ah, you're packing," Gardiner said, coming into the room. He stood by the window looking out across the rolling landscape. "I shall regret leaving."

Gertrude turned to him. "I regret leaving Mary True."

She's been good for the girls," he agreed.

"And especially good for Mabel, Gardiner. She has a childlike curiosity towards life herself and is blessed with an unusual ability to communicate with children of any age. She treats them as equals and teaches them at the same time. She will make a rare find for some school board. I only hope they'll realize what a treasure they are getting!"

"She is special."

"More than special. She joins the girls in their games, and she knows how to bring Mabel out of her shell. She walks with her in the woods and tells her about birds and insects. She loves botany and knows ever so much about the plants that grow around here. She gives Mabel credit when she learns something new and then helps her to find answers to her own questions so she can learn on her own. Gardiner, I want to take her back to Boston with us. I want her to teach the girls."

"Are you certain?" He had intended to suggest that himself if she hadn't.

"I'm quite certain. If we looked for an age we wouldn't find anyone as right for them just now."

"It's obvious that Mabel adores her. She calls her, 'Miss Rue,'" Gardiner chuckled.

"I know, all I hear is 'Miss Rue' this, and 'Miss Rue' that. Finding someone who Mabel relates to well is half the battle of teaching her.

She needs someone who understands her, and someone she can understand."

"I'll talk to her. We'll see if she's interested in becoming the Hubbard family's live-in governess."

Gertrude smiled. "I knew you'd agree. Please, go and talk to her now. I know it's short notice, but perhaps she can even return with us."

"I'll see to it straightaway," Gardiner promised.

The Hubbard house in Cambridge had a special room in which the children studied. It was littered with books, pictures and projects. A large shelf held various things the girls had collected in the woods—pressed leaves and blossoms, unusual rocks and the white-weathered skeleton of a squirrel. Mary used as many tools as possible when she taught. Her classes were formal, with no nonsense.

On this day, she had asked Gertrude to come and talk about Mabel. She was at her desk correcting exercises in the girls' copybooks when Gertrude came in.

"I don't mean to intrude. If you're busy we can talk later."

Mary waved aside her concern. "I'm nearly finished. Please, sit down."

"You're doing a wonderful job," she told Mary, who beamed at the compliment. "You had something to tell me about Mabel."

Mary nodded. "Mrs. Hubbard, I believe that to achieve her full potential, Mabel should have a special teacher for the deaf. I can only teach her the way I have been taught to teach. But I am not qualified to teach her properly. She needs a specialist. I will of course continue teaching her until one can be found."

Gertrude appreciated Mary's candour. "Thank you for being so frank. As you know, Mr. Hubbard and I do not hold with the idea that education is for men only. We intend to see to it that our daughters receive a well-rounded education to university level—and beyond if they are inclined to it. Moreover, we want Mabel to be treated the same as her sisters."

"She should be," Mary agreed. "She's as sharp as a tack, Mrs. Hubbard. But there is a problem."

"Which is?"

"Berta, Grace and Marion grasp my lessons easily, but Mabel tends to fall behind. Not because she can't learn, but because it takes her a little longer."

"What do you suggest?"

"I thought that we might formulate a special program for her."

"I have some ideas," Gertrude allowed, then added, "but we may discover that the best program is no program at all. I've always found that Mabel learns best when she's allowed to discover things for herself."

Mary nodded thoughtfully. "I think I shall try something new. When I've dismissed class tomorrow, I'll take Mabel out on a field trip. When we get back, I'll quiz her on whatever we did. I could have her make maps tracing our outing."

"Yes," Gertrude agreed enthusiastically. "And never stop reading to her. She's getting better at learning to read lips. Be certain to look at her when you're speaking."

Mary had an infectious laugh. "Oh, I've already discovered that. The other day when I didn't look at her as I spoke, she took my face in her hands and turned it towards her."

Gertrude smiled proudly. Mabel was learning the importance of demanding that people pay attention to her.

"Still, despite her progress, she does need special training."

"The Hartford School won't take her till she's older, though Gardiner doesn't like the place much in any case. He simply bristles at the thought of so many deaf children being brushed aside by boards of education across the country. He says it is always easier for so-called experts to do nothing than invest the time and effort needed to help a handicapped child. He is convinced that the day will come when every deaf child in America will learn to speak."

"I'm sure he is right, if Mabel is any indication. She's so quick-witted. Did you know that when she can't find just the right words to answer a question, she uses a substitute idea."

"Such as?"

"Yesterday I asked if she could explain a grammatical conjunction. She answered, 'Oh, yes, a conjunction is like an isthmus, it joins the peninsula to the mainland.'[2] She learned that from her maps and made the connection. Of course, she is quite right—a conjunction connects the two clauses of a sentence in the same way that an isthmus connects a peninsula to the mainland."

"Oh, Mary, she is so bright," Gertrude replied after a moment. "We must find a way of teaching her—not just for Mabel, but for the others like her."

"Amen, to that!" Mary concluded.

Gardiner sat slouched comfortably in his great easy chair, eyes glued on the fire. He and Gertrude were deep in conversation. Shadows from the dancing firelight spilled across the walls of his study.

"Dunderheads," he muttered darkly. "It never ceases to amaze me! The quality of people who manage to get themselves elected to the legislature even in this, the enlightened state of Massachusetts. It is appalling, my dear, simply appalling."

"They do seem unprogressive," she responded sympathetically.

"Unprogressive? A monumental understatement. They are utterly backward! Well, most of them anyway."

Gertrude looked at her hands folded tightly in her lap. Poor Gardiner. He had gone before the state legislature repeatedly and each time had encountered scepticism and hesitation. He was not a man to take inaction lightly. He believed in ploughing ahead, whatever the difficulty. The people at the Hartford School for Deaf Mutes were backward. He appealed to the legislature for an independent charter that would, through public funding, establish a small institution to teach deaf children to speak. There were hearings and Gardiner had—in her quite prejudiced view—presented his case with passionate eloquence. She had been proud of him. He was a most effective speaker, and Gertrude thought he cut quite a figure with his long fair beard, imposing stature and booming voice. He knew just when to remove his gold-rimmed spectacles for effect.

He had spoken his piece, and then the tight-lipped representatives of the Hartford School for Deaf Mutes, led by their prejudiced principal, presented a rebuttal. They voiced strong opposition to any new school—in whatever form—as a thinly disguised attempt to duplicate or thwart their own efforts on behalf of America's deaf. Whereas Gardiner had made his own case, the defenders of the status quo were many—and the legislators took their side. In any case, money was tight as the country had until recently been at war.

Gardiner returned home, seething with frustration. Then he tried again. This time the state agreed to set up a small, privately funded, non-chartered experimental school for the deaf in Chelmsford. It was not exactly what he had fought for, but it was better than nothing. The school's subscribers hired Harriet B. Rogers—a trained teacher of the deaf—as principal.

But they decided not to send Mabel to Chelmsford, preferring to teach her at home and adamant she be taught among normal children and be treated as an equal. Their decision proved a wise one. None of the children at the school, despite being older, came even close to Mabel's level of comprehension or had acquired her basic education.

Gardiner continued lobbying for the deaf. His opponents wanted proof that the oral method of teaching deaf children worked and was superior to signing. Patiently, Gardiner pointed to the success of the new Chelmsford School, but the legislators said the experiment was too short and too small a demonstration to be valid.

Support for the cause came unexpectedly. In the midst of the legislative submissions, a deaf businessman from Northampton, John Clarke, offered fifty thousand dollars[3] to help start a school for the deaf. He wanted to provide deaf children with the opportunity for a good education, something he had missed as a boy. But even with a backer, Gardiner was unable to change the opinions of the conservative-minded legislators.

"They say they are a serious-minded government body, not a speculative assembly of well-intentioned dreamers. Fools!" Gardiner said.

Gertrude drew in her breath. "I hardly expect men of this calibre to discourage you, Gardiner."

He turned from the fire and looked into her eyes. It was quite true that he considered himself a first-class promoter and he damn well hated failing at anything. "Mrs. Hubbard, I need some sort of spectacular display in order to succeed. I need something that will silence the critics, convince the legislators and enlist public support. Something simple, something that everyone can understand."

"It seems to me that your best advertisement for the oral method is, at this moment, asleep upstairs."

"Mabel?" he raised his brow and removed his spectacles.

"Yes, our Mabel."

Gardiner's eyes twinkled, "Of course, you're right." He frowned slightly, "But would it be right—proper to use her in such a way. After all, she is only eight years old."

Gertrude nodded knowingly. "Who is better qualified? Talk to her about it. I think she'll do it."

~

If only he could get the papers to print something like, "Eight-Year-Old Deaf Girl Faces Legislature," Gardiner thought as he looked about for the representatives from the major newspapers that he had notified in Boston, New York and Washington.

Mabel was wearing her best dress; she clutched Mary True's hand as they followed Gardiner and another man through the halls of the legislature.

This was an honour, she thought silently. Her mother had explained carefully that the gentlemen who wanted to talk with her were deciding if they should allow a proper school for the deaf to be built—like the one in Chelmsford. "They want to meet you and they want you to tell them about yourself. Can you do that?" her mother had asked.

Mabel had agreed straightaway because she thought it sounded like fun, and because it also meant she could journey to the gold-domed state house atop Beacon Hill.

"The men will want to ask you questions. Now don't be nervous, just try to answer as best you can." Then her mother and Mary had explained what the legislature was and what it did.

They stopped and for a moment stood before a huge door. The man she didn't know opened it and announced them each by name. They were conducted into a large wood-panelled committee room, packed with spectators.

At a long table, a grey-bearded man held a large wooden mallet. He hit it on the table and though Mabel couldn't hear it, or the noise in the room, she saw that people closed their mouths and sat up straight.

"Miss Mabel Hubbard, will you step forward?"

Mary guided her to a huge wooden chair in front of the dais at which the man with the wooden mallet sat. She climbed into the chair, startled that her feet were so far off the ground. She gave the grim looking men a big smile then crossed her hands in her lap as Mary had told her.

At first, the men seemed strangely uncomfortable. One of them reminded her of Billy Goat Gruff, but she didn't laugh at him.

It was just like a quiz game. They asked her about geography, history, grammar and arithmetic. She watched their lips and read them, then she answered each question. After many questions they asked her to step down. The man with the mallet banged it again and it appeared as if everyone in the room was talking at once.

"Incredible," one of the legislators said to her father. "She's a wonder!"

"As you can see," Gardiner answered, "when children lip-read and talk, they can communicate with anyone. When they only sign, and can only read sign language, they can only communicate with other deaf children or someone who knows how to sign. Clearly there is a great advantage to the oral method."

"It would seem you're right, Mr. Hubbard. We'll have to revisit our previous decisions in the light of your daughter's testimony. Hubbard, you've made history."

When the man turned away, her father winked at her, and Mabel smiled. She knew that she had helped.

⁓

A huge plate of buttermilk pancakes, crisp bacon and an enormous jug of maple syrup had been laid out for breakfast. Gardiner Hubbard sat at the head of the table, Gertrude at the foot, the girls on either side with Mary True next to Mabel.

"T'is a day like no other!" Gardiner proclaimed as he unfolded the *Boston Globe* carefully.

"Indeed a day to celebrate," Gertrude said.

Mabel took a big bite of her pancake. It did seem like a special day. The sky was ever so blue and a big sunbeam was shining straight into the breakfast room.

Gardiner turned to her. "It's a special day because of you. What do you think of that? You have changed things, you made those men listen."

"What have they done?" she asked. "Will there be a school?"

"Yes, there will. Thanks to you, the Massachusetts Legislature passed two bills ... into laws. A charter authorizes the founding of the Clarke Institution for Deaf Mutes at Northampton. The second bill will provide state funds for the education of all deaf children at the Clarke school or any other school for the deaf within the state of Massachusetts. Because of you, Mabel, from now on all deaf children will be taught to speak and lip-read—they'll be freed from the restrictions of sign language!"

Mabel smiled happily and clapped her hands together. She always clapped, like her sisters, and always wondered what clapping sounded like. She felt proud, as proud as her father and mother seemed to be of her.

"Good," she said brightly, then, "I have something to ask."

"Ah, now we'll pay for her help. Are you holding us to ransom?"

Mabel shook her dark curls and laughed.

Gardiner waited. "Well, what do you want to ask then?"

"Miss Rue wants to know if I can go to spend the summer with her in Maine."

"All summer?" Gardiner asked. "That's a long time." He liked the idea and his daughter's sense of independence.

"I think it's an excellent idea," Gertrude said, looking at Mary. "Of course we'll miss you."

"I'll write faithfully," Mabel promised.

"I know you will," Gertrude smiled.

"Are you in favour of this visit, Mrs. Hubbard?" Gardiner asked formally.

"I think it will be good for her. Yes, I am in favour of it."

"Good! Then that's settled. Mabel, you will go to Maine," he announced.

Again, Mabel clapped, then hugged Mary. "We'll have such fun, won't we?" she said.

⁓

The lazy summer days melted into one another. Mabel loved the countryside and the long wonderful walks that she and Mary took together. There were no lessons to be learned and no rush to get anything done. Each day they went for a long walk and collected things. They read books sitting on Mary's front porch, swaying on the comfortable wooden swing.

"You astonish me. You've learned so many new words," Mary told her one afternoon.

"And it has been such fun," Mabel replied, moving the white swing ever so slightly.

"Oh, there's the mailman." Mary pointed down the tree-lined street. "Maybe there's a letter from your mother."

The mailman walked up the front path and handed Mary a letter. "All the way from Boston," he announced importantly.

Mary took the envelope and turned it over. Mabel leaned over to examine it. She recognized the handwriting. Clearly it came from her mother. But it was addressed to Mary, not to her.

"I'm sure there's something in it for you," said Mary, sensing Mabel's disappointment.

Folded inside the letter was a note addressed to Mabel, but Mary saw the request, underlined, at the beginning of the letter.

"Please read this, before giving Mabel my note."

Mystified, she held the note in her hand as her eyes moved quickly down the page. Then she bit her lip and shook her head.

"What's the matter?" Mabel asked. Mary looked as if she were going to cry. "What's wrong, tell me. Give me my note, please."

"Wait," Mary said, holding Mabel's hand. "Your mother wants me to speak to you first."

Mabel's face knit into a look of deep concern. "Is someone sick?" she asked.

Mary drew in her breath, "Your little sister, Marion. She was ill, very ill ... Mabel, she died.... I'm so sorry."

Mabel stared at Mary. "Died?" she repeated. She took the note from Mary. In it, her mother told her sadly about Marion's illness and death.

"I loved her! I want her!" Mabel cried. Her large brown eyes filled with tears. "What does 'died' mean? Will I never see her again? Tell me, Mary, tell me why she died?"

Mary stood up and took Mabel's hand. "Come with me," she said gently.

With tears running down her cheeks, Mabel followed Mary to the back of the house and out into the fields. They walked in silence. Mabel felt the breeze on her wet cheeks, and still the tears fell from her eyes.

They reached the big apple tree that was their favourite climbing tree. Mary began to climb, and Mabel followed. They reached the uppermost branch.

"See the wind moving the leaves?"

Mabel nodded. "Why did we come here?"

"Because this is the highest branch of the tree. It's as close to heaven as we can reach. As close to Marion's spirit as we can get."

"She's gone to be with the angels, hasn't she?" Mabel asked.

Mary nodded. "We all die sometime," she said slowly. "And we go to heaven and sit with the angels."

"I will miss her."

"Then you must climb a tree and speak to the wind. She can hear you."

Mabel wiped her cheek. "Growing up is hard," she said finally.

⁓

By the autumn of 1869, Mabel's education had progressed to such an extent that Gertrude felt confident enough to try and enrol her in a public school. Mary agreed to stay on as governess and provide whatever extra help Mabel would need to keep up with the other children. Public school meant formal lessons and a classroom filled with students. There would be distractions and she would not always be able to see the teacher's face. Before enrolment, she was interviewed by one of the school board directors. "I am surprised at the readiness with which she reads from the lips, as I have never talked with her before, and she understood me without difficulty."[4] The board of examiners discovered, to their amazement, that eleven-year-old Mabel was more advanced than most students her age.

As the opening day of school approached, Mabel felt uneasy. Her family, friends and relations accepted her disability. But how would a roomful of strangers her own age react? Would they laugh, or tease her, or turn away with embarrassment? She had observed such reactions from strangers during her travels with Mary and her parents.

To smooth her way, the principal addressed the student body at the first assembly of the year, advising them that a deaf girl would be attending classes. For the first few days, Mabel was the school's curiosity. It took time for both the teachers and the students to understand her flat speech. But most were able to attune their ears quickly. Those who couldn't were provided with instantaneous translations by those who could. Within a week, Mabel had been accepted by everyone. In class, she sat in the front row where she could see the teacher's lips. Occasionally, one of the teachers would forget in mid-sentence and turn to write on the blackboard, leaving Mabel cut off. Whenever this happened, Mabel raised her hand and the teacher would repeat the missing words. Later in the school year, her classmates shouted reminders at the teacher to stop talking when facing the blackboard. This acceptance by her peers boosted Mabel's self-confidence and taught her to never be afraid of facing the world with her disability.

In the summer of 1871, Gardiner and Gertrude took the Hubbard family to Europe to expand their daughters' education. Berta and Grace were enroled in a Swiss private school while Mrs. Hubbard and eldest daughter, Gertrude, spent the winter in Paris. Mabel was enroled in a school for the deaf in Vienna run by Herr and Frau Lehfeld. The Lehfelds had persuaded the Clarke Institute to send its principal, Miss

Rogers, with Mabel so that she might learn more about their teaching methods. Mabel, who had turned fourteen, seemed less than enchanted by the proposed arrangements. In her journal of 2 September 1871, she described a discussion with her mother.

"When I came in Mama's room, I found her waiting to speak to me. She began very guardedly but I saw at once the end. It was for me to go to Vienna for the winter. 'I know what you mean but I won't go.' Mama said she only wanted me to think about it. I was to do as I pleased in the matter. They thought that if I went there, I would learn German more thoroughly and that it would be much to my improvement; it would help me to speak and understand much better and faster and besides Cousin Copley and Cousin Mary would be there [but not at the Lehfelds' school] as well as Miss Rogers, who would stay at the same house with me. I might go to Rome in the spring. The children would go to a boarding school in Geneva and Mama and Sister would hover between us. On the whole I think I had better go to Vienna for Mama says it concerns my future welfare. I will try and decide like Charles V of Germany and see if after all 'I may not be glad afterwards.'"[5]

It turned out to be a thoroughly satisfying arrangement for everybody. The family lived in Europe for three years, although Gardiner had to make several trips back and forth across the Atlantic to attend to his business interests. While in Vienna, Mabel wrote a series of long letters to her mother describing the events of the day. She and the gregarious Miss Rogers spent most of their free time exploring the city, visiting its art galleries and places of historical interest. After a trip to one gallery, Mabel described a painting in her journal: "Above, resting in a reclining attitude on a cloud, was God. He had a long grey beard and grey mantle. I don't like to see him thus represented. No one knows that he is an old man."

She met a friendly adversary at the school in Vienna with whom she competed. Buba, a Hungarian Jew, took an interest in her. Mabel seemed amused. "I don't suppose you would like to have a gentleman of who you know scarcely anything tuck you under the chin, pat your face. It is different with the others who wouldn't dare to be so familiar. If they were, Buba would be sure to scold them, for it seems he will let only himself play with me."[6]

Often, she found her lessons frustrating but drew some comfort from the fact that Buba, despite being a few years older, had difficulties too.

"I did not have very good lessons this morning but after relearning them, I got them very well without mistakes. Buba did not seem to have much better lessons and I was much pleased as it is nicer to have somebody as bad as I than to be alone."[7]

Still, Mabel felt very much cut off from the rest of the world and sent frequent requests to both parents for American newspapers. When Miss Rogers returned home she arranged for copies of the Northampton papers to be sent to Mabel. But its pages were filled with stories of purely local interest. The Viennese papers weren't much better and required a laborious translation. Mabel longed for some real international news written in English to tell her what was going on in the world.

"I wish those papers would tell me more about Europe. I really don't know if the Queen of England is dead or alive; if Napoleon is Emperor or not and that vexes me very much."[8]

She was also beginning to feel homesick. It had been months since she had seen any of her family. Cold winter winds began to chill her enthusiasm for Vienna. "I feel sometimes so forgotten here ... and wish April was almost here."[9] Removed from the protection of family and friends she became more aware of the disadvantages to being deaf. "As I grow older, I feel my loss more severely. At home I don't remember the idea ever entering my head to wish to hear, but here where I am thrown more into the society of strangers, I feel somewhat discontented. Only somewhat, thank God. I am getting to understand more strangers without help."[10] In January, her spirits rose when rearrangements were made for a March visit to Rome with her mother and sister. The weeks dragged by until in a haze of green the Viennese trees began to bud. One morning soon after, her mother and sister Gertrude appeared with a coach and porter to collect Mabel and her luggage. They bid the Lehfelds *dankeschon und auf weidiershen* and took the train to Rome.

The British Prince and Princess of Wales were visiting the city. When it was rumoured that they might be attending Sunday service in an English chapel, Gertrude arranged for some of the Hubbard clan to be on hand. Mabel recorded:

"Sunday morning was very unpleasant but nevertheless we went to the English Chapel hoping to see the Prince and Princess of Wales. We were successful and I liked them very much but I did not think the former very devout because at prayers when I looked up for a moment from my prayer book, I saw him turn his head all the way around in a way that reminded me of a naughty little boy."[11]

A few weeks later, her sister arranged an audience with the Pope. Gertrude decided that Mabel would look too young in a coloured dress—coloured dresses were worn on children, not young ladies—so Mabel borrowed one of her mother's black dresses for the occasion. "Didn't I feel fine! They say I looked twenty years old."[12]

At the end of May, the family left Rome for Florence to meet Berta and Grace who had completed their finishing school in Switzerland. For the first time in nearly a year, the sisters were together. Each of them realized with wonder and a little regret that they were no longer girls. Their childhood had ended. The European visit and its schooling had turned them into self-assured young ladies. After a few days taking in the sights of Florence, they started the journey home.

When Gardiner Hubbard first returned home he delivered an extensive report to the Clarke School about European methods for teaching the deaf. New advances in the field were being developed constantly. One that fascinated him was something called "Visible Speech," developed by a Scot, Melville Bell. Gardiner and Melville finally met at a dinner party in 1868, given by Thomas Hill, president of Harvard University. The thirty guests were a mixed bag of academics, physicians, scientists, politicians, lawyers, and several special guests like Gardiner who shared a fascination for the subject. Gardiner was instantly attracted by the tall bearded Bell who, with his perfect diction and commanding stage presence, was able to keep the audience on the edge of its seat for over two hours. Bell's innovative ideas on Visible Speech were astonishing. The brilliant Scot had devised a visual alphabet of basic phonetic sounds consistent with every language on earth. He demonstrated this consistency of vocal sounds in French, English, German, Basque and Hindi. The implications for teaching the deaf were intriguing. Gardiner's fertile imagination came alive. He wanted to hear more. When the lecture ended, he pushed his way through the congratulatory circle of well-wishers and seized Bell by the arm, dragging him away for a private discussion. The results of this meeting would, ultimately, change the history of the world in a way that neither of them could ever have imagined.

CHAPTER FIVE

London, Summer 1865

After Alexander Ellis left the Bells', Melville had danced about. "We've conquered the last sceptic, my son!" he told Aleck joyfully. Melville believed that Mr. Ellis was a link in a chain—a chain that would finally bring funding to his Visible Speech project.

Mr. Ellis had hardly escaped the front door when Melville optimistically began writing letters. He wrote to every conceivable government department and when those letters went unanswered, he tried to go around the bureaucracy. He approached Lord Palmerston, who listened politely to his case for Visible Speech but uttered only vague comments when discussing government support. Frustrated, Melville next sought access through the Foreign Affairs Office, which referred him to another office, then another and another. Finally, Melville tried in vain to present his request directly to Queen Victoria. The request was promptly denied.

Aleck decided the problem was that neither Palmerston's government nor any previous British government had considered creating an official office to oversee the support of research and development. Pure research was considered best left to the nation's foremost academic institutions such as Oxford and Cambridge. Engineering and mechanical research were usually funded by public or private companies and sometimes, if the end product had military use, the War Office would provide money. As a result of this policy, many found themselves in a sort of creative straight-jacket. Visible Speech was accepted by his father's academic peers, and even *The London Illustrated Times* had observed, "We cannot pretend even to guess at the horizons opened up by such an alphabet in the training of the deaf, the dumb and the blind."[1] But no matter how great the praise for Visible Speech, there was no money to encourage the system.

Bitterly disappointed, his father returned to Edinburgh with his family. He began teaching privately again while his manuscript on Visible Speech made the rounds to various publishers.

A few months later, Grandfather Bell died in his sleep. Aleck was grateful that he died peacefully. He was close to old Alexander—perhaps closer to him than to anyone in the family. After all, his grandfather had been the first to treat him as an adult. He had been a wonderful companion and as long as he lived, Aleck knew he would never forget his grandfather's melodic voice or his dancing eyes.

After Alexander's death, Melville held a family conference. It was decided that they would move permanently to London—to the house on Harrington Square. Aleck and Melly would continue their rotation of teaching and learning. Soon after, Melville closed up shop in Edinburgh and travelled to London with Eliza, Edward and Aleck. Melly remained in Elgin working his turn as a student-teacher.

At the end of the summer of 1865, the two older brothers again traded places. Aleck went back to Elgin to teach at Weston House, this time as resident assistant-master, while Melly travelled to London and moved in with his parents on Harrington Square. Melly had worked himself hard in Elgin and was in poor health. Melville and Eliza worried that Aleck might do the same. Melville dispatched a letter of advice.

> *Don't lie down heated on the ground*
> *Don't go crawling into caves*
> *Don't go psalm singing in a choir*
> *Don't forget tomorrow in today*
> *Don't bother your brains about ideography*
> *Don't neglect English Literature and history*
> *Don't forget what you know of languages*
> *Don't fail to rank music last in your accomplishments*
> *Don't let a week pass without writing to us*

Don't hate London—for home's sake—if you can't love it
Don't gloom at my doubts, and
Don't doubt the constant affection of

Your fond father

Aleck's interests continued to centre on speech and the production of speech. Before Aleck left for Elgin, Melville made the discovery that if a series of vowels were whispered in a particular order, the effect would be an ascending musical scale. Aleck disagreed and said it was a descending scale. Either way it was a curious phenomenon and remained fixed in Aleck's mind. Why did vowels change their tones? How? He decided the only way to find out for sure was to perform a physical examination on himself as he whispered the vowels. This exercise required him to make various exaggerated facial contortions while he tapped the front and sides of his throat, searching for the changing tones and pitches. After some personal experimentation, he moved to a series of bottles, each filled with different levels of water. When he blew over the top of each, the results varied from the high pitch of a full bottle to the low foghorn sound from an empty one. He decided instinctively that the throat cavity worked in a similar fashion.

He discussed his findings with Melville when he came home for the Christmas holidays. Although intrigued by his son's work on the musical vowels, Melville was distressed by Aleck's decision to continue his professional work while studying for a degree at the University of London. Melly's health had only just returned to normal after overworking himself. Melville suggested firmly that Aleck do one thing at a time: a year at the college and then maybe start his professional career. The argument was cut short when Aleck returned to Elgin to finish the school year. However, his mother had the last word. After he had left, she wrote: "I think you should implicitly surrender yourself to papa's judgement in this matter."[2]

Yet he continued to overwork, teaching not only at the Elgin school but part-time at a girls' school nearby. The result was fatigue and terrible headaches. He wrote to his mother for advice. She suggested that he stay off pickles, sip some beer, and try cool water on his eyes. She sent along some medicine for his sleeplessness.

Aleck continued at his frantic pace; teaching at the two schools and, with whatever free time he had left, continuing his experiments on the harmonic vowels. By March of 1866, he was confident enough about his experiments to share them with the master and sent a letter describing his findings to Alexander Ellis, asking for an opinion. Ellis replied promptly. "I find, you are exactly repeating Helmholtz's experiments for determining the musical tones of the vowels."[3] He wrote that Helmholtz had gone further, managing to synthesize the vowel sounds. Aleck felt deflated. He had believed himself to be on the verge of an original discovery. Despite the disappointment, he took consolation in the fact that, at nineteen, he had independently worked out the same theory as a leading professional in the field of phonetics. Ellis expressed some interest that Aleck might widen his experiments by trying to repeat Helmholtz's vowel simulation with vibrating tuning forks. He offered to lend Aleck a copy of Helmholtz's book describing the experiments. Unfortunately, the book was in German. Aleck decided that a visit to Alexander Ellis would be the next best thing.

As the remaining months of the school year passed, his health began to improve. Warmer spring weather gave him an opportunity to explore the countryside. A centuries-old ruined building that had once housed an order of monks lay within walking distance from the school. It seemed an appropriate spot to go and sort out his thoughts. His days in Elgin were happy and he decided that his future held great promise. At Miss Gregory's girls' school he had fallen in love with one of his pupils, Anna Duan, who was nearly the same age as Aleck. However, social restraints dictated that his appreciation had to remain at a heart-breaking distance. It would have been scandalous for a teacher to become involved with a student. He contented himself with the girl's picture and carried it with him for many years.

The school year ended, and again his students did remarkably well. As he arrived for his last class at Miss Gregory's school, the room fell silent. Aleck stood at the front, curious about the unusual silence in the normally bubbly group. Shyly, Anna Duan got to her feet. The rest of the class giggled. Had they discovered his yearning for this lovely creature? Aleck trembled at the thought. Disgrace and ruination were now only a heartbeat away.

"Professor Bell," Anna began, "with our thanks for your patience and understanding when we were supposed to be seeking wisdom from you (more giggles) and for your perseverance in making certain that we would, we would like to present you with this writing case." She carried it to the front of the room and handed it to him. The students clapped and shouted their approval. Aleck was speechless. For many years, he looked back upon the event as being "the first present of the kind I had ever received and I was very proud of it."[4]

Although Aleck left Elgin with a few regrets, he was still excited about visiting Mr. Ellis in London. Indeed, he ended up spending most of the summer with him, eagerly soaking up all the information about Helmoltz's experiments that he could.

Meanwhile, Melville had been teaching at London's University College and giving private lessons in elocution. The lack of government support for Visible Speech depressed him. On an impulse, he explained the entire system in great confidence to Alexander Ellis. Ellis had been overwhelmed. "Bell ... makes a prior analysis which suits the special case with remarkable exactness. And he also enables a learner to train himself to read his combinations with singular accuracy."[5] Ellis saw a problem with the difficulty of explaining how the system worked. In spite of Melville and his sons learning the system in a matter of weeks, Ellis felt sure that anyone of average intelligence would be hard pressed to learn it at all. Such comments discouraged Melville. Copies of the Visible Speech brochure had been sent out to several American scholars, all of whom expressed their interest in learning more about it. "What was wrong with Ellis?" Melville groused to himself.

As Ellis's interest in Visible Speech waned, his enthusiasm for Aleck's efforts increased proportionately. Ellis transcribed most of the German text of Helmholtz's book for him. Unfortunately, the descriptions and diagrams were minutely detailed and too complicated to understand. Neither Aleck nor Ellis had sufficient knowledge about the electronics involved in Helmholtz's experiments. As a result, Aleck came to several faulty conclusions. Nevertheless, he continued to search for all available information about electricity in order to try to understand its properties. His search continued into the next school year when he began a new teaching position at Somersetshire College, in

Bath. The town was similar to Elgin, only much closer to London and his parents. He continued his frenetic dawn to dark work pace—teaching, experimenting and learning a variety of things, from the French language to the principles of electricity. His mother wrote often, concerned about his health and pleading with him to slow down.

Melly was away in Edinburgh lecturing on elocution and doing quite well financially and Melville had planned for Edward to go to Elgin for the 1866–67 school year. However, his youngest son was too weak to attend classes. "I suspect that Edward has grown too fast for his own strength." Edward once commented to his mother that he felt he had no backbone. However, his weakness came from another source—tuberculosis. He spent the winter in bed, often too weak even to write to his brothers.

During his year in Edinburgh, Melly had met and fallen in love with Caroline Ottoway, "Carrie" as she liked him to call her. The two promptly announced their upcoming engagement. Aleck was thrilled for his brother's good fortune but somewhat depressed by his own lack of female companionship. "I only wish I were as fortunate as Melly is!!!"[6] He often looked at his picture of Anna Duan and wished he had said something when he had the chance. But it was too late for regrets and so he threw himself into his work. The fierce headaches and sensitive eyes returned to cripple him. "... In fact the only idea I can form of this past week is one immense headache."[7] Again, he received letters from his mother suggesting various headache remedies and imploring him to slow down. When the school year ended, Aleck returned to London. As the English spring emerged from the melting snows of March, Aleck's strength returned. Sadly, however, his youngest brother lay dying.

As Edward's life slipped away with every laboured breath, Aleck wrote to Melly: "Ted is truly ill, Melly. Please come to see him as soon as you can." Aleck's dark eyes filled with tears as his gaze moved around the room. His beloved younger brother's shepherd's cap hung on the bedpost and on the shelf of his bookcase, Ted's favourite skull stared at him with hollow eyes.

Aleck's journal for 17 May 1867, described his brother's last hours: "Edward died this morning at ten minutes to four o'clock. He was

only eighteen-years-and-eight-months-old. He literally 'fell asleep'—
he died without consciousness and without pain, while he was asleep.
So may I die! (signed) AGB."[8]

⁓

Melville took Eliza on a vacation to Scotland during July to recover
from Edward's death. Here, he worked on the finishing touches for
his book on Visible Speech. Aleck had the house to himself and the
place became a refuge for lost souls. Adam Scott, a friend of Aleck's
moved in. Adam had been orphaned as a baby and raised by a spinster aunt. He enjoyed Aleck's company and often invited him to come
for daily walks. "We several times arranged to meet at half-past six in
the morning at King's Cross for a stroll before breakfast, but he never
turned up, and it always ended in my going on to Harrington Square,
and finding him dead asleep in his bedroom."[9] Aleck was not a morning person. Throughout his life, he struggled to stick to what society
called 'normal working hours' without success. He saw no great need
to rise with the sun. He preferred to work all night when there were
no distractions, then fall asleep shortly before dawn.

A former student of Melville's, James Murry,[10] also lodged at the
Harrington Square house. Murry had suffered through the death of
his wife and only child and had come to London to escape the memory
of his family. Aleck provided great therapy and lively companionship
for the poor widower. When Melville returned from Scotland, he
invited Murry to a meeting of the Philological Society. At the time, the
society was struggling over its goal of producing the first-ever
absolute dictionary of the English language. The project had faltered
miserably. Murry took it over and with great enthusiasm turned it into
a resounding success. The final result, almost forty years later, was to
be the *Oxford English Dictionary*.

Melville Bell's book was finally published. It was called *Visible
Speech: The Science of Universal Alphabetics*. The secrets of Visible
Speech were now available to everyone. The book contained ex-
cerpts of all known languages, including a section on translating the
Zulu dialect that Aleck had completed during the summer—after a
series of discussions with a Zulu sailor he had met on his travels
around London. The opening pages gave a heartfelt dedication to

Edward and his efforts in exposing Visible Speech to the general public. He wrote:

"To the Memory of Edward Charles Bell, one of the first proficient in 'Visible Speech,' whose ability in demonstrating the linguistic applications of the system excited the admiration of all who heard him; but whose life of highest promise was cut off in his nineteenth year."[11] The first edition was well received by the intellectual community who hailed it as another step in the quest for a universal alphabet. However, their general opinion was that it could not be considered as the definitive version of the universal alphabet because of its complexity. Everyone agreed that the system was extremely good but too difficult for everyone to master.

Great changes had occurred in 1867. An ocean away, in America, the Civil War had ended and the president, Mr. Lincoln, had been assassinated. The British North America Act had established the Dominion of Canada as a bulwark against further continental expansion of America. Each year, dozens of new inventions and innovative ideas appeared. They were coming faster than the mind could grasp. It was an exciting time to be alive!

The transatlantic cable had finally been completed and American trains now had sleeping cars. A wondrous new household tool called the carpet-sweeper was being sold in London stores. Every month new advances were being made in medicine and science. Aleck's head was filled with so many ideas that he could hardly concentrate on one. He felt linked to what seemed a new spirit of invention.

Some months later, in 1868, Melville had a pamphlet published called *English Visible Speech for the Millions*. It was his answer to the critics. The pamphlet described how anyone could use Visible Speech with relative ease. Unfortunately, however, people weren't especially interested, having little use for such a system. The intellectuals were silenced but unhappy that a public pamphlet proved them wrong. It seemed that no matter how he tried promoting his brainchild, Melville couldn't win. The government refused to help, the general population showed no interest and his peers were certain that something better would come along in due course. It was all very discouraging.

The only bright spot in Melville's life was Aleck's growing interest in elocution and speech research. Since the experiments with his own vocal cavities and the various sounds from different sized bottles of liquid, his curiosity had intensified. He studied the vocal organs of some of his father's students to see if a stammering child might not have a slightly different arrangement or sizing of the throat and vocal organs. After deciding that there was no obvious difference, he began to wonder if other mammals might also have the same physical capacity for speech. His attentions turned to the family dog, Trouve. Aleck recounted that "I found little difficulty in teaching the dog to growl at command. His food supply was limited, and he soon became delighted to growl for food. He would sit up on his hind legs, and growl continuously until I motioned him to stop. He was then rewarded with a morsel of food. I then attempted to manipulate his mouth. Taking his muzzle in my hand, I caused his lips to close and open a number of times in succession while he growled. In this way he gave utterance to the syllables "ma ... ma ... ma." He soon learned to stop growling the moment I released his mouth in anticipation of the expected reward (which was never withheld). After a little practise, I was able to make him say, with perfect distinctness, the word 'mama,' pronounced in the English way with the accent on the second syllable."[12] After another set of manipulations, the dog was able to sound an audible "ga." If the two sounds were combined: "he gave utterance to ga ma ma; by practise this was made to resemble in a ludicrous degree the word 'grandmamma' (pronounced ga ma ma). A double reward followed this result, and the dog became quite fond of his articulation lessons."[13] After some more lessons the dog's vocabulary increased to include the sounds of "oh" and "ow." With great effort all the sounds could be combined and the dog would politely inquire "How are you grandmama?" (pronounced ow ah oooh ga ma ma). The lessons went no further but news of the Bell's talking dog soon spread to family friends and became a topic of incredulous gossip. The story escalated to a point of absurdity where it was claimed that the dog could carry on lengthy conversations.

Aleck decided to switch his attention to teaching Visible Speech. The possibilities of teaching the deaf to speak using the system appeared promising. Although Melville had discussed the idea some time before with Susanna E. Hull—another Bell student and teacher at a deaf school in South Kensington—no practical application of his theories for teaching the deaf had ever been put to the test.

⁓

Aleck walked down the hall of the South Kensington School for the Deaf. The sound of his footsteps echoed eerily in the strangely silent building.

He counted the doors along the corridor under his breath and, as directed, stopped at the fourth door on the left from the end. A small plaque read, "Miss S. Hull." He knocked.

"Mr. Bell?" Susanna Hull gave him a bright smile and motioned him into the small cluttered office.

She seemed a bright woman, with sharp observant eyes. She studied him through her glasses. "Your father has told me a great deal about you."

"I believe you were once a student of his."

"He is a very talented teacher. Are you also a talented teacher, Mr. Bell?"

"I am a good teacher," Aleck replied. "And I want to teach deaf children to speak. I suppose there is a degree of talent required to do that. Although I have never really thought about it in that way."

"Teaching children to speak but not to use sign language?" She raised her brow, then looked about, "Oh, forgive me. I'm being rude. Please do sit down."

Aleck sat. "To answer your question—I want to free children from the closed world of signs. There is a larger world with which they can communicate if they can learn to read lips and speak."

"That's very ambitious, Mr. Bell. Tell me, how do you propose to teach these deaf children to speak?"

"Like my father, I believe his Visible Speech system has great potential for teaching the deaf. I want to try this method on a few students."

"You mean you want to *experiment* on students."

"Putting it bluntly, yes." He looked her in the eye, hoping she was daring enough to help him. Then he added, "It is not an experiment that could do harm."

Susanna Hull wet her lips and sat considering the proposal. Finally, she picked a list of names from her desk and scanned it with her finger. She looked at him thoughtfully.

"I have two students—Lottie and Minna, who might benefit. I'll turn them over to you … to start your experiment. Let's give it a month and see how things work out. After that we can discuss the matter again. Will that suit you, Mr. Bell?"

"Thank you," he said, knowing full well that her respect for his father had determined Miss Hull's decision.

"You may come three days a week if that is satisfactory."

"Perfectly satisfactory. But you will have to drill them on certain exercises between my visits."

"I'll help in any way I can. Show me what to do."

⁓

Melville Bell lowered his newspaper to look up at Aleck, who stood in the doorway of the study. "Come in, my boy. Tell me how the experiment is going. Two weeks now isn't it?"

Aleck nodded and sat down. Melville had been away on a lecture tour. "My four pupils are remarkably intelligent and happy," Aleck told him.

"You have four?"

"Miss Hull gave me two more—Kate and Nelly. I guess she thinks that there is some possibility I may be right."

"Well done! Now that is progress. And how did you proceed?" Melville prodded.

Aleck took a deep breath. "In order for them to understand the Visible Speech system they needed first to understand the symbols themselves. I began with a lesson on basic anatomy, sketching a face on the blackboard and then explaining with signing that I would next draw the inside of the mouth. They were all highly amused, and I might say delighted, to see what the inside of their mouths looked like."

"And how could you tell they understood?"

"They touched their lips, their tongue and so forth. Then I erased the drawing except for the lower lip, the point, the front and the back of the tongue and the glottis.[14] I'm wonderfully encouraged—they made great progress on their first day. Now, Katie can say, very clearly, 'I love you, mama.'"

Melville beamed. "Splendid, Aleck. We'll show the world that my system is useful."

~

It was an ordinary rainy Sunday in August. Aleck was surprised to see roast lamb for dinner—a rare treat in London. His mother had put out the best table linen. Fresh flowers filled the vase on the table's centre-piece. There must be a secret cause for celebration, thought Aleck.

He looked at his father, whose delighted expression portended good news. "I'm going to America!" Melville gleefully exclaimed. "Your uncle David has arranged a lecture tour."

David Bell, his father's older brother, had always been very enthusiastic about the potential of Visible Speech.

"Since Melly is married and living in Edinburgh, I'll have to leave you in charge of the business here. I trust you're up to the responsibility?" His father looked at him quizzically. "Well, my boy, you needn't look so stunned."

"You do tend to treat me like a child at times, sir. Now you propose to leave me in charge of your business. Am I up to it? Of course I'm up to it."

"A challenge," Melville said. "David has convinced me that the British are not yet ready for the possibilities of Visible Speech. He insists people are more apt to take chances in America. The British are so cynical. For months the academics have insisted that Visible Speech is a work of genius, while at the same time condemning it as too difficult to be of practical use. You have already proved them wrong."

"Not quite. I need to do more work," Aleck protested. "Certainly I believe in its value. There's no question that it works and that it's ideal for teaching the deaf."

Melville brushed aside these reservations with a wave. "More important at the moment is, will you agree to handle the business while I'm away?"

"Of course," Aleck replied. It would be a lot of work, along with his own teaching, but the chance to test himself and prove to his father once and for all his worth was too great an opportunity for him to refuse.

"Then David and I shall set forth to conquer America," Melville announced grandly.

⁓

Aleck sat at his desk, writing notes—attempting to do what he didn't do well—organize himself. Rain lashed the windowpane. The winter of 1868 had been particularly cold and damp in London. He had set himself a backbreaking schedule; nonetheless, he had succeeded in running his father's business, teaching his own deaf pupils, attending university classes in physiology and anatomy and attending regular viewings of operations as a member of the Medical Society.

He had taken a brief vacation to Dover earlier in the year to meet his mother and grandmother. However, it couldn't have been enjoyable as he later wrote: "Rather sorry I went, was introduced to people I would not care to recognize if I went there again."[15]

During the summer of 1868, he embarked on an enthusiastic relationship with Marie Ecclestone, a handsome, slightly older woman. It appeared to be a serious affair. But Eliza expressed doubts: "I am more and more convinced she [Marie] would need to marry somebody with a purse and I doubt if she could sit down contentedly to home duties—without extra excitement.... I think it would be better ... if he selected somebody more like Carrie."[16] His mother needn't have worried. Aleck was much too busy for a long-term female relationship.

Yet, as tired as he was, each letter from his father renewed his energies. The most recent correspondence was very enthusiastic. At Yale university, Melville had encountered what he called as "academic sour grapes" from one of the faculty members, Dr. William Dean Whitney. But then David and Melville were invited by the dean of Harvard University to attend a dinner and give a lecture on Visible Speech. At the dinner, Melville had met an influential Massachusetts lawyer, Gardiner Greene Hubbard. Mr. Hubbard, who had a deaf daughter, was overwhelmed by the possibilities of Visible Speech.

"I met Gardiner Greene Hubbard," Melville wrote. "He is very anxious for me to visit his school ... and this Hubbard and I seem to be of one mind. We both believe signing is limiting, whereas children taught to speak can truly communicate."[17]

⌒

"Are you hiding in your study again," Melly asked as he opened the door a crack. He and his wife, Carrie, had come to London for a short visit.

"Not hiding," Aleck replied. "Just trying to find some things." Melly looked tired, even more tired than Aleck felt.

"I have a bit of a surprise for you," Melly allowed.

"I like surprises—I'll qualify that: most surprises."

"Carrie's going to have a baby. You're going to become Uncle Aleck."

Aleck jumped to his feet and embraced Melly. "Wonderful!" He hugged his frail brother tightly. "This is cause enough for a celebration."

"I think just a good dinner and perhaps some song afterwards will be enough."

"My pleasure," Aleck said. He grasped his brother's shoulder. "I wish you lived here instead of in Edinburgh."

"I have my teaching. And now with a baby coming there's even more need for hard work."

"You need rest," Aleck told him seriously. Melly's pale complexion and thin body reminded him of poor Ted, as did the periodic fits of uncontrollable coughing.

"Is that your advice, little brother?" Melly forced a smile. "Since father left you've been working night and day. You're the one who is near collapse."

"Work invigorates me, really."

"Me too," Melly replied without conviction.

Aleck pressed his lips together and nodded. He didn't want to say more, though he felt he should. It was clear that Melly was far from well.

⌒

Melville Bell stepped off the boat train to London into a sea of bobbing hats and sobbing relatives reunited with loved ones. He squinted against the bright sunshine pouring through the glass dome. It was late August and the weather was surprisingly warm for London.

"Father!"

Melville turned towards the sound and saw Aleck tall and straight striding toward him. As he drew closer, Melville could see the lines of weariness around his son's eyes. Clearly, the boy had been overworking himself, probably staying up half the night as usual. But oh my, it was grand to see him again after so many months. They locked into a mighty embrace, then parted, each regarding the other warmly.

"Where's your luggage?" Aleck inquired finally.

"I sent most of it through to the house. It'll arrive in due course. We were late leaving Liverpool. The train seemed to take forever to load. Every passenger must have had a dozen steamer trunks."

They walked towards the exit. Aleck gave him a sideways glance. Their eyes met and both of them laughed.

"You look well father." It was true. The trip had done him a world of good. His cheeks were rosy, and he looked fit as a fiddle.

" I can't tell you how much more healthful their climate is than this London air!" As they stepped outside he sniffed the air and wrinkled his nose. "Disgusting!"

Aleck laughed. "Doesn't it get unbearably cold in the winter?"

"And hot in the summer! But, in spite of the extremes in temperature, it evidently agrees with most of our countrymen!"

"Just our countrymen?" Aleck asked with an amused twinkle in his eye. His father was a true Scots. He considered the Scots a race apart—a race with special needs as well as special tastes, extraordinary intelligence, perseverance and just plain common sense. Not that his father belittled other nationalities. He didn't. Simply stated, he believed that when God made the Scots he made them a wee bit better than anyone else on earth. And that was that.

"No, everyone I suppose. But I have no way of judging the others. I was thinking of those old friends who emigrated to America some years ago. Unbelievable, Aleck! McCleary ... I don't think you would

remember him ... left here ten years ago. He doesn't look a day older!
Not one day!"

Aleck smiled tolerantly.

"And let me tell you, not a few of those who left have had wonderful financial success! North America, Aleck! It's the future of the world!"

"Perhaps one day I can see it all."

"Soon," his father vowed as they walked towards the waiting line
of carriages. They clambered up into a cab. "Harrington Square, Driver!"
Melville shouted and they were off. He settled back in the seat. "My
boy, Ted's death made me realize more than ever that we need to
find a better climate before all of us die. I am planning to move the
Bells to North America. All of us. What do you think of that?"

Aleck didn't know what to think. His father's determination took
him aback, although moving overseas was not an idea that he found
objectionable. From everything he'd heard, Americans were more open-
minded, more progressive than the straight-laced conventionalists of
the British Isles. America, he knew, advocated opportunities for the
common man, and that attracted him.

"To the United States?" he asked.

"Actually, I was thinking more of the new Dominion of Canada.
They're giving land away there! It's a huge place of wide-open spaces,
fine fresh air, forests and clear lakes. Moreover, Aleck, the country is
overflowing with Scots. Including the prime minister himself! Surely if
Canada is good enough for the likes of John A. MacDonald[18] and
Sandford Flemming,[19] it's good enough for the Bells."

"And when had you thought we might move?"

"As soon as it can all be arranged. After all, there are two businesses to be wound down—ours and Melly's in Edinburgh—as well
as a thousand arrangements to be made. But I intend to write to your
mother tonight."[20]

"There's a new Bell to be moved as well," Aleck said.

His father's brows shot up. "Good heavens! Carrie! Is she all right?
I thought I'd be back in time."

"The baby came in August, while you were en route. You're the
grandfather of Teddy Bell."

"And young Teddy's health?"

The cheerfulness faded from Aleck's face. "He's frail, sir, but he's a fighter."

Melville nodded, realizing that the baby had been born prematurely. "And Melly?"

Aleck couldn't lie. "He needs a long rest, he's overworked and I'm afraid his health is deteriorating."

"We must move," his father exclaimed with urgency. "It's imperative." He gazed moodily out the widow at the cacophony of city sounds and crowds of sweating people unaccustomed to such severe summer heat. "Damn this dreadful climate that sweeps away the best!"

⁓

Aleck glanced out the window. Heavy rain pelted the sidewalk but did nothing to dissipate the smoke that lingered over industrial Edinburgh. His father had been right. It was unhealthy on these islands, at least for members of his family.

Nor, he reflected, did spring seem like spring. He had passed the holidays in London, celebrating the New Year of 1869 with his parents. Then, as soon as the spring rains began, he received an urgent letter from poor Carrie. Not only was tiny baby Teddy still sickly and barely clinging to life, but Melly's coughing fits and sleepless nights alarmed her. She reported that there was blood on his pillow nearly every morning. Could someone help her? Aleck took the first train to Scotland.

"Oh, Aleck, I'm so glad you could come."

Carrie met him at the door, looking pale and close to exhaustion.

"You must be weary. All night on the train is enough to make anyone tired. I'll make us some tea."

"I could use some tea. Have the maid make it extra strong."

"Where's Melly?" Aleck asked when she returned.

She pressed a finger to her lips. "Upstairs. He's had a terrible chest cold. The doctor has given him some sleeping powders."

"You look as if you could do with a rest yourself."

"Oh, I'll be all right. It's just the strain. The baby's sick too, and Melly is ... well, stubborn, Aleck. He won't rest. He no longer has the energy to operate the school. Consequently, there is no business."

"And of course no money coming in."

"We're living on our savings. What's left of them."

The maid brought in the tea and placed the tray on the small table between their chairs. Carrie poured from the china pot.

"He's lost so much weight," Carrie lamented.

"Well, stubborn or not, the three of you have got to leave here. If you don't Melly will end up like Teddy."

"But he worries so about what's left of the business."

Aleck took a deep breath, "Look here, I've been operating father's business for the better part of a year. I'm sure I can deal with what is left of Melly's for a few months."

"Oh, Aleck, would you? I think that would relieve him enough to make him give in."

"Do you have a place where you can go?"

"Yes. One of my uncles owns a farm in the lowlands. It's ideal, I know he'll get better there."

"Then as soon as he wakes we'll tell him that the three of you are leaving tomorrow morning."

"He'll argue."

Aleck forced a smile as he reached over and squeezed his sister-in-law's hand. "Of course he will. But you'll see, it won't do him a bit of good."

⁓

Aleck sat in the study of the house on Harrington Square and reread his brother's letter slowly, then he read Carrie's pleading letter again.

When Melly, Carrie and baby Teddy had returned from the lowlands at the end of September 1869, Melly had appeared totally recovered. Aleck had been elated, not just because Melly seemed so much healthier, but because the strain of overwork had worn him out. He waved aside their gratitude, and in a state of exhaustion returned to London and a less demanding routine.

His father, still planning the move to Canada, had had to interrupt those plans when he was invited to America for another lecture tour. His first visit had stirred up such academic controversy that his defenders insisted he return to support their fight for Visible Speech.

Once more, Aleck had to manage the family business. Not that he minded helping his father, but the extra work meant that he had to curtail some of his experiments in sound.

There was always so much to do and so little time in which to do it. The worst part was his abysmal ignorance in the field. Sound, electricity and the operational components involved in creating human speech were not subjects that could be learned at university. Information was only to be found in obscure research papers, limited edition publications and the occasional report in a foreign language— usually French or German. He was fluent in neither. He felt like a caterpillar inching its way into oblivion.

Then, on the first day of April—All Fool's Day—he received a heartbreaking letter from Melly that changed everything. Baby Teddy had died, and Aleck's older brother pleaded with him to keep in touch.

"I do wish you would give me a line now and then.... Is it that your scientific attainments are so much further advanced than mine that you can take no interest in the little I can say on such subjects?... As for your fighting shy of me, because I sometimes make fun of such of your ideas as strike me as ridiculous; it is absurd to give such a reason; and I suspect that this is the foundation of all I complain of. Write soon like a good chap."[21]

The letter had made Aleck feel very guilty. He knew that he should have written more often, but somehow the time seemed to fly. True, Melly did tease him sometimes, but that was not the reason he hadn't written. He had been selfishly wrapped up in his own frustrations about being unable to do what he wanted because he had his father's business to run.

The next letter had come from Carrie. She pleaded with him to come to Edinburgh. He replied immediately and arrived in Edinburgh to find her close to physical exhaustion and Melly near death.

He had booked them all on the first sleeping car to London. His parents were in absolute shock. For three days they sat, stone faced and silent next to Melly's bed in the front room. The doctor came and went, but there was nothing anyone could do. Throughout the days and nights, Melly's breath came rasping and laboured, each bloody cough painfully racking his emaciated body. He died on 28 May and was buried that morning in Highgate Cemetery, next to his brother Teddy and Grandfather Alexander Bell.

Aleck wiped his brow. He felt emotionally drained and completely exhausted from everything that had happened.

"Aleck!" Melville, still dressed in his funeral clothes, entered the study and sank into a chair with a groan.

Aleck looked up. His eyes were moist.

"We are leaving this abominable country," his father said. "This time we shall not postpone the trip. I've made arrangements to depart in July. I'll not lose you too."

Aleck nodded. He was too tired to reply.

Some time before his death, Melly had developed an interest in the spiritual afterlife. He sent his father books on the subject and, after a serious conversation with Aleck, a promise was made between father and sons that whichever of them died first would try to communicate with the other. After Melly's death, the memory of the pact remained fixed in Aleck's mind. Later he wrote: "I well remember how often—in the stillness of the night—I have had little seances all by myself in the half-hope, half-fear of receiving some communication ... and honestly tried my best without any success whatever."[22]

Aleck looked pale, thin and tired—not at all well—and, as usual, terribly busy trying to do too many things at once. Friends and relations who had attended the funeral shook their heads in the certainty that the Bells were about to lose their remaining son. The listless Aleck already looked more dead than alive. Melville insisted that the fresh Canadian air would work its wonders if Aleck came to the New World with the rest of the family. Aleck considered his options. It meant starting all over, giving up the businesses, leaving contacts and students. As well, it would mean leaving Marie Ecclestone. It had been his intention one day to marry Marie. In the end, Aleck returned unhappily to Edinburgh to sell the house, wind up Melly's affairs and help Carrie pack her things for the overseas move. He wrote to his father:

The dream that you know I have cherished for so long
has the heart not to let me know it. I do not wish to have
it referred to again. Do not think me ungrateful because
I have been unhappy at home for the last two years.
I have now no other desire than to be near you, Mamma,
and Carrie, and I put myself unreservedly into your hands
to do with me whatever you think for the best, I am
dear Papa

Your affectionate and only son, Aleck.

He sent a goodbye note to Marie, together with two pictures of himself appropriately inscribed with sorrowful notations claiming that he would still think of her despite the ocean between them. Marie's response startled him. Her cheerful tone and well wishes for his future were not at all what he had expected.

"Don't grieve about your examinations, &c—all the degrees in the world would not make up for ill-health ... Make a name for yourself away. Don't get absorbed in yourself—mix freely with your fellows— it is one of your great failings. How I shall miss you all!... I scarcely expect you will return, England would be too slow for you after America."[23]

The letter was a blow to Aleck and, some years later, he recalled the incident observing that "I had created an ideal which had no existence, still I believe that I should have learned to love her had I not awakened to the conviction that she cared nothing for me—that she merely wished to give me sufficient encouragement to keep me— in case no other came forward." The conclusion that Marie had been simply biding her time with him was a humiliating experience. "Ever since Papa's unintended conduct in the matter of Marie Ecclestone made me feel so bitterly ... it has almost been impossible for me to approach him confidentially."[24] Although there was no elaboration as to the native of his father's interference, it was implicit that Melville Bell had spoken at length with Marie, perhaps making it clear that if she were not serious about his son then she should do the honour- able thing and break off the relationship. References to his father in her farewell letter no doubt tipped Aleck as to what had transpired.

With nothing left to hold him in England, he and the other members of the Bell family, Melville, Eliza and the widowed Carrie, together with their belongings, hopes, and memories of the land from which they had come for generations, set sail on 21 July 1870, for the Dominion of Canada.

CHAPTER SIX

Brantford, Ontario, Canada, 1870

Aleck adjusted the pillows under his head, then rolled on his back and stared up at the old tree on the hillside. Its branches formed a leafy barrier between him and the blue sky. The effect was pure art as the bright sun filtered through the leaves to scatter on the grass beside him in dancing, lacy patterns.

His surroundings—the rolling hills, the fields of wildflowers and the orchard—lay warm and beautiful in the summer sun. His health had returned. Even his headaches had subsided. And yet a sense of guilt crept into all this thoughts. Why, he asked again and again, had he been the one to survive?

They had sailed for Canada late in July. It had been an uneventful crossing. Aleck had sat on deck staring at the gulls and wondering at the grace of their flight. The ship docked at Quebec City on the first day of August, and they had waited most of the day while it unloaded and their trunks and boxes were transferred to another vessel for the trip up the St. Lawrence River to Montreal. From there, they had taken an overnight train four hundred miles farther inland to Paris, Ontario.

"How I wondered at this land!" Aleck said to himself. It was a huge country with a scattered population of less than three and a half million. A deserted paradise. They had come to Ontario because his father had met the local vicar, the Reverend Thomas Henderson, during his last lecture tour. Henderson had talked to Melville about immigrating. He had offered to house them until they could find a suitable house and acreage.

The district around Paris had been settled by English, Scots and Irish immigrants who clung tenaciously to their cultural and social values. His father researched the area, and decided it was the right place for them to settle down. "We should be near our own kind," he had proclaimed.

There had been many family discussions on the subject in which Aleck seldom participated. He didn't care. Now that they were here, one place was as good as another. Melly's death had depressed him to the point that he had become mentally and physically lethargic, almost indifferent to his surroundings. If his father had suggested moving to the Sahara or Timbuktu, he would have gone without a murmur of protest.

At his father's urging, he had finally agreed to the two of them riding out in the Reverend Henderson's buckboard to find a place for the family to live. After a week of clopping up and down dusty concession roads, they had found a farm near the neighbouring town of Tutelo Heights. It looked like an ideal farm; ten and a half acres of tall stately trees, flowering shrubs, a fine garden and a sizeable apple orchard. The back of the property ended at a bluff where an assortment of enormous elms, their leaves constantly aflutter, rustled softly in the wind. It became Aleck's favourite spot for hiding from the world. He came to it regularly—with blankets, pillows and books.

After the stench of London's sulphurous air and the noise of that huge city, their little farm was a peaceful wonder. When they had first arrived he had been ill, worn out from the previous year. But now he knew he was stronger, even though thoughts of Melly's death and his own self-doubts still depressed him from time to time. The two feelings were clearly connected. Losing his brothers had not only saddened him but for the first time in his life made him sharply aware of his own mortality.

What had he accomplished in his life thus far? When he stopped to reflect he felt that he had achieved nothing. Why had he not succeeded? Succeeded at what? He didn't even know that. He hadn't married. He had failed to find the love of a good woman. He had given up his teaching and his research. Now all he did was read, rest and help his mother and Carrie with repairs to the homestead. His father had left them almost as soon as they had moved in. He wanted to use what was left of the summer to make enough money to see them through the winter.

"And what can I do?" he asked aloud. The wind rustled the tree branches above. He got to his feet and stretched. Was he really isolated in the middle of nowhere? He'd been here for months, and except for house hunting, had hardly explored the district at all. This wouldn't do. "God helps those who help themselves," he muttered, gathering up his things.

As he strolled down the hillside he tried to recall what he knew about the district. It hadn't interested him before, but his curiosity was reawakened. Hadn't his mother said something about an Indian Reserve in the area? What language did these Indians speak? Could their language be put into Visible Speech? Why not? Suddenly, a host of questions began popping into his head like tiny Chinese firecrackers. He realized that it was the first time since Melly's death that he had felt the least interest in anything. He picked up his pace, walking briskly toward the house, his arms full of pillows, blankets and books. The more he thought about the Indians the more excited he became until he began to run. He would leave everything on the porch and start exploring at once.

Aleck stopped to read the crudely painted sign nailed to a tree trunk at the side of the dirt road. It informed the visitor that he was entering the Indian Reserve. He had seen some of the local Indians when his family had arrived in the district; once, while shopping in town with his mother he saw a few of them hanging about on street corners. They dressed poorly and were always on foot. The adults tended to avert their eyes when white people passed, but their children were curious and bright-eyed, with shy smiles. He felt certain that their dress, behaviour and general manner resulted from the way they were treated. He had talked to a few neighbours about the Indians and concluded that they were deeply despised, and for the most part, ignored.

"Indian," he whispered as he walked along. It wasn't at all correct. These people were no more Indian than he was, but had been misnamed by a lost and somewhat confused explorer.

He came to a stop a few yards down the road at a small house. It was built of logs and clearly had only one room. Two children played out front on a rope suspended from a tree branch. He tried to approach, but when they saw him they stopped playing and stared at him suspiciously.

"I'm looking for your chief," he said as clearly as possible. He supposed they did have a chief —he knew almost nothing about Indians except what he had read in books and that had been precious little.

The pair giggled, their eyes shinning like bright new shoe buttons. "Is there a chief?" He spoke slowly, distinctly.

They nodded in unison.

"And where might he be?"

One pointed further down the road. The other spoke in a near whisper. "It's the big house."

"Thank you very much," Aleck replied with a wink.

He proceeded down the road, passing four more small shacks before coming to a proper house. With considerable self-resolve but without the slightest idea what he was going to say, he climbed the porch steps to the door and knocked.

A powerfully built man with a severe expression opened the door. He had thick dark hair and magnificent, high cheekbones. Aleck looked him in the eye and held out his hand.

"Good afternoon. I'm looking for Chief Joseph."

"I'm Chief Joseph."

The chief refused the handshake and didn't invite him to enter. Aleck withdrew his hand. "I'm Alexander Graham Bell."

"And what can I do for you, Alexander Graham Bell?" the chief asked without much interest.

"I'm a teacher," Aleck replied. "I last taught in England."

Chief Joseph looked sceptical, but he stepped aside and motioned Aleck to follow him.

The central parlour was comfortably furnished with an inscribed portrait of King George over the mantle. Aleck peered at it.

"Joseph Brant was my ancestor," Chief Joseph explained. "He translated the Book of Mark into our language—Mohawk. The king gave him his likeness."

Aleck returned his eyes to the chief. "I know almost nothing about your people, except what I read. I want to learn from them. Can you help me?"

"To what purpose will you put such knowledge?"

Aleck half smiled, "First, to improve my own knowledge. Second, I am interested in languages. My father has invented a system of writing all languages phonetically. The ability to write my language in your language would enable us to translate many works."

Chief Joseph considered his visitor carefully. He decided that the tall young man had an open and honest face with curiosity beaming from his eyes. He thought most white men were interlopers, but this one seemed genuinely interested in learning, and that, Chief Joseph believed, was a quality that should be encouraged. Aleck waited quietly while the chief made up his mind.

"Very well, I will instruct people to answer your questions."

Aleck nodded enthusiastically. "Can we begin now?"

"We'll begin at the school," he suggested. "It is the proper place for learning."

⁓

"I didn't think you would make it," Eliza said as Melville stomped the snow off his boots in the hallway and then began the laborious job of taking off his top two layers of clothing.

"I didn't think I would make it either, my dear. I've never seen so much snow, never!"

"It's our first of the year," Eliza said. "It won't be our last." She hugged him awkwardly. They had never been given to outward displays of affection, particularly in front of the children, but the relief of his safe arrival through a howling blizzard overcame her inhibitions. "Oh, I'm so glad you're home." She was nearly in tears from joy.

Melville held her tightly for a moment then chuckled. "Let's all go in and sit by the fire." He rubbed his hands together.

Aleck and Carrie followed them into the living room. "There's fresh pie for you," Carrie announced. "We preserved so many apples after the harvest that none of us wants to see any apples again."

Melville laughed.

"The house smelled of apples night and day for weeks," Aleck told him.

His father sank into his favourite armchair. "I feel as if I never want to leave this house again."

"With all the snow, you may not be able to," Carrie said—only half joking.

"No matter. I've made more than enough money to see us through the winter. And ... I have a surprise, a real surprise."

Aleck repeated his father's words into his mother's ear.

"Before leaving, I applied for a teaching job at the school here in Brantford. To my surprise, they have accepted my application. I do not have to go on the lecture circuit again."

Aleck looked surprised. "But what about your Visible Speech?"

"My boy, I've spent my life on Visible Speech. I do not intend to spend the rest of my life trotting the globe explaining it. My only regret is that I'll have to cancel my spring lecture tour. On the other hand, teaching in Brantford will allow me to remain at home." He looked at Eliza and nodded with satisfaction.

Aleck stared out the window at the snow. It was still falling, more snow than he had ever seen before. He thought about the Mohawks. His few months of work with them had been a fascinating experience, and he was making great progress with their language, but he knew that it was not enough. He needed to escape. He felt trapped by the snow and isolated from the world of ideas. He turned suddenly to his father and tried not to sound overly anxious to escape. "Father! Why not have me take over your lecture tour?"

For a long moment Melville did not speak then his face seemed to light up. "Of course! Why not?" he said. "It's a grand idea. I'll write to the Reverend King at once, recommending you as my substitute."

⌒

Aleck alighted from the train. He felt a new man and, for the first time in a long while, his own man. Not only was he taking over his father's lecture tour, but he had been offered a teaching position at the Boston School for Deaf Mutes at the princely salary of $500 for the school year.[1]

From what he had seen through the train window, spring came much earlier to New England than to Ontario, where winter was still retreating slowly. In the deep woods thin crisp snow clung to the earth in the shadows of rocks and trees. Pools of ice-encrusted water lay in the lowlands and ditches. But in Boston the air was warm, the snow had gone and daffodils were already in bloom.

He stood in the crowded North Station under the clock where he had been instructed to wait. "Mr. Alexander Graham Bell?"

Aleck turned to confront a pair of inquiring grey eyes and the kindly face of a tall, slim elderly gentleman with excellent posture.

"I'm Alexander Graham Bell."

"Dexter King." He held out his hand and Aleck shook it firmly. "I've brought my carriage."

Although he avoided snap judgements, Dexter King liked the look of Melville Bell's son. He had a ready smile, and a friendly, though perhaps slightly mischievous expression. His nose was long and straight and his inquisitive dark eyes twinkled with good humour. His beard, King noted, was a bit sparse and his hair was groomed in the current fashion—oiled and pasted flat to his scalp. He was certainly no fashion plate; the English cut of his dark suit was out of style but acceptably conservative. Teachers were not, after all, expected to be dressed in the most recent fashion.

"Did you sleep well on the train?"

"Like a baby, lulled by the singing rails."

"Ah, you are a poet then, or a romantic at least? Well, since you are well rested, and as it is early in the day, I shall first transport you to your lodgings at Miss Fisher's Boarding House. Then perhaps you would care to accompany me on a walking tour of our city?"

"That sounds most agreeable," Aleck said with a grin. He already felt at ease with the Reverend King—and a good thing too, he thought, to get along with one's new employer.

"You'll discover that Bostonians are inordinately proud of our city."

The carriage rattled over the cobblestone streets. They arrived at number 2 Bullfinch Avenue, which, King informed him, had been named after Charles Bullfinch, the famous architect who had skillfully transformed Boston from an eighteenth-century English style town into a nineteenth-century American city, and whose son, Charles, was one of America's leading writers, known chiefly for his work in mythology.

When they reached the boarding house, Aleck was introduced to his new landlady and left his case in his modest but adequate room. Dexter King then had his driver take them to the Boston Common where they began their walk. They strolled along Tremont Street bordering the common. Across the common, atop Beacon Hill, sat the State House with its oddly garish gold dome. Then they turned down State Street toward the waterfront and historic Faneuil Hall and the old State House.

King kept up a running history lesson as he pointed out the various sights. "Two hundred and fifty years of American history in the making," he stated with pride.

Aleck smiled, but kept tactfully silent. To be sure, Boston reeked of American history—what there was of it—and indeed it seemed an extraordinarily fine town. But two hundred and fifty years of history was nothing to a Scotsman. Edinburgh traced its history to the seventh century.

"One if by land, two if by sea," his guide intoned. "There are four churches, one on each corner of the city. That's from 'Paul Revere's Ride' by Longfellow. Revere rode out to warn the citizens that the British were coming. There was one lantern to be hung in the church tower if they were coming by land and two lanterns if they were coming by sea." He waved his hand at the stark white, clapboard North Church. They turned up Summer Street and headed back toward the common. "Boston is granite and pudding stone; brownstone and bricks. Bricks and more bricks."

The common and the Boston Public Gardens were separated by Charles Street, which bordered the Charles River. A long park with half-moon bridges lay along the river bank. Graceful willows dipped into the water, shielding the scores of sleeping ducks from the spring sun. Across the river, on the other side of the Harvard Bridge, lay the Massachusetts Institute of Technology (M.I.T.).

When King pointed out the famous institute Aleck stopped to stare. During his months in Canada he had had no access to the latest technical books and publications. Just seeing the greystone buildings of M.I.T. excited him. Oh, how he longed to roam its library and have time to read all the articles on the most recent inventions.

"Are you free for dinner?"

"I'm afraid not, sir." Aleck replied. "I'm meeting the Munroes—friends of my father."

"Then some other time soon," King suggested. "And of course I shall see you bright and early Monday morning at the school."

"You shall indeed."

"Then we should finish our tour. I shall leave knowing that you've seen at least a part of Boston." He gave a cheerful laugh and slapped Aleck on the back.

"I have enjoyed it. Thank you."

He indeed liked what he saw. The flowers in the public gardens were well laid out, the trees were engulfed in the light green foliage of spring, and nature itself seemed to be greeting him with the same warmth as the Reverend King. After they parted though, the only sight that remained firmly fixed in his mind was the buildings of M.I.T. The thought of them made him hunger to get back to his real work—of satisfying his curiosity and working with language and the science of sound.

⟿

Dinner that evening was roast duck, bread dressing, plum sauce, squash, potatoes and a rich raisin pudding for dessert. Not only was the food excellent, but the conversation proved stimulating and raised Aleck's hopes for the future. He had been hesitant about visiting strangers, but he'd been welcomed warmly and treated with such great respect that he was somewhat embarrassed. He felt himself unworthy of such treatment.

Mr. Munroe leaned over intently. "Your father tells me you've been dabbling in the science of sound for a number of years."

"My brother and I once tried to make a talking machine."

"And how did it turn out?"

"Not very well," Aleck answered. "But it was great fun."

"You seem a fellow of fine good humour. I suspect you built your machine for more than fun."

"I did. And I do understand how speech is made. It is the principle I use when teaching the deaf to speak." He saw a glint of scepticism in his host's eyes. "It's true, I once had hopes of reproducing the human voice mechanically. I still cherish that dream."

They moved from the dinner table to the study. It was a large room with enclosed bookcases, a fine highly polished mahogany desk and several comfortable, overstuffed chairs. Munroe poured the brandy.

"Are you familiar with the work of Hermann von Helmholtz?"

Aleck nodded. Helmholtz was one of the most respected scientists in the entire world. He had made important contributions in many areas including sound. "I've read some of his papers, but I've been out of touch for the last year."

"We have a Helmholtz sound apparatus in the lab at M.I.T. Why don't you come around and we'll give you a demonstration."

Aleck felt a surge of excitement. He would gladly forgo the dessert and brandy and visit the M.I.T. laboratory immediately, but his host lit his cigar and leaned back in his chair.

Aleck decided it was important that he appear sensible and restrained. Not everyone appreciated impulsive behaviour. "I should like very much to see it, and at the earliest possible date," he said quickly.

"I daresay before seeing a demonstration you ought to do a little homework, so to speak. Have you read Dr. John Tyndall's latest work?"

"The Irish physicist?"

Munroe looked pleased, "Yes, the same. He's at the Royal Institution in London."

"I'm familiar with much of his work, although he's written a great deal."

"Quite so. Quite so. But his latest book is on sound."

"As I said, I've been isolated. I am behind on my scientific reading."

"Well then you must catch up. I have his book here. I'll lend it to you."

Munroe carefully withdrew a volume from a bookcase and handed it to Aleck.

"I shall read it this very night."

Munroe laughed, "All of it?"

"Every word!" Aleck promised.

"I would call that a real hunger for knowledge. Tell you what. Meet me at M.I.T. tomorrow and I'll arrange a demonstration of the apparatus for you."

"I'll be there," Aleck promised. "Name the time."

"Shall we say one o'clock?"

"One o'clock it is then."

With that, Munroe handed him a snifter of brandy. "To tomorrow!" He toasted. "And to all the tomorrows after that."

On Monday morning, Miss Sarah Fuller met him at the door of the Boston School for Deaf Mutes. She was a bustling little woman who exuded warmth and kindness.

"I can't tell you how very happy I am that you have accepted the position to teach the term, Mr. Bell."

Aleck assumed that she would have preferred to see his father in the position, but if she felt any disappointment at his arrival, she covered it admirably.

"And I cannot tell you how pleased I am to be here, Miss Fuller."

"Come along then," she said. Aleck followed her into the red brick building, down a corridor and out onto the playground.

Two boys were squabbling, their sounds understandable, but typical of those who could not hear. Aleck paused a moment and watched as Miss Fuller broke up the argument with a rare combination of kindness and resolve. Almost immediately he felt himself to be in the company of an extraordinary person. Her face was a perfect blend of love, goodness and firmness.[2]

"Ours is the only speech day school for the deaf in Boston," she told him.

"It feels alive," he said grinning. "Much better than all the other schools for the deaf I've visited."

"The followers of Mr. Gallaudet's sign language method are freely predicting our failure. Sometimes I think they hope for it so they can be declared the greater experts."

Aleck shook his head vigorously. "You won't fail, Miss Fuller. I doubt that you often fail at anything."

She looked him straight in the eye. "Are you trying to flatter me, Mr. Bell?" Her expression softened momentarily. "It's true, that I don't give up easily. I believe in what I'm doing here, and I believe children learn in different ways. One method may not be right for every child. As teachers, we must learn more flexibility."

They stood for a moment looking at one another as if each recognized some vital quality in the other. Then, a large red ball rolled towards him, and a young girl ran after it. "Can I beat the brushes after class?" she asked. Her words were carefully formed, but she spoke with hesitation and without expression or tone.

"Yes, you may beat the brushes after class," Miss Fuller replied.

Aleck watched the young girl run away.

"You see, Mr. Bell, these children are deaf, but they're not helpless. Teach them to speak. But above all do not pity them."

"I'll do my best."

"As soon as the bell rings—though only we shall hear it—I will take you to a classroom and you can begin."

The classroom Miss Fuller took Aleck to was small. His young pupils filed in silently and took their seats, waiting expectantly. Miss Fuller remained in the room, taking a seat at the back.

Aleck went to the blackboard and—as he had done with his star pupils, Kate and Nelly, at Miss Hull's School in London—began by drawing a huge absurd-looking face. The children laughed and he laughed with them. He wrote the first of the speech symbols on the board and then illustrated them. The children responded to Aleck quickly. By the end of the afternoon, they had mastered the first four groups of symbols.

When the time came to dismiss them, he felt almost sad to see them leave. Their minds were so eager, they seemed so ready to learn more.

"Oh, you dear man, you have exceeded my wildest expectations!" Miss Fuller's face glowed with such admiration that Aleck flushed with embarrassment.

"I had thought it would take hours!" She shook her head. "Oh, Mr. Bell, I must beg your forgiveness. When the Reverend King and Mr.

Gardiner Hubbard told me that you would be coming instead of your father, I was ... well frankly, I was disappointed. I even doubted that you could be as good. You see, I had heard him speak, and had already prepared myself to work with him. But you're just as gifted a teacher as he—perhaps more so."

For a moment, Aleck was taken aback by her honesty. "Given your doubts, I'm surprised you accepted me in the first place."

"Like the Reverend Dexter, I have faith," she answered, looking him in the eye. "There is a group of older students who are much less manageable. Those you will take on this evening."

"I look forward to the challenge, Miss Fuller."

She smiled and took his arm. "Come along. We'll have supper together and plot and talk."

~

"I made a mistake, a most ignominious failure!" Aleck paced back and forth in Miss Fuller's parlour, chastising himself.

The days had blended into each other leaving him little time for anything except teaching. His experiments with the Helmholtz machine at M.I.T. had been put on hold. Initially, his students' progress had been so quick that he'd thought they would all be speaking in a matter of months. But he realized now that he had been too optimistic. He had tried to teach all of them at the same pace, and in the process he had left most of his more mature students far behind the young ones in his day class.

He looked at Sarah. She reserved comment on his self-criticism. "My older students can only make the most lamentable squeaks imaginable.[3] I've simply pushed them beyond their capabilities."

"You wanted the best for them."

"And now I have given them nothing."

"You're being too hard on yourself."

"But all they can utter is babble talk!" As he continued to describe the problem, he suddenly thought of a possible solution. "What if I tried to write the symbols for the sounds that they do make and then compare those to the symbols for the sounds that they should be making?"

Sarah's eyes twinkled, "I think you may have hit on something."

Aleck laughed, "They're teaching me!"

"Learning, Aleck, is always a shared experience between student and teacher. When we forget that, we fail."

"You're a wise owl, Sarah," he told her.

"And you, Aleck, are a very good teacher."

Perhaps I'll have more time after tonight's lecture, he thought hopefully, as he closed his book of notes. This was the last in the lecture series he had taken over for his father. He glanced about the room and realized that he would not get away early. Those who had sat attentively through his talk were now preparing to swarm around him. He didn't mind answering questions relating to the lecture, but he was disturbed by ardent admirers who just wanted to meet him.

"Oh, that was so stimulating Mr. Bell!" a middle-aged woman gushed. She reached the podium first, even before he had finished putting away his notes. "I think your work is remarkable, simply remarkable."

"Thank-you, Madame."

"Can any deaf child learn to speak?" a tall man asked him.

"Any child who is taught properly," Aleck replied.

"Mr. Bell!" A deep penetrating voice spoke from the fringe of his admirers. "Gardiner Hubbard," the gentleman announced.

Aleck remembered his father telling him that Hubbard had done a great deal to raise money for educating the deaf. "It's good of you to come, sir." Aleck offered his hand.

The others must have recognized the Hubbard name because they drew back and began, as if on cue, to talk to one another.

"Come, come, Mr. Bell. I want to talk with you privately. I have my carriage outside. May I drive you home?"

"That's very good of you," Aleck said. He shook a few more hands on his way out of the hall as Hubbard cleared the way for him. When they'd escaped into the night air. Hubbard waved to his carriage, and in a moment they were trotting off toward Mrs. Fisher's Boarding House.

"I have a deaf daughter," Gardiner Hubbard began without preface.

"My father has mentioned her."

"She's thirteen now, and I must say, something of a miracle. Mind you, she's a bright child— extraordinarily bright." He gave Aleck a wry smile in the dimly lit coach. "But then I suppose all fathers think that their children are bright. However, I assure you that I am not alone in my opinion."

Aleck smiled. "I have heard others comment on her intelligence."

"And her stubbornness? Mabel has been deaf since she was five. She had scarlet fever."

"It's fortunate that she had already learned to speak," Aleck said. "It makes it easier."

"I know—but of course she wasn't very old, nor was her pre-deaf vocabulary very large."

"And it is a terrible setback when you can no longer hear yourself form words," Aleck told him seriously. "She must have been very frightened when she discovered she was deaf."

"I assume she was ... but she was such an extraordinary child! At first she seemed more angry than frightened. Then she became frustrated. Though I must tell you, Mrs. Hubbard and I were more frustrated. We thought she had brain damage as well. We even considered putting her in a home. But heaven smiled! We discovered she had a fine brain, and after that it was primarily a matter of patience. Mrs. Hubbard's patience, I might add."

Aleck felt a thrill as he listened to Hubbard recount Mabel's story. The precise moment when a spark ignited that kindled a deaf person's comprehension always excited him. He had seen the eyes of his pupils at that moment of understanding, just as Gardiner Hubbard had seen it in his daughter.

Hubbard went on to explain how he had sought funding for schools for the deaf. Then he added, "But we didn't send Mabel to a special school. Perhaps we were wrong. We educated her as if she were normal."

"From my own experience, I'm sure you had a difficult time, but I think you were right. Pity and pandering is not the same as compassionately teaching the deaf to stand on their own feet and be independent."

"Sometimes it was a battle of wills. She howled with rage. Floods of tears and violent tantrums."

"But you succeeded?"

"Mabel succeeded." Gardiner Hubbard replied. "Mabel and my wife."

"She must have built on her pre-deaf vocabulary," Aleck guessed.

"Exactly," Gardiner said. "Mind you it took a great deal of patience. Fortunately, Mrs. Hubbard has the patience of Job. And as she learned to speak, my daughter learned also to read and write."

"Did your wife educate your daughter alone?"

"No. We have other children. A governess works with all of them. In this regard fate smiled on us again; we were able to engage an exceptionally gifted young lady directly from Teacher's College—Mary True." Hubbard paused, for emphasis, before getting to his main point.

"My daughter's education is still incomplete. I could send her to Europe for a year or two to study. But I'd like you to teach her. Knowing your father and his teaching system, and hearing you tonight, I sense that you could do much to improve her tone, make her speech less flat."

"I'm flattered, sir, that you would ask. But I can't possibly take on a private student at the moment."

"I would pay you well," said Hubbard as the carriage came to halt in front of Mrs. Fisher's.

"Believe me, it's not the money. I have obligations to fulfil my contractual agreements."

Hubbard sighed in disappointment and pressed his lips together. He was a man used to having his way, but he understood.

"She is very fortunate to have you for a father, and I do look forward to meeting her one day." Aleck said.

"You may count on it."

CHAPTER SEVEN

Boston, Summer 1871

Gertrude Hubbard had a spacious, airy room. Even in the heat of a Boston summer, it was cooler than the rest of the house. Mabel paused in the doorway. Her mother's room always evoked a nostalgic feeling that she couldn't describe. Perhaps the faint odour of perfume, perhaps the cool blue in which the room had been decorated, or maybe it was some long-lost memory of infancy.

"Mabel," Gertrude faced her to speak, and held out her arms.

"Yes, mama?"

"Darling, I want to talk with you."

Mabel came into the room and sat on the corner of the big four-poster bed.

"The school year is ended. Did you enjoy it?"

It seemed an odd question. In spite of a tenuous beginning, her year in a normal school, filled with normal students had been highly successful. "Very much," she replied, feeling that she was stating the obvious.

"I was certain you did. I know it was awkward at first, and certainly it wasn't an easy decision for us—I mean we weren't sure how the other children would treat you."

Mabel smiled. "Once they got used to me, they treated me as an equal."

"And I think that has given you a great deal of self-confidence."

"I'm not afraid of meeting strangers if that's what you mean. Most people are quite helpful, once they understand."

Mabel smiled, remembering how when her teacher turned to write something on the chalkboard while continuing to speak, her classmates shouted a reminder to him to turn around so that she could read his lips.

"And how do you feel about next year?" her mother asked.

Mabel wondered if her face showed the surprise she felt. "Why, I want to go back to school."

"Your father and I have been thinking," Gertrude began guardedly. "We feel that it's time for you and your sisters to study in Europe."

Certainly it was what all young ladies from good families were expected to do, Mabel knew. But why now when she was so happy with all her new school chums? "I don't know what you mean, and I don't want to go," she said forcefully.

Gertrude's expression remained neutral. Coaxing her daughter always worked better than ordering her. Mabel was by far the most stubborn of her children. Most of the time she considered it a great asset, given Mabel's deafness. But at other times, it was simply a stumbling block that had to be overcome. "We thought that if you went to school in Vienna you could improve yourself by learning German. Besides, Cousin Copley and cousin Mary will be there—and Miss Rogers as well."

Mabel shook her head and studiously fixed her gaze on the carpet.

"Perhaps you could go to Rome in the spring. Your sisters would be in boarding school."

Mabel still said nothing.

"Of course we won't force you," her mother said, leaning over and touching her lightly on the arm. "I only want you to think about it."

"But can I decide? Will it really be my very own decision?" she asked, looking up suddenly.

"Yes, you can decide," her mother promised.[1]

Mabel left the room, her mind filled with conflicting thoughts. Perhaps her mother was right. Perhaps she should go to Europe. On the other hand, she did like her school and her friends. She went to her bedroom and sat down to consider the alternatives. Her mother always wanted the best for her. If she refused the trip to Europe she might regret it later. It wouldn't hurt to think about it awhile longer. She laughed, realizing that she was already beginning to relent.

⁓

Aleck withdrew his pocket watch and checked the time. He was expecting Sarah Fuller with a prospective new student. He surveyed his room to see whether the worst of the clutter had been cleared away. When he'd returned from Canada the previous September he had rented larger rooms at 35 Weston Newton Street to give him enough space to conduct private lessons. The premises were reasonably priced and ideal for his needs. He had his bedroom and another in which to meet his students. At the moment, he was teaching three: Theresa Dudley, Susanna Hull and Jeannie Lippitt—all cash customers.

He looked around again, admitting to himself that no matter how large an area he occupied he invariably managed to fill it with books, papers and the bits and pieces of his various inventions. Lectures, classes and tutoring filled his days. He was busier than he had ever been. He knew he had made the right decision in returning to Boston.

The summer of 1871 had been a joy. At the end of the school term, Sarah Fuller invited him to spend the summer at the home of her married sister. The Jordans had three youngsters, all of whom took an instant liking to Aleck. Within the first week they were calling him "Uncle Allie." He passed his days with long walks, overnight hiking expeditions and reading. With the luxury of leisure time he reviewed his teaching performance, considering carefully what had worked and what had not. When September arrived, he'd come back to the school physically refreshed and bursting with new ideas.

During the first term, he worked with both teachers and students. There were five teachers on the faculty: Annie Bond, Sarah Fuller, Ellen Barton, Mary True and himself. Mary True had come on the recommendation of Gardiner Hubbard. His frenetic pace began again. He went to Northampton to discuss Visible Speech with the principal of the Clarke School, Harriet Rogers. He met Lewis Dudley, who had a special interest in his methods and promised to send his daughter, Theresa, to Boston for private lessons. News of his success at the

Boston school spread around the state. The program he organized to demonstrate student progress at the annual presentation of the school body to the leaders of the Boston Education authorities was such a resounding success that it was reported in both the Boston and New York newspapers. When the term ended he hurried off to teach for a few months at the Clarke School. At Lewis Dudley's insistence, he took Theresa Dudley home with him to Tutelo Heights as a boarding student. Besides being paid handsomely by Dudley for giving his daughter individual attention, it gave him an opportunity to visit his parents, and above all, to rest. When he went back to Boston with Theresa, she had improved so much that her grateful father urged him to "stay at the Clarke School with April to compare notes with the other teachers."

When summer came again, bringing unbearable heat and humidity to Boston, he escaped to Canada for a long rest.

Aleck had continued giving a lot of thought to where he was, what he was doing and what he wanted to do. He knew that he enjoyed travelling, lecturing and tinkering. After some consideration, he came to the conclusion that his life's work, like his father's, lay generally in the field of phonetics. But Canada, with its conservative British traditions, and a cultural suspicion of anything new, was not, it seemed, the place to develop innovative ideas or business concepts. The United States, on the other hand, had flexible attitudes and a pioneering hunger for any worthwhile discovery.

Though he kept trying to find better ways of teaching the deaf and providing the skills needed to help them speak, he grew ever more passionately interested in the science of sound—especially in an idea he had sketched for using Helmholtz's principles to create a harmonic telegraph. He was certain that technical advice and financial support would be much easier to find in the United States than in Canada. He was offered a job in Washington, but after due consideration decided to return to Boston where he already had a reputation.

Aleck stopped daydreaming when he saw Sarah coming up the walkway with a small boy in tow. He went down to meet them.

"Sorry, we're a little late," Sarah said. "I hope you're not put out. I know how busy you are."

"Not to worry." He looked down at the boy she had brought him. "This fine lad must be Georgie Sanders." Aleck bent down until he was at eye level with the sandy-haired-five-year-old.

"He was born deaf," Sarah said. "But he's as bright as a new button. I know he can learn."

"But too young for the Boston School for the Deaf."

"Which is why I have brought him to you. I've spent some time with him myself trying to teach him but I think he would benefit more from your tutoring style."

Aleck looked up at Sarah's earnest face. He wanted to say no, to tell her how busy he was, but he couldn't.

"Georgie's father lives in Salem. He's a wealthy leather manufacturer. So fees are no problem. He adores the boy and wants to try and make a normal life for him. Spend a few minutes with him, Aleck, and see what you think."

"Will you wait downstairs so I can be with him alone?"

"Of course. I brought something to read." She left the room at once, closing the door behind her.

Aleck lifted Georgie into a chair and positioned himself directly in front of him. Very slowly and with great care, he began to test the lad's level of comprehension. In less than an hour, he called Sarah back. "He's certainly everything you said, a very teachable little boy ... a lovable little fellow. For the best results I'll have to teach him for two or three years.[2] Is his father prepared to make that sort of commitment?"

Sarah nodded. "I'm certain he will. But more important, will you have the time to devote to Georgie?"

His head swam at the thought of his work for the coming year. He sighed. "Tell me, Miss Fuller, why did God allocate us only twenty-four hours between one day and the next?"

He smiled when Sarah laughed.

⁓

"I can hardly believe you've been away three years!"

Mabel's dark, quick eyes followed Mary True's lips. Mary's lips were always easy to understand. It seemed to Mabel as if Mary had always been a part of her life, and she realized how much she had missed her friend and teacher.

Mary had been teaching at the Boston School for Deaf Mutes, while Mabel and her sisters were away in Europe, but they had kept in touch. Mabel was now almost sixteen.

"Your mother is worried about your articulation," Mary said, careful to mouth the word "articulation" clearly, so that Mabel could understand.

"People understand me," Mabel replied stubbornly.

"I want you to meet someone," Mary persisted.

"Who?"

"A friend of mine. Professor Alexander Graham Bell. He knows your father."

Mabel stood looking out the window over Mary's shoulder. Mary touched her arm, and her gaze returned to Mary's lips. "Professor Bell teaches something he calls, Visible Speech," she finished.

It was lovely outside, a perfect day to go to the park. Mabel felt herself rebelling against any more lessons, or more practice. She had been studying constantly under the tutelage of her European professors and she was sick of it.

"I know what worries mother," Mabel said, "I've seen her talking to father."

Sometimes her parents forgot she could read lips from a distance. "I know Mabel's knowledge has expanded and I know she's unusually intelligent," her mother had said. "But my dearest, what difference does it all make if she is unable to make herself understood to others?"

Her father had agreed, though he appeared only mildly interested. He had been very busy attempting to get the Hubbard Bill through the Congress of the United States. More than half his time was now spent in Washington. Gardiner's legislation had been designed to break up the monopoly held by Western Union, so that he could legally establish his own firm, the United States Postal Telegraph Company. In fact, he was so busy that he had closed their Cambridge house and moved the family to Washington. Mabel had moved to Boston temporarily to live with her cousins.

Mary touched Mabel's shoulder again. "Don't you want to meet Professor Bell?"

Mabel shrugged. "We live in Washington now. What's the point of my meeting Mr. Bell if he's in Boston and I'm in Washington?"

Mary was not one to take no for an answer. "It's important that you meet him."

"I know all about him. Father asked him once to give me lessons. He was too busy."

"That was before you went to Europe. Now he's a professor at Boston University, and I think he has more time."

Again Mabel shrugged. She gave Mary a half smile. "What's the point of objecting. You'll just go on arguing."

Mary laughed. "I knew you'd give in! Come along then. I told him that he could expect us this afternoon."

"You're more stubborn than I am."

Mary laughed. "That would be impossible."

⁓

Feeling completely at ease about meeting Professor Bell, Mabel walked beside Mary as they climbed Beacon Hill's steep incline. They seldom spoke when they walked, because conversation meant stopping to read Mary's lips. She wondered whether Professor Bell would treat her as an equal, the way Mary did. She reasoned that since he had taught the deaf he was used to them. She sighed. It wouldn't be like meeting a stranger who was unprepared. Strangers reacted in one of three ways. Either they ignored you because they thought you were really stupid, or they were surprised you could communicate at all, or they became condescending, trying to cater to non-existent needs.

The pattern of people's reaction was all too familiar: at first they were surprised to learn she was deaf, then they were disbelieving, then they tried to understand, and finally they showed her pity. It was the pity that she disliked most of all.

What kind of man was Alexander Graham Bell? Mary had given her few hints. She considered him a good teacher. She seemed to think that his Visible Speech could help. But how? There were so many quacks, so many who sought to take advantage of the deaf with miracle remedies and absurd contraptions that were supposed to help the deaf to hear. None of them worked, and most of the so-called new methods didn't work either.

"This is it," Mary announced.

Inside, an old gentleman sat behind a desk.

"Professor Alexander Graham Bell," Mary said.

"Miss True? Upstairs, first door on the left. He's expecting you. Go on up."

They climbed the steep narrow stairs and entered a room with dark green walls and a grimy window.

A door leading into another room opened and a tall, thin, raven-haired man emerged. Mabel studied him. He was dressed carelessly in a dark suit made of horribly shiny broadcloth. It was expensive, but not at all fashionable. His hair seemed too shiny. Mabel tried not to frown or appear to disapprove, although he looked as she had feared—like a snake-oil salesman. Moreover he looked old, terribly old! Why he must be over forty, she thought to herself.[3]

After the introductions were completed he motioned them to be seated. Mabel studied his face. At least there was no pity in his eyes. He began speaking, and she read his lips, interjecting an occasional comment on what he said. He explained the principle of Visible Speech. She had been prepared to reject the entire idea outright, but what he said and the way he said it interested her. As he spoke, his face took on an entirely different expression. His physical presence was spell-binding, his eyes steady and earnest.

They talked for half an hour. "You are a most proficient lip-reader, Miss Hubbard. Still, your speech needs considerable improvement. I can help you. And, if you agree, I will give you lessons."

Mabel tried not to allow her expression to reveal her thoughts. It's odd, she thought. I both like and dislike him. Something about him makes him look as if he is not quite a gentleman—yet he acts like one.[4] And there is kindness in his eyes—kindness and something else—a devilish quality. Yes, that was it, he had a teasing, devilish quality.

"So, Miss Hubbard. Would you like me to teach you what I know?"

Mabel held out her hand and forced herself to enunciate, as clearly as possible, "Yes, Mr. Bell, I believe I would, but I will have to see if arrangements can be made for me to stay with my cousins. My father has moved to Washington."

He took her hand, held it for a moment, and then he smiled. "I hadn't realized that. But if you can make the necessary arrangements, I think you will benefit."

Perhaps, she thought, she might like him better once she got to know him. There was something intriguing about him. But what it was exactly she could not define. And why did she feel attracted and repelled at the same time? It was really quite odd. Still, none of that really mattered. What mattered was that she believed he could help her to speak more clearly and that was reason enough to put up with any of his idiosyncrasies.

⁓

Aleck stood at the grimy window watching them leave. Mary True had worked with him as a colleague; she was a talented, caring teacher. He would have to thank her for bringing him such and extraordinary student. Miss Hubbard seemed a trifle young, but because she appeared so poised and confident he couldn't guess her age. Moreover, she was beautiful! Her dark eyes, her angelic face and even her speech—flat and toneless as it was—had a wonderful sweetness to it. On top of everything else, she seemed intelligent with an intense interest in the world around her. He smiled to himself as Mabel and Mary turned the corner and disappeared from view.

But why in heaven's name did he feel so elated at taking on another student? "I haven't enough time now," he said aloud. It had been a busy year for him and one of his best financially. The same could not be said for the country's general economic situation, which was dreadful. The nation was in the grip of one of its economic depressions.

He picked up John Tyndall's latest book from his desk. He had been attending a series of lectures at M.I.T. covering a wide range of topics from zoology and geology to experimental mechanics. The mechanics course had been the most interesting. He reread and studied John Tyndall's first book on electrical experiments. His latest book delved into the science of acoustics, a field about which very little had been written.

"I'm really two people," Aleck thought. One persona poses as a teacher, the other manifests itself as an inventor. Which was he? His lifelong love of inventing was perhaps the stronger desire. Lately it seemed that all the money he earned from his teaching went to pay the costs of the paraphernalia he required for his experiments. So far he hadn't invented anything. Nevertheless he'd had a lot of fun trying. No, that wasn't true. He had invented the wheat-husking machine at the Herman's mill, and he and Melly had invented a machine that could actually talk—well, at least utter a few words.

The possibilities for the electrical transmission of sound fascinated him. He couldn't leave the subject alone. So much was happening in the field, and so many people were involved. He needed to learn much more about electricity. Music, languages and ancient history were all very well for a well-rounded education, but Aleck realized now that he should have insisted on studying science as well—alchemy, as his father called it, making it sound only slightly more respectable than witchcraft. Aleck had built his own version of Helmholtz's wonderful harmonic telegraph. He hoped that eventually it would have the ability to send various tonal pitches over a single wire and decode them at the other end.

On the other hand, as a teacher he was happy boarding with Georgie Sander's grandmother in Salem. Mrs. Sanders had offered him room and board in exchange for continuing to tutor Georgie. It meant commuting by train to Boston University, but he didn't mind. He got on well with Mrs. Sanders. She was the sort of independent woman who encouraged lively conversation and argument.

⁓

His father had come to Salem for a visit and surveyed his experimental "toys" with suspicion.

"I shall tell your mother that you are in good health and keeping decent hours, even though I have suspicions to the contrary," Melville had told him as he scanned Aleck's makeshift laboratory.

At that moment he believed that he could make his father understand. He had gathered up a jumble of tuning forks and wires.

"I told you about that trick, remember? The singing piano—this is the same principle. If I send a current from a battery through a wire,

I can interrupt it with several tuning forks, each with its own frequency." Quickly, he demonstrated his discovery. He saw the distress in his father's face.

"For what purpose, Aleck? Why are you doing all this? You stay up all night and never get enough rest. For what?"

"Don't you see? If I tap codes in different pitches, I can send them all down the same wire simultaneously. Multiple telegraph messages. What do you think?"

The question hung in midair. His father had simply shrugged, "I must be going, Aleck, or I'll miss my train."

"But I have to know what you think."

"I think you've become self-indulgent and muddle minded."

His father had turned and headed out into the hall for the stairs. "What about Visible Speech?" he muttered. "You said you would tour the country. We must promote our method ... otherwise ..."

"Visible Speech is limited," Aleck had snapped. "It isn't the answer to everything."

"It's my life's work!" his father thundered.

"But not mine," Aleck had shouted.

"No, yours is tinkering and daydreaming and never settling down." Melville turned his back and started down the stairs.

"It's a *continuation* of your work, father. You work with the sound of words, I'm trying to work with the sounds themselves." He knew his father was listening even though he continued down the stairs.

"I believe sounds can be collected and dissected and moved around. Sent down a wire, maybe ... or maybe visualized for the deaf. Imagine, a born deaf child speaking as freely as the two of us."

"I hope there is understanding as well as speech," Melville said, pointedly. "Aleck, the goal of Visible Speech is the creation of a universal language. That's important enough. Will you come and lecture with me?"

"No, father."

Melville had turned and looked him in the eye. "Well, that's it, then. Goodbye and good luck with all this."

Aleck had watched him go. They were both stubborn. But he has his path and I have mine, Aleck had reminded himself.

He resumed his hectic routine—nights working on the harmonic telegraph, days teaching and afternoons tutoring private students. Once again he had overloaded himself by accepting another private pupil. But Mabel Hubbard seemed special and an inner voice told him that he should take her as a student.

~

"I doubt that a single one of our students will appear today." Miss Locke spoke with conviction as she peered out at the falling snow. It was wet and dense, perfect for building snowmen although that was not what was on her mind. "A typical Boston winter," she murmured. "A wonderful Indian summer through until Christmas—and then February. Always the worst time of the year here. Always!"

"I daresay you're right," Aleck agreed. She had become his student-teacher in training and acted as his assistant, giving lessons to some of the pupils. She was, he recognized, a great help and very competent. His students had prospered under her teaching. The arrangement benefited both of them. She was learning more about teaching the deaf, and he was able to take on more pupils.

"Hello! Is anyone here?"

Mabel's flat voice echoed the hallway.

"Good heavens!" Aleck opened the door. Mabel stood at the foot of the stairs in the foyer, looking for all the world like a living snow girl. In spite of her hat, the fringe of dark hair that framed her face was white with melting snow crystals. Her long lashes were similarly encrusted. Her cheeks were as rosy as two apples.

"You're surprised to see me," she called. "You didn't think I'd come?"

Aleck wanted to embrace her, but held his emotions in check, reminding himself how young she was and that she was his pupil. She enchanted him. Her agile mind was like a sponge, absorbing everything he told her. He taught her speech, but her lessons also embraced a wide and eclectic range of other interests.

"Are you all right, Mr. Bell?"

Her smile was so sweet and lovely that he had to force himself not step closer and take her in his arms. But no! He told himself again that it was his responsibility to maintain the proper teacher-student relationship. Should the fates allow, he thought, there would be time enough.

"I assure you, I am quite all right," he smiled. "Miss Mabel, you are quite charming with your rosy cheeks and your hair full of snow-flakes." He spoke lightheartedly so she would not consider his flattery entirely serious, or see it for what it really was—words spoken by a man smitten.

Mabel blushed. She was never certain about him, never entirely sure when he was serious. Sometimes his lips said one thing, but she could see something else in his playful eyes. She turned away and removed her waterproof cloak and veil.

Over the past months she had come to know Professor Alexander Graham Bell rather well and soon realized that he wasn't at all a snake-oil salesman, as she had thought upon first impression. She found him endlessly stimulating, but she was not drawn to him, she told herself, the way she thought a girl might be drawn to a man if romance were to blossom. No sooner had the thought entered her head, then she wondered why she had even thought of it. It was him. Sometimes she felt as though he wanted a romance to develop. Or was she only imagining it? Certainly his actions were most proper at all times.

As it turned out, he was not as old as she had originally believed. Indeed, he was not all that much older than Mary True. He just looked older because of his beard. Her cousins, with whom she lived now that her father had moved the family to Washington, were always giggling about love. She knew that, while she enjoyed Professor Bell's company almost more than that of anyone else, she did not feel at all giggly about him.

"We should get started," Aleck told her. "The storm is getting worse. If you're to get home, you will have to start soon."

"No matter, I didn't want to miss a lesson that costs so dearly."

"You could well be a frugal Scot, Miss Hubbard," he said playfully. "Surely, you don't think I would charge you for a lesson missed be-cause of Boston's inclement weather?"

Mabel brushed past him, her eyes twinkling, "I shall remember that the next time there is a blizzard," she laughed.

Aleck followed her up the stairs. Today, he thought happily, they might discuss the phenomenon of snow. Was it true that no two snowflakes were alike?

To Aleck, their hour together passed much too quickly. It was as if time itself had been compressed into one fleeting moment. He wanted the lesson to last forever. He must learn to control himself. He wondered is she had any idea at all of the effect that her presence had on him.

"Scissors ... sssss ..." he said positioning his tongue on the top of his mouth and hissing slightly through his teeth. It was exaggerated, but that's what was required. Mabel repeated the strange sound.

"Like a snake," she said. "I read that they hiss."

"Exactly—like a snake." He glanced at his pocket watch. They had already gone overtime.

"My time is up," Mabel surmised.

"Yes, but I insist on taking you to the streetcar."

"It's not necessary, Mr. Bell."

"Then I shall go for pleasure. I think I can use some fresh air, a nice brisk run down the hill in the snow."

They went downstairs and with his polite assistance she put her winter coat, veil and boots on. He bundled up too and they stepped out into the swirling snow.

"Oh, it's so lovely!" Mabel exclaimed.

"As white and pristine as all innocence," he agreed. The snow gave everything a magical quality. The trees looked dressed, the houses clean and fresh, the lawns and cobbled sidewalks virgin territory. Not a single carriage-wheel track on the street.

"I'll race you to the bottom!" He plodded forward; although much shorter, she raced beside him, gamely keeping up with his giant steps. They ploughed through the deep snow, laughing as they went. The snow spilled over the top of his overshoes. Mabel could feel it on her knees as it melted against her long stockings.

"It's up to my knees!" Mabel cried out.[5] "I can hardly hold on to my coat and veil! Gracious!"

His hat flew off and spun away on the wind. He chased it into a snowbank and collapsed in laughter beside it.

When they reached the bottom of the hill he helped brush the snow off her coat.

"Ah, just in time. Here's the streetcar."

He helped her climb aboard and stood watching as the tram whisked her away. He started back to the classroom humming happily. Mabel Hubbard seemed to him a friend as well as a student—someone he could even laugh with. The thought made him a little giddy.

CHAPTER EIGHT

Boston, 1873

"Ba!" Mabel replied, imitating the position of Aleck's lips.

He shook his head, "Not so explosive, you're accidentally adding the sound of 'a' so the noise you're making sounds rather like a sheep.

He demonstrated the position of the lips and tongue again, and again Mabel tried to make the sound. This time he smiled and she knew she had succeeded.

"That's better. Much better!"

"I think I'm improving as we get to know each other," she replied.

"I must say you seem more relaxed."

"I'm wonderfully happy," she confided. "My father, mother and sisters were all in Washington most of last winter. Then Papa started talking about selling our house in Cambridge. I was so afraid he would."

"You like living in Cambridge?"

"It's my home. Our family was separated three whole years while my sisters and I were away studying in Europe, and again since they went to Washington. But now papa's plans have changed; he's reopened our Cambridge house and we're all going to be together again—at least for most of the time. Professor Bell, I want you to be one of our first guests. You will come, won't you?"

Wild horses couldn't have kept him away, though he reminded himself that his welcome would be only as Professor A. G. Bell.

Unhappily, as Aleck Bell, prospective suitor, he would probably be thrown out on his ear. Holding his emotions in check while walking the narrow line of propriety was not easy. But he had no choice.

"Of course, I'd be delighted," he replied casually, holding his eagerness in check.

⁓

Aleck walked up the long drive to the Hubbard house on Brattle Street. It was clearly the residence of a wealthy family. Lush lawns and tall elms surrounded the place, and the garden had obviously been attended to in the few weeks since the house had been reopened.

He arrived at the imposing front door and knocked. An older woman wearing a grey dress and a white dust cap answered and motioned him inside.

"Professor Bell," he announced.

"Yes, you're expected, sir." The maid still had her wonderful Irish brogue. He had concluded within his first three months in the city that all the house servants in Boston, as well as most of the police, were Irish. It seemed as though most of Ireland had come to Boston during the potato famine of the 1840s.

Aleck surveyed the foyer. Solid mahogany carved banisters followed a winding staircase that rose to the third floor. All the gas fixtures were shaded with sparking crystal. He caught a glimpse of the dining room. It had crimson velvet wallpaper with matching damask drapes that hung from gilt valances. It seemed evident that Mabel's mother had fine and suitably expensive tastes.

He followed the maid into a large and comfortable drawing room. The drapes were drawn back and the windows open. allowing the soft evening summer breeze to cool the room.

"Professor Bell! Delighted, absolutely delighted!" Gardiner Hubbard rose from his easy chair and strode across the room to shake hands.

"The ladies will be joining us in a few minutes." Can I offer you a cool sarsaparilla?"

"That would be most welcome," Aleck replied carefully.

"Mabel has been telling me some astounding things about you, Professor Bell. I knew—have known for some time—that you were a gifted and talented teacher of the deaf, but I didn't know that you were an inventor as well."

Aleck smiled shyly. He had told few people about his research. He had confided in Mabel, though he knew she didn't understand everything he told her.

"I've been dabbling in modifications to the Helmholtz apparatus," he said, trying to sound casual.

"The Helmholtz apparatus!" Gardiner exclaimed. "Well, we do have something in common. I'm sure Mabel has told you of my efforts to break the monopoly held by Western Union. Yes, sir, I have a vital interest in telegraphy."

Aleck confided, "I've always conducted my experiments in absolute secrecy. There's a lot going on, and frankly I worry about someone stealing what few ideas I have."

Gardiner looked thoughtful. "I appreciate your fears. Have you ever thought of applying for patent protection?"

"I can't. I'm still a British subject."

Gardiner rubbed his chin. "The usual procedure in the United States is for an inventor first to file a complete description and purpose, as well as a model of the intended invention. The procedure is called filing a caveat. It gives the inventor priority for patent application over anyone who might file for a similar invention at a later date. But you're quite right. As you're not yet an American citizen, you're not entitled to such protection or priority status."

"As you see, sir, I have no choice but to work in secret."

"You could, of course, still apply for a patent if you provided a working model of your invention with your application."

Aleck shook his head. "That's the essence of my problem. I'm not as good with my hands as I am with my head. I'm afraid my lack of electrical knowledge and the sloppy, home-made appearance of my apparatus would be totally unacceptable for such an official procedure. I feel trapped. To make my invention presentable I'd have to hire an electrician who might steal the idea. So I've done nothing. Naturally, I'll submit my experiment to the British government eventually."

"The whole field of telegraphy is very competitive," Gardiner warned him.

"Telegraphy is all I hear about," Gertrude Hubbard interrupted as she and Mabel came into the room. Mrs. Hubbard was an elegant woman, well dressed and wearing expensive but tasteful jewellery. Mabel wore a light-coloured summer dress. Her dark hair had been drawn up and pinned back so that the thick ringlets fell just below her shoulders.

"Now that he knows you're interested in telegraphy," Gertrude warned, "my husband will monopolize you all evening."

"Perhaps he would enjoy discussing it all evening," Gardiner protested.

"Then the two of you can discuss it at some other time. You won't be discussing it tonight, not if I can help it. Now Professor Bell, I've heard that you play the piano."

"I do indeed."

"Then Gardiner may talk to you about telegraphy before dinner, but after dinner I insist on some music and song from you."

Aleck sat down and leaned back in the comfortable armchair. He already felt at ease in the Hubbard house. "That sounds like a splendid evening to me," he replied to his hostess, although his gaze was fixed on Mabel.

The Christmas holiday season passed quickly into 1874. Aleck continued to work, teach and visit the Hubbards. Visiting the Hubbards became his only recreation. He seemed always to be hurrying somewhere, and the faster he ran, the less he accomplished.

He hurried up the steps of the Sanders' house in Salem, where he lodged. Once out of the bitter February cold, he took off his heavy winter coat and boots in the anteroom.

"You're late," Mrs. Sanders observed, poking her head out of the parlour. Her grey hair was pulled back in a huge bun and secured with a long silver pin. She had wrapped herself in a dark blue, heavy winter robe. "I saved you some dinner. Oh! And you had two letters in the post."

"It was very good of you to save dinner." He followed her into the parlour where a fire burned slowly in the hearth. "I was detained at the university."

"No need to apologize. I do hope you aren't going to stay up all night again working. You need your rest." She treated him as a member of her family.

"You sound like my mother."

"I take that as a compliment." She went to the desk, pushed aside a few papers and produced two letters.

Aleck glanced at them. One was from the British government, the other bore the Hubbards' return address.

"Something important from England?" Mrs. Sanders inquired.

"Just a routine inquiry," he told her.

But it wasn't just routine. He had sent a letter describing his idea to the British government in order to see if there were some way to protect his work. But even before opening the letter, he knew it wasn't good news. It was too slim a letter.

"I'd best go upstairs," he told her. "I have a lot of reading to do tonight."

"Then take your supper with you. You must be hungry."

"Thank you."

Aleck headed to the pantry where he picked up his plate of cold roast beef, potatoes and cabbage. With the plate in one hand, a glass of milk in the other and the two letters between his teeth, he hurried upstairs. He opened the letter from the British government first, reading and rereading it. His temper rose. The response—written in clear, but absurd bureaucratic language—illustrated why America had long since displaced England as the land of inventive opportunity. It stated that: "If you will submit your invention it will be considered on the understanding, however, that the department is not bound to secrecy in the matter, nor to indemnify you for any loss or expense you may incur in the furtherance of your object, and that in the event of your method of telegraphy appearing to be both original and useful, all questions of remuneration shall rest entirely with the postmaster general."

"Idiots!" he muttered and put the letter aside.

To his delight, the second letter was an invitation to a Valentine's Day party at the Hubbards. It was to be Mabel's first formal dance.

⌒

The furniture in the drawing room had been pushed back against the walls, and there were bright heart-shaped decorations on the table in the dining room, where an enormous punch bowl and refreshments had been laid out on ornate platters.

"Oh, Aleck, I'm so glad you could come. We need a competent pianist." Gertrude greeted him warmly. She was dressed in blue and wearing a pearl necklace. She looked about. "So many young people! I love having them in the house. Poor Mabel, she wanted to have all her friends, but Edith and Annie Longfellow[1] couldn't make it."

Gertrude Hubbard was not intentionally name dropping, it was simply a fact that in Massachusetts, either she or her husband knew members of every prominent family in the state.

"I'm sorry I shall miss meeting them."

"And Gardiner did ask me to give you his best regards. He's off to Washington again."

Aleck looked around. Mabel had not yet appeared. He supposed that since it was her party she wanted to make a fashionable entrance.

"Everyone is here. Can you play a tune Aleck?"

"I'd be pleased to. What kind of music will be suitable for Mabel's arrival?"

"One of your highland tunes," Gertrude suggested. "You seem to play those with the most gusto."

He sat at the piano and began to play, "I Love a Lassie." Through the open doors of the drawing room, he caught a glimpse of the edge of a peach gown as it descended the stairs. He quickened the pace of the music.

Mabel entered the room, her face aglow. She looked absolutely beautiful and resplendent in her peach gown. A young man to whom Aleck had been introduced, Harcourt Amory, stepped forward. "A waltz, Professor Bell, if you please!"[2] Harcourt ordered.

Smarting from the young man's insolence, Aleck hesitated a moment, then struck up a waltz. Amory took Mabel by the hand and led her onto the dance floor.

Aleck's fingers moved automatically across the keys as he played the tune he knew so well—but his eyes were on Mabel, whose eyes were on Amory. Was this precocious young man interested in her? For the first time in his entire life he felt a twinge of jealousy; it was not a pleasant sensation. He wanted to be Harcourt Armory—wanted to be dancing with Mabel. He wanted to have her look at him the way she was looking at her partner. He continued playing, knowing it would be fatal to his hopes and dreams to cause any sort of a scene or betray his feelings in any way.

Why, all of a sudden were things going badly for him? First the absurd letter from the British government, and now he had to put up with this pompous young man who seemed to have stolen Mabel. There was no justice.

———

"Twenty-seven!" Aleck muttered aloud. He felt ancient, almost middle-aged. According to the life insurance tables the average life span was fifty years. "Good God, my life is more than half over. I'm getting senile," he thought. He was talking to himself. But then he had always talked to himself. Pre-senility then, starting when he was still a teenager? Was such a condition possible? He should investigate.

He turned the corner for home, fervently hoping that the infernal carpenters Mrs. Sanders had engaged to do some remodelling had finally left. Twice this week he had returned home to the distraction of saws and hammers. In addition to the noise, there was now the horrid smell of paint and wallpaper paste that made him slightly ill.

He opened the front door cautiously and paused to listen. No, he couldn't hear them, perhaps they had finished.

He took off his coat and hat and opened the parlour door. Suddenly a chorus of voices greeted him.

"Happy Birthday!"

Mrs. Sanders held up a large cake blazing with candles. Little Georgie Sanders stood by her side. Georgie's father was there together with all of Aleck's pupils, including a blushing Mabel Hubbard. Aleck's heart skipped a beat. Mrs. Sanders wore a dark dress trimmed in lace. All his young female students were wearing party dresses in various shades of pastel.

"We surprised you!" Mrs. Sanders exclaimed with satisfaction.

"We were all afraid you'd decide to work late." Mr. Sanders said.

"I don't know what to say!" He felt like crying.

Mrs. Sanders set the cake on the table. "We won't have the cake till you've opened your presents," she said.

"I'm embarrassed," Aleck said, sinking into a chair.

"Well you needn't be," Mrs. Sanders told him. Students always give their teachers little gifts."

"But rare is the landlady who bakes birthday cakes," he countered, then he gave her a big hug.

"I trust I am a little more to you than your landlady, Professor Bell."

"You are indeed!"

She pressed her lips together, "I have two surprises for you."

"Two? You mean in addition to this party?" He glanced upstairs to where the remodelling had been going on, "The silence of the carpenters' hammers would be gift enough, I assure you."

Mrs. Sanders laughed, "Ah ha! That's my surprise. And I did it all right under your unsuspecting nose."

"Tell Professor Bell, Georgie. Tell him what his birthday present is." She spoke slowly, allowing Georgie time to read her lips.

Georgie grinned. "Grandmother is giving you your very own study!"

Aleck's mouth opened in surprise. "A study!"

"Yes, your very own study. A place for you to work without keeping me up half the night. A special place for your experiments."

Aleck felt as if he were truly going to burst with gratitude. He went back to Mrs. Sanders and again he hugged her. "A study," he said honestly, "I simply couldn't have wished for a better gift."[3]

"It was a defensive measure on my part," Mrs. Sanders told him mischievously.

"And these," Georgie added, handing Aleck a tiny box.

Aleck opened it carefully. Inside were a pair of gold sleeve-buttons. "They're elegant," he said. "I don't deserve so much."

Mrs. Sanders laughed. "You deserve whatever you get and nothing more."

Each of his students presented him with a small gift. There was a pouch of aromatic pipe tobacco, a hand-knitted scarf, a pair of gloves and from Mabel a pair of warm wool socks.

"Thank you. I am astonished," Aleck said, looking fondly at them all. There were tears in his eyes. "This is one of the best birthdays I've ever had."

～

As if it wasn't enough to have his wonderful new study at Mrs. Sanders', he had also been presented with a new laboratory at his parent's home in Tutelo Heights where he had returned for the summer. He wondered how his father would react to his latest invention. It was far from completion, but the principles he had used in its construction were sound. Melville Bell was not always patient about nor interested in his tinkering, though the attitude seemed to depend on circumstances. Aleck recalled how, in Boston, his father had disparaged his work on inventions and urged total concentration on his teaching. But at home, when Aleck was supposed to be relaxing, Melville didn't seem to mind all that much.

No matter where he was, multiple transmissions over one wire had become Aleck's all-consuming passion—more than a passion! "You try to do too much at once," Mrs. Sanders had scolded him in the weeks before he'd left Salem. And Mabel, who knew him even better, told him solemnly, "You can't go on lecturing, teaching and then stay up all night experimenting. You're close to physical collapse."

Her warm, dark eyes had flickered with deep concern, but still he had gone on pushing himself. Then Mrs. Sanders had spoken to him again. This time she minced no words, made no suggestions. Hands on her hips, eyes and voice steady, she had told him emphatically: "Aleck, you are going to fall over from exhaustion. You're going to get sick, and you're going to die. And that's what you're doing to yourself, young man! But now there's me to consider. Whenever you stay up all night, you keep me up all night. So even if you don't need your sleep, I need mine. If you don't take a good long holiday, I'm going to ask you to leave."

There was no choice, and since the summer was at hand, he had gone home to Ontario where he would be restored to health by the wonderful climate and the attention of his parents.

For the first week of his visit he had only slept, eaten and read. His strength and energy returned, which set his mind buzzing again. Best of all, there was no need to hesitate. Now that he had a laboratory, he could work almost as well in Canada as in Boston. For the four weeks before coming to his parents' he had been trying to construct a phonoautograph.

"We're here," Melville said. He and Eliza stood in the doorway.

Aleck uncovered his invention. "Here it is!"

His parents considered the creation carefully.

"Fascinating," his father pronounced finally, after admiring his son's handiwork.

"Grotesque," Eliza muttered.

Aleck smiled at his mother. She was referring not to his apparatus, but to the human ear. He had made a hurried trip to Toronto to borrow the ear of a cadaver from a friend who was attending medical school.

"Explain it to me again," Eliza said, her curiosity overcoming her revulsion.

"The idea for the phonoautograph was originally developed by a Frenchman name Leon Scott," Aleck said bending over his model. "It operated on the principle that when words were spoken into this end—the one with the wooden cone, here—the sounds of speech vibrated a thin membrane stretched over the opposite end. See, I've used the real membrane from a human ear rather than something artificial."

Eliza nodded, waiting for him to finish. When her son spoke, she could almost see his mind working. Even now, as he spoke, she felt certain something had just occurred to him, perhaps an idea born as the result of explaining the phonoautograph to her.

"You see this small rod attached to the centre of the membrane? It will pick up and magnify the vibrations. The tiny bristles affixed to the end of the rod and resting lightly against this piece of smoked glass will create a set of etchings on the glass—each one will be characteristic of whatever sound is produced."

"And?" his father asked, a questioning look on his face.

"And ... what is so fascinating is that the total sum of a series of complex sounds can be reduced to a single set of etchings ... and that such a very thin membrane can move a set of bones connected to it, despite the great difference in weight."

"Yes, dear, it's very interesting, but what does it all mean?" Eliza wanted to know.

Aleck shrugged, "I hope it might mean that one day human speech can be transmitted over wires."

His father muttered into his beard and continued to look sceptical.

Aleck stared at the phonoautograph. His mind raced, teeming with ideas—other experiments that had to be made. "I've got to perfect this," he said after a moment.

"Before the end of summer, no doubt?" his father suggested.

"Yes, before the end of summer," he agreed.

"Good! Then perhaps you can return to Boston with the single purpose of teaching the method I've spent my life devising."

Aleck did not answer. He was making no promises.

~

October was always the most beautiful month in Massachusetts. The grass stayed green in the Boston Common, late blossoms still bloomed in the public gardens, while the first frost left a palate of colour in its wake: red sumac, gold, orange and red maple, deep green bushes with scarlet berries and the russet hues of high cranberry.

Aleck sat at the piano in the Hubbard parlour. Gertrude had asked him to play for them.

"He's so good," Gertrude had once remarked to Gardiner when she thought Aleck had been out of earshot. "I always marvel at how a person with hands so large can produce such delicate airs. And he is never the prima donna! He's always so willing."

Aleck knew that he could have become a concert pianist if his grandfather hadn't persuaded him that there was infinitely more to life than music. Playing relaxed him. It had become one of his greatest pleasures. He had a vast repertoire of classical and popular music committed to memory, which would have gone to waste if no one ever asked him to play. In Gertrude Hubbard he had found a grateful admirer of his musical talents. He sat now playing a sweet nocturne by Chopin. He knew she loved Chopin. Midway through the piece, he stopped suddenly.

"Is something the matter?" Gertrude Hubbard looked concerned.

Aleck shook his head. "No. I just had a thought—something I discovered, and it occurred to me that I've never told you. Gardiner, did you know that a piano will play back the same notes as are sung into it?"

"Is this a new parlour trick?"

"Not at all. Let me demonstrate." Aleck pressed the mute pedal and in a strong clear voice sang a note into the piano. After a moment he stopped. The piano echoed the same note clearly. "See? Or should I say, hear?"

Hubbard bit his lip. "Very clever. But to what purpose?"

Aleck shrugged. "Perhaps none—but consider this: did you know that if a tuning fork tuned to 'C' is struck near a second fork turned to 'C' the second fork will begin to vibrate on its own."

"I still don't see the point," Gardiner admitted.

"The point is, sir, that it means several messages can be transmitted over a single wire," Aleck told him.

Gardiner considered this possibility. If Aleck meant a telegraph wire then this was new! An idea that no one had thought of before. A smile slowly spread across his face. His eyes twinkled. "Your idea might be the one golden treasure in the sea of modern communications."

"Perhaps. Certainly not until I can prove it."

"I still don't understand," Gertrude sounded confused. "With all the various vibrations resulting from human speech, how would it be possible to transmit more than one sound over a single wire? Surely it would take a lot of wires?"

Aleck shook his head, "How do my words travel to your ears?"

"Through the air, of course. Aleck Bell, are you making fun of me?"

"Not at all, ma'am. My vocal vibrations, as complex as they are, travel through only one element—that element is air. If there is only one air, there need be only one wire." It was an oversimplification, he knew, but it might help her to understand the principal.

Gardiner rubbed his chin thoughtfully. Aleck could see his mind churning. For four and a half years he had been fighting to break the Western Union monopoly, convinced that the company was restricting free enterprise. He believed fervently that if private competing companies were allowed to flourish, consumer costs would decrease, general usage increase and everyone would benefit. Aleck had heard Gardiner expound on his pet subject, many times. He knew also that William Orton, the feisty president of Western Union, disagreed and had fought Gardiner tooth and nail to retain the precious monopoly.

"My critics all say that more than one company will not change things because all the improvements that can be made to the telegraph have been made by Mr. Orton's purchase of Mr. Edison's latest inventions. But what you've just illustrated could change everything again."

"Possibly, but there is no guarantee that what is theoretically possible can be turned into a physical reality," Aleck cautioned.

Gardiner waved aside his concern. "I must do some research on this point."

Gertrude, weary of having her pleasures interrupted, walked between the two of them. "The importance of this does not escape me, but there is no research to be done tonight, and I would like to hear more Chopin."

Aleck smiled and swung around on the piano stool. "And so you shall," he said cheerfully. "And so you shall."

He began to play, thinking that he had done the right thing confiding in Gardiner. Hubbard was only the second person he had taken into his confidence. He admitted that he needed help. Would one of his two confidants provide it?

CHAPTER NINE

Boston, 1874

The grandfather clock in the hall of the Sanders' house in Salem struck six.

Thomas Sanders, Georgie's father, had until last night been Aleck's only confidant. Now Sanders stood before Aleck with a shocked expression on his face.

"You told Gardiner Hubbard? You explained your discovery to that old reprobate? Good Lord, man, have you no sense? Mother has warned that because you stay up all night and work all day that your mind would become addled. I thought your lack of common sense was restricted to your own physical well being. I never dreamed it extended into areas of business."

"Gardiner Greene Hubbard is an influential man," Aleck protested. He did not add that he was also the father of the young woman he loved.

"He is a man whose reputation has changed over the years. He used to be a courageous legal crusader for the deaf, now he's heavily in debt and known as a market speculator."

"I didn't know, and I still don't believe he'd do anything to ... to compromise my work."

"You don't believe? Aleck, you must protect yourself with a patent."

Aleck shook his head. "There's nothing I can do without the money for a patent lawyer. Besides, I need an electrician to help build a suitable model."

"I have faith in you," Sanders said sincerely.

"Even though I have no common sense." He gave a rueful smile.

"Yes. I'm only being hard on you because I want you to be protected. You've changed my son's life. Since you've lived in my mother's house I think that I've grown to know you ... Aleck, let me offer you a business proposition. For a half interest in your harmonic telegraph invention, I'll pay all costs to secure a patent."

"You would do that?"

"Yes, and you can start tomorrow."

Aleck sat down on the sofa. The offer stunned him. Accepting it would mean he'd have to put more time into his invention. The temptation was overwhelming. He felt he was on the verge of a very important breakthrough in his work. Was he close enough to success to take the risk?

"Well?" Sanders demanded.

"I accept," Aleck replied.

The small tea house on the scenic banks of the Charles River across from the Massachusetts Institute of Technology was nearly deserted. Aleck, who seldom found time to frequent tea houses, sat across from Dr. Clarence Blake. Aleck and Blake had co-authored an article on the phonoautograph. As they waited for their tea to arrive, Blake told Aleck why he wanted to see him.

"I've been asked to invite you to attend a convention of the Boston Society of Medical Sciences."

"Really? I'd be pleased to attend," Aleck told him enthusiastically.

"Not just attend, Aleck—participate. I want you to join me on the platform to answer questions about our published notes."

"I'd be very happy to do that too." He felt more flattered than his response conveyed.

Their tea and buttered scones arrived. Dr. Blake smiled and sipped some tea, then told Aleck confidentially, "Before the meeting it might be wise to read the work of Elisha Gray—Mr. Gray allowed me to review his experiments on the transmission of speech a few weeks ago."

Aleck felt himself rooted to his chair. Experiments on the transmission of speech! He had never even spoken to Dr. Blake about his own work on the transmission of speech—was someone else doing the same work? Had that someone beaten him to the idea? Had he filed his patent too late?

"You look quite pale," Dr. Blake leaned toward him. "Are you ill?"

"We must go immediately to your office. I've been secretly working on the transmission of speech for three years now. I never dreamed—it never even crossed my mind—that someone else had been working on the same idea."'

Now it was the doctor's his turn to be surprised.

"I had no idea! I'm astonished," Dr. Blake muttered.

Aleck gulped down the rest of his tea. "Come," he said anxiously. "I must see this man Gray's notes and I must tell you about my own work."

⁓

"You are making yourself ill with anxiety." Gardiner Hubbard looked Aleck in the eye.

"I can't help it. I've worked so hard ... "

"And you shall continue to work hard. I have just spent an endless amount of time scouring the patent office attempting to find anything that even resembles your invention. And even with my considerable connections, I can find nothing."

"Yet," Aleck reminded him miserably, "even as we speak, a finished invention may be ready."

"I doubt that. You are on the verge of something extraordinary—something that may well change the current method of mass communication forever."

"But it will only be valuable if it's protected."

"True. Therefore, I have a business proposition for you. For an equal share in the invention, I'll support all the costs of your experimentation."

"I already have a partner."

"Ah yes, the good Mr. Sanders, who probably considers me a shameless opportunist. Then you had better tell him about Mr. Gray and my search at the patent office. You can tell him also about my offer. I'm willing to consider two partners."

"I don't know that he'd be willing." Aleck didn't reveal anything, but he remembered his conversation with Mr. Sanders. Gardiner must have read his thoughts.

"Thinks I'm the devil himself, does he? Well, I have something to offer. Let Mr. Sanders put up the money, I'll put up the legal, business and organizational knowledge that is required. And you ... will put up your genius. How does that suit you? Mind now, you'll be obligated to fulfil your part—to develop the technical ideas—under a business contract."

Aleck studied Gardiner's face. He thought about Mr. Sanders. "I'll speak to him right away," he promised.

"And when you've finished talking to him, apply for your American citizenship. At least that will help solve the problem of applying for a caveat."

Aleck nodded. He felt sure that Mr. Sanders would agree. He had been touched by great good fortune. At this moment is seemed as though everything he had ever wanted was about to be granted: financial security, funds for experiments, astute financial, legal and business partners, and it even seemed possible that one day Mabel might return his feelings. In any case, he had heard no more about his competition for her affections; that alone made him hopeful.

"I'll come and see you as soon as I've talked with Mr. Sanders."

Tonight, Aleck knew, he would write home and let his father and mother know how wonderfully well things were going for him.

⌐

"Up and down, then down," Aleck said aloud as he studied his father's letter under the lamp. What had seemed endless good fortune a short time ago, was now turning to muck. The problem was time. He didn't have enough of it to get everything done.

There were his professorial lectures at the School of Oratory, and his list of private students had increased to thirteen. The only time he could spend on his experiments was Sundays and evenings. Gardiner was unhappy and lectured him severely at every opportunity. "You are not," he told him repeatedly, "devoting sufficient time to the harmonic telegraph."

The latest barb came in a letter from his father.

"Your wisest course, would be to sell your plans to Messrs. Sanders and Hubbard. You can't work out the scheme without neglecting your other business. Get what you can get at once."

As usual, Melville regarded Visible Speech and teaching the deaf as the family's main business interest.

Aleck muttered under his breath, searching for an appropriate expletive. "I will not sell anything. I will not stop work and I will not give into the nagging of anybody's father, including my own!" Unconsciously, he doubled his fist and brought it down on the desk. He put the letter aside and considered his recent conversation with the patent lawyer, Anthony Pollock.

Gray had published an article describing his invention of a "Musical Telegraph." Happily, the date of reference given for the invention's conception gave Aleck's invention priority by several months. His first reaction was that the race was not so tight as he had believed. Or was he mistaken? Pollock said that he was.

In fact, on Mr. Pollock's advice, his own caveat had now been withdrawn. "Gray filed a caveat that dealt with part of your harmonic telegraph idea. If Gray were to discover a similar caveat on record, he might well figure out what you're up to, Aleck. Then you'd lose everything. I want you to finish, and then we'll apply for a patent on the entire invention, thereby overstepping Gray's caveat on the grounds of priority of conception. We have the proof. We have your papers and the letters you wrote to Gardiner Hubbard and to your mother."

Aleck had agreed, though he wondered why everything had to be so infernally complicated, and why his own father—who had not the slightest idea what was really going on—had to be so conservative, so stubborn and so short-sighted. He would just have to work faster and harder.

He stood up and stretched. It was late, but if he worked steadily, there were still a few good hours before sleep would overcome him. "If only I had help from a really good electrician." It was a thought that came to him again and again.

He did have Moses Farmer to consult, and Farmer was a fine electrician. But consultation was not the same as having someone beside him, someone better with his hands than he was. Success, he had discovered, was based as much on recognizing shortcomings as recognizing strengths.

⁓

"Happy ruddy New Year," Aleck thought dismally as he strode through the freshly fallen snow. He tried to avoid the places where it had drifted during the night. "Filthy white stuff," he grumbled. His prospects at this dawn of a new year were looking very bleak.

The most recent difficulties had begun when his electrical consultant, Moses Farmer decided to move himself and his business to Newport, leaving Aleck without anyone to help solve his electrical problems. Whatever he tried created another problem, and everything ended up taking more and more time. He'd cut back on his sleep in order to get more done but it hadn't worked. He felt like a man drowning, sinking deeper and deeper.

He expelled a frosty breath and paused in front of the Charles Williams's Machine Shop. He and Farmer had contracted Williams for much of their work. Perhaps Williams could help him.

He pushed open the door to the old brick building and climbed the dusty stairs to the workrooms. The interior of the machine shop felt chilly—like an old barn.

"Morning, Professor Bell."

Aleck waved at young Tom Watson. They'd met on a previous visit. "Good morning to you. Is Mr. Williams about?"

"In his office."

The office, as Tom called it, was a cubbyhole, with only makeshift walls separating it from the rest of the shop where some two dozen men laboured. They were all specialists and could make anything out of wood, metal, glass or wire.

Aleck poked his head into the cubbyhole. "Have you a few minutes, Mr. Williams?"

Charles Williams looked up from some drawings and motioned Aleck in. "What progress on your experiments?"

"Slow, I'm afraid. It's all very frustrating."

"You have a specific problem?"

"I need a permanent electrical consultant. With Mr. Farmer gone, I've been left high and dry."

Williams tugged at his moustache and stared thoughtfully at his papers.

"You know, I think young Tom Watson might be just your man," he suggested after a few minutes. "I don't generally consider myself a matchmaker," he said with a wink, "but there is something about you two—something I suspect will work. Did you know that he began his career by changing jobs with the seasons. Then, while attending commercial college, he appeared here one day asking for work. I guess what we do suited him. No two jobs were ever the same—lots of variety. He's turned out to be one of my best men. I kept him on in spite of the depression. He's what I call a self-starter. He spends all his spare time studying the principles of electricity and reading up on the latest scientific advances."

"Tom Watson," Aleck repeated. "By heavens, he might be just the man for me."

⁓

A March wind blew the rain in great sweeping sheets across the city. But at least New York was cool, and that was a blessing. Not at all like Washington, which was either too hot and humid or too damp and cold. He had taken his invention to the patent office a few weeks earlier and learned to his astonishment that Gardiner had arranged for William Orton, the peppery head of Western Union to drop by for a demonstration. Only the month before, Aleck, Sanders and Hubbard had officially entered into a commercial partnership. The Orton presentation would be the first for the new partnership.

Aleck had been panic-stricken at the time. Somehow, he had managed to demonstrate the apparatus successfully to Orton, who then demanded that it be repeated under commercial operating conditions, using Western Union's telegraph lines in New York City. Aleck and Gardiner had agreed.

There were, as they had expected, problems with the patents. Mr. Pollack, their patent lawyer, told them of a potential conflict with Elisha Gray's submission. He had proceeded with three separate submissions, two were rejected because of the apparent conflict, but the third was approved. Pollack felt confident that Aleck would be awarded the remaining two as well.

Back in Boston, while preparing his harmonic telegraph for the New York demonstration, Aleck continued to dabble in the irresistible—his theory that the human voice could be transmitted through a wire. He wrote home: "Such a commercial idea as telegraphing vocal sounds would, indeed, to most minds seem scarcely feasible enough to spend time working over. I believe, however, that it is feasible, and that I have got the clue to the solution of the problem." His parents encouraged him, but Gardiner did not. His partner approved wholeheartedly of the idea of transmitting speech, but continually reminded him that he and Sanders had their money tied up in the harmonic telegraph, and that it was the harmonic telegraph that could bring the quickest cash return to all of them. Feeling obligated to both of his partners, he had continued to work on the harmonic telegraph, but the concept of the telephone intruded perpetually into the back of his mind. The idea seemed to cry out to him continuously. Then, late in March, Orton notified him that arrangements had been made for the test and Aleck had taken the train to New York.

"Mr. Orton is ready for you now," an officious middle-age man in a drab grey suit announced. He crooked a finger and motioned Aleck to bring his equipment. Aleck followed him through a maze of halls and into the nerve centre of Western Union, one of America's most powerful companies.

"Set it down right here," Orton ordered without bothering to shake hands. Aleck did as he was told. An electrician stood by nervously as Aleck readied the equipment. He could feel his heart beating so rapidly that for one absurd moment he thought its sound might somehow interfere with his transmission. Finally, he had it all hooked up. "Ready, sir" he said.

The electrician threw a switch and the demonstration started. Aleck clenched his fingers tightly in his palms determined to betray no emotion. It all went like clockwork. His signals came clearly through the two hundred miles of circuits.

Orton rubbed his chin. "Impressive," he said slowly. Aleck stood for a moment. Now what?

Orton checked his watch. "Bell, can you come back after lunch?"

"Yes, sir."

"Come directly to my office—the top floor."

They shook hands and Orton hurried away. Lunch? Although his appetite was usually very good, he was far too excited to eat. Would Orton buy his invention?

He walked down the street feeling as though he were walking on air. It had even stopped raining. The March winds were drying the streets, and a weak sun glimmered through a break in the clouds. New York was a city of immigrants, of growing industry, of parks, markets and museums. There were fine hotels such as the Belmont, the Metropolitan, the Fifth Avenue and the famous Astor. If only he weren't so excited, if only he were hungry. He stopped outside an oyster saloon and peered in the front window at the long, narrow room, well furnished and divided into snug little boxes, separated by curtains. There was a semi-circular bar near the entrance, where people had congregated to drink and to eat their oysters.

But he wasn't hungry, nor did he have the time to visit the Metropolitan or Natural History museums. Instead, he walked to Central Park and stopped in the Dairy for a glass of cold milk. Orton was waiting for him when he returned to the Western Union building.

"Come in." William Orton pointed to a chair near his massive desk. Before Aleck could sit he inquired, "Tell me, Professor Bell, have you ever heard of Elisha Gray?"

Aleck felt his stomach churn. What a fool he had been. He'd been almost certain that Orton was genuine ... that things were going smoothly. Now he felt a foreboding.

"I know of him," Aleck replied honestly.

"I met him at lunch hour. He brought me his invention. It's over there on that table. I think you'll agree that it looks much like your own."

Aleck left his chair as if he'd been stung and went over to inspect the apparatus. The instrumentation was far more sophisticated than his.

Orton leaned back in his chair and eyed him critically. "Western Union has enormous power, Bell—more power than most men ever dream about. With Western Union's backing, the weak can be made strong."

Aleck studied him. Orton's bombast sounded like the prelude to an offer, but perhaps he had already made an offer to Elisha Gray. Then the businessman dropped his bombshell. "I know he's a friend of yours, but is Gardiner Greene Hubbard involved with you in a business sense?"

"He is one of my partners," Aleck answered.

"You must understand that Western Union will never take up any scheme that will benefit Mr. Hubbard."

Aleck stared at Orton dumbfounded. Of course! It was the Hubbard Bill presented to Congress that would have broken the monopoly of Western Union and done too much damage to be overlooked by Western Union's stockholders.

"If that's the way you feel, sir," Aleck told him frostily, "then I shan't take up any more of your valuable time."

He left the office, furious at his naiveté for not realizing that Orton's only interest in his invention was to compare it with Elisha Gray's. Orton had never been serious about buying into a competing idea, especially one with Hubbard's name attached to it. What a fool he had been!

⁓

That summer the air turned exceptionally hot and thick as it enveloped Boston in a windless haze. And as if the heat outside weren't bad enough, the suffocating claustrophobic humidity in the miserable attic over Williams's workshop was even worse.

Aleck wiped his brow and stared at his equipment. He felt a mounting frustration. He and Watson had rigged up three transmitters in this room and three others in the adjacent room. Those in the other room were monitored by Watson. When he touched the wires connecting the first two transmitters it caused the two in the other room to sound. But the third transmitter refused to function.

He was devoting more time now to experimenting with the telephone because the harmonic telegraph—for all intents and purposes—was a dead issue—although Gardiner still didn't think so. When Aleck returned from New York and related what had happened in Orton's office, Gardiner at once offered to resign from the partnership. Aleck refused. Instead, they approached Western Union's competitors. Suddenly, out of the blue, Western Union made them an offer, but promptly withdrew it when they heard that Aleck had started dealing with the competition. When the competitors turned down the invention the three partners were left high and dry.

If that were not bad enough, Aleck now found himself strapped for cash. He realized rather ruefully, that he should have taken his mother's advice and banked some of the money that he had earned the previous year. Why did everything in his life have to revolve around money? There was never enough.

"Drat!" he muttered, tapping the equipment in front of him. "Watson!" his voice boomed through the hot attic.

"Here!" Watson shouted from the other room.

"Check and see whether the transmitter reed has stuck against the electromagnet."

Watson leaned over, "Indeed it has," came the reply.

Aleck blinked in astonishment then stared as his transmitter reed began vibrating on its own. He waited a second then ran to the other room. "What did you do just now?" he demanded.

Tom Watson looked up surprised, "What you told me. I plucked the reed."

Aleck sucked in his breath. "Do it again—but with all the transmitters, until I tell you to stop."

Watson nodded.

Aleck dashed back to his stool and watched the three transmitters. One by one they were vibrating, unaided and unaccompanied by a whining tone. Then he tried a reed not attuned to the ones Watson kept plucking. "Heaven sent! I've got it!" he whispered as a chill shivered down his spine in spite of the heat. He prayed that his eyes were not deceiving him. The vibrations and sounds of the reeds were being transmitted along the same wires as the tones and pitches of human speech. A year before he had suggested this very idea, even though most electrical engineers and academic theorists believed it to be impossible. Today's success proved that the basic principle of his telephone was valid! Now, he thought, it needs only to be perfected.

His room was in its usual chaos; the desk was littered with scribbled notes on electrical circuitry and the countless other ideas that continually invaded his thoughts in the dark of night.

All three chairs were piled high with books. His clothes were spread in disarray across the bed. He lifted the books and papers from one chair and moved them to the end of the bed.

"It needs only to be perfected," he muttered and sat down. He had said the same thing weeks before. It had been a moment of ecstasy following a breathtaking success. But the moment had faded, leaving only the routine of daily experimentation and failure, or experimentation with limited success—so limited that progress seemed static.

Aleck admitted, unhappily, that his world was steadily shrinking. He had few real confidants and practically no social life. His greatest joy—teaching—had been cut back in order to work on his invention. For months now, Mabel had been the only person with whom he talked about anything besides his invention. To her, he confessed his innermost thoughts. She was so bright, so beautiful. He loved her more now than he could even admit to himself. It was the one thing they never discussed.

The question of what to do about their relationship haunted him; during their two-year association they'd become close friends, but he still had no idea how Mabel really felt. Did she know how he felt? Did she even suspect? At times he felt that his heart would break. At the moment his emotions bordered on desperation. Mabel would be leaving Cambridge for the summer and going to Nantucket to spend three months with her cousins. What was he to do without her? Who would he talk to? Maybe now was the right time to make his feelings known. Yet ... she was so young.

He stared a moment at the papers on his desk, then, as though in a trance, began rummaging for a clean sheet of stationery. That was it! he decided. He would write to Mrs. Hubbard telling her how he felt and seeking her advice. After all, he couldn't conceal his true feelings forever. Nor should he. It wasn't fair.

He began by saying that Mabel knew nothing of his feelings and that, indeed, he had no idea at all how she felt about him. "I have discovered," he wrote, "that my interest in my dear pupil has ripened into a far deeper feeling ..."[1] He ended the letter with a commitment, "I promise beforehand to abide by your decision."

He reread the letter, then folded it carefully and tucked it into an envelope. He would send it by messenger. No point prolonging his agony.

He started a second letter, this one to his parents, telling them about Mabel. "She is as intelligent as she is beautiful and has the most gentle and affectionate manner I have ever encountered." And he added, "She has travelled abroad and comes from a most respected Boston family." He wondered whether his father remembered meeting Gardiner Hubbard. Almost as an afterthought, he ended with news of his experiments. "I've made a new and startling discovery. Musical signals can be transmitted without any battery at all." The next step, he told them would be the transmission of vocal sounds. "At last a means had been found to render such a transmission possible."

When he had finished he went out into the warm June evening in his shirtsleeves to cool off.

As soon as Aleck stepped inside the Hubbard house he began feeling like one of his stretched and taut transmission wires that might at any moment begin to vibrate.

Mrs. Gertrude Hubbard was not as tall as Mabel, nonetheless she was a slender, attractive woman with an unusually pleasant face and smile. Where he was concerned, she was almost indulgent. She had always liked him and he had always liked her. He considered her a friend.

But today Gertrude didn't smile. She appeared terribly concerned and intent on trying to make him understand. She told him to sit down while she paced the drawing room, speaking slowly, avoiding his eyes except when she wanted him to acknowledge a point.

"I realize you're Mabel's friend and that the two of you have seen a great deal of each other. I certainly know you well enough to accept that you have kept that relationship on a pupil-teacher basis and that you have at all times been proper in your actions."

"I most certainly have," he interjected quickly.

"Oh, I know, I know—don't you see? That is why your letter so unhinged me." She glanced at him, then returned her gaze to the design in the oriental carpet that covered the floor. "And of course I know that you and Mabel have discussed all matter of things—that is, I know that her education has not been confined to elocution under your tutelage. I know you've talked of philosophy and science, music and literature—and I certainly don't want you to think that I'm ungrateful in any way for all you've done for her."

He sat on the edge of his chair, waiting for that excruciating moment when Gertrude, who apparently had not spoken with Gardiner, would drop the other shoe.

She cleared her throat. "Let me say that I appreciate your honesty. But I'm not quite certain how to make you understand my position. You see, Aleck dear, although you think you know Mabel, you do not know her as I know her. To you she is a poised, well-educated young lady, a brave young lady who has fought to overcome her deafness. Yet in spite of all of that, in spite of her European education and travel, Mabel is woefully naive for her years."

"I was not suggesting any immediate action," he stammered. It was a lie. He wanted immediate action. Most of all he didn't want Mabel to be away for the entire summer.

"Aleck, you said that you would abide by my wishes. I must ask you to promise me that you will not speak to Mabel of your feelings for a year. Give her that much more time to grow. Then if you still feel as you do, you can tell her so."

He felt immediately despondent, but realized that Gertrude had left him a glimmer of hope. Did this mean that she would not be opposed to him as a son-in-law? Certainly she would be easier to satisfy than Gardiner.

"A year seems like an eternity," he whispered.

"It seems entirely proper to me," she replied. She had finally stopped moving about the room and now sought his eyes as well as his promise.

He withdrew his pocket watch and examined it thoughtfully. Its gold casing glimmered in the candlelight. It was nearly eight o'clock. He closed his watch and replaced it. "Time moves slowly for those bound by such promises."

"Then you will promise?" she pressed him.

He nodded slowly, trying desperately to look on the bright side. She hadn't slammed the door of possibility, and perhaps he would be able to concentrate more on his work now that he had taken this step. It had been an exciting day—July the first. He would remember it. Earlier in the day he had written in his work journal: "A grand telegraphic discovery today, transmitted vocal sound for the first time.... With some further modification I hope we may be enabled to distinguish the 'timbre' of the sound. Should this be so, conversation viva voce by telegraphy will be a *fait accompli*."

"Will you promise?" Gertrude repeated.

Aleck nodded. "I promise."

CHAPTER TEN

Boston, 1875

Aleck shivered in spite of the heat and the wretched July humidity. His chill was not caused by illness, but by excitement and anticipation. He and Watson were on edge, consumed with energy, as they prepared to continue the series of critical voice tests. For a long moment, he studied his apparatus. He had changed his equipment model to resemble a human ear, using a membrane and an aperture in the hope that it would transmit clear vocal sounds. The concept, which he had first tried during a summer in Ontario on the harmonic telegraph, had worked to a degree. For the first time, he and Watson had been able to hear faint sounds of speech through the transmitter. He had reported this exciting fact to Hubbard, who had missed the point entirely—he was still preoccupied with the harmonic telegraph— and answered crisply, "I am very much afraid that Professor Gray has anticipated you in your membrane attachment."

Never mind, Aleck thought. Soon Gardiner Hubbard wouldn't miss the point and neither would anyone else. He leaned over and spoke clearly into the transmitter. This time he and Watson were using similar diaphragms on both the transmitter and the receiver.

In a moment Watson burst into the room, his face filled with excitement. "I could almost make out what you said! I could hear your voice plainly!"

"Let's change places." Aleck hurried to the other room and listened. It was important to make certain that what Watson heard was not noise from the street. But he heard nothing. Again, he examined his equipment. It would work. It had to work. The theory was right.

"No success?" Watson asked. He was framed in the doorway, perspiration on his brow.

"No," Aleck muttered, aware that his emotions were in a constant flux between the mountain top of hope and the valley of despair.

"It will work in time, " Watson said, echoing Aleck's conviction.

Aleck bit his lip. "I'm worried about competition, Watson. I'm going to apply for a patent anyway. The principles are right."

"I think that would be wise," Watson agreed.

⌒

The Nantucket beach was wide and sandy. Mabel sat in the shade of a striped beach tent. A broad-brimmed hat protected her from direct exposure to the scorching August sun. She was reading, but only fitfully, as she kept glancing up to watch the gulls float, seemingly without effort, on the drafts created by the breezes. Immediately she thought of Professor Bell. It was he who had first pointed out the gulls to her and discussed the wind currents that enabled them to stay aloft for so long without so much as the flap of a wing. How magnificent to be able to fly, to take wing, to look about and see all that was below. She tried to imagine how that might be, then—forcing herself back to her book—resumed her reading. But she could not concentrate. In her mind's eye, she saw Nantucket from above, imagined she was flying over it, just as the gulls did.

Mabel decided she liked Nantucket Island even better than Martha's Vineyard, which lay fifteen miles to the east, across the Muskegat Channel. Nantucket was fifteen miles long and three miles across at its widest point. Its beaches were not so rocky as those on Cape Cod or the mainland, and the island was steeped in history. There were a thousand places one could walk and many different places to explore.

The village's cobblestone roads were lined with small shops and distinctive homes. Many a sea captain had built his house on Nantucket facing the ocean. They were wonderful old houses with third-storey attic rooms surrounded by a widow's walk. Legend had it that the wives of the seamen paced these walks, scanning the horizon and the unforgiving sea for a sign of their men returning from voyages that sometimes lasted several years.

"You're not reading," her cousin—Mary Blatchford—observed, as she plopped herself down on the warm sand. Casually, she arranged her long green cotton skirt around her.

"Have you come to talk?" Mabel asked. She closed her book, wondering at her cousin's expression. Whenever Mary sought her out, it was to have a conversation and more likely than not to gossip.

"Well, I've come to ask you about your Professor Bell."

Mabel read Mary's lips. "*My* Professor Bell?" she asked, perplexed.

"Yes, your Professor Bell."

Mabel frowned, "Why do you call him mine? He's my teacher. He's a very good teacher and a very interesting man."

"And what else? " Mary asked. "I think you must be hiding something from me."

Mabel tilted her head and studied her cousin's knowing expression, "What else should there be?"

"You're being coy," Mary accused.

"I'm not!" Mabel insisted. "I really don't know what you're hinting at."

"I find that very hard to believe."

Mabel laughed. "No matter how you find it, I haven't the least idea what you want to know."

"Well, I want to know how you feel about him and how he feels about you?"

"Apart from thinking I'm a good pupil, which he tells me often, I don't know how he feels."

"You mean it's true! You mean you really don't know? You don't have a single tiny, tiny inkling of how he feels? "

Had Mary taken leave of her senses, or was she misreading her lips? "I've nothing to add, " Mabel said flatly.

"Well, how do you feel about him?"

"I told you, he's a good teacher, a very interesting man."

"And he's never told you?"

Mary's face was flushed, and her eyes were absolutely wide with curiosity. At that moment Mabel realized that Mary, always a dreadful gossip, knew something she did not, and was in fact on a fishing expedition. But what could Mary know about Professor Bell?

"Apparently not," Mabel said, knowing that her cousin couldn't keep a secret longer than ten minutes under the best of conditions.

"Well, then, I know a secret."

"And how do you know it's a secret?" Mabel asked.

"I didn't know it was, till just now."

"Oh," Mabel replied, as she pretended to return to her reading.

"Don't you want to know?" Mary pressed.

Mabel shrugged and tried to appear disinterested.

"Well, I'll tell you. I heard my mother reading a letter from your mother to my father. Your Professor Bell has written a letter to your mother. He declared his love for you, that's what. He said he loved you and wanted to court you!"

Mabel let the book fall into her lap and felt her face redden as if she had been sitting in the bright sun all day. "What?" she murmured in disbelief.

"He said he loved you and wanted to court you."

"When was this letter written?"

"Oh, the end of June I think. Your mother wrote that he'd promised he wouldn't declare himself to you for at least a year. But I just couldn't believe you could see someone so often and not know he was in love with you. Honestly, Mabel, you must be almost unconscious."

Mabel slammed her book shut and abruptly stood up, brushing the sand off her tan walking skirt.

"Are you mad at me?" Mary asked, all wide-eyed and innocent.

Mabel shook her head. She wouldn't ask Mary to promise not to tell anyone else as that would guarantee the looseness of her cousin's tongue. She felt her anger rising. How dare her mother not tell her of this letter from Professor Bell. How dare she keep her it from her.

Not that she felt anything for Professor Bell—except for liking him and finding him interesting—but it was her life and her decision. She and she alone should have had the right to accept or reject him. Certainly not her parents! It was outrageous.

"I shall write to mother immediately!" she said to herself as she stomped across the sand towards the house. "I shall write and we shall straighten this matter out at once!"

⤳

Aleck stood before the familiar door of the Hubbards' Cambridge house. In spite of the threatening clouds it was a pleasant summer day, and he had walked all the way from Boston University—taking the Harvard Bridge over the Charles River. As he knocked, he wondered why Gertrude Hubbard had summoned him. Her note had seemed slightly more curt than usual and certainly it contained no hint as to why she requested to see him so urgently.

The butler answered the door and ushered him inside. "Mrs. Hubbard is waiting for you in the parlour."

Aleck entered the parlour where Gertrude was sitting in a gold wingback chair wearing a plain dark dress with lace trim. She nervously fingered a long string of pearls around her neck.

"I received your note," Aleck said.

"Please, sit down." Gertrude seemed to be collecting her thoughts. I asked you to come because I've received a letter from Mabel—a letter I think you should read."

"Does it concern me?" Aleck asked, his heart suddenly leaping.

"Yes. It seems that your intentions are known to her."

Aleck frowned. "I kept my word. I have said nothing to her."

"I know. Please, don't misunderstand. I am to blame. I wrote to my sister and apparently Mabel's cousin, Mary, overheard her mother reading my letter. In any case, Mabel knows and has written. I'm afraid this letter will not make you happy, Aleck."

Gertrude leaned over and passed him the letter.

Aleck unfolded it. The paper was light blue and smelled lightly of lavender.

It read, in part: "I think I am old enough now to have a right to know if he spoke about it to you or Papa. I know I am not much of a woman yet, but I feel ... my whole future life in my hands.... Oh, Mama, it comes to me more and more that I am a woman such as I did not know before I was. Of course it cannot be, however clever and smart Professor Bell may be; and however much honoured I should be by being his wife I never ever could love him or even like him thoroughly.... Oh, it is such a grand thing to be a woman, a thinking, feeling and acting woman.... But it is strange I don't feel at all as if I had won a man's love, even if Professor Bell does ask me I shall not feel as if he did it through love."[1]

Aleck reread it carefully, then folded it and looked up at Gertrude. "I should go immediately to Nantucket to talk with her," he announced.

"I ask you not to go. You did promise not to declare yourself for a year."

"What does that promise mean now? Mabel already knows of my love and I've not been the one to tell her." Sadly he added: "I've upheld my end of the arrangement and see where it has gotten me."

Gertrude Hubbard nodded. "Of course, I can't stop you. But please consider your position carefully before you go to Nantucket."

Aleck said as he stood up. "Thank you for letting me know." Yes, he would think about it, but it seemed essential that he see Mabel himself—see her and talk with her.

Aleck paced his rooms, grateful that Mrs. Sanders was out and thus unable to ask questions about his mood and restless behaviour. He glanced at his small satchel on the end of the bed. It held his essentials, the few items he would need for a few days on Nantucket. He sighed. There were things he hadn't said to Gertrude Hubbard, things he had only thought of on the way home. Why was it always so impossible for him to speak his thoughts about Mabel without some prior reflection. Writing came easier. He stopped pacing and sat down at his desk. Rapidly, he penned Mrs. Hubbard a note.

"The letter you read me yesterday was not the production of a girl, but of a true noble-hearted woman—and she should be treated as such" he wrote. "I shall not ask permission from you now, but shall merely go."[2]

He supposed that Gertrude wouldn't be at all surprised by his decision. He hadn't promised her anything; nevertheless he had sat all night considering his course of action. The effort of it all had left him exhausted, but filled with nervous energy. He folded the letter and hurried downstairs, deciding to post it immediately.

~⌒

Aleck had spent a restless night in the oceanfront bed and breakfast hotel on Nantucket. Not that he could complain about his room; it was cozy and comfortable and had a fine bay window that offered a good view of the ocean. And the salt air was wonderful! Had he felt better, he would have enjoyed this respite from Boston's miserable, humid summer heat. But this was not a vacation; it was a mission that at the moment was being thwarted by a capricious display of Mother Nature's force.

He had awakened from his troubled sleep to a pounding rain. He considered walking to the Blatchford house where Mabel was staying, but he knew he would arrive soaked like a drowned rat and that his wet clothes would smell horribly. The rain was heavy and relentless. He had waited all day, and finally, feeling totally frustrated at not being able to fulfil his mission, he went to the writing desk and penned Mabel a letter.

"I have loved you with a passionate attachment that you cannot understand, and that is to myself new and incomprehensible. I wished to tell you of my wish to make you my wife—if you would let me try to win your love."[3]

He confessed his earlier promise to her mother to keep his love a secret for a year, and he wrote that he would abide by her wishes, whatever they might be. "It is for you to say whether you will see me or not. You do not know—you cannot guess—how much I love you.... I want you to know me better before you dislike me.... Tell me frankly all that there is in me that you dislike and that I can alter. I wish to amend my life for you."[4]

He finished the letter and placed it in an envelope, then he stretched out on the bed again. Tomorrow, he decided, the weather would be better. It had to be. It couldn't get any worse. He thought about what he had written. It was consistent with his final words to Mrs. Hubbard. In spite of what he had written to her, he had stopped at the Hubbard house on his way to Nantucket to tell her that he would at all times obey Mabel's wishes. If Mabel did not want to see him, he would not pester her, but would return home. It was obvious to him even when he spoke to Gertrude that she would eventually accept him as a suitor if Mabel were willing, but that Gardiner regarded him as too old. Well, he supposed that men were always cautious where their daughters were concerned, but in the end, it was Mabel's opinion that mattered.

He continued thinking—rehearsing what he would say to Mabel—then fell into a troubled sleep.

⌒

Aleck had gotten up, dressed and eaten hurriedly. It had rained all night but finally stopped. He thrust the letter he had written into his pocket, trudged down the stairs, and began his trek across the waterlogged landscape to the Blatchford house.

He approached the big clapboard structure slowly. He paused on the stoop to smooth his hair and brush off his suit. Then he knocked.

Mary Blatchford answered the door. She wore a light gingham dress and had her hair pulled back and tied with a ribbon. Mary was no stranger. In the beginning, when he had first taken Mabel on as a student, she had lived with her cousins, and Mary had often accompanied Mabel to her lessons. But it had been some time since he had seen her.

"Miss Blatchford. You may not remember—I'm Professor Bell. I've come to see Mabel, if that's possible." He didn't feel at all himself. He felt wretchedly nervous. And the unmistakable expression of "knowing all" on Mary Blatchford's face did not put his nerves at ease.

"I'll tell her you're here, Professor Bell. Please have a seat in the parlour."

He sat tentatively on the edge of a white wicker chair with a gaudy flowered cushion. The room was not furnished in the manner of a proper Boston parlour, but casually, like the summer retreat it was.

Mary Blatchford was gone an interminable length of time. Finally she returned.

"I'm afraid Mabel is hesitant about seeing you," she said, her face flushing slightly.

Hesitant? Had he done the wrong thing? He felt panic in his heart. Quickly, he withdrew the letter he had written Mabel and handed it to her cousin. "Then please give her this letter."

"Gladly," Mary said sympathetically.

"Goodbye, and thank you," Aleck muttered. He felt dreadful, a proper fool. He felt like running all the way back to his room in the bed and breakfast.

⁓

He didn't run, but he walked as quickly as he could, taking long strides and feeling his shoes sink into the soggy grass along the side of the road.

When he got back, he retreated to his room in misery. For a long, long while he sat staring out the window. It was hardly a perfect summer day. Storm clouds again threatened. He watched as the gulls circled, heading closer to shore as the storm's backside approached. The dark ocean heaved and roared on the rocks below. Should he stay a few more days, or return to Salem? What on earth did Miss Blatchford think? What did Mabel think? Would she read his letter? His mind was a muddle, and this time it had nothing to do with his invention.

⁓

Hours passed. Aleck's hands were cold and he felt restless. Then, making a split-second decision, he stood up. He would go for a brisk walk along the shore to clear his mind. Damn the wind and the rain. It was mild compared to the summer storms at the Scottish seaside.

He hurried downstairs.

"Professor Bell?" the desk clerk called out to him.

"Yes?"

"There's a letter here for you. It just came by messenger. I was about to bring it up."

Aleck all but snatched the letter from the bespectacled old gentleman. The writing on the envelope was unmistakably Mabel's. His spirits soared.

He opened it. The words she had written danced before his eyes.

"Thank you very much for the honourable and generous way in which you treated me. Indeed you have both my respect and esteem. I shall be glad to see you in Cambridge and become better acquainted with you. Gratefully, your friend, Mabel G. Hubbard."

He felt himself grinning from ear to ear. He would have his chance! He felt confident that he could win Mabel's love, given the opportunity. And what relief to have her know his true feelings! Things were indeed looking up, and now he was ready to return to his work with a vengeance.

Bostonians take Thanksgiving more seriously than any other holiday of the year. Aleck supposed this was because the celebration was said to have originated in the Bay Colony. It was recorded that in the year 1621, the governor of the Massachusetts Bay Colony, William Bradford, invited the neighbouring Indians to join the Pilgrims in a three-day festival of recreation and feasting to celebrate the bounty of the harvest. The feast had been celebrated every year since. But, as Aleck had read, it had only been made an official holiday twelve years earlier in 1863, by a proclamation of then president, Abraham Lincoln. This year, he thought happily, Thanksgiving had a special significance to him. This year, it fell on the last Thursday of November, the 25th, which by coincidence happened to be Mabel's eighteenth birthday.

Aleck tried to keep a cheerful perspective as he walked towards the Hubbard house. Gardiner had asked to see him, even though he would be there again two days hence for Thanksgiving dinner and to celebrate Mabel's birthday. He was especially looking forward to the holiday because he had been so busy lately, so overburdened with work, that the promise of one day of recreation made his spirits rise. And Mabel's birthday was indeed a special day!

Besides his lectures at the School of Oratory and his private lessons, he had recently founded a school to educate teachers of the deaf in the Visible Speech system. His time was now divided among the university, Georgie Sander's special lessons, work on his inventions, teaching the deaf and courting Mabel.

Despite all his activity he had very little money and was under constant financial pressure. He was trying to get enough funding to apply for European patents, hoping he could make money from them. His agreement with Sanders and Hubbard covered only the United States, leaving him free to try to patent his inventions elsewhere. But so far no funding had been forthcoming, and daily he grew more dismayed over his financial situation. Nor could he approach Gardiner Hubbard in this case. If they were only business partners he would not have hesitated to broach the subject, but he felt that he could not take advantage of his personal relationship with Mabel in order to cage a loan.

Pursuing his idea of European patents, he had contacted the Brown brothers—George and Gordon—in Toronto. George, owner of the *Toronto Globe* newspaper, and his brother Gordon had agreed to try to find financing for the overseas patents on two conditions: first, he was to provide them with written particulars of his inventions; second, he was to promise to do nothing with the U.S. patents that might in any way damage the patents abroad.

Aleck had agreed to this arrangement when he was home visiting his parents, and he had finally—in October—prepared and sent off the detailed account of his inventions, including a description of his concept for the undulating current.

He and Gardiner had argued about applying immediately for an American patent. To begin the filing process in Washington carried grave risks for the European patent rights. If a British patent were issued on the basis of a U.S. patent, and if the American one were later contested, then the British patent would be lost together with the investment made to obtain it. He worried even more that his patent idea would be exposed to others, and that his invention would be picked up and perfected by someone else. He argued that priority of concept would see him victorious, but Gardiner was furious.

Nothing was going as planned. The Browns had been unable to secure financing, and he was still broke. His school to train teachers for the deaf was successful, but it was also time-consuming and kept him away from his inventions. And of course there was Mabel! Did she love him? He had no idea whether his campaign to win her love was succeeding or failing.

Aleck reached the door. He shook his head as though to dispel darker thoughts. Gardiner had summoned him, and he was peeved because he felt an obligation to come despite his busy schedule. He knocked loudly on the door. Hopefully, whatever Gardiner wanted would not take too long.

The butler directed him to Gardiner's study.

"Good morning, sir."

"Good morning indeed," Gardiner replied without so much as a smile. "Frankly, I'm surprised you're here. I thought you'd be gallivanting about."

"I do not gallivant!"

"Really? You don't spend much time in your laboratory these days," Gardiner snapped.

"I have lessons to give, teachers to train."

"And ten thousand excuses for not finishing your work! Our work! The work I invested in!"

Aleck looked into Gardiner's eyes—they were small dark eyes; sometimes they seemed almost predatory. He often wondered how Gardiner could possibly be related to Mabel. And at this moment not only did Gardiner's eyes snap, he was puffed up like a turkey strutting before a hen. "I have to earn a living," he said evenly.

"Oh, so that's the excuse. Well let me give you a choice, my boy."

Aleck felt himself stiffen. He hated it when Gardiner adopted this tone, especially when he called him, "my boy" in such a patronizing manner.

"Either you teach Visible Speech and tutor, or you work on our telegraphy project and court Mabel! You absolutely cannot continue to do all four! Should you chose Mabel and telegraphy, I'll finance you—assuming she marries you—until you're financially secure. I'll finance all your inventions too."

Aleck stared into Gardiner's eyes. What cheek! Who did he think he was? Aleck pulled himself up to his full height of six feet four inches. "How dare you try to force me to make such a decision! It is precisely because of Mabel that I want no favours! As for teaching Visible Speech and teaching the deaf, I cannot, will not give it up! I have been blessed with an ability to free children from their silent world—to offer them limitless possibilities by teaching them to speak and lip-read. Until I find a teacher who can replace me, I will most certainly continue teaching."

Aleck stopped talking, but continued to glare at Gardiner who didn't retreat and apparently didn't intend to back down.

"So, you're giving up Mabel, then?" Gardiner barked.

"I am not," Aleck replied angrily. "If she loves me, and I feel certain she does, she will marry me despite anything you might have to say."

"Is that your answer?" Gardiner fumed.

"It is!" Aleck stormed. "Don't bother seeing me out. I have work to do. I could have done without this visit, which has not only been insulting, but a waste of my precious time!"

He strode down the hall, opened the front door and stepped into the brisk morning air. He had been there so short a time he hadn't even taken off his coat and scarf. "Drat," he muttered as he headed for the tram line and directly back to Salem.

Boston, 25 Nov. 1875

Aleck stood in front of the glassed-in bookcase in the library. A fire flickered in the fireplace, giving the room a cozy, homey feeling. Mabel, looking absolutely beautiful, stood a few feet away, her eyes seeking his. It was as if they were communicating without speech.

To his relief, dinner had gone off with no harsh words between himself and Gardiner. He presumed this was because he had thought better of their argument and written an apology. In it, he had tried to explain the forces that drove him, and he had thanked Gardiner for his interest and concern. He must have struck the right note, because Gardiner did not mention the argument, nor attempt to repeat his ultimatum.

"You look lovely," Aleck murmured, taking Mabel's hands in his.

"Do you think it strange that I asked you to come here with me?" She tilted her head and smiled.

He felt for all the world like crying—the firelight seemed to catch the highlights in her rich dark hair, her eyes danced, and at that moment she seemed closer to him than ever before. "Not strange," he answered, "just unusual."

"When you came the other morning, my mother and I were in the next room. My mother overheard everything that passed between you and my father. She told me."

His heart sank. Was this what she wanted to talk with him about? He had challenged her father, he had even expressed his certainty as to Mabel's love for him. It was a bluff, of course. He was not certain at all that she loved him. He started to open his mouth, but she lifted a hand and placed her fingers on his lips to silence him.

"Aleck, I was furious that my father attempted to use me to make you work harder. It was unfair of him, as unfair as it is of me to keep you guessing."

This was it then. She was going to tell him she did not love him. How would he ever bear it?

"Aleck, I love you better than anyone—with the exception of my mother, but that is a different kind of love. Aleck, I think we should become engaged immediately."

He looked at her speechless. She had spoken slowly, distinctly, but had he really understood her correctly? Or was his imagination playing tricks on him? "You ... you love me?" he managed.

She smiled again, "Yes, I love you."

He took her hands and drew her into his arms. He bent forward and kissed her tenderly on the lips, "I can scarcely believe it," he whispered.

"It is true," she whispered, as she leaned against him.

"I'll be afraid to sleep tonight, afraid that I'll wake up and find this was all a dream."

"You're such a romantic," Mabel said smiling. She squeezed his hands, "We must go and tell father and mother."

Aleck nodded. He felt inside as though he could walk all the way home to Salem without his feet touching the ground. Mabel would be his. No matter what else happened, he had won the heart of the woman he so passionately loved.

CHAPTER ELEVEN

February 1876

Four months had passed since his engagement to Mabel—another period of ups and downs. "A pattern I should be used to by now," he told himself aloud. He looked around—his apartment was more cluttered than ever. His training school for teachers for the deaf was going well, so well that he had trained one teacher to take over Georgie Sanders' tutorials. He had decided in January that it was time to move back to Boston. He found a suitable apartment in Exeter Place for only sixteen dollars per month and another five dollars for meals.

Today, however, had been all downhill. He had received a dispiriting letter from Gordon Brown, who had returned from England with Aleck's patent specifications still in hand. Brown wrote that he had taken the package to several electricians and to the patent office. Everyone had agreed that the autotelegraph idea was sound, but no one seemed to think it was commercially viable. Brown hadn't even shown Aleck's other invention—the telephone. The letter went on to cancel their business arrangement and politely explain that the financial gains would never offset the initial cost of the venture.

Next, came a frantic wire from Gardiner, who had only yesterday decided to file a U.S. patent. He discovered that Elisha Gray had filed a patent shortly before and, as the wire said, "It is amazingly similar in its concept to our submission." Aleck was stunned—hardly able to believe the message.

Gardiner went on to rant about the delays and distractions caused by Aleck.

Finally, there was a letter from Mabel that made him look inside himself.

"I love you so much, dear Aleck, I cannot bear that anyone should write to you and with too much justice, as my father has done. And I cannot bear that procrastination should rob you of the fruits of hours of hard study and the great abilities God has given you. I know that ill health has the last week or two prevented you from working as hard as usual. But it seems to me when the thing to be done was so very important, when if it failed, you lost the reward of past toil and suffering, you might perhaps have put even that aside for the time."[1]

She was so right! He sat down to write back to Mabel at once. "Procrastination is indeed my besetting sin, help me, Mabel to conquer it. I will not disguise from you dear what a blow this misfortune has been to me—for I had looked to this new patent to avoid all conflict with Gray and to place the control of the new system of telegraphy entirely in my own hands. I feel it more deeply than anything that has ever before happened to me—except one thing! And you know what that is!"[2]

He signed the letter and leaned back in his chair. Instead of peace of mind, he was faced with yet another fight—against his own irresolution and discouragement, which could cost him dearly in the patent fight against Gray.

⁓

Gardiner Greene Hubbard's Washington drawing room was furnished with fine mahogany chairs and sofas—many upholstered in deep red velvet. Gardiner sat on the settee, and his faced looked to Aleck as red as the velvet. He was animated, joyful and, for once, satisfied.

"I never thought we would win! Never!" he admitted. "By Jove! It was touch and go!"

Aleck thought that an understatement. Perhaps the lowest moment had been when they learned that on 14 January, Thomas Edison—who had been hired by Orton of Western Union to develop a better invention than either his or Gray's—had filed a caveat at the patent office. This development tied everything up until a new hearing could be arranged to decide between the conflicting claims.

Aleck had desperately clung to the fact that their application had priority of concept, but for most of his stay in Washington his mood fluctuated between moroseness and feeling utterly helpless. But today, on his twenty-ninth birthday, the perfect present had arrived. After what seemed an interminable length of time, an official letter from the patent office informed him that the investigating officers for the telephone submission had cleared the patent in his name. Patent number 174,465 was issued to him on 7 March 1876.

"David has overcome Goliath!"[3] Mabel maintained. She meant, of course, that he had trimphed over the giant—Western Union.

"You'll be going right back to Boston, of course," Gardiner suggested.

"Yes, I have to sort things out. I'm satisfied that the school for teachers of the deaf is progressing satisfactorily. I'm going to devote my time now to perfecting my invention."

"That's what I wanted to hear!" Gardiner grinned.

Whenever Gardiner turned jovial Aleck thought he had a puffed-up appearance.

"And I'm going to ask Tom Watson to join me full time."

"I look forward to real results," Gardiner announced enthusiastically.

Aleck didn't answer. He felt there would be results, but he knew also that they had only won some time. The race to develop the telephone was far from over.

⁓

Outside their workshop, the March wind blew vigorously. Sometimes when they were working together intently, he and Tom Watson seemed like ships that passed in the night. They had just finished preparations on the telephone apparatus in one room, then silently moved to the next room to work there.

Aleck turned on the power, glanced at Watson and crossed his fingers. He left the room, returning to his set. He pulled out the chair and sat down. As he reached out to turn on the power, he spilled a bottle of liquid on the table. Annoyed, he took out his handkerchief and began mopping it up. "Mr. Watson, come here. I want to see you," he called.

Aleck continued mopping and when he looked up, Watson was standing in front of him expectantly with a wide incredulous smile on his face. "You heard?" Aleck stammered. "Over the telephone?"

"Yes! You said, 'Mr. Watson, come here. I want to see you.'"

Aleck was beside himself, "That's what I said, it's exactly what I said! I wasn't even thinking, I spilled this stuff—my God, Watson! Are you sure, absolutely certain, that you heard me through the machine?"

Watson nodded emphatically. "*Yes,* Professor Bell. It works!"

Aleck leaned back in his chair. He turned around and fumbled through the mess of papers on his desk for a book. "Here, take this and go to your piece. Read to me, and speak distinctly."

Watson nodded and hurried away.

Aleck leaned down, he pressed the receiver to his ear—articulate sounds came through. He made out "to" and "out" and "further" then he heard Watson say quite clearly, "Do-you-un-der-stand-what-I-say?"

"Yes!" Aleck boomed back. He closed his eyes. Today, 10 March 1876, he thought gleefully, the telephone has spoken.

⟿

The American Academy of Arts and Sciences meetings were held in a large hall. Aleck thanked heaven for his training in elocution. His booming voice could easily be heard all the way to the last row. He looked out eagerly on the sea of grey beards and white heads. Tonight they would have an experience they would never forget. He felt confident as he began speaking on the subject of new telephonic theories. He knew that his learned audience expected an illustration of voice transmission. Rumours about his invention were rife in the academic community, and they had been greeted with great enthusiasm by some and extreme scepticism from others.

Aleck knew that vast improvements had yet to be made. Again, the elation of success had quickly dissipated in the face of the work still ahead. He yearned at times to take a professorship and teach Visible Speech—to bury himself in his teaching. He knew that he was still handicapped by his own disorganization, and that he worked too many nights. And yet, each improvement to his telephone made the sound clearer. He was certain that soon all the difficulties would be resolved.

He had decided against a voice transmission; instead, he would transmit music on his invention. He finished speaking and moved dramatically to the apparatus. For a moment he bent over it; the audience fell silent, as if holding its collective breath. He signalled William Hubbard, Mabel's cousin, with whom he had rehearsed the demonstration. Suddenly, and quite distinctly, the small box on the platform table began to emit the sounds of the popular song, "Old Hundred." It was loud and distinct, and the audience of academics gasped almost simultaneously. A ripple of whispers filled the hall then faded into momentary silence. Suddenly everyone was on their feet clapping and whistling. Aleck tried not to show his pride openly, though he certainly felt it. He bowed graciously and there was more clapping from a thousand academic hands. It was sweet music, indeed, to his ears.

As Aleck left the platform, crowds formed around him. "Amazing!" was the most frequent exclamation, but he thrilled, as well, to "fantastic" and "futuristic."

"Professor Bell." A distinguished looking greybeard of medium height moved through the crowd of admirers. "I'm from M.I.T.," the gentleman said, offering his hand. "Extraordinary, Professor Bell. Clear sound—music from a little box that appears to be attached to practically nothing!"

"Thank you," Aleck managed.

"Professor Bell, I would like to have you give a demonstration before the university's Society of Arts."

"I should be delighted," Aleck agreed. "But I have to check my calendar first."

"Of course. Please get in touch with me." He handed Aleck his card.

At that moment Aleck felt as though borne on a rising tide.

⁓

Aleck sat in the Hubbard parlour, his hands folded tightly in his lap. Mabel had wanted to talk with him, and he could guess about what.

Gardiner Hubbard had arranged to have himself appointed to the three-member board organizing the Philadelphia Centennial Exhibition. Visible Speech was to be a part of the Massachusetts display on education, and Gardiner had spent more than an hour urging Aleck to enter the telephone in the exhibition's electrical section. "The transmissions are still too indistinct for public presentation," Aleck had argued.

Gardiner's stubborn insistence had forced a compromise. In the end, Aleck had told him to demonstrate the telephone himself and Gardiner had agreed. Days before, Aleck had shipped the apparatus to Philadelphia on the clear understanding that Gardiner was in charge of the demonstration. Soon after, Gardiner had wired him, saying that hotel arrangements had been made and urging him to come and demonstrate the telephone personally, adding, "If you don't come, Elisha Gray may receive all the accolades."

Aleck had steadfastly refused to go. He hated appearing before the public. He wired Gardiner: "You know as well as I how the machine works, you demonstrate it." He seethed with anger at his partner's relentless pressuring. He was tired, busy beyond all belief, and he didn't want to go to Philadelphia in spite of his success before the Academy and at M.I.T.

The parlour door opened and Mabel came in. She looked wonderful—as always! She was dressed in white and her thick hair tumbled over her shoulders.

"I came as fast as I could," said Aleck.

Mabel came to sit beside him on the satin settee. She took his hand in hers. "Aleck, I asked you to come so we could talk about Philadelphia."

Aleck felt himself tense, but he couldn't take his eyes off her eyes. She looked intent and very serious.

"You must go, Aleck. You must stand up for your invention."

"I have work to do for the teachers at the school—a pile of exam papers. And ... Mabel, the apparatus is not ready."

"You were wonderful at M.I.T. Aleck. The newsman from the *Boston Transcript* wrote rave reviews about your invention."

True enough, he had. He had reported that "Vowels are faithfully reproduced; consonants are unrecognizable. Occasionally, however, a sentence would come out with startling distinctness, consonants as well as vowels being audible."[4]

"He was reporting on a demonstration to academics. And such demonstrations are different. I don't dread them so much because men of science have some idea what goes into such an invention. They know this is not the finished product, so they don't expect perfection. They are satisfied with a demonstration that shows the theory is sound."

"Aleck, this is important to me—to us."

Her face seemed unusually pale; her large eyes filled with great tears and he felt as if his heart would break.

"Please, Aleck. I beg you. Let mother and I take you to the train now."

Aleck reached out for her. He held her for a moment, smelling the sweet spring in her hair. "Yes," he whispered. "Please don't cry, Mabel. I'll go."

He held her for a few more minutes. He felt like someone floating in a trance.

Gertrude and Mabel took him to the North Station in the Hubbard carriage and before he knew it, he was on the train to Philadelphia.

～

Aleck fought to control his nerves, though he felt calmer now that William Hubbard had arrived to assist. William had helped him at M.I.T., and in response to Aleck's desperate request, he had agreed to help again. Aleck wiped his brow. In spite of the high ceiling, the Philadelphia Centennial Hall was airless. Everyone there suffered in the terrible heat. Time passed excruciatingly slowly because he was waiting to have his precious invention judged. Aleck tried to think of other things. He acknowledged to himself that he was elated to be at such an important exhibition. If he hadn't come, he would have felt cheated.

On the first day he had wandered through the hall. The scope of the exhibition was prodigious, its dimensions staggered him. He found the Chinese exhibits fascinating and wrote Mabel, observing how presumptuous Americans were to think themselves superior. Another exhibit that caught his eye was a Brazilian table made of solid silver—weighing 4,002 pounds. The logic of constructing such an object escaped him, though it was undeniably beautiful.

He had, of course, examined some of the electrical exhibits and met Sir William Thompson, one of the electrical judges. Thompson turned out to be a splendid, genial, good-hearted and wise-headed man, and, Aleck noted comfortably, he was also a Scot. He also met his arch rival, Elisha Gray, who seemed an honourable man. As things turned out, Sir William had not been able to judge Aleck's invention on schedule, which was fortunate because it had been damaged during shipment. It took him hours to repair the instruments.

This morning—26 June—he had awakened in the hothouse that was the city of Philadelphia. Dear God, how he hated the humid heat! Every building looked on the verge of wilting.

He and William had hurried over to Centennial Hall, where Elisha Gray's exhibit was the first to be judged.

Gray had made several factual errors and to Aleck's scarcely concealed delight had to be corrected by the judges. Among those present was Dom Pedro, the Emperor of Brazil. He caught Aleck's eye and waved. Aleck waved back. Dom Pedro knew his father and had visited Aleck's school in Boston only a few weeks before. Seeing a familiar face helped Aleck to relax while awaiting his turn.

"I think they're finished," William Hubbard whispered, nudging Aleck in the ribs and jolting him from his thoughts.

The judges returned to their table. Perspiration dotted their brows, and their shirts—like his own—were wet. After putting their heads together they made an announcement: "Owing to the extreme heat and humidity, all further judging will take place tomorrow."

"Oh, no," Aleck muttered. "I can't stand this waiting." He bit his lip and wiped his brow again. He was already a wreck. This meant another night's lost sleep. "I just want to get it over with," he muttered.

"Professor Bell, weren't you to be next?"

Aleck looked into the eyes of Dom Pedro.

"I was," he answered, "but it seems I've been put off."

"I can see you're disappointed. Let me have a word with the good judges. I think I can prevail upon them to sacrifice themselves to one more judgment." With that, Dom Pedro winked at Aleck and went off to confer with the judges.

In a moment there was another announcement. "We have decided to judge one more exhibit today. Professor Alexander Graham Bell, please."

"We're on," William whispered.

Aleck led the officials to the Massachusetts corner. He offered Sir William a chair. The invention was set up on the table in front of him.

"Sir William, please put your ear next to the small box receiver."

Sir William did as requested. "By George, I can hear the sound of music—carnival music from ... yes, from outside."

Suddenly the box spoke, "Do you understand what I say?"

Sir William jumped from his chair, nearly knocking everything over. He looked at the other judges. "Did you hear what I heard?" He shouted into the box, "Yes! Do you understand what I say?"

The box replied, "Yes. I understand!"

Sir William turned and embraced Aleck. "Wonderful," he said loudly. "A wonderful invention! Quite the most wonderful thing I've seen in America."

After examining the other exhibits on the following day, the judges' decision was unanimous. Alexander Graham Bell's invention of the telephone received first prize and the gold medal.

~

Aleck felt a mingled sense of success, relief and exhaustion. It seemed he'd been back and forth to Washington a hundred times, and although he had been working day and night, he missed Mabel terribly. She was on a transcontinental tour. He envied her and wished he were with her. But as usual, he was much too overburdened with lectures and patent work for a vacation. However, he was now on his way home to Boston and Mabel would be returning soon.

Shortly after the triumph in Philadelphia, a patent conflict arose. He had gone to Washington to sort out the dispute between himself, Western Union and Elisha Gray. For six hours he testified on his priority of conception after which the Western Union lawyers withdrew, leaving Aleck and Gray to settle whatever differences still existed between them. The two inventors had developed a respect for one another.

Meanwhile, Watson had continued working in Boston. He wired to Aleck his latest suggestions on how the transmissions might be made clearer, and Aleck, in turn, advised him to make models with the changes and send them to Washington. Watson soon informed him that the new instruments exceeded all expectations and advised Aleck to apply for a patent without delay. The drafts for the final telephone patents required intensive work and he worked on them day and night. By mid-January he had finished the final patents and delivered them to Anthony Pollock, the patent lawyer.

Letters and accolades poured in, but no money.[5] He and Gardiner discussed how to market the telephone. A demonstration was arranged for Elisha Converse, president of the Boston Rubber Shoe Company. Aleck sent music over an eighteen-mile wire with Watson at the other end, then Watson spoke to a stunned audience. The newspapers picked up the story, and for the first time the public learned about the telephone and understood why it was so named.

The Chicago Tribune wrote a galling article claiming Gray had invented the telephone, but in March, Gray himself wrote, "I do not, however, claim even the credit of inventing it, as I do not believe a mere description of an idea that has never been reduced to practice—in the strict sense of that phrase—should be dignified with the name invention."

Aleck had read and reread Gray's letter. It seemed that Mr. Gray had given up all claim to having invented the telephone. Still, court hearings on disputed patents continued even though the invention was not yet marketed.

Aleck, Hubbard and Sanders formed the Bell Telephone Company and the first line was installed in April 1877, between Charles Williams's Boston workshop and his house. After several unsuccessful attempts to raise capital, the partners decided nonetheless to keep control in their own hands. The company's initial five-thousand shares had been divided among the owners—Aleck, Hubbard and Sanders. Hubbard suggested that they try to interest entrepreneurs from other cities in introducing the patent.

~

Cambridge, 11 July 1877

A cool evening breeze rustled the trees in the garden, relieving the heat and humidity of the day. The Hubbards' elegantly furnished drawing room had become as familiar to him as his own living quarters. He had often been a guest, and it was in this room that he had asked Mabel to marry him.

The candles in the ornate silver candelabra flickered as the guests mingled. They talked softly and wished the newlyweds health and happiness. There were endless toasts. But nothing mattered to Aleck except that moments ago he and Mabel had been married, pledging themselves to one another for a lifetime. He inhaled the sweet smell of the Madonna lilies that filled every vase in the room, and his gaze strayed again to his beautiful bride. She wore a gracefully simple white gown; her dark hair curled round her lovely face; she looked to Aleck, like an angel. She was speaking with one of her mother's friends when she glanced up and their eyes met. She touched the cross that hung round her neck as though sending him a silent signal.

He had given her the cross, exquisitely made of eleven round pearls. It was as delicate as she, he thought. He smiled back at her across the room. Aleck and Mabel could communicate silently on more than one level—she always knew his mood, his thoughts, his desires. From their engagement nineteen months before, until they had recited their vows to one another today, they had ridden the roller coaster of success and near-defeat together. It had taken twenty months of overwork and uncertainty before finances stabilized enough that they were able to set a wedding date. It had been a simple wedding in the Hubbard home. Aleck invited only Miss Fuller, his long-time friend.[6]

With Mabel at his side, Aleck had a real partner—in every sense of the word. His wedding present to her was all but ten of his 1,507 shares of the newly formed Bell Telephone Company. He offered it as proof of his marriage vow, "With all my worldly goods I thee endow." But he knew, as well, that Mabel was a much better manager of his affairs than he could ever hope to be. She had good business sense and would never do anything financially foolish.

He sipped some wine and then walked towards the piano.

"Yes, Aleck play for us!" Gertrude, dressed to the nines and coiffed elegantly, floated toward him. "You should play at your own wedding."

Aleck played "Old Hundred" for its symbolic meaning to him. Then he played another tune and another. He sang while the guests joined in. He laughed as his fingers danced across the keyboard. Tonight marked a new beginning, and Aleck could feel the tension of the last twenty months dropping away.

Gardiner touched his shoulder after a time. "However much my wife and our guests enjoy your playing, Aleck, this is your wedding night and if you don't stop, you will miss your train."

Aleck nodded and played a spectacular glissando to end his performance. The timing was perfect. Mabel appeared, dressed in her travelling suit. Aleck rose from the piano stool and bowed to the guests. He gazed at Mabel lovingly even as her friends and family hugged and kissed her.

"It's time," she told him softly, her eyes shining. "It's time to go."

~

Their carriage moved at a leisurely pace down the dirt road. "What if your mother doesn't like me?" Mabel asked, seeking his reassurance.

Aleck hugged her, then kissed her cheek. "Everyone likes you. In any case she won't just like you, she'll love you as I do."

"I'm nervous, Aleck."

"You don't need to be."

She took a deep breath of the dry, warm, summer air. Canada was indeed different from the United States. The houses were far fewer and the space between them much greater. In fact, it seemed to be on the edge of the wilderness—rolling farm country practically uninhabited.

Aleck tapped her shoulder and Mabel turned to read his lips, "What do you think of Canada?" he asked.

She smiled. It was not the first time he had asked a question about the very thought she was having.

"For one thing, I think Canada has the best part of that natural wonder, Niagara Falls."

"But the U.S. side has the best inns."

They had begun their honeymoon at Niagara Falls; after a few days of strolling the banks of the Niagara, examining the falls from all angles and enjoying quiet dinners together, they took the train to Brantford and the Bell home at Tutelo Heights.

"Another bend in the road," Aleck said, looking at her.

"Oh, I'm so nervous," Mabel repeated.

She had hardly finished the sentence before the carriage creaked to a halt. Aleck, long-legged and energetic, climbed down and lifted her to the ground.

Just as the two of them started down the flower-bordered path toward the homey looking two-storey house, the front door opened and Mabel stopped short. A smallish, plump women dressed in calico and wearing a crisp white apron ran toward them. Her hair was pulled behind her head, though wisps of it had escaped, framing her round face. She held her long skirt with one hand so as not to trip; in the other she carried a cake. But she did not carry it to present it, but rather at shoulder height, in one hand, as though to propel it through the air.

Mabel's mouth opened in shock as the woman reached her. Suddenly, and for no apparent reason, the woman dumped the cake on Mabel's head, crumbling it as she did so, and laughing heartily.

Mabel stood stunned, unable to summon words. In the doorway a large man appeared, roaring with laughter as Mabel fought back tears. She turned to see that Aleck too was wild with laughter, and even the lunatic woman was now smiling and attempting to embrace her. What manner of family had she married into?

Then she felt Aleck's large hand on her shoulder. She faced him, wide-eyed.

"My dearest, it's an old Scottish tradition! That's an oatcake and to have it broken over your head the first time you enter your husband's home ensures that we will never go hungry."

Mabel read his words and now realized that the woman must be Aleck's mother. Eliza Bell smiled kindly and hugged Mabel warmly. "Welcome," Eliza said. "Welcome to our family."

Melville Bell took Mabel's small hand in his. "I've arranged a dinner in honour of your marriage to my son. Every leader in the province is coming, and Chief Johnson has also promised to attend."

"Chief of the Mohawk Indians," Aleck explained.

"I'm honoured," Mabel replied.

"Let's stop lollygagging out here and go into the house." Eliza propelled her along. She felt drawn to Eliza and curious about this woman who was her husband's mother.

Mabel remarked on her new family when she wrote her mother.

"Mrs. Bell is just as nice and kind as she can be, so bright and quick. I do think she enjoys this life in Canada though I understand why Aleck feels so badly about it (her having to give up her life in London for the sake of Aleck's health.) "It is so funny to see him here. He is so different from them all and actually seems a great dandy."[7]

⁓

The honeymooners started back to Boston at the end of the month. The summer of 1877 was one of the worst on record for Indian attacks, riots and robberies on the railway. By the time their train reached Montreal, Aleck became so alarmed by hair-raising stories that Mabel reported: "We were so doubtful of our chances of reaching Boston undisturbed that Aleck bought a revolver with ammunition enough to kill a hundred men, he said. I think he was rather disappointed not to have a chance to show it off."[8]

When they reached Boston, arrangements were made for a board of directors meeting for the company.

"The first official meeting of the Board of Directors of Bell Telephone," Aleck said proudly, as he pulled out a chair at the long table for Mabel.

Gardiner nodded at his daughter. He smoothed down his vest in a characteristic gesture, and then, with flourish, withdrew his gold watch and checked the time. All the board members were present, but he had decided not to begin one moment sooner than scheduled. When the big hand reached the Roman numeral "II" on his handsome Waltham watch, he began. "For a company that was in dire straits a few months ago, everything is now going very well indeed."

"There are now two hundred telephones in operation," Watson reported, "and not one has failed in a single instance."

"And we have orders for hundreds more," Sanders put in.

"What about the President's statement?" Aleck inquired. "Will it affect our sales?"

Rutherford B. Hayes, nineteenth president of the United States, had, after trying the telephone line linking Washington to Philadelphia stated to the press: "That's an amazing invention but who would ever want to use one of them?"

Gardiner brushed Aleck's concern aside with a wave. "If anything his remark has helped sales. He did say it was an amazing machine. That's the important thing. If the poor man can't see the advantages to using it then he is to be pitied. Others can and do and are willing to buy it."

Aleck leaned back in his chair. He was, at this moment, filled with optimism. Soon, he hoped, the financial benefits of his invention would relieve all his personal economic difficulties. He leaned toward Mabel, and shielding his mouth so only she could read his lips, he whispered, "Now we can continue our honeymoon in England—I long to take you to Scotland, my love."

Mabel answered with a nod. Aleck was as relaxed and as happy as she had ever seen him. "I do love him," she thought, "I really, truly do."

Melville Bell, 1819–1905.
"My life's work," he called the
universal phonetic system that
he laboured twenty years to
create.

Eliza Bell, 1809–1897. "She was
so kind and gentle, so loving
that during the fifty-two years of
our companionship, I never saw
a frown on her sweet face."

Aleck (left) at fifteen,
with his brothers and
parents. Teddy (right)
died of tuberculosis
at eighteen as did
Melly, the eldest son,
at twenty-five.

Alexander Graham Bell—
the sixteen-year-old
teacher of music and
elocution.

Aleck (top right) moved
from Canada to Boston to
teach the deaf to speak,
using his father's universal
phonetic system—Visible
Speech.

By age thirteen, Mabel Hubbard was well-travelled, well-educated and confident—and soon to meet the teacher who would change her life.

Gardiner Greene Hubbard (1822–1897) was a lawyer, businessman and promoter. He became Aleck's business partner before becoming his father-in-law.

Aleck worked to exhaustion as a teacher of the deaf and an inventor. New ideas were always coming to him and there were too few hours in a day.

Mabel and Aleck with their daughters Elsie (left) and Daisy, in 1885, the year of their first visit to Baddeck.

The telephone made Aleck famous—and rich—but he longed to put it behind him and pursue new challenges.

Mabel plays with her granddaughter Carol.

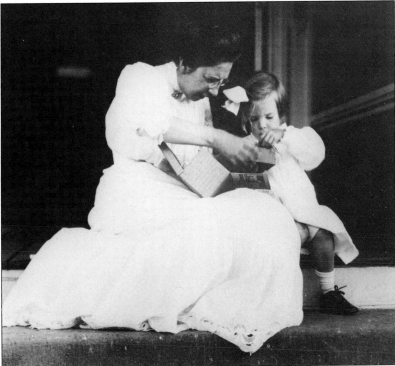

Beinn Bhreagh, the Bell's estate at Baddeck. "It's what I've always dreamed of," said Aleck. "A house with everything a man could desire, and bounteous nature right outside the doorstep."

1907 Sep 1

Family group gathers at lodge porch, 1907.

Mabel wrote, "Just now ... flying ...
appeals more to the imagination,
but ... the water highway will
resume interest. Fifty years later, the
Canadian navy's hydrofoil, *Bras
D'or,* won international acceptance.

The HD-4 "resembled a sixty-foot-
long grey cigar on pontoons."
Its phenomenal speed record was
unbroken for eleven years.

Douglas McCurdy's *Silver
Dart* was the last A.E.A.
airplane. In February 1909,
at Baddeck, McCurdy made
the first airplane flight in
Canada.

Mabel at work. In response to the tragic Halifax Explosion in 1917, she mobilized the people of Baddeck to gather food and make clothes, which Casey Baldwin and twelve townsmen took to Halifax by sea.

Bell with granddaughters Gertrude, Lillian and Mabel Grosvenor, 1909.

Aleck at his old school—the Royal High School—1 December 1920. "The next day ... the newspaper proclaimed that not even the city's association with Sir Walter Scott had brought as much pride and honour as did Alexander Graham Bell."

Part II

CHAPTER TWELVE

On 4 August 1877, nearly seven years to the date of his arrival on the North American continent, Aleck and Mabel set sail for England on board the steamship *Anchoria* to continue their honeymoon.

While at sea Mabel allowed Aleck the luxury of rising early, taking a hot bath, eating some breakfast and then crawling back into bed until noon. Efforts to have him conform to what she considered a normal schedule were to last throughout their lives together. The voyage was pleasant; dancing and parties every night. The Bells were seated at the captain's table where Aleck did a sales job on the advantages of a shipboard telephone system connecting all departments. The sceptical captain listened politely but tactfully expressed no opinion. In the evenings Aleck played for the other passengers while Mabel danced with the captain. Unlike the other passengers, her deafness and lack of inner ear balance kept her from becoming dizzy or seasick. She relied on her sight to maintain balance. But when night fell she needed someone to guide her.

As the steamer approached land, Aleck's excitement grew. "I cannot tell you what a longing I have to see the places I remember so well, London, Bath, Edinburgh and Elgin. I don't know how it is, but Elgin bears the palm with me."[1] When the ship docked in Greenock, Scotland, their first stop was the city of Glasgow. Mabel noted her husband's sudden change of character. "Here we are safely on shore again in Alec's[2] beloved 'ain country.' The poor fellow is perfectly wild over it and is so anxious to have me like everything because it is Scotch and especially anything that is from Edinburgh, it is really pathetic. He almost went down on his knees to beg me to like Edinburgh breakfast rolls."[3]

Aleck arose each day with the watery Glasgow sun, ate his breakfast and was off to visit old friends. He returned several hours later like an excited school boy with a group of his buddies, who would burst into the hotel and run up the stairs to play with the telephone. An invitation arrived from Sir William Thompson's brother to come to Plymouth for a meeting of the British Association for the Advancement of Science. Aleck couldn't have been more pleased. For the first time since their marriage Mabel began feeling inadequate at being married to such an internationally famous man.

"Tomorrow we will be in Plymouth, probably at the centre of attention, and I am so frightened to think how ill I can act my part as Graham Bell's wife. This is the only name Alec is known by here. Oh, I wish I were safe at home, I'd give up all hope of ever being Lady Bell and all the glories of being the wife of a successful inventor, everything but just being Alec's wife, to come home to quiet humbleness. Not that I am not enjoying myself nor that everyone is not very kind.

Who do you think asked to be introduced to Alec today but Sir Willoughby Jones. He brought Alec up to Lady Jones and they seemed very proud to meet him. They invited us to dine with them tomorrow but we had to decline because we are dining with Sir William and Lady Thompson on their yacht. Lady Jones will call on me tomorrow morning. Alec is really the chief person here. Everybody seeks to do him honour. He has been introduced to all the great people, Lord this and Sir that, and all are anxious and eager to speak with him."[4]

During their first four months Aleck gave ten lectures and demonstrations. They resulted in wonderful publicity. Every newspaper in the country praised the telephone. While on the lecture in Edinburgh, Aleck took Mabel to see his old house on Charlotte Square. He pointed out the opaque window in the school for girls next door. One of its windows had faced his bedroom where he and his brother Teddy had stood in their nightgowns making silly faces at the girls. After several warnings to cease and desist, the headmistress installed opaque windows to protect her young ladies.

Aleck decided to take a holiday trip to Covesea, a seaside village in the north of Scotland. Mabel shuddered at the thought. The cold September air blowing in off the North Sea seemed to go straight into her bones. They planned their stay in a fisherman's cottage, determined to rough it—man and his woman against nature. Aleck thought it all sounded very romantic. Although they anticipated bringing a large supply of food with them, they had decided that their main diet would be the fish that they caught from the sea. Aleck had never caught a fish, much less cleaned and cooked one. But he felt that it couldn't be all that difficult. Mabel wasn't so sure.

"We engaged the funniest little room you ever saw. The ceiling is so low that Alec's tip-top curl almost brushes against it. The room has tiny diamond-paned windows. The green painted walls are covered with countless little pictures from newspapers, giving the room a most fantastic air. We are to provide our own food and fuel, and how I am to manage cooking on a little grate I don't know and Alec is so aggravating in his sublime ignorance of any difficulty in the matter. A pleasant-faced woman offered to do anything for us and Alec actually told her he thought all we would need was hot water. However, Mrs. Cameron supplied us with some nice fresh milk and eggs. We have bought a little portable tea kettle and broiled our tea and eggs in it but alas two trials were sufficient to break Alec's courage and now to my great joy, Mrs. Cameron boils our eggs, tea and potatoes for us. The only thing Alec won't trust her to do is to prepare his beloved smoked herrings. He did them himself at first but the fire gave him a headache so he allows me to do it.

Alec insisted that a loaf of bread, half a pound of sugar and a pound of butter was quite enough to last us the week. I am rather triumphant for this morning Mrs. Cameron's lassie had to walk three miles to Lossiemouth for some more. Alec meant to have gone this morning at six, but of course when Mrs. Cameron called him, he turned over on his side and went to sleep again. My sugar ought to have lasted longer but that husband of mine wasted six or seven good lumps trying experiments to find out if it was the sugar itself or the air in the sugar that exploded when melted in a cup of hot tea or water, causing little fountains of water at the surface.... He decided it was the air. Ever since Saturday we have been out on the rocks each day. Saturday we carried provisions but quarrelled so over them and found them so heavy that yesterday we left all behind. What a man my husband is! I am perfectly bewildered at the number and size of the ideas with which his head is crammed. Flying machines to which telephones and torpedoes are to be attached occupy the first place just now from the observation of seagulls, and the practicability of attaching telephones to wire fences.... Every now and then he comes back with another flying machine which has quite changed its shape within a quarter of an hour. Then he goes climbing about the rocks forming theories of the origin of cliffs and caves, which last problem he has solved to his satisfaction. Then he comes home and watches the sugar bubbles. Starts out the next morning after rabbits, but I have no doubt he pays more attention to the seagulls but seems as anxious to prove himself as good a shot as any schoolboy."[5]

While at Covesea cottage they took walks along the beach. Mabel sat in the sand and waited while Aleck examined the lapping shore line. He waded into the chilly water, watching the seagulls floating on the air currents overhead. They squawked and dipped closer in search of food. Mabel thought the scene too picturesque to pass up. She had brought her sketching pad. "I tried to sketch him as he stood still for a few moments thinking of a rhyme, his feet bare and rather far apart, his hands outstretched. The sketch was a failure so far ... as any likeness was concerned, but I wish you could have seen him. He was so wild and full of fun, though rather ashamed that the inventor of the telephone should go wading, but I persuaded him that he should not be a slave to his own position."[6]

On the trip back to London Mabel began suffering from upset tummy each morning. Aleck suggested a doctor. The doctor told her that she was two months pregnant. Aleck was elated and presented his wife with a tiny pair of blue baby socks.

At another lecture in Glasgow, Aleck collected fifteen pounds, ten shillings. Such prompt payment pleased Mabel. Other lecture organizers still owed substantial fees. It appeared to her that the scientific community, while highly intelligent and responsible for pushing the wheels of progress, was most unbusiness-like in its financial dealings. Of the Glasgow lecture she wrote that "I am glad to have it settled beforehand, for the Aberdeen people have not said a word about payment now that their lecture is over."[7]

They settled into one of London's fashionable hotels. Aleck thought that as the inventor of the telephone, he should put on a good show since people would expect it. Mabel agreed reluctantly, although she failed to see how spending money would make Aleck more scientifically acceptable. By mid-November she was homesick and tired of hotel life. Originally, they had planned to return home in November but decided to stay on rather than risk a rough ocean passage while Mabel was pregnant. "You have no idea how tired and homesick I have been, living here with nothing to do to induce me to try and keep our rooms looking nice. It is no use, Alec has no room for his papers and they are always scattered about the room on chairs and on the floor and every day the piles increase in spite of my daily sorting. The only writing table is small and will not hold half the things Alec is always wanting, so he uses the dining table and at mealtime the waiter sweeps the papers all together and piles them up here and there, creating greater confusion and putting Alec out and destroying my work of hours of arranging. Then Miss Brooks, the proprietress, does not like the telephone. Alec wants a house where he can run wires from top to bottom to rooms out of earshot and where he would be free to do as he likes. Of course, in a place like this, the owner would always be interfering and Alec's nightly labours make trouble. People don't like to have men striding up and down over their heads all night long ... Alec is quite as anxious, if not more so, then I am, to have a home of our own."[8]

In late November they moved into a home that they could call their own, a four-storey mansion in South Kensington with seventeen rooms. The rent came to £225 a year. Two servants were hired to look after the place. Mabel worried continually over their expenses. She asked her mother for advice on leftovers. "I should like your recipe for whips and floating island as I do not like the English puddings. How do you make fish balls? What can I do with the remains of cold chicken? Could I serve it up with curry the next day? I don't want to waste anything."[9]

She was not happy in London. Settling in one place provided an illusion of permanence, yet she missed her family. One of their servants, Mrs. Home, had been with the Bell family off and on for nearly forty years. She had worked for Melville before the family sailed for Canada. Mary held a tight reign over the household and accompanied Mabel whenever she wanted to go shopping. Mary acted as translator for the sales clerks, who usually had difficulty understanding Mabel's strangely toneless voice. These trips often left Mabel feeling self-conscious and embarrassed. Nevertheless it was better than shopping with Aleck, who hated to leave a store without buying something. When she begged him to try and control himself, he would argue and then buy some useless article. In her opinion, Aleck spent far too much money.

Colonel Reynolds still owed £500 for the British patents and as pleased as Mabel was that Reynolds and Aleck were working together on the English Bell Telephone Company, she had some reservations about Reynolds's business competence. "We have ever so many applications, some very important ones, and I wish he would see about them, and take some of the work off Alec."[10]

Reynolds, although a likeable enough fellow, had absolutely no business sense. When capital was required for the formation of the English production company, Reynolds promised to take care of it. Instead, he engaged a rubber company to manufacture the telephones. Product demand grew so rapidly that cheap imitations began sprouting all over England and Europe. Aleck wrote to Gardiner that he found business "hateful ... at all times."

Their financial situation worried Mabel constantly. "Well, I am glad that we have decided to go without housekeeping, for it will teach me the value of money and I think I will be more careful now. Oh Mama, to think of having to spend more than a hundred dollars and not being able to save a cent. Of course, I must have spoons and forks to eat with and salt cellars to hold the salt, sheets and table napkins are necessities, and yet I can't bear to buy them for our money does run out fast and the balance is getting so low. I know Alec is dreadfully anxious for some regular employment. If the English company could only be formed, they would have to refund five hundred pounds to us and that would make everything straight, especially if they give Alec the post of electrician, but we have heard little of it of late. I am sure Papa is right in saying that Alec is not suited to this work. Alec says he will not wait until his money is gone before he gets some more. Oh dear, I do wish the Bell Telephone Company would earn enough money to at least pay for all the time and work Alec put on the telephone last winter. It is so dreadful to see him worried and all his chances of working and improving the telephone gone for the present while he has to earn his bread and butter."[11]

The new home made life a little less stressful. "Alec says he is glad he took this house for I am so much better and happier than in those rooms [at the hotel]. I hate the thought of them. Alec himself is happy in this land of dreams or will be as soon as his secretary comes to take the correspondence that weighs him down. He has failed to get a satisfactory one yet."[12]

Gardiner tended to side with Mabel on the matter of Reynolds owing the money and wrote to Aleck saying so. But it would take another month before Reynolds finally paid his debt. "Colonel Reynolds yesterday gave Alec a check for the full amount he owes. Now Mama darling, I do hope you and Papa will feel better about Colonel Reynolds. The gentlemen were to have met yesterday to consider the terms of the new company and to settle everything. I fear something went wrong or there was some delay for Alec did not receive the telegram Colonel Reynolds promised to send."[13]

The distance between the continents was about the same as the gulf between Aleck and Gardiner Hubbard. They did not see eye to eye on anything unless Gertrude or Mabel intervened. "I really do not think there is any danger of Alec doubting how hard and faithfully Papa works for us all. If it seems so at any time, remember Alec was not well in health, and anxious and worried in mind, distracted between his feverish anxiety to experiment and feeling that he could not do it for the want of a little money. Everything conspired to make him unreasonable and doubtful of everybody and everything, but he is better now and I think Papa would be satisfied if he could know how much Alec loves and honours him."[14]

Aleck had been under enormous strain, most of it self-made. His name was well known throughout Europe, and although his lectures remained profitable, the money from them seemed to disappear. Mabel tried to curb their spending. "To think that not only a whole week but Christmas Day has passed without my writing you. I am so sorry, I thought I would have all day yesterday to write and it is not my fault or Alec's but his two hundred and one pounds that kept me from doing so. Why, Mama dear, he had his wedding trousers made larger some time ago and who would have thought that they would so soon be tight again in that they'd burst. My afternoon went in darning that terrible tear that grew larger the more I stitched.... Was it not horrible later on in the evening, when Alec stooped to put out some Christmas candles that had caught fire, they should burst again in the very same place and all my hours of work lost."[15]

Married life suited Aleck. Since summer his weight had increased nearly forty pounds. "Alec ... is perfectly happy with his Edinburgh rolls, Scotch oatmeal porridge and red herring. Last night he swallowed a whole dish of finnan haddock which was intended for us both. In fact Alec is growing tremendously stout, and can hardly get his wedding trousers on now. I remember your warning long ago and scold just as hard as ever I can, but it is no use. Alec proposes buying a book, teaching fat men to grow thin!"

Her scolding over his waistline had little effect on his eating habits and he remained a little overweight for the rest of his life. Carping about his sleeping habits produced only temporary results. Initially, she told her mother, "He would complain of sleepless nights and a bad headache and I never had the heart to pull him out, in fact I couldn't." But as the months passed she insisted that Aleck get up and have breakfast with her. "He often feels cross and headachy when I awake him, and begs hard to stay in bed, but if I am firm, after breakfast the headache has quite disappeared, and he is bright and thankful he has been awakened. It is hard work, and tears are spent over it sometimes." In the end she admitted to her mother that "Alec is just as loving as ever he could be and instead of finding more faults in him, as they say married people always find in each other, I only find more to love and admire. It seems to me I did not half know him when I married him."[16]

In the New Year Aleck received an request from the Queen's secretary asking when it would be convenient for him to give a private demonstration for Her Majesty. Aleck suggested that Thursday or Friday of the following week "would be most convenient, but awaited Her Majesty's commands—this last he put in much to my Republican disgust to show that he was the Queen's subject."[17] They decided that Mabel would need a new dress for the occasion. Aleck insisted on nothing less than the best and ordered a gown from Paris. Despite her strong Republican feelings, Mabel was excited by the prospect of meeting Queen Victoria. Then disappointing news arrived.

"I know you are all waiting anxiously to hear all about our visit to the Queen, so I may as well begin by saying that Sir Thomas Biddulph has refused to permit me to accompany Alec. He says he doesn't see how it could be managed without asking Her Majesty and he does not like to do so. Well, I am disappointed, principally I think because it would be fine to write you about. Alec goes down to Cowes on Saturday to see that all is in readiness, as the presentation had been changed to Monday, and immediately afterwards, he leaves for Paris where he is to remain at least a week. I am anxious to go too, it is so dreadfully dreary without him. I don't see how I can survive a week's solitary confinement as it will be. I am justly indignant that the pains and labour bestowed in getting my dress ready for the Queen will be thrown away. It was not to have been finished until the 15th, but I wrote on Friday and it is promised for tomorrow. Do you know about the hardest part of not going to see the Queen is that you will all be disappointed."[18]

To compound her disappointment, when the black silk dress did arrive from Paris and on time, it wasn't what she wanted. Mabel wrote to her mother about her disappointment.

"Well, with some shortening of the train, I could wear it and not feel too gorgeous although it is heavily trimmed with jet. But I am afraid it is altogether too old for me. I am so vexed I could cry.... I now see what a goose I was to use the words "long train" to a dressmaker, but you used those words to me.... I said my dress was for ceremonious calls and receptions; that I wanted a handsome dress but it must be very simple; I wanted something that would be handsome but not showy. Well, if it isn't a showy dress, I don't know what is. What shall I do? I thought I was going to see the Queen and I knew I must have a dress even if I did not go. I think I did not use language descriptive enough, but I feel so helpless and ignorant. The worst of the thing is the good rounded sum there will be to pay."[19]

Aleck went to see the Queen. Several different lines had been set up to transmit conversation and music for the royal ear. One transmission line to Cowes for the singers and musicians broke down and could not be fixed in time for the demonstration. For this reason he had insisted on having several lines available to avoid a repeat performance of his Boston fiasco the year before. The lines running through the Queen's Osbourne Cottage worked perfectly and Queen Victoria was able to converse with ease. Kate Field, an American writer and singer, had been engaged to sing "Kathleen Mavourneen" for the occasion, but at the moment when she was to begin her song, the Queen happened to be looking in another direction. Aleck, accustomed to his Mabel's deafness, touched Her Majesty's hand to get her attention and then offered her the telephone receiver. Touching the Queen was the worst possible social *faux pas*. No one touched the Queen. Not ever. However, Queen Victoria's diary for the day made no mention of Aleck's error and called the telephone demonstration "most extraordinary." He described the Queen to Mabel as "humpy, stumpy, dumpy" and told her that she had not missed very much. The British press disagreed. News of his touching the Queen circulated quickly to all Royal watchers and a generally horrified British Commonwealth.

The telephone became so popular that "Wherever you go, on newspaper stands, at new stores, stationers, photographers, toy shops, fancy goods shops, you see the eternal little black box with red face, and the word 'Telephone' in large black letters. Advertisements say that 700,000 have been sold in a few weeks."[20] Cheap imitations started flooding the market. Reynolds began a series of lawsuits against the most audacious of these manufacturers. But there was a hitch; Sir William Thompson had published an article in 1876, after the Centennial, that provided a complete description of the inner workings of the telephone. The Bell telephone patents in Britain were in danger of cancellation. However, a photograph of the telephone, damaged from the trip to the Exhibition, saved the day. Since the telephone shown in the picture was not exactly as the one described in the British patents, the authorities decided that the Bell patents would stand. This problem—brief as it was—swiftly dampened the enthusiasm of prospective financial backers. To raise capital, Reynolds was forced to sell fifty-five per cent of the patent rights to backers for the paltry sum of £10,000 down, and a further £10,000 within a year, out of the estimated half a million pounds they had planned on getting. It was a disappointing turn of events. Aleck took it in his stride.

He chose Sundays as his day of rest. But even on Sundays there were things to do, as Mabel explained in an apologetic letter.

"I am afraid you didn't get as many letters as usual from me. I have no regular time for writing and always look forward to Sunday as the day set apart for letter writing....We have not been to church regularly or often since we came here. First, because it hurts Alec to sit still and then for one reason or another. Now he says I shall not go any more until after the baby is born. Alec considers Sunday emphatically his day of rest. He refuses to get out of bed until after ten. We have dinner at three and Colonel Reynolds comes every now and then, and Mr. Holmes almost every Sunday evening, bringing a friend or two with him; Chester Bell [a cousin] once in a long while. So you see we are not alone on Sundays. I like it, for it is like old times in Cambridge when your house was so full. We like Mr. Gaulie, a friend of Alec's, very much. Berta and Grace might laugh at him but he is very pleasant with plenty of talk and very careful always to speak to me so that I can understand what he says, which is more than most people take the trouble to do."[21]

She missed her sisters and parents and suggested to Aleck that they could invite the family over for a visit until the baby was born. Aleck agreed immediately and invited Gertrude Hubbard to London.

"Mabel has hitherto been so much part of you that it seemed at first like tearing her life to pieces to remove her from your sheltering care. If there is anything that can console me for this cruelty, it is the feeling that the temporary separation has brought her nearer to me— that it has made us more truly man and wife than we could ever have hoped to become in America—and that it has converted the helpless clinging girl into the self-reliant woman. Still, I think we both agree that we have had enough of the separation and you will be assured that no mother could receive a more hearty welcome from her children than you will receive from us."[22]

Gertrude arrived two weeks later and reported to Gardiner that "Mabel is looking so well. The house is simply furnished with exquisite taste; just the house in every respect that we could have wished for them, and both are so happy and preside with so much ease and grace. Mabel was never half so charming and fascinating, and as for Aleck, you would be more proud of him than ever. He has grown stouter—209 pounds—and seems very well. His mornings are spent with his secretary or in his laboratory. He dines at seven and his evenings are given to Mabel. She retires about ten and he studies until one. Mabel superintends her household as quickly and with as much ease and self-reliance as though she had been mistress of a house for years."[23]

Although Gertrude sounded pleased with things in general, Mabel's articulation concerned her. When she asked Aleck to try and improve her speech he refused, explaining that as man and wife, Mabel and he were now equals. He could not return to the student-teacher relationship because it would place Mabel in a subordinate position. Aleck considered her articulation to be very good and suggested that a year without hearing her daughter speak had dimmed Gertrude's perception of Mabel's articulation. The issue was dropped.

On 8 May 1878, Mabel gave birth to a baby girl. Aleck wrote home. "Such a funny black little thing it is! Perfectly formed, with a full crop of dark hair, bluish eyes, and a complexion so swarthy that Mabel declares she has given birth to a red Indian!" After two weeks of more or less continual argument, they decided to name the baby Elsie May Bell. Elsie, for the short form of Aleck's mother, Eliza, and May, which was Mabel's nickname as well as the month of the baby's birth. She wrote that "Alec is at once so fond of it and yet so afraid of the poor little thing, and he hardly knows how to hold it." If he lacked instant parental knowledge he made up for it by ensuring "that all its organs of speech and sight and hearing are perfect."[24]

This was his first encounter with a baby. All his experience had been limited to dealing with three-and four-year-olds. "I do so love little children, and I like nothing better than being among them. I can hardly wait for Elsie to quit the baby stage ... and to be old enough for me really to love her."[25] Fatherhood was a new and puzzling affair, and even if he wasn't too sure about what to do with his daughter, she was at least more interesting than business.

He and Reynolds continued organizing the patents and the company. All American and some of the foreign patents were held in a trust by Gardiner Hubbard. Income from the trust was arranged to be given to Aleck and Mabel up to the sum of three thousand dollars, everything beyond that was to be put aside into a separate account for their children. This excess income was to be deposited into the children's account until it reached $300,000. After that, Mabel and Aleck were to receive all monies. When the trust was first organized shortly after their marriage, Aleck promised Mabel not to meddle in financial affairs, leaving the management to her father. Under Gardiner's management the children's trust grew handsomely ... at least for the time being.

CHAPTER THIRTEEN

Colonel Reynolds's business operations were a succession of peaks and valleys. Adam Scott, one of Aleck's old London friends, offered to help. Aleck felt so confident about his friend's business abilities that after only a short time, he turned the entire company management over to him, whereupon Aleck no longer concerned himself with business meetings, letters, appointments or anything else that he thought Scott could handle. Unfortunately, this lack of interest in the business by Aleck caused a lack of confidence among the other shareholders. They began to pull out. Worse, by neglecting to keep his eye on the company's business, the acting manager, McClure, managed to swindle the firm out of a considerable sum. McClure had gone off to pursue his own idea of selling telephones outright, instead of under lease. The whole key to the company's strength lay in its leasing policy. Scott notified Aleck, who wrote a letter at once to the Board of Directors, calling for McClure's dismissal. In the same letter he praised and recommended Scott as a suitable replacement. McClure was fired, but instead of Scott, Colonel Reynolds filled the vacancy. Reynolds was trustworthy but hopelessly inept in business matters. The corporate future looked bleak. Aleck's earlier excitement over the telephone business was beginning to pall. He was fed up with the constant stream of problems that seemed to accompany the invention.

Mabel's sisters came to London for the summer and rented rooms in a Middlesex hotel. Mabel spent idyllic days with her mother and sisters, "lying on shawls spread out under the shade of some great tree in the meadow." These restful sunny days of picnicking among the English fields and flowers ended with a thunderclap. *The Times* published an article denouncing Aleck's claim to be the inventor of the telephone. It suggested that he had stolen the idea from someone else. Aleck was indignant. But the worst was still to come. During a telephone sales trip to Ireland *The Times* printed another article authored by Elisha Gray and Thomas Edison. Prompted by Orton at Western Union, the pair had suggested that Aleck was a scoundrel, a thief and that the originality of his inventions was questionable at best. Mabel read the item and was outraged by the injustice of it all.

"I have been working all evening on my needlework and have plenty of time for thought, which I have used to work myself up into such a state of indignation over that horrid letter in *The Times*. The more I think of it, the more it seems like a deliberate attempt not only to rob you of all credit in your own discovery, but also to convey the impression that you are a thief and purloiner of other men's ideas.... Altogether the article gives a most disagreeable impression of you and is a reflection on your honour which no man of any spirit could stand. For your own sake and for all our sake's, please do something. Cannot you write a note to the Editor and if he will not publish it, write to *The Telegraph* or some other paper that may be glad to take up anything against *The Times*. Don't you see how the unanswered insinuations of all these attacks must be injuring you in the eyes of all honest but imperfectly informed people?"[1]

Aleck didn't want Mabel worrying about what the papers published. It did not matter to him, so long as they knew the truth. But he was wrong. It did matter. The bad press was discouraging investors who did not, as Mabel pointed out, know any better. He wrote back: "The more fame a man gets for an invention, the more does he become a target for the world to shoot at. I am beginning to be quite troubled too, just because you are. Let the press quarrel over the inventor of the telephone if it pleases. Why should it matter to the world who invented the telephone as long as the world gets the benefit of it? Why should it matter to me what the world says upon the subject so long as I have obtained the object for which I laboured and have got my sweet darling wife? And why should it matter so very much to you and to my little Elsie so long as the pecuniary benefits of the inventor are not taken from us—and so

long as you are conscious of my uprightness and integrity?...
Truth and Justice will triumph in the end. Let others vindicate my
claim if they choose but keep me out of the strife."[2]

This was not the reply that Mabel expected. Her husband's naivety
and lack of business sense in general were never more apparent. Not
only was the press slandering him but he didn't seem to be objecting
to it. Rather than calming her, Aleck's letter prompted Mabel's sense
of indignation to explode. The difficulty was that Aleck simply wanted
nothing more to do with the telephone. It wasn't fun any more and
certainly not worth the worry and upset.

In the United States, Hubbard had instigated a legal action by the
Bell Telephone Company against Western Union. He needed a statement from Aleck. But Aleck ignored his telegrams and letters, hoping
privately that somehow the entire mess would go away. Gardiner's
letters continued to arrive and Aleck continued to ignore them. One
letter from Greenoch, Scotland, however, caught his eye—a request
for help in finding a teacher for a small school of deaf students. The
school's trustees hoped that he might know someone willing to teach
for a few months. Here was something much closer to Aleck's heart
than the telephone. He offered himself for the job and in late August
took a train to the small community on the river Clyde. Mabel was
less than enthusiastic. It made no sense to her. Aleck was needed in
London. She needed him. Couldn't he see that? More disturbing telegrams arrived from her father. Her husband appeared to be running
away from his responsibilities. She wrote begging him to return home,
for the sake of the business and baby Elsie. The idea of taking second
place in Aleck's priorities to a group of country school children annoyed her. His prompt reply caught her off guard.

"I do not consider myself as working so many hours a day 'for
a couple of babies'—but as inaugurating a revolution in the methods
of teaching deaf children in this country. I do not see in this school
the two or three children actually present—but the 30,000 deaf mutes
of Great Britain.... I trust you will see that I am needed and my presence or absence may mean the success or failure of the new method
of teaching articulation in this country. I have been waiting for months
past for something to do. I have been absolutely rusting from inaction—hoping that my services might be wanted somewhere. Now

I am needed and needed here. I am not going to forsake my little school just when it is struggling for existence—though the telephone should go to ruin—and though my wife and child should return to America and leave me here to work alone. I shall make this school a success if I have to remain until Christmas. It is a sorrow and grief to me that you have always exhibited so little interest in the work I have at heart—and that you have neither appreciated Visible Speech nor have encouraged me to work for its advancement.

Of one thing I am quite determined and that is to waste no more time and money on the telephone. If I am to give away any more of my time—it must be for the object that is nearest my heart.... I am sick of the telephone and have done with it—excepting as a plaything to amuse my leisure moments. We cannot live for many months longer as we have been doing and I must go to work at something that will pay me and at the same time be doing some good in the world. I never would have commenced to work on the telephone had it not been for the temptation of assistance from your father and Mr. Sanders. I never would have continued to work on the subject had it not been that I wished your father and Mr. Sanders to be repaid for the money they expended.... And I never would have succeeded in perfecting the telephone had it not been for the hope of getting you, my sweet wife; the struggle is ended now and I long for peace.... If my ideas are worth patenting, let others do it. Let others endure the worry, the anxiety and expense. I will have none of it. There is too much of the element of speculation in patents for me. A feverish anxious life like that I have been leading since our marriage would soon change my whole nature. Already it has begun injuring me and I feel myself growing irritable, feverish and disgusted with life."[3]

His wish to have nothing further to do with the telephone was something over which he had been brooding for some time. Two months later he made up his mind to return to Tutelo Heights for a rest before returning full time to the profession that he loved best, teaching the deaf to speak. He handed in his resignation to the English Telephone Company, stating that his decision came as a direct result of "the gross mismanagement of the Company's business and the personal discourtesy with which I have been treated by the Board of Directors and by the Acting Manager." Colonel Reynolds was the acting manager. Since McClure's ouster, the business had been run honestly but remained in a dreadful state of disorganization. Aleck's earlier doubts about Reynolds were realized as the business spread itself in all directions and accomplished nothing. He washed his hands of the entire mess, and in November with Mabel and the baby, sailed for Canada.

Mabel's attempts to get him to file a statement for the American Bell Telephone Company had been fruitless. Without Aleck's statement the company was in danger of loosing its own lawsuit. Time was running out. In one last-ditch effort Hubbard sent Watson to Quebec City to meet the boat when it docked. Watson went aboard the vessel and after much pleading and tears from Mabel, Aleck agreed to go to Boston, not for the sake of the telephone but for his wife and then only after he had seen Mabel and Elsie safely settled with his parents. Watson accompanied them. He intended sticking to Aleck like glue until he got him to Boston. Mabel wrote to her mother after Aleck and Watson had left.

"Poor Alec has been suffering terribly since we landed, with abscesses. Yesterday and the day before, he nearly fainted several times, and yesterday he had two shivering fits that frightened me very much. Today he is suffering less or he could not have gone; but he is very weak and looks dreadful and I am frightened. Oh, if I could only be with him as I am so worried for the whole responsibility of his going is mine; he would not have gone but that I felt so strongly about it. But now that he is gone, Papa will be very kind to him, won't he? Alec is not like Papa, he cannot go on working steadily, and particularly through all suffering, as Papa does. He cannot help it if he is not so brave."[4]

By the time they reached Boston, Aleck's condition had deteriorated. Watson took him to the Massachusetts General Hospital where, from his hospital bed, he dictated his statement on the telephone patent from memory.

This patent conflict was only a small part of a much larger lawsuit which had its origins when the American Bell Telephone Company filed legal actions against Peter A. Dowd on 12 September 1878. Dowd, representing the Gold and Stock Company [a Western Union affiliate] had been selling telephones that he claimed were invented by Elisha

Gray. Western Union, as the parent company, was defending the case on Dowd's behalf. Aleck's eleventh-hour statement managed to save the day. Hubbard, Sanders and Watson heaved a sigh of relief. Their next problem was keeping Aleck in Boston because the moment he left hospital, Aleck intended heading straight back to Tutelo Heights and beginning work at once with the deaf. Hubbard stepped into the breech and offered him the position of company electrician [chief engineer] at a salary of $5000 a year plus expenses. He promised Aleck that the work would be minimal and that he could do as he pleased as long as he stayed around Boston and made himself available to give testimony whenever he was needed. Reluctantly, Aleck agreed and wrote Mabel the news. She couldn't have been happier. The new arrangement meant a steady income and would bring her back to the arms of her family. He asked where she kept the key to the box where she stored his letters to her. "Not that I have the remotest intention of publishing any of my love letters! I am only anxious to discover any statements that may help me to fix dates."[5] He was in the midst of a frantic search for anything relating to the telephone that might be used as proof of priority in the Dowd Trial.

They moved into the Hubbard home in Cambridge temporarily until they could decide whether to stay in Boston or go to Washington. Although the Bell Telephone Company's office was in Boston, for the foreseeable future Aleck would be needed in Washington to give testimony during the long and drawn out court case with Dowd and Western Union. Whichever city they chose, Aleck would have to spend much of his time away on business. Ultimately, they decided that Washington would be the lesser of two evils. At least there Mabel would have her parents and sisters for company while Aleck was away. They moved to the capital and rented a small brick house a block away from the Hubbards. It made her long separations from Aleck easier. The emotional strain of these partings was something with which both of them had to come to terms in order for their marriage to survive. By March of the following year Aleck saw the problem as a threat to their happiness.

"Don't let us consent to being separated any more; help me darling to prevent it now. Let us lay it down as a principle of our lives that we shall be together, that we shall share each other's thoughts and lives—and to be to one another all that a husband and wife could be. Letters cannot speak as we can face to face—heart to heart.... Fragments of our lives must inevitably drop out of each other's knowledge if we are separated. In spite of daily interchange of written thought little by little the breach will widen until at length we lose the sense of unity of life and learn to live apart."[6]

Living apart was not the problem, it was not knowing how long they would be apart. The future appeared filled with uncertainties. The telephone had brought them together. Now it was forcing them apart.

"Yesterday Alec left us for Boston, to be gone no one knows how long. It is all on account of that wretched lawsuit, the Bell Telephone Company versus the American Telephone Company, alias the Western Union Telegraph company. All day long he worked over old letters trying to find something that will throw a light of any kind on the lawsuit. Sitting on the floor in the midst of all the confusion I had created with drawers opened and their contents strewn all around on table, chairs and bed, Alec and I got into a long discussion on riches. I say I want fifteen thousand a year, my fine house and carriage. Alec says five thousand a year is a handsome income and that I would be able to keep a carriage on that.

'Well, if you want me to give up scientific work and devote myself to making money, you can probably lie in your carriage and dress in velvet, etc.'

'What is there higher than making money really?' asked I rebelliously with unfelt frivolity.

'Science, adding to knowledge, bringing us nearer to God,' answers he, sitting upright and speaking enthusiastically. 'Yes I hold that is the highest of all things, the increase of knowledge making us more like God. And will you bring me down and force me to give up my scientific work?'

'No, only I want money too if I can get it.'

'So you shall my dear,' declares my husband turning suddenly around, 'and doubtless you will by and by.'"[7]

The thought of continuing to live a hand to mouth existence was not her idea of security. Not long after their discussion on riches she wrote to him about the prices of the telephone stocks.

"Enclosed please find a blank power of attorney to sell seven hundred of my shares at sixty-five dollars immediately. Mama says Papa and Mr. Morgan both think this is the time to sell, so please sell out immediately, please, please, please, please, please, PLEASE, PLEASE, PLEASE. Are you sufficiently impressed by the importance of the subject now? If you love me do something right away the moment you get this."[8]

There is no record of Aleck having complied with Mabel's request. Morgan's financial advise turned out to be bad. Within months the value of the stock had tripled. Aleck continued digging for more letters and papers to help with the trial. Often, he spent the entire night up in his office sorting and cross-referencing. When Mabel called for him to stop for the night he would beg to be left to his work. He tried hard to explain his peculiar work habits.

"I have my periods of restlessness when my brain is crowded with ideas tingling to my fingertips when I am excited and cannot stop for anybody. Let me alone, let me work as I like even if I have to sit up all night or even for two nights. When you see me flogging, getting tired, discouraged or my work done, then come in and stop me, make me lie down, put your hands over my eyes so that I go to sleep and let me sleep as long as I like until I wake. Then I may hang around, read novels and be stupid without an idea in my head until I get rested and ready for another period of work. But oh, do not do as you too often do, stop me in the midst of my work, my excitement with 'Aleck, Aleck aren't you coming to bed? It's one o'clock, do come.' Then I have to come feeling cross and ugly. Then you put your hands on my eyes and after a while I go to sleep, but the ideas are gone, the work is never done."[9]

His letter was a sincere effort to make his wife understand. She vowed in her journal, "Well I will try and do better. I begin to think he is right myself; I know I have not acted with proper tact about the question of his going to bed regularly. Our worst quarrels have always been about that. No, the first rank belongs to the all important one of getting up in the morning but this follows close behind."[10]

Trying to run the household along American lines created a problem with their British staff. They had brought Mary Home and Elsie's nursemaid, Annie, with them when they returned from England. But the adjustment to the American way of life and working with the black house staff was more than the two could handle.

"It is hard living above a crater never knowing when the explosion may take place and I do long to see more of my little girl than Annie lets me. I want a good capable nurse for Elsie and nothing more, not one so very smart and knowing that I have nothing to do. I don't want things made easy for me. I would rather struggle through until I know how to make them easy for myself."[11]

Annie gave her notice a few weeks later. Aleck remained blissfully unaware of the household problems, preferring to leave everything to Mabel to sort out.

"Alec has just come upstairs flourishing the poker and wanting to know what to do as the new servants have let the fires go out. A mild suggestion on my part that he may go down to the cellar and bring up some coal does not seem to meet with his approval. He is going to leave the fires as they are so that they may remember the next time."[12]

Aleck wasn't much of a handyman around the house, nor did he subscribe to traditional social values outside his home. He refused to attend church because he considered Sunday his day of rest. Mabel used this weekly omission to persuade him to go out on afternoon calls with her. He agreed grudgingly, considering the exercise a waste of time and always seemed able to manage different ways of stalling their departure until it was too late to go anywhere.

"This afternoon I spent getting ready to make some calls. My maroon dress came home in time for me to wear it, but when Alec saw me in it he utterly refused to make calls with such a gorgeous person and I had to go down on my knees to him before he would hear of it, then to put on his things myself. By the time we got to Mama's it was pretty late and most of the callers at the different receptions had gone."[13]

Mabel's debut into Washington society was arranged at the home of their patent lawyer, Anthony Pollock. But when the date arrived for the dinner party, Mabel couldn't go.

"Alas for my hopes of a good time at Mrs. Pollock's party! Alec was summoned to Boston to a meeting of the stockholders of the New England Telephone Company and of course I could not make my first appearance in Washington Society without him. I hoped Alec might come home Friday and go with me to Mrs. Blaine's reception last night but no, a telegram said 'All working satisfactory, leave Monday night.' I decidedly did not think it satisfactory."[14]

Two weeks earlier, before Aleck had left for Boston, the Bells had attended a reception at senator Sherman's home.

"Just returned from a reception.... Mrs. Lander was there and told Alec apropos of his question as to when [Sir Henry] Irving would be here, that she hoped no one would make the mistake of inviting Ellen Terry to meet him; that recently in New York, Irving asked permission to bring her to a home to which he had been invited, and was told that his host would be glad to see her, but the ladies would be [put] out! Such a mean thing to do or say. Because of a fault committed years ago and repaired as far as possible by devoted care of her children, Miss Terry is to be excluded from all good society while Irving, about whose past there are stories and who is certainly divorced from his wife, is received and feted everywhere. The reply I suppose would be, if you think so, why don't you invite her to your house? I would, privately, but not publicly.... My own position in society is not yet secure and I have no right to injure my husband or children for what after all would be no pleasure to her.... I do think our laws are so hard on women in such cases.

Some time ago talking of divorce, Alec said he did not believe in it when there were children. I asked would he force a lady to live with her husband if she knew him to be a libertine? He said no, he would have no divorce granted, but he would have the gentleman put in prison. Think what a sensation that would make, a gentleman at hard labour! I think it would have more deterrent effect upon gentlemen villains than legal separation from a woman of whom they were tired."[15]

As the trial of Bell versus Dowd continued to drag on, Aleck's credibility as an inventor came into question. He did not have any massive piles of written experimental details that other professional inventors produced as a matter of course. Members of his own company and some of those involved in the trial process felt that his telephone invention may have been a fluke.

"Oh Mabel dear, please, please make me describe and publish my ideas that I may at least obtain credit for them and that people may know that I am still alive and thinking. I can't bear to hear that even my friends should think that I stumbled upon an invention and that there is no more good in me. You are the mistress of my heart and sharer of my thoughts (haven't I become poetical?) so I send you a few ideas—as they come to me—to be added to the list of unwritten inventions and upon my return to be written out by us my dear."[16]

Unknown to Aleck, the Board of Directors of Bell Telephone was planning a move to push him and Gardiner out of the company. It had started in the summer of 1878, when Hubbard had been desperate for operating capital. Since he was president of both the Bell Company and the New England Telephone Company, the two corporations were in the same financial bind. Aleck and Mabel had been away in England developing the British Telephone company. Aleck's apparent lack of interest in his American companies and Hubbard's financial crisis were enough for Board members to lose confidence in both men. They demanded Hubbard resign. Aleck didn't know what to do. How could he agree to fire his own father-in-law as president of his own company? "I am troubled and anxious and don't know what to do. I love your father and am proud of him as head of this Company—and yet, even I feel that his name stands in the way of our obtaining the financial support we require and threatens financial ruin to the Company. I wish you would put your arms around my neck and tell me what you wish."[17]

Mabel quite naturally was upset, but realized that in the end her father would have to go as president of the twin companies. She knew also that he would not do it willingly. Gardiner Hubbard was a stubborn man. Like Aleck, Mabel understood the feelings of the Board members. To try and solve the impasse she and her mother called on Mrs. Howe, wife of one of the Board members. Gertrude knew that the only way to calm the storm was through the wives who knew everything their husbands did, but unlike their husbands, were willing to talk about it.

"For an hour poor little Mama sat and talked, hearing Mrs. Howe's complaints, explaining things, admitting others, and generally managing to cheer Mrs. Howe and get the blame off Papa's shoulders. I told her I thought it was a shame she had to do all the comforting, not only for her own family but everybody else besides; she had to carry the burden of cheering the whole Bell Telephone Company on her shoulders and no one to comfort her. I never realized before how much she helped Papa, standing by his side ready to defend him and explain, and smooth the ruffled feelings of those who may feel hurt by anything he may have done."[18]

Later that summer, on a train in North Carolina, Aleck was confronted with an amusing aspect of public faith in the telephone as a mystery of science. The train had stopped in the middle of nowhere. The conductor approached Aleck. "Are you the inventor of the telephone, sir?" Aleck replied that he was. The conductor gave a sigh of relief. "Do you happen to have a telephone about you? The engine has broken down and we are twelve miles from the nearest station."[19]

CHAPTER FOURTEEN

Aleck decided to write a book on electrical telegraphy. It would be a compilation from his years of correspondence and lab notes. He suggested to Mabel that they sell a few of their telephone shares to support themselves until the book was completed. Mabel was not so sure.

"I must confess I do not like to live on my capital; if I could invest in some paying concern and live on the interest, I should be only too glad to agree, but I don't know what is more important just now, the book or a new invention. However, if what is rumoured is true, that Mr. Edison has gone to Europe, that leaves us in peace for awhile and I know however hard and faithfully Alec may work on his book, he cannot prevent ideas entering and overflowing his brain."[1]

In the end, his book never amounted to more than good intentions and a few roughly organized papers.

Summer arrived, painting the landscape in a bright green. It was time again to escape the punishing humidity of the capital. They returned to the Hubbard home in Cambridge. Mabel, two months pregnant with her second child, worked hard maintaining the house and entertaining a succession of visitors. "This has been a very busy summer for us all. Lena and Augusta [McCurdy cousins] have been here since the beginning of July, and I now find that their father has shut up his house leaving them on my hands until September without a 'By your leave.' Then Papa and Sister are in England, the one on Telephone business, the other to see and enjoy all she missed last year. Mama, Berta and Augusta going off on short visits to the seaside now and then. Now at last Grandpa [McCurdy] has come and right glad I am to see him for his own sake. He is very feeble."

They went back to Washington in September. The Dowd lawsuit dragged on. It was no longer a case of who had more money to finance the trial, or whose side was stronger, but who had the patience and persistence to slog through the masses of documentation. By November William Orton and Western Union had run out of patience and accepted the obvious: the Bell patents were flawless. Orton tried for a compromise. Aleck declined. They met face to face. The irony of the situation was not lost on Aleck as he studied Orton across the oak conference table in his attorney's office. Only a few years had passed since he had tried to sell the idea of the telephone to Orton and had been summarily dismissed. Now he had the upper hand. He liked the feeling. Although Western Union promised to stay out of the telephone business, it still owned a number of valuable telephone-related patents. After weeks of negotiations and numerous shouting matches, on 10 November 1879, an agreement was reached. All of Western Union's patents were to be handed over to the Bell Telephone Company. In exchange, Western Union would receive twenty per cent of all telephone rental profits for a period of seventeen years. It was a handsome deal for the Bell Company. Aleck breathed a sigh of relief. But Western Union was only one of a series of court actions that would haunt the telephone for another two decades. The Bell claim to inventing the telephone would be tested in over six hundred different cases. The settlement with Western Union was the most important because it provided the linchpin of corporate stability that the Bell Telephone Company had been seeking for so long.

One of the strangest infringement actions brought against the Bell Telephone Company came from Antonio Meucci who had filed a caveat in 1871 for an invention that he called the telephone. Meucci, a veteran of Garibaldi's army, was enjoying retirement on Staten Island making candles and sausages. The caveat described something he called the telephone but upon closer examination turned out to be little more than a child's toy employing two tin cans and a connecting string. The only similarity between Alexander Graham Bell's telephone and the one described by Meucci was the name. Meucci's claim was enough for Dr. Seth R. Beckwith to swing into action. Beckwith had earned the reputation of a man with big ideas; a super salesman who could fire up everyone he met on any project and then disappear just before it collapsed. He specialized in creating telephone corporations. Beckwith leaped into the fray on Meucci's behalf. On the basis of name only, he claimed infringement by Bell on the Meucci caveat. When, under Beckwith's Globe Telephone Company of New York, the claim failed, he presented it again under the newly formed Meucci Telephone Company of New Jersey. The Bell company lawyer wrote to Aleck. The "whole story is a piece of fraud, supported by a forgery.... Meucci is the silliest and weakest imposter who has ever turned up against the patent."

When poor old Meucci did finally get to the witness box he was unable to explain even the basic principles of electricity or telegraphy, nor could he describe his own caveat with any degree of clarity. Aleck laughed as he read the court transcripts, partly from relief because every new trial caused him some anxiety, and partly out of amazement at the gall of Meucci for even attempting such a lawsuit against his company. Beckwith vanished into the pages of history. Meucci returned to Staten Island and his sausages. Each lawsuit in the years that followed only served to strengthen the foundations of the Bell patents.

At Christmas 1879, the Dowd case had ended. The future looked bright. The Bells couldn't have been happier. That winter, Mabel's sister, Gertrude, became engaged to Maurice Grossman, a handsome Hungarian actor from New York, who had suddenly forsaken the stage to take up law. It was love at first sight. They were married in the first week of the New Year. Mabel wrote to Aleck's mother about their newest family member. "I wanted to tell you all about my 'Hungarian brother' as he calls himself, as our heads and hearts were so full of him and my sister, but I could not manage it. Now I will only say "he came, saw and conquered." He was so cordial, so friendly and determined to love all my sister's family and friends. He is so full of life, love and boyish spirits that it was quite impossible to do otherwise than like him."[2]

A month later she wrote, "I have been waiting until after the wedding to tell you the whole story. I suppose Alec told you why they changed their minds so suddenly. Maurice found it would take him at least five years to qualify as a lawyer and they were neither of them young enough to wait all that time. Maurice could easily make plenty of money by acting, but neither he nor Papa wanted him to do that, so at last it was decided that he should go to Germany as head of the International Telephone Company, a new Company which Papa started. Maurice had of course little acquaintance with the business details of the organization of companies, but he has many influential friends in the chief European capitals, and in many ways will be of much assistance to the business managers. He is very much interested in the telephone and a very clever, clear-headed man and we all think he will do very well. The managers were to start last Saturday and Maurice had to go out at the same time if he wanted the position. He refused to go without Sister [Gertrude] nor would she let him, so a week ago Sunday it was decided and Saturday she was married.

Such a breathless race as it was to get everything ready. Two hundred and fifty "At Home" cards to be ordered, addressed and sent out with only two days notice, wedding dresses to be ordered from New York and made up in the same length of time, presents bought, friends invited and received and housed here, there and everywhere, flowers brought from Cambridge and arranged, etc., etc. And all was done and ready by 8:00 P.M., only half an hour late!"[3]

Two weeks later Aleck and Mabel had something of their own to celebrate when their second baby—a girl—arrived.

"I am on the sofa for the first time this morning and must try and give you an account of my little one, as I fear Alec has been far too busy with his own baby [another invention] to talk or write much about mine. What his baby is I leave him to tell you, sufficient to say, he thinks it more wonderful than the telephone, though he cannot assert it is more marvellous than this little living, human mite lying so quietly in her dainty blue and white bed by my side. My little girl has long thick black hair but is not so dark as Elsie, though still far from fair. Even Alec, who could not endure my poor little Elsie at this age, thinks her pretty. I want to name her Marion Hubbard but am not perfectly sure that Mama likes it. It was the name of my youngest sister; she says yes, but so quietly I am waiting to see if she can stand it after a day or two's trial."[4]

Ten years had passed since Mabel's sister, Marion, had died suddenly. It had been the first real sorrow of Mabel's life. Mary True had tried to explain God and His mysteries. Mabel decided to name her new baby Marion. Aleck nicknamed her Daisy, because she reminded him of a beautiful summer flower.

In April Mabel's younger sister, Berta, became engaged to Aleck's cousin, Charlie Bell. Charlie had been working as Aleck's secretary until a suitable position opened up in the telephone company. It was a wonderful year of family celebrations. Then the bubble of happiness burst. Aleck branded Gardiner Hubbard as the ogre.

When the Bell Telephone Company was formed, Aleck had made Hubbard trustee of all the patents and of a special trust for the Bell children, arranged to accumulate to $300,000. In the summer of 1878, when the English Telephone Company was about to collapse, Hubbard went overseas and managed to save the company. He was given $12,000 in cash and stock as a reward for his services. He placed this windfall in the trust for the Bell children. Less than a year later the amount had grown to over $100,000. In his efforts to save the British company Gardiner had suffered severe financial losses. He asked permission to borrow from the trust. Not keen on the idea, but not wanting to say no to his father-in-law, Aleck agreed, albeit reluctantly.

Since the formation of the trust, Aleck had promised himself to rely on Hubbard's financial judgement. Now, he began to harbour dark doubts. As he had never inquired about the trust, Hubbard assumed that, like most business matters, his son-in-law simply wasn't interested in the details. Consequently, he had never provided a financial report. When Hubbard wanted to borrow money from the trust Aleck became suspicious. He wrote a scathing note, accusing him bluntly of gross mismanagement of his children's money. Hubbard was taken aback. If he had not saved the English Company there would have been nothing to put into the trust *to* manage. So what was the problem? In his reply he defended his position, reminding Aleck that he had gone to England and saved the British company after Aleck had abandoned it and sailed for home. They were instantly at loggerheads, neither one speaking to the other. Gertrude Hubbard and Mabel were aghast at the conduct of their stubborn husbands. Something had to be done swiftly before a permanent break developed between the two families. Mabel explained Aleck's thoughts on the matter to her mother.

"He thinks it is far better to be perfectly frank and open and he is perfectly willing to admit that Papa may be entirely in the right but he does want to have the opinion of some other business person. His greatest concern is not what was done or not done but simply that Papa never volunteers any information concerning the affairs of the Trust.... Well, I have found out for myself that Alec is a very hard man to deal with. The only thing I can do is make the best of matters but you may be sure that there is no one more true and loving than he in spite of everything."[5]

The split between the families was more than she could bear. She loved both men dearly and could not stand seeing them at odds. To Aleck she wrote, "Did you read Mama's letters? Somehow they all left a feeling of sadness in my mind, especially any reference to my dear father. I feel as though Mama were half unconsciously and indirectly trying to change what she feels is your unjust opinion of Papa. I may be all wrong but it does seem to me as if Mama were unhappy about you and Papa.... Poor little Mama has much to … worry her. I feel as if they were both trying very hard to do everything they could for you.

Oh, Alec Dear, if you would but write to them. If not to Papa because of the questions that must be opened, then to Mama. Just a bright kind loving playful letter such as you write to me so often. Nothing I could do or say would give her so much pleasure as that. Please do my Darling for my sake and for hers. She has done so much for you and you do not know how she loves you. I don't believe she could love you more if you were her own son."[6] Aleck responded to her plea. In time, the families were reunited. As the years passed they grew closer together, and a new understanding and stronger relationship developed between them.

The Christmas edition of *The New York World* that year carried a special note of good wishes from Mark Twain. "It is my heart-warm and world embracing Christmas hope and aspiration that all of us— the high, the low, the rich, the poor, the admired, the despised, the loved, the hated, the civilized, the savage—may eventually be gathered together in a heaven of everlasting rest and peace and bliss—except the inventor of the telephone." The article prompted a rebuttal by Hubbard which was followed by another write up in the paper, entitled "To the Father-in-Law of the Telephone." Twain explained that his gripe was with the Hartford, Connecticut telephone system. It was horrible, "and if you try to curse through the telephone, they shut you off. It is this ostentatious holiness that gravels me. Every day I go there to practice, and always I get shut off." Since it had been Hubbard's son-in-law that had invented the contraption, Twain held him personally responsible. As well the abomination called the telephone had most certainly given Bell a reserved position in Hell. "For your sake, I wish I could think of some way to save him, but there doesn't appear to be any. Do you think he would like me to pray for him? I could do so under an assumed name, and it might have some influence." Aleck thought the whole episode amusing and good publicity for the telephone.

In September of 1880, the French Government awarded Aleck the prestigious Volta Prize for inventing the telephone. Aleck sailed for France to collect it. The prize, set up in honour of Italian scientist Alessandro Volta, had only been given a few times. A cash award of fifty thousand francs [$10,000 U.S.] accompanied the prize. Aleck used the money to finance the Volta Laboratory for scientific experiment. His cousin, Charlie Bell, and associate Sumner Tainter, became his partners in the venture. The three men worked on a variety of projects but their main interest was the photophone and phonograph, a precursor to Edison's Gramaphone.

One interesting experiment resulting from the windfall of the Volta Prize was undertaken by Albert A. Michelson. During the Victorian era it was believed that something called "ether" was responsible for the transmission of light and sound. Scientists believed that ether was necessary as a medium for both light and sound waves. Michelson wanted to study the "ether effect." Unfortunately, he lacked the funds. His associate, Professor Newcomb, of the Smithsonian Institute, wrote to Aleck requesting assistance. Still flush with his ten thousand dollar prize money, Aleck sent him five hundred dollars. Michelson objected, saying that he was too "young and therefore liable to err" with such a large sum at his disposal. He did not want him to regret his largesse. Nevertheless, Aleck insisted, recalling the faith that Hubbard and Sanders had had in him when they backed the telephone. Michelson began his experiments. His conclusions were not at all what he had expected. "The experiments concerning the relative motion of the earth with respect to the ether have just been brought to a successful termination. The result was however negative, ... showing that the ether in the vicinity of the earth is moving with the earth." Even more startling was the possibility that there was no ether. He gave Aleck a detailed expense account with his report, promising to return the remaining three hundred dollars as soon as possible.

Aleck was fascinated; no ether? This amazing revelation changed all conventional wisdom. Scientists around the world would have to readjust their theories. "I think the results you have obtained will prove to be of much importance," he wrote to Michelson, insisting that he keep the remaining money for more experimentation. Even though Michelson's discovery was refined by scientists in later years, its implications in the world of physics were profound. His work affected Albert Einstein's theory of relativity. Three years later, in 1907, Michelson became the first American to win the Nobel Prize for his efforts in experimental methodology and studies on the properties of light. With the help of Einstein's detailed reasonings, Michelson's initial experiments proved to be correct. There was no ether.

The Hubbard family, finally free from financial difficulties, decided to take an extended European vacation. Aleck and Mabel were offered the Cambridge house for the summer and following year. They accepted. For Aleck the house held memories as the place where he had played the piano, sipped tea as a bashful suitor, fought with Gardiner and married Mabel. For Mabel it was a return to her childhood home. The house embraced an eerie combination of the past and present. Her childhood games and memories were embedded in the worn wooden floors.

"In the old house again, welcomed by your and Papa's cable and note. It is so lovely to be here again and yet so sad. All around marks of your presence and yet you are not here. Alec and I love this old house so very much and are so glad to have our children here that they may love it too.... I think it feels more really home to Alec than our own home.[7] How did you manage to exist here all alone when

Papa was in Washington? My husband is in Washington now and he too promises to have his work done in a fortnight. Will he keep his promise as well as Papa did his I wonder? To think that I am "Mama" now in the place where I was a little girl, that my babies run around where I ran, sit in the same high-chair at table, and play about the same games as I did—I can hardly realize it all.

If I could be as much to my children as you have been to me my mother—I am getting rather anxious about it—Elsie says so little to me and so much more to others. She very evidently sees the difference and points out things to me instead of saying them. I fear she may learn to give her confidence and tell her little stories to others until it will be too late for her to care to come to me with them. I know she is fonder of me than anyone but she does not talk to me as she does to others—from what her nursemaid says, she must be full of childish prattle and pretty dictatorial ways—all of which I see nothing as she talks so indistinctly, hardly moving her lips."[8]

Aleck cancelled his business commitments for the rest of the summer, hoping to spend a couple of lazy months sitting on the front porch with his books and romping in the fields with his children. The vacation was cut short when, on 2 July, President James A. Garfield was shot in front of a crowd at Washington's main train station. The gunman, Charles J. Guiteau, a deranged political appointment-seeker, had been passed over by a selection committee as being too unstable to hold public office. He was immediately whisked away by the authorities and the President rushed back to the White House. Miraculously, Garfield survived the gunshot. However, the bullet remained lodged in his body, although where exactly no one knew. Röntgen's discovery of X-Rays lay a dozen years in the future. The president's doctors were reluctant to attempt exploratory surgery without knowing where the bullet had lodged. Garfield might die. But if the bullet were left he would die anyway from infection. How to find where the bullet lay? The problem was presented to Alexander Graham Bell.

Some years earlier, Aleck had experimented on something he called an electronic probe. The instrument was designed to detect metal within the human body. This was the "baby" that Mabel had referred to in her letter to his mother. The instrument had not yet been perfected. Now it was desperately needed. Aleck offered it to the

President's doctors who agreed to try as soon as it was ready. Aleck brought in Professor Newcomb and Professor Trainer, close professional friends, to help. They worked around the clock. Time was running out. Mabel, pregnant with her third child, wrote to Eliza.

"Alec I have hardly seen the last few days, he has been hard at work day and night on an apparatus for the use of the President's physicians. He thought he would have it finished and be off to Washington last night, but alas an accident happened and from the heights Alec has gone down to the depths. However, he has gone to work again and hopes perhaps to get off tonight."[9]

The hot humid summer air of Cambridge was almost too thick to breathe. While Aleck worked on his probe, Mabel escaped to a summer house at Pigeon Cove on the Massachusetts coast with the children. She wrote to Aleck daily.

"I cannot begin to tell you how anxiously I watch for news of you and your doings, how you are succeeding. Oh, how I hope you will be able to find the bullet, it would be such a triumph for you. Of course I want it for the President's sake also but I want you to be the man to do it, my own dear boy."[10]

Aleck brought his equipment to Washington. Things were tense in the Capitol. Everyone seemed on edge, waiting for the latest news about the President. The city was strangely sombre and unbearably hot. He reached the dying President's bedside. A smell of disinfectant assailed his nostrils from the suppurating wound. Dead air hung like a humid shroud. He set up his equipment. Aleck thought Garfield "looked so calm and grand he reminded me of a Greek hero chiselled in marble. He has a magnificent intellectual looking head, as you know, with massive forehead. As I remember him of old, his florid complexion rather detracted from his appearance, giving him the look of a man who indulged in good living and who was accustomed to work in the open air. There is none of that look about him now. His face is very pale—or rather it is of an ashen grey colour which makes one feel for a moment that you are not looking upon a living man. It made my heart bleed to look at him and think of all he must have suffered to bring him to this."[11] Garfield seemed terribly small and frail, not at all the ruler of the world's greatest republic.

Aleck arranged his equipment as quietly as possible. Instructions had been given to remove all metal objects near the bed to prevent signal distortion. The probe was activated. Aleck passed the instrument lightly over the President in sweeping motions. A hiss of fluctuating static erupted. He tried again, his heart pounding. Sweat trickled down his forehead. The second attempt produced the same results. The president saw Aleck's frustrated frown. A gentle smile of thanks passed across his ashen face. Garfield's eyes closed.

The doctors ushered everyone from the room. The president needed to rest. Aleck sat in a stiff-backed chair trying to decide what had gone wrong. A sudden thought occurred to him. He asked one of the president's doctors of what material the bed was. A hair mattresses on a wooden bed frame, he was told. What about the bed springs, were they wood too? The doctor shook his head. Wooden slats would have been too uncomfortable for the president. Aleck exploded angrily. No wonder the probe hadn't worked. Interference from the steel bed springs had scrambled the signals. He demanded that the doctors move Garfield to an all-wood bed as soon a possible, certain that a second attempt with his probe would be successful. The doctors refused and the papers reported that Alexander Graham Bell's experiment had failed. There was even a suggestion that Aleck was in some way responsible for the President's condition. Mabel read the news stories with a heavy heart.

"You poor boy, how sorry I am for you in your disappointment. I can imagine just how chagrined and mortified you must have felt when those horrid noises [from the steel coils in the bottom mattress] prevented you being sure what you heard. Never mind, courage; from failure comes success, be worthy of your patient and don't lose heart even if all others are discouraged. I have not the least doubt but that you will eventually succeed. You have never yet failed and will not now. Only I wish I could be with you to help try to cheer you.

How excited you must have been to go into the President's bedroom. Thank you very much for telling me all about it, and taking so much pains to draw the plan of the room. I almost feel as if I had been there too. I am glad you admired the President so much. Don't you think he will live? I wish you had seen Mrs. Garfield too; she must be so brave to keep up through everything as she does. Oh dear, why couldn't I have been invisible to see everything too, but I don't know but that I prefer you to tell me about it."[12]

She received news that he was making second attempt with the electronic probe. "I am sorry I did not write you yesterday but I sent a telegram instead. I am so glad to hear that you are improving your apparatus. I hope the second attempt will be successful. I know you deserve it and poor Mr. Garfield must wish it. I have been looking over the old papers of the first few days of Garfield's illness and wonder how he lived through them. There seems to have been so much confusion and everybody who liked had admittance to him. At one time it seemed that the whole Cabinet called upon him and all their wives were his nurses. I should think all that crowd would literally have worried him to death. My heart and mind are constantly occupied with you and the wish for Mr. President's recovery.... I long to have you near to tell me all about it. No wonder you are exhausted and headachy. I only hope it won't make your nervous trouble worse."[13]

Having the imperfect results of his inventive efforts placed on public display in the newspapers made Aleck ill with worry. His probe was only a crude prototype. Adjustments still had to be made. The public could not possibly understand the complexity behind the instrument.

On 15 August, Mabel gave birth to a baby boy. They had decided that if it was a boy to name him Edward, after Aleck's brother Teddy. Sadly, the child arrived two months premature and lived only a few hours, gasping out his short life. Mabel was heartbroken. Aleck wired that he would leave Washington at once, but she insisted that he stay where he was needed most and finish his work for the President's sake. Unfortunately, Aleck never got the chance to make a second attempt at finding the bullet.

Garfield died on 19 September 1881, as the result of infection from the bullet. The autopsy showed the bullet was too deeply embedded for Aleck's instruments to detect.

"Poor Garfield had gone, I hope indeed that there may be an immortality for that brave spirit.... If prayers could avail to save the sick, surely the earnest, heartfelt cry of a whole nation to God would have availed in this case."[14]

What had started out as a summer of relaxation for the Bells had ended in the birth and death of their son, the death of the President and public ridicule for Aleck's attempts at trying to save him. They decided to get away and join the Hubbards in Europe. Mabel wrote to Eliza Bell trying to explain why they had to go.

"You know Alec has not been well for nearly a year past and the doctors say entire rest from mental labour is necessary to avert serious constitutional trouble. We hoped he would … rest this summer but the President's illness prevented it. While in Washington he seemed better but on his return, he felt the effects of the long excitement and my illness coming on top of that, has thrown him completely back and our physician says he resumes his winter's work at his peril; that a journey in Europe with an ocean between him and his work will do more to restore him to complete health than anything else.

Though I have been very well, I am not yet strong, in fact I have had to go back to bed twice and am still there now. The Doctor says it will be some months before I can hope to regain complete strength. So for me too, he advises European travel. My children are just the age for such a journey, too young to mind the travel and yet not so young but that I can leave them with Mama for days at a time while we go off alone. In all probability I shall never have such a chance to travel until my children are grown up and married. Alec will never go without me, so that in every way this seems too good an opportunity to be lost; especially as my family are in Europe and may be there for years and I may not see them otherwise. As Alec says, we now have money enough to do it and never may again, as with each year our expenses increase and soon we shall have houses to maintain. It was he who proposed this plan…. I never want to cross the ocean again." Aleck decided to add a P.S. to Mabel's letter. "What never? Hardly ever. Dear Mama don't believe half [of what] my little girl has said. I am all right, although I need rest, but a European tour is a thing Mabel and I longed to make and as she says, we do not know when we may be able to go again."[15]

CHAPTER FIFTEEN

Europe, Autumn 1881

In the true fashion of a Victorian Romance, Aleck and Mabel sailed away into the Atlantic sunrise to escape their problems. They arrived in England and went to visit Mabel's mother and sisters, Berta and Gertrude—now Mrs. Charles Bell and Mrs. Maurice Grossman.[1] Both were expecting babies, a bitter reminder to Aleck and Mabel of their own recent loss. "I would like a boy, oh so much," Mabel told her sisters. However, the joy of seeing her family again helped compensate her depression over the loss of baby Edward.

They went to Paris where Aleck was again presented with the Diploma of Honour from the French Government for inventing the telephone. Although the second award held no monetary benefit, he enjoyed such an official recognition after his summer of emotional disasters. It came like a pat on the back and did much to raise his spirits. He and Mabel were still hurting from the loss of their little Edward. Aleck commissioned a French artist to paint a picture of a small infant surrounded by flowers in a casket in memory of the baby.

Idly, he began sketching an experiment for something he called a "Vacuum Jacket." It was to be a device that would induce artificial respiration when needed. After hearing Mabel's description of baby Edward gasping for breath Aleck was sure that he could have saved his son's life by mechanical means. Experimentation on this device would span the next two decades and lead eventually to the invention of the iron lung.

While in Paris Mabel revisited many of the places she remembered from her youth. Nothing much had changed. To her mother in the spring of 1882, she wrote, "I am overwhelmed at the idea of getting my own clothes alone, what shall I do? I am making decidedly more use of Alec's Secretary [Mr. Johnson] than Alec is just now, as he goes on all shopping expeditions with me. If I took Alec he would be sure to have a bad attack of heart trouble in the first shop, and make me buy all I didn't want. At present, not being bothered, he is very well. Just now he has gone off hunting for caterpillars as he had an idea that he can find a method of preventing them climbing trees! Alec says I am to have a dress from Worth's, but I think I will get Papa to take me there as Alec would never let me set a price or bother about how the dress is to be made. And yet, no one is more critical of the effect when finished."[2]

Worth's was one of the finest shops in Paris where all proper ladies had their dresses made. Aleck wanted nothing but the best for Mabel and his daughters. Not only were they able to afford the trip abroad, but could maintain a comfortable lifestyle while they were in Europe. Their days of financial problems and nit picking over expenses were finally over. Aleck had written to his father that his income from all American sources for the year of 1880 was in excess of $24,000 [half a million in current dollars]. "We should be able to live on that," he commented sarcastically. This was a far cry from his discussion on riches with Mabel a few years before.

However, it was not Aleck but Mabel who took care of the household finances and managed the income from their investments. The Bell Telephone Company had been officially reorganized into the American Bell Telephone Company in 1880. The original 73,500 shares were exchanged for shares from the founding company at a rate of six to one. Mabel's 2,975 new shares accounted for four per cent of the new company. The Bells would never have to worry about their finances again. A year after he had written to his father their annual income had jumped to $37,000. By 1882, their investments amounted to over $900,000. Translated into current inflationary dollars, the Bells had cleared nearly fifty million tax-free dollars from the telephone. They could afford to travel about Europe as long as they wanted. However, they decided to return to America in that spring and spent the rest of the summer and early fall in Newport, with Mabel's grandfather McCurdy.

Aleck became restless. He was thirty-seven, in the prime of his productive life and anxious to get back to work. They began house-hunting in Washington. After a few weeks of scanning the city they found a house at 1500 Rhode Island Avenue. It needed massive renovations before they could move in, but appeared to have everything they were looking for. The grounds covered an entire city block with an enormous three-storey house that had everything: separate rooms for the girls, a proper laboratory for Aleck, a library, a music room complete with grand piano, an oratory and even a fair size conservatory. The property was covered by trees with flower gardens framed by a velvet carpet of grass. They bought it for cash and began renovating.

In the summer of 1882, Aleck received a copy of the latest *Science* magazine from its editor, John Michels. The magazine boasted that "*Science* is essentially the medium of communication among the Scientists of America.... *Science* enters into competition with no other scientific journal; it was established to fill a void that has been long felt."[3] Michels had given Aleck the option of buying the journal during the summer that he was busy trying to save President Garfield. Michels now offered him a second chance. Aleck thought the matter over and, after discussing it with Hubbard, decided to accept Michels's offer. The idea of owning a scientific magazine appealed to his imagination. Hubbard agreed to manage the enterprise while Aleck acted as financier and occasional contributor.

Although the magazine's intentions were good, its subscription rate fell far short of the six thousand needed to break even. Aleck's new frontispiece stated boldly that "The aim of the journal will be to increase the knowledge of our people, to show our transatlantic friends our real activity, to gain among intelligent people a knowledge of the true aims and purposes of science, and to elevate the standard of science among scientific men themselves."[4]

Over the years, he sank close to $60,000 into the magazine, Hubbard $20,000—all in the name of *Science*. Additional large subsidies were obtained from the AAAC[5] Its list of subscribers grew. It was taken over eventually by James Mckeen Cattell but not until 1899 did it begin making a profit. Michels's conviction that *Science* would fill a void in the scientific community had proved correct. The magazine became the scientific bible and the main artery of information for respected scientists and researchers across the United States.

Aleck was finally able to include himself as an American scientist when, on 10 November 1882, he became officially a citizen of the United States of America. Never one to hurry, he had first filed his citizenship papers back in 1874. However, faced suddenly with the enticing prospect of nomination to the prestigious National Academy of Science, he concluded his citizenship paperwork in record time.

Mabel worried continuously that things were not being done properly during the refurbishing of their Washington house. The workmen were not following her instructions. Frustrated that they were taking far too long to get the job done and, in the process, were probably ripping them off, Mabel complained. "Alec told me not to work so hard but what was I to do—the moment I left the men an instant, some mistake was made and the work had to be done all over again. The children caught cold and I got up night after night to assure myself they were all right and properly tucked in. I caught cold myself, had a cough for the first time in my married life. Alec went to the meeting of the National Academy in Hartford. Mama went to New York on a shopping expedition. I sent for the doctor who thought nothing of my cold, merely told me to be careful of drafts.

Was awakened in the morning by Elsie's kiss to find myself cold and shivering and feverish. The doctor sent me to bed but assured me it was all right and there was no danger for my (expected) baby. Sister came and insisted on staying all night. After a rather restless night, about two I called Sister and thought she had better send for the doctor as I was not feeling well. Well, he was out so I sent over to my neighbour, Mrs. Poe, to ask if she knew of another physician nearby. She did not, but came herself.... My true friend in time of need, doing all for me and my poor [new] little one that a physician could have done. Poor little one, it was so pretty and struggled so hard to live, opened his eyes once or twice to the world and then passed away. The little one whom we called Robert, came November 17th.... Alec knew nothing of what had happened until he reached Washington three hours after my baby had come and gone.... Alec had been giving the premier presentation of his work "Upon the Formation of a Deaf Variety of the Human Race" to the National Academy of Science in honour of his new membership.

What we should have done without Mrs. Poe, my poor sister and I cannot bear to think, the only wonder was that Sister was not ill herself, not being strong naturally and borne down by long anxiety about her husband. Poor Maurice, he grows weaker all the time. When I was able to be on the sofa, he and Sister went to Philadelphia, leaving their baby for the first time, and met the physicians in consultation there. The doctors decided the he was suffering from a tumour which could not be removed without killing him."[6]

Two years later, Maurice Grossman died of cancer on 16 October 1884, at the age of forty-one, leaving a wife and baby daughter. The Bell and Hubbard families were profoundly shocked. Maurice had been such a live wire, full of life and laughter. It did not seem fair that he should be taken away from a family that needed and loved him so much. Later that month, Mabel recorded the strange quietness that had fallen about the house.

"He was so intensely alive. We seem such a quiet ordinary family now. Alec is a man out of the ordinary certainly, but he is quieter in general life. He never shocks and takes away our pride with his overflowing spirits and utter disregard of conventionalities as Maurice sometimes did. We are all so quiet-mannered and self-restrained. He must have been like a breath of fresh air to my sister, all her life more or less an invalid [tuberculosis]. I think he must have carried her completely by storm. He needed her so much, needed her calm almost masculine judgement, her strength of mind. She needed him so much, his constant tender watchfulness and care of her, and his bright and joyous spirits to bring brightness to a life before rather sad and quiet."[7]

The death of her husband hit sister Gertrude hard. The following day, she sat by the huge bay window in her house and stared at the dripping rain. Angry black clouds raced above trees and rain poured down. She stared out the window, not really looking at anything in particular, yet hoping for answers. Her daughter, Gypsy, tugged at her skirts. "Mama, what are you looking at?" Gertrude turned. "Nothing. I have nothing to look at now." Maurice had left no will. Without a will, under state law, his property went to his heir. Gertrude was dumbfounded. Maurice's heir was their daughter, Gypsy. Mabel's heart went out to her sister.

"Sister [Gertrude] said to Mama: 'Gypsy cannot have this house. I cannot let her have it. I shall hate her, I know I should, if I thought she had Maurice's home.' She does not know the further storm in store for her, his jewelry, his books and such things which have value only for him and her are also not hers. It seems to me almost more bitter than death, at least to add a terrible sting to it. It has come so fearfully home to me what suffering there may lie in the neglect to make a will that I have induced my own husband to go upstairs into his study and draw up a will. I hope as I am writing these lines that he is writing his will. He is safe enough, for I have made my will leaving him everything I have.

Alec has just brought me his will signed and witnessed. Now I am wondering if the document is legal being written on Sunday. Alec says 'Yes, I am glad you did make your will but I would not have asked you to do so.' Perhaps not, but he would have regretted not doing so all the rest of his life if he survived me. My making my will meant the loss or gain to him of more than half a million dollars; his making his will gives me the privilege, justly mine, of carrying out his wishes which I certainly know better than anyone else and which would be more sacred to me than to anyone else. God knows I hope it will never be needed."[8]

Gypsy wasn't old enough to understand that her father had died, nor of legal age to become the owner of property. The estate was placed in trust with an executor, who decided to sell it off. Gertrude was heartbroken. If everything was sold she would have nothing. At this point Gardiner stepped in and offered to buy the house and contents for her. Although Gertrude lived only two more years before succumbing to tuberculosis in 1886, thanks to her father's generosity, she was able to remain in her own home surrounded by the mementos and memories of her beloved Maurice. After Gertrude's death, the house and contents were sold. Gypsy was taken in to be raised by her grandparents.

Over its four years of operating, the Volta Laboratory had used most of its funding. It had produced several inventions for recording sound. The most interesting of which was a wax-coated cylinder that used a thin stylus to etch sounds onto the surface of the wax. The etchings could then be used to reproduce sound. The founding partners, Charlie Bell, Sumner Tainter and Aleck, had formed the Volta Graphophone Company in Virginia to be the official owner of various patents that the men had procured over the years. The company was later absorbed into the American Graphophone Company, which issued shares to pay for the acquisition. These shares were divided four ways: one-quarter to each partner for his inventive work in the company and the remaining quarter going to Aleck as the financier. Soon after receiving it Aleck sold his stock for $100,000. The money was put into a trust, with Melville Bell as the trustee, and used to help finance research projects relating to the deaf. Over the years the trust would be the lifeline for hundreds of experiments and work that resulted in a new understanding of the deaf.

Besides establishing the trust fund for research, Aleck appealed to the National Education Association for the Deaf. He proposed the use of day schools for deaf children, to keep them from being separated from their families and homes. It was a long uphill battle of the kind Aleck enjoyed. The public needed to be educated to the fact that deaf people were not mentally deficient. He pointed proudly to the Boston Day School for the deaf, operated by Sarah Fuller, as a shining example of what could be achieved by teaching children to lip-read and speak, rather than using manual signs. Although sign language was easier to learn, especially for young children, he maintained that the continued use of signing was the equivalent of mental imprisonment. Children would be limited to communication only with others who knew signing, the rest of the world would remain inaccessible.

Because the principles of sign language were based on the limited and imprecise expression of ideas by symbols, Aleck became chief advocate of the movement for the oralist method of teaching children to speak and lip-read. However, when he gave his lectures, he did provide a simultaneous version in sign language. There was no point in trying to pretend that sign language did not exist, nor that many of the deaf could only communicate using signs. He offered both versions, yet staunchly maintained that the oral method of teaching provided the greatest scope of opportunity for the deaf to lead normal lives in a world of hearing. His views were in direct conflict with Edward M. Gallaudet, leader for the method of sign language.

Edward Gallaudet and Aleck were similar in many respects. Gallaudet's mother had severe hearing problems, and he had spent much of his early adult life in the shadows of a famous father who had founded the first deaf education centre in the United States. Edward rose to become head of the Columbia Institution for the Deaf and Dumb in Washington. When the first push for the use of speech-reading appeared, he thought the whole idea rubbish until Gardiner Hubbard and representatives of the Clarke school proved him wrong. Gallaudet took a year off in 1867, to make a tour of the European institutions for teaching the deaf. Wherever he went he was con-fronted with the success of lip-reading and deaf students speaking. Upon his return home he made a number of changes to the Columbia school curriculum, incorporating the use of speech-and lip-reading. However, Gallaudet was not a complete convert to the oral method. He maintained the usefulness of signing and advocated the combined use of both methods. The oral method was a difficult one to teach and Gallaudet felt that signing should not be abandoned, but rather used as a major component in the general educational program for the deaf. Aleck disagreed emphatically, calling Gallaudet's "Combined Method" a thinly veiled excuse to promote signing. The two men agreed to disagree and continued their work helping the deaf, each in his own way. Their paths would cross again.

Washington, July 1885

Aleck and Mabel had planned another European trip for the summer of 1885. Unfortunately, Mabel's sister Berta fell ill. She had been sick for many years with the same dreadful tuberculosis that had killed Gertrude. She died while giving birth to a daughter. The families went into mourning again. Reflecting on her relationship with her sister, she wrote that "Berta and I had very little to do with each other after my illness as a child. She was too active and practical. I am inclined to romantic fancies with which her practical mind had no sympathy. When she was fourteen she caught the measles, being the last of us to have them and although she was not very sick, it was succeeded by that terrible trouble [tuberculosis], which now after twelve years has cut short her beautiful young life. She had exquisite colouring, big saucer eyes and soft cheeks breaking into dimples when she laughed."[9]

Mabel sat in front of her dresser, brushing her hair as her mind wandered. Her plain black cotton dress made her look even smaller than she was, and her eyes showed that she had been crying. "Poor Berta," she whispered under her breath. In her mind's eye she visualized her sister's oval face. Now she was dead. Tears flooded Mabel's eyes again as she thought about Berta. She had died only three days before on the fourth of July. It would have been tragic at anytime, but somehow on that day, a day usually devoted to family celebrations and daylong picnics, it seemed even worse because the children—cousins and the like—didn't understand and continually asked for explanations. Only there weren't any.

It wasn't birth that had killed Berta, but tuberculosis, the same disease that threatened her older sister, Gertrude, and which had killed both of Aleck's brothers. It seemed to Mabel that the family had been in constant mourning. Last October, her sister Gertrude's husband had died of cancer. Shortly after that, she herself had lost a baby, and now Berta—who had married Aleck's cousin, Charlie Bell, five years ago—was dead too. Before the succession of dreadful disasters, there had been an ongoing struggle over the future of Aleck's wonderful invention—the telephone. Its obvious value led to many court challenges over his patents. Aleck hated court cases and the accusations that he hadn't really created the telephone. He had tried to run away from trouble, lamenting that his wonderful invention was no longer fun. For a time, he turned his back on it, but invariably his pride rallied his spirit to fight on—both for the credit of his invention and his just rewards.

Aleck hated business—though he loved spending money. Her father, on the other hand, loved business and adored a good fight. These two men—the driving forces in her life—were the antithesis of one another, and both she and her mother were constantly intervening to try and keep the peace between them.

For some years, she and Aleck had been beset by financial problems. Now, by any standard, they were wealthy, but it seemed they were being stalked by death. Mabel forced these black thoughts from her mind by conjuring up the image of her two darling daughters. She had lost two children but had two others who were happy, healthy and normal—and for that she was grateful. She vowed to mourn Berta, but also to focus on the living.

"Hah! I thought I'd find you hiding in here," Aleck opened the door and stepped into the room. Mabel saw his reflection in the mirror. She turned suddenly and tried to smile.

He had grown a trifle more stout. Adding his girth to his height, he seemed to fill the room. He was, she decided, a handsome man. How strange that she hadn't loved him instantly—that after all these years she was learning to understand him. Alexander Graham Bell was a man of many moods and complicated character, often given to boyish daydreams and a young man's delight.

Aleck bent down and kissed her cheek tenderly. "There are people downstairs," he said.

"I'm sure. Papa has a lot of friends in Washington."

"They've just come to pay their respects."

Mabel nodded and pulled herself up, smoothing out her skirt. Aleck took her arm and together they descended the winding staircase.

They paused on the landing. Aleck turned her face towards him. "I know you're still terribly upset. I think we should reconsider getting away for the rest of the summer. It's even more important now than it was before."

Mabel drew in her breath as she thought of the mourners downstairs, of the impropriety of going off to Europe as they had planned. "Oh, Aleck, we can't go to Europe now—it ... it wouldn't be right."

He frowned, but didn't scowl. Nor did he move, and she knew that meant he had more to say on the subject. He was merely thinking of how to phrase it. But surely he understood her objections, surely he could see that a trip to the continent would be most improper under the circumstances.

"My dear, this family has been in mourning for some time," he said slowly. "We have to get away —we need to get away."

Was he going to insist? She hoped not. He could be most stubborn.

"I know," he said suddenly. "You're quite right. A trip to the continent wouldn't be at all proper, but I think a shorter voyage would be acceptable."

"A shorter voyage?"

Suddenly a smile crept across his face, "Yes! I have it! Years ago my father spent a summer in Newfoundland. Let's take the family and explore the isle of his lost youth!"

"I'm not sure," she hesitated knowing full well that to hesitate with Aleck was to lose.

"It would be quite proper! Hardly like running off to Paris on a shopping expedition! It'll be a nature holiday, a holiday in the sun, a holiday away from the dreadful August heat of Washington. You know how I hate the heat. Lord, how I yearn for the ocean breezes!"

She looked into his eyes and saw how taken he was with this new idea. His childlike curiosity and love of nature and the outdoors had never waned. She smiled slowly. "If that's what you want," she said. "I suppose it would be an acceptable compromise."

Gardiner Hubbard ran his fingers through his beard. Gertrude sat on the sofa beside Mabel, while Aleck stood across from Gardiner. For once, the two were not squaring off as adversaries.

"Yes, it would be quite improper to go to Europe while the family is still in mourning, still a trip of some sort is in order. Yes, I think Newfoundland would be an excellent choice. Excellent."

"I'm glad you agree," Aleck said, pulling his jacket down and already savouring the ocean air.

"I have an idea," Gardiner said suddenly, and knowing how her father's mind worked, Mabel guessed immediately that he was about to suggest conducting some business during their trip. Whenever her father arranged an itinerary there was little time—even on a vacation—for anyone to relax.

"You know—well, perhaps you don't know—that I own stock in a mining company on Cape Breton Isle in Nova Scotia, the Caledonia

Coal Mines. You would do me a great favour, Aleck if you could make a little side trip to Nova Scotia and inspect those mines for me. I have a considerable investment in the venture."

"Nova Scotia ..." Aleck sounded hesitant, but only because he was talking to Gardiner and he would never allow his father-in-law the satisfaction of knowing that one of his ideas sounded appealing.

"It's not far out of the way, you know."

"Possibly, but it's not on the way either," Aleck pointed out. He enjoyed letting Gardiner dangle.

"Oh, of course it is. You have to go to Cape Breton Isle to get a boat to Newfoundland."

"Unless we sail from New York, Boston or Halifax," Aleck countered.

"You'll enjoy a side trip," Gardiner insisted.

Aleck appeared to be considering the proposal carefully, although he had every intention of agreeing. "I read a book once ... by Charles Dudley Warner. It was called Baddeck and that Sort of Thing. Warner described an extraordinary woman named Maude who lived in the Telegraph House Hotel in Baddeck, a village on Cape Breton Isle. I think I should like to see this extraordinary woman for myself."

"I can read your lips from this angle," Mabel said, lifting her brow as she spoke.

Aleck chuckled, "This trip is your father's idea. Besides, Maude is no doubt fictional and, therefore, should not be the object of jealousy."

"I'm not jealous," she said, flatly.

"My idea is that you should visit a coal mine, not a femme fatale described by some errant travel writer," Gardiner huffed. Aleck could hardly keep from laughing at Gardiner taking the turn of conversation so seriously. "In any case, this Baddeck is hardly out of the way of your coal mine," Aleck observed, mocking Gardiner's earlier comment.

But Gardiner wouldn't bite. "I suppose not."

"How do you feel about going to Nova Scotia, Mabel?"

"I've never been there, so I'm not sure."

"Nova Scotia, New Scotland—I wonder how much of it looks like Scotland."

"A great deal," Gardiner put in. "I've heard it said that they're more alike than not. For all I know there are more Scotsmen there than in Scotland."

"Then it must be a very special place," Aleck laughed. "All right, we'll make a side trip to Nova Scotia."

Mabel smiled slyly at her mother. Both knew that Aleck had intended going all along.

~

Moonlight streamed in through the porthole of their stateroom, illuminating the bed where the children slept. Mabel stood a moment and looked at them sleeping so peacefully. Nothing, she thought, was as innocent and as sweet as the face of a sleeping child.

She turned away just as the door to the stateroom was flung open by Aleck. Even though she could not hear him, she knew instinctively that he was being noisy, so she pressed her finger to her lips. He looked beyond her, and seeing that the girls were asleep, motioned her outside onto the moonlit deck.

"Well, what do you think? Isn't it beautiful!"

Mabel watched his lips and the movements of his hands. She could tell when he was enthusiastic.

"What I can see of it is certainly beautiful," she replied.

"Look at those stars, my dear. You could almost just reach up and grab one. And today? What did you think about today, the scenery—everything!" His arms swept across the night in a proprietary gesture as if he had created it all for her.

"It was breathtaking," she replied honestly. That was surely the only way to describe the boat trip through the land-locked, saltwater Bras d'Or Lakes. They had taken a ship to Halifax, then a carriage across town to the rail station. They'd travelled by rail to the Strait of Canso where they had boarded the SS *Marion* for the trip though the lakes and then onward to Sydney. Aleck had slept through much of the train trip, but she had been enchanted with the land. It was covered with thick virgin forests intersected by crystal streams and rushing rivers.

"I think it all looks exactly like Scotland! The cliffs, the sea! Even the deer, though at home we call them roe. And to be sure they're a different breed, our roe deer are smaller," Aleck informed her.

"In a moment you'll begin reciting Bobby Burns to me."

"No, in a moment I'll be walking down that wooden wharf and right onto that road. I'm off to explore the village of Baddeck. Join me. It's a perfect night."

Mabel smiled at him. His eyes were twinkling and she could sense his spirit of adventure. Whenever he felt curious and adventurous, whenever there was a new world to conquer, a mystery to solve, or a good question to answer, he fairly lit up with energy.

"I can't leave the children," she replied.

He frowned, then a mischievous smile crept over his face. "I'm bound to find the beautiful Maude, you know."

"The beautiful Maude?" Mabel repeated.

"You remember, I spoke about her. She's mentioned in Warner's book about Baddeck. She's the daughter of the keeper of the Telegraph House."

"Ah, yes, the beautiful Maude," Mabel said slowly. She sighed, "Well, I'll have to risk losing you then, because I really can't leave the children."

"And what if I run off with this ravishing creature?"

Again Mabel sighed in mock bewilderment. "Then I shall just do the best I can to raise the poor deserted children alone."

Aleck grinned sheepishly and kissed her on the cheek. "I really do fancy a late supper in this place. Are you sure you won't come exploring with me?"

"Not this time," she replied.

"And you don't mind?"

"I wouldn't dream of trying to stop you. For one thing you would never stop talking about your lost opportunity to see this legendary creature."

Aleck smiled broadly and then tipped his hat to her. "I shall be off then."

He strode down the gangplank. Mabel stood on deck and watched his tall silhouette shrink down the wharf. She hoped that he would find the beautiful Maude. Whenever Aleck set his mind to anything, he threw himself into it. If it became boring, he would immediately drop it and run. Yet other times, he plunged on, dogged by the need to succeed.

Mabel reflected that although the telephone was a wonderful device, Aleck had other wonderful inventions —many of them designed to help save lives. Those were the inventions he loved the most.

She walked around the deck several times; the water, silent to her ears, lapped against the side of the boat. She watched it for a moment and wondered how it sounded. Then, slowly she turned away and went back to their stateroom. When Aleck returned, he would be full of stories to tell her, and his joy in telling them always gave her the greatest pleasure.

Aleck, swinging his walking stick and whistling happily, reached the end of the wharf. He paused, looked both ways down the dirt road that ran parallel to the lake shore, and then, spying a sign in the distance that read, "Hotel," he headed toward it.

Baddeck seemed an idyllic little village. Nestled in the hills above the lake, it sprawled along the shoreline. Each and every house had a fine view of the vast lake and the islands and inlets that gave the shoreline character. He imagined brilliant sunsets such as the one that they had seen that evening, and in his mind's eye, he could even conjure up a silver day when the lake would be grey blue, its water rippling softly in a fresh breeze.

And so much to explore! The woods were full of secrets; the rocks told the story of the ages, the birds were too numerous to catalogue.

He approached the hotel, a hundred questions on his lips. Were there many guests in the little hostelry? How many people lived in this village and in the surrounding area? Was the hunting good? What did people do when the icy cold of winter came? And most important of all, was this the place so wonderfully portrayed in Warner's book, or was the book more fictional than it claimed? So far, everything looked quite as described.

At that point Aleck stopped. Next to the hotel was another building. In faded letters it said: "The Telegraph House." Without hesitation, he strode up to the door and entered the premises. A woman wearing a crisp apron stood clearing one of the tables inside the small dining room. She looked up and smiled warmly. "You must be off the *Marion*."

"And how did you know that?" Aleck asked.

"We don't get many people from away, but when the *Marion*'s in port, people tend to wander ashore to explore."

"Well, that's exactly what I'm doing, exploring and visiting."

"Would you like some supper?" she asked.

"I would indeed, especially if that supper might include a fresh piece of berry pie for dessert."

The woman grinned, "Would blueberry be to your liking, then?"

"Oh, it would indeed. I'm Alexander Graham Bell," he offered.

"And I'm Mrs. Dunlop," she replied matter-of-factly.

She showed him to a table, then disappeared into the kitchen. When she returned, she brought him tea, and while his supper was being prepared they talked. She tried to answer all his questions.

When his dinner arrived he ate it with enthusiasm and was in the process of devouring his delicious dessert when an old man and a most beautiful young woman entered the Telegraph House.

Mrs. Dunlop turned. "Ah, Mr. Bell, I'd like you to meet my daughter, Maude."

Aleck put down his fork. "The beautiful Maude from Mr. Warner's book! I am indeed honoured."

The girl blushed and Aleck laughed gently. "No need to worry. I'm quite married and the father of two beautiful daughters of my own."

The old man rubbed his chin. "You're the fellow who's invented that newfangled contraption they call a telephone, aren't you?"

"I am. How did you know?"

"I heard you sailed in on the *Marion*, and I saw your picture once in the newspaper."

"News travels fast here," Mrs. Dunlop explained.

"That means you have no need of my invention," Aleck replied cheerfully as he stood up. "I'm afraid I must go. I can hardly wait to tell my wife of the accuracy of Mr. Warner's book."

"Come again," Mrs. Dunlop said, as Aleck paid for his dinner.

"I will," he promised, thinking of the beauty of the area. "You can count on it."

—⁓—

They looked a motley bunch as they trudged along the dirt road that followed the rocky barren coast of Newfoundland. The crew of the *Marion* led the march, followed by a wagon bearing most of the women and children passengers, while a scraggly line of men and a few women brought up the rear. Aleck refused to walk in line. He walked beside Mabel, more or less apart from the others, and midway between the crew and their fellow passengers.

"I can't believe this!" Mabel said, lifting her skirts as she walked. "Do slow down. Your legs are so long I have to take three strides to each of yours."

Aleck slowed slightly. "You could ride in the cart."

"I don't want to ride in the cart. My shoes are perfectly good for walking and I am not decrepit."

"Nor do you want to be like the other women."

"That's true. Besides, I enjoy walking."

"What an adventure! A trifle inconvenient, perhaps, but I can't recall when I've had a better time."

Mabel suppressed a smile. Inconvenient was hardly the word, still he was right—it had been quite an adventure. She glanced at her daughters. They were riding in the cart. "I think I'd have been happier if the people in that village had been more hospitable. Imagine telling us to move on! After being shipwrecked!"

"There's simply no accounting for people's actions or reactions, especially people who live by and depend upon the sea. Their moods change with every tide."

"How philosophical! And I might say, charitable as well. And what if the people in the next village are as anxious to be rid of us? Will we have to walk all the way to St. John's?"

"I don't think the inhabitants of the next village will be as inhospitable as those of Portugal Cove. Apparently they have a reputation for peculiarity."

"You learn so much, in so short a time," Mabel said. "I envy you the ability to eavesdrop and talk at the same time."

"Pshaw, all I did was to overhear the captain talking about the people of Portugal Cove."

"Well, I don't care how peculiar they are, or even why—as long as we get help soon."

"Hasn't this been just the most wonderful trip? Baddeck was exactly as described! Even Maude was real!"

Mabel noted that he paused and waited for her reaction. He was a terrible tease. She didn't respond.

"A magnificent voyage complete with a shipwreck—well, run aground on the rocky coast of Newfoundland to be entirely accurate."

"Aren't you glad you won't have to be entirely accurate when you weave your tale for our dinner guests when we get home—if we ever do," she said mischievously.

"True enough," he allowed. "You know, the only bad part of this vacation has been the trip to the coal mines at Sydney."

"Those poor people living in such terrible conditions," Mabel frowned. "No wonder my father's stock yields such high dividends. It's immoral and I shall tell him so when we get home."

"What, ho!" Aleck said, stopping in his tracks. A young lad appeared running down the road. When Aleck stopped, everyone walking behind him stopped too, even the cart clattered to a halt.

"Are you the people from the Marion!" the lad shouted, breathlessly.

"We are," the captain answered.

"We're preparing food and lodging for you for the night," the boy told them. "And a boat's coming in the morning to take you all to St. John's."

Aleck turned to Mabel, "There see, we are rescued." He repeated the lad's words for her.

"I suppose there'll be no hot bath till we get to St. John's," she lamented.

"Probably not," he agreed, then, stroking his beard, he looked into Mabel's eyes. "As pleasant as I find it here in Newfoundland, I was more taken by Baddeck. Mabel, let's consult with the rest of the family about returning there for the rest of our holidays."

"Not because of the lovely Maude?" Her eyes twinkled and he leaned over and kissed her cheek. "No, because I've fallen in love with the place. And if it proves to be as wonderful as I think," he said slowly, "we might consider it for something more permanent. During the summer heat of Washington, we could make good use of a summer home in the cool of Cape Breton Isle."

Mabel nodded. As unconventional as it had been, this was the first holiday since their honeymoon that she'd felt really free. Moreover, in Baddeck they could be alone. She imagined long days hiking in the woods with Aleck, and she smiled. "It does seem ideal."

"A place to find refuge, my dear," he added. "A place of our own making."

CHAPTER SIXTEEN

Washington, 1885

The great iron engine rested by the station platform, panting steam as it prepared to back out of the station and start its journey to Washington. The cool, early morning air mixed with the steam, the smell of smoke, perfume and the aroma of hot coffee as it drifted from the dining car. Outside the curtained windows of the Bell family's first-class compartment, hundreds of busy travellers could be seen milling about on the platform. Women in fashionable dresses, draped in light, knitted shawls and wearing ornate bonnets, carried hatboxes and bags as they tried to herd their children together to board the train. Distinguished looking men in tall hats gathered in small groups to enjoy a cigar before climbing aboard. And porters pushing overloaded baggage carts wove in and out of relatives and well-wishers who huddled together to see passengers off to the nation's capital.

The Bell family occupied a large compartment with six red plush seats—though they only needed four. Each seat had a headrest covered with a spotless white lace doily.

"Oh I do love trains," five-year-old Daisy cried to no one in particular. She explored the various pockets on and near the seats, the brass lamps that were positioned over the window and the other assorted gadgets intended to make the traveller's trip more enjoyable. There was even a little slot in the door where a gentleman could place his shoes; they would be taken by the porter and returned, cleaned and shined so beautifully that you could see your face in them. And during the trip, after dinner in the dining car, the porter would bring hot tea and a bowl of hot towels to freshen up. Yes, there were hundreds of things to look at, and in addition, there was the scenery beyond the window. Daisy thought the view from the window particularly fascinating as they were leaving or approaching a big city. Flapping clotheslines faced the tracks. The rows of shabby wooden tenements lining the outskirts were so close that she could look right into people's rooms and see what they were doing. Sometimes her parents talked about these "new" Americans and how badly they were forced to live. But Daisy didn't understand their conversation very well, and it wasn't nearly so interesting as the sights to be seen.

Seven-year-old Elsie squirmed in her seat and shook her hands as though expelling her excess energy. Daisy remained glued to the window. Both girls were dressed in bright summer pinafores, with their thick hair drawn up and held by ribbons. They had inherited their father's dark hair and eyes. Mabel often called them her two little gypsies.

"Do try to sit still, Elsie," Mabel said, touching her daughter's shoulder lightly. She was still standing, surveying their hand luggage, which had been placed on the metal racks above their seats.

Aleck had folded himself comfortably into his seat, with his long legs taking all the space between his seat and the empty one facing him.

"I guess it will all stay up there," Mabel said uncertainly, sitting down next to him.

"Of course it will."

"Will you be glad to get back to Washington?"

"You know better than to ask that," he said wearily. "But I suppose it will be more bearable now on two counts."

"Which are?"

"It's already cooler and I know that from now on I will absolutely never spend another summer in the eastern United States."

Mabel smiled sympathetically. Every year the heat and humidity drained his energy. Once he had been able to escape to his parent's home in Ontario, but they had now moved to Washington to be near their grandchildren.

"I'm absolutely elated with our decision," Aleck said, adjusting his feet to make himself more comfortable. In his mind's eye he conjured up the green velvet hills and gentle ocean breezes of Baddeck that cooled his body and refreshed his mind.

Mabel reached over and took his hand. They had talked about it for weeks. On the boat back they had made up their minds. As soon as they got home, Aleck would write to Mrs. Dunlop for advice on buying a cottage in Baddeck. Washington and Boston were necessary for business, but a cottage in Baddeck was where the fullness of life could be enjoyed.

"I can hardly wait to go back," he said, closing his eyes. "I want Elsie and Daisy to be able to roam the countryside, learn from nature."

Mabel glanced at her oldest daughter again. She was wriggling about, and this time she had kicked off one of her shoes. "Elsie, please try to sit still."

Aleck opened his eyes and looked at Elsie. "Perhaps you should take her to the doctor," he suggested.

Mabel nodded. Elsie simply couldn't sit still, she slept badly at night and seemed frantic with activity. The younger Daisy was much calmer. "I suppose a check-up couldn't hurt."

"We are going to the dining car aren't we?" Daisy asked brightly. "I love the dining car."

Mabel looked at her youngest child indulgently. Daisy loved the silver serving sets, the crisp white tablecloths, and the fact that you could eat while looking out the window. She also loved all the little things, and that her father had to write down what each of them chose from the huge black and gold embossed menu. The waiter brought a little tray with a pencil and a pad and it was all properly recorded.

Just as the train jolted backward to move out of the station there was a loud knock on the door.

"A bit early for the conductor," Aleck observed.

Mabel leaned across his legs and unlatched the door.

A young boy, hardly older than Elsie, stood before them with a pile of papers under his arm. He wore a funny little tweed cap, knickers, a vest and crumpled shirt. He looked a trifle grimy and unkempt.

"Got the Washington papers," he announced. "Right off the train that just got in."

Aleck fumbled in his pocket for change and handed the lad a coin.

As Aleck unfolded the paper, Mabel saw the headline. "Oh, good heavens!" she gasped.

The bold black headline read: "Alexander Graham Bell Guilty of Fraud, Bell to Be Charged with Perjury, Bell Not the Inventor of the Telephone!"

Aleck's fingers tightened on the page as he read.

"Who says that?" Mabel asked. "Who is accusing you of fraud?" Her face was pale.

"The Pan-Electric Company," he answered.

Mabel's dark eyes widened. "Who are they?"

"Damnable crooks!" Aleck exploded.

Mabel glanced at the girls. Daisy was intent on looking out the window. If she had sensed their outrage or noticed her father's language she didn't show it. Elsie was much too busy moving about and too lost in her own world to notice. Mabel turned back to Aleck. His lips were pressed together. She could see that he was fighting to control his anger.

"Pan-Electric is one of the thieving groups being investigated for patent infringement," he explained. "The Principal Secretary of Pan-Electric is the Attorney General of the United States. Their entire charge is based on nothing. It's just a case of corruption and greed emanating from the office of the Attorney General."

"Oh, Aleck—I know how awful this is for you." She squeezed his hand.

Aleck faced her. What would he do without her. He shook his head. "Seven years ago a British electrical experimenter forecast all this, Mabel. His name was William H. Preece, and he wrote, 'Once a new thing is shown to be true, a host of detractors delight in proving that it is not new. The inventor is shown to be a plagiarist or purloiner or something worse—Professor Bell will have to go through all this.' He was right, Mabel. Sometimes I think that I'm not the inventor of the telephone. Every new battle requires more testimony, more proof, more energy! I'm so busy fighting court battles that I can't get back to teaching the deaf."[1]

"You did invent it, Aleck! You must fight for what is yours."

"It's like an endless series of bad dreams."

"From which we will eventually awake," she whispered. "Aleck, think about Baddeck, think about next summer."

He closed his eyes and leaned back. He hadn't even reached Washington and it had all started again! His head pounded painfully as anger surged through him.[2] He tried desperately to force it all from his mind and to concentrate on his memory of the Nova Scotia wilderness. Gradually he began to relax.

⁓

Mabel sat nervously in the doctor's office. She hated hospitals, they always smelled of vinegar and formaldehyde—an odious gas that had been used in hospitals for the past ten years to kill germs. Poor little Elsie. She remembered that wonderful May morning seven years ago when Elsie had been placed in her arms for the first time. Aleck had been enthralled. He had written home immediately, but had read her the letter first. "Such a funny black little thing it is! Perfectly formed, with a full crop of dark hair, bluish eyes, and a complexion so swarthy that Mabel declares she has given birth to a red Indian!" They had argued for two weeks over a name, then settled on Elsie, after Aleck's mother, Eliza.

Aleck had been wonderfully funny, she reminisced—so fond of little Elsie, yet afraid too. Elsie had been his first encounter with a baby. He hardly knew how to hold her. But what he lacked in parental knowledge, he made up in scientific knowledge. He ensured that all the baby's organs of speech, hearing and sight were perfect. What wonderful hopes they'd placed in their dear little Elsie. But something was wrong with her. Mabel knew it and could hardly conceal her concern.

A doctor entered the room. His rich black beard was flecked with white. He wore a dark suit with a cravat and starched wing collar. Through rimless spectacles his eyes appeared large and penetrating "We've finished our examination," he said, looking directly into Mabel's eyes ... I understand you're deaf, Mrs. Bell."

"I can read your lips perfectly well," Mabel interrupted.

"You speak very well," the doctor said. He seemed surprised.

Mabel ignored him. She was here because of Elsie, not because of her problems. "Elsie," she pressed. "Tell me what's wrong with her."

"A common problem—distracting I fear, but all too common." He shook his head.

"What is it?" She felt irritated and wished that Aleck were with her.

"St. Vitus's Dance, I'm afraid. The medical name is chorea. It's a nervous disorder. As you have noticed, she makes irregular, involuntary movements. Actually, Mrs. Bell, her case is quite severe."

Mabel bit her lip and tried not to cry. "What can I do?" she asked softly.

"First we must put her in the care of a good neurologist. She needs lots of rest. If her condition gets any worse she might need to go away to a rest home."

"I'd rather keep her home for the time being," Mabel said, horrified at the thought of sending Elsie anywhere.

"She may well outgrow it. And you must realize how common it is. More common in young ladies than in men. I think it's the female constitution."

Mabel stood up. Her own experience made her wary of doctors. She wasn't interested in listening to any nonsense about the female constitution. "Thank you, we'll do as you suggest and find a neurologist."

"I could recommend one."

"That won't be necessary," Mabel said straightening up. "My husband, Professor Bell, has many friends at the Massachusetts Institute of Technology and the Harvard Medical School."

The doctor looked surprised. "Oh, you are that Mrs. Bell?"

For once Mabel felt rather happy to be the wife of a famous man. "I am indeed," she replied as she left.

⌒

Their carriage moved slowly up Pennsylvania Avenue, the great dome of the Capitol looming in the distance. L'Enfant, the French engineer who had laid out the original plan for the capital city in the 1700s, was a man of vision. The dome was visible from almost everywhere, and the concentric circles and parklands gave Washington a spacious air. It was a city designed for a nation of stature.

"I'm glad we chose to take the long way home," Aleck said, spelling the words out on her hand. In the dark, it was the way he communicated with her. He leaned back against the soft leather seat of the carriage and placed his arm around Mabel. To a casual observer they would have seemed to be courting, rather than an old married couple.

"I'm so proud of you, Aleck."

"An honorary doctor of medicine! Do you think I'll become an insufferable medical bore?"

"No, of course not. You know you won't be."

His eyes took on a thoughtful expression. "Perfecting this invention meant a lot to me, Mabel."

"I know—because of President Garfield."

"Yes. It was too late for him, but I know it will save other lives."

"It's being used everywhere. It's already saved lives."

He thought about his medical probe. If only he had perfected it sooner. "Yes," he added. "This is the only kind of invention that is truly rewarding because I know it will help people."

Mabel smiled up at him in the dark. He didn't seem to realize that the telephone could save lives too. It was a milestone in communication, yet he turned away from it, tired of all the wrangling. Not that she didn't understand. The legal battle with Pan-Electric had drained him for much of the previous year. She had hardly seen him at all.[3] And much to his sadness, he had been forced to close his school for the deaf because he couldn't devote sufficient time to it. Thus, his recent success—perfecting the telephonic probe—meant more than anything else to him at this moment.

"Now that things have calmed down a bit, I'm going to begin petitioning for more schools for the deaf," he told her.

She squeezed his hand. "Don't get too heavily involved so that you can't leave Washington. We'll be going to Baddeck soon."

"I can hardly wait," he told her as their carriage turned the corner and drew up in front of their house. "We're home," she announced.

"No, my dear, Baddeck is home."

Aleck was dressed casually in a morning coat. He sat in a favourite leather chair in his study, a smaller and less formal place than the drawing room. He rarely received guests in the drawing room, which he found cold and impersonal. The visitor he was waiting for was a stranger to him, and Aleck felt more self-assured in his cozy study when meeting someone for the first time.

The butler opened the door and ushered a well-dressed gentleman into the room. "Captain Arthur H. Keller," he announced.

"Show him in."

Aleck could see that Captain Keller was a man of rigid posture. He attributed the man's alert stance to his having been an officer in the Army of the Confederacy. Military men, Aleck had observed, were never quite able to forget their basic training; they stood straight as sticks long after their service had ended. Such was the case with Captain Keller, although he was now a newspaper editor in his hometown of Tuscambia, Alabama.

"I know it is a great imposition, Professor Bell, and truly I want to thank you for taking the time to see me."

Aleck listened to the man's refined southern speech with interest. America's regional accents fascinated him. He was relieved, as well, that Mr. Keller's visit had nothing to do with the telephone or the patent battles that plagued his existence.

"Not at all. My secretary informed me you've come about your daughter."

"I brought her with me," Keller said. "She's in the foyer with her nurse. I wanted to speak with you first."

Aleck motioned him to a chair and proceeded to light a cigar. Mabel hated his cigars, but he couldn't do without them—or more to the point, he didn't want to do without them.

"I know that you are the leading expert on teaching and training the deaf as well as a talented inventor. I've come to beseech your advice, and perhaps your counsel, on my daughter's condition."

Aleck leaned forward. A man so set on helping his daughter must indeed be a devoted father. "Tell me about your daughter," he said.

"Her name is Helen. A few years ago she became ill. The illness was undiagnosed, but it left her both blind and deaf. And possibly ... "

He hesitated, and Aleck watched him carefully. The pain in Keller's face was obvious. He could hardly say the words,

"And possibly mentally impaired," he finished in a near whisper.

"Deaf and blind," Aleck said carefully. "What a dreadful tragedy."

"We're just not sure if she can learn—she's developed into a wild animal. My wife and I can no longer control her, and naturally there is no communication."

"How old is she?"

"Six."

Aleck nodded. "Please, go and bring her in here."

"I warn you, sir, she's very strange, quite unpredictable ... "

Aleck smiled kindly. "I am prepared to take my chances, Captain Keller."

Keller left the room and returned leading a small girl by the hand. Aleck noticed how tightly she held her father's hand using her free hand to feel air, stroking with curiosity whatever she touched. She sniffed the room like a basset hound. As she came closer to the ashtray that held the smouldering cigar, her face grimaced with distaste.

"Bring her here and transfer her hand to mine, finger by finger so she will know you approve."

Keller looked doubtful, but he did as he been asked.

Aleck squeezed the small hand gently—once, then twice. In a second, he felt her respond with a hesitant squeeze of her own. He lifted her gently to his knee and gave her the watch from his vest pocket. She turned it over and over in her hands with interest, then held it against her.

"She can feel the vibrations," he told Keller. "Look how interested she is in it. And she squeezed my hand just as I squeezed hers. There is most certainly no problem with her mental capacity. Your poor child is trapped in a dark, silent world, Captain Keller. She needs a teacher to guide her back into our world."

"Can it be done?" Captain Keller asked.

Aleck noted that the captain's facial expression had changed completely, as if some great weight had been lifted. "Of course it can be done. I suggest Michael Anagnos, Director of the Perkin's Institute. He can recommend a good teacher. Indeed, we were recently discussing one of his star pupils. Now let me think—ah, yes. Her name is Annie Sullivan. She might be just the person to help your Helen."

"Are you quite certain Helen can learn?"

"As certain as I can be," Aleck answered. Again, he squeezed Helen's hand and received another squeeze in return.

"My dear professor Bell, I can't thank you enough for the hope you've given me."

"Do keep me informed. Bring Helen again, let me know how her education progresses."

"I will indeed," Keller promised.

Aleck walked them to the front door. "You must try to stimulate her interest, encourage her curiosity. Use the senses of touch and smell and one day I promise she will break out of her empty world and communicate."

"I'll do my best."

Aleck took Helen's hand in his and spelled "good-bye" into her palm. She didn't understand, of course, but she seemed to realize that he was trying once again to communicate.[4] He watched as the girl and her father walked toward their carriage, and as always, his heart ached for all the children he couldn't reach.

⁓

A cold January wind blew off the Potomac, and dark clouds threatened rain.

Mabel lay curled beneath the quilts in her giant four-poster bed. Not fully awake, she flailed at her dog who had jumped on the bed and started nipping at the sheets as she tried to draw them closer around her. Suddenly, Mabel sat bolt upright and stared at the dog. Clearly, it was barking. She sniffed and smelled smoke.

She fairly leapt out of bed and ran barefoot down the dark corridor banging on doors and rousing the household. The smoke was stronger now, but she didn't know where it was coming from.

"I hear the fire trucks!" Elsie, shouted. She turned to her mother and mouthed what she had said. In the dim light, Mabel read her daughter's lips.

"Bundle up the children, take them across the street!" she ordered the maid, "I'll make sure everyone else is out."

The terrified maid scooped up Elsie and Daisy and hurried away.

Mabel wrapped herself in a robe, flung her coat on over top, and thrust her feet into a pair of stout shoes. This was no time to be fashion conscious. She met the firemen at the front door.

"This is the home of Alexander Graham Bell, the inventor. You must try to save his library—you must!" She tried to speak as clearly as she could.

"You'll have to leave, Ma'am!"

Mabel shook her head and followed the firemen back into the house and down the hall. Her heart pounded. What if Aleck's papers were destroyed? What if his notes burned? What might be lost to the world? But the smell of the acrid smoke was suffocating and she began to cough. Finally, she admitted to herself that it was no use. She hurried out of the house and across the street where the children and household staff stood huddled beneath a street lamp.

Daisy tugged on her mother's skirt. Mabel bent down to see her youngest daughter's lips. "Our house is burning down," Daisy wailed.

"No, it will be all right. We'll rebuild it."

Daisy sniffed. Elsie simply stared at the conflagration. Yet even in all this excitement, Mabel noticed that Elsie could not stand still. She was fidgety and seemed wider awake than the others, in spite of the late hour. It was her condition, and Mabel knew that once excited, it would take hours to calm her down. Elsie was turning more and more inside herself; the chorea seemed to be getting worse.

"Where will we go?" Daisy asked.

"To grandmother's house. I'll have to wire your father." Aleck, as usual, was away on business; now he would have to return.

～

They stood in the blackened, cold foyer of their once magnificent home. Aleck held Mabel close and kissed her hair. "God, when I think of what could have happened! I should have been here."

"You were where you had to be."

"Thank the Lord that no one was hurt. What a smart dog!"

The house was covered with a thick coating of soot and ice from the fire hoses. Mabel walked about, touching this and that and shaking her head sadly.

"The fire department must have arrived very quickly," Aleck observed, when again she turned to face him. "It's a horrible mess, but the library survived and, thank heaven, so did my notes."

"They told me a policeman saw the smoke pouring from the third floor. He called the fire department. They were here within minutes."

Aleck shrugged helplessly. "Where do we start?"

"We start by getting help," she said firmly. "I've already contacted a local boarding house—a place where casual labourers stay. I've offered a fair wage and the workmen I saw yesterday will begin tomorrow. Naturally, sorting through your library and notes will require a special person—someone with intelligence and patience. Do you want to see to that?"

"No thank you. I'll leave it all to you. I can't organize anything."

She suppressed a smile in spite of the gravity of the situation. At least Aleck knew his weaknesses even if he was unable to reform himself.

"The workman I have in mind is a Charles Thompson. He's an unemployed black man from Virginia who arrived with the others yesterday. He seems brighter than the rest, and he can read and write. Besides that, he has a wonderful smile. He is really quite charming."

"He sounds ideal. I'll have to work with him for a while. He must understand that nothing with writing on it can be thrown out."

"You'll like him," Mabel predicted. "He can do the job."

Aleck surveyed the damage. He knew that there was no need to worry—Mabel would set everything right. As delicate as she looked, and as ladylike as she acted, she was firm, organized and strong, with a backbone of solid iron. She could make decisions and carry them out. Without her he would be utterly lost.

⌐

Washington could be fearfully warm, even in June. Today it was hot and humid again. At times it seemed as if a breeze would never come to relieve the airless oppression. Aleck was away so much promoting day schools for the deaf throughout the United States. Mabel believed that he contrived to be away when the weather was so unpleasant, though in her heart, she knew she couldn't blame him. Not that Aleck's absence and the weather were the principal source of her discontent. At the moment, Elsie was her greatest concern.

Her daughter's illness had grown progressively worse. The neurologist proposed a rest cure, but it would mean taking her away for at least a year. Mabel suggested that they wait another year before making that decision. The doctor agreed. But had she done the right thing? Daily, she wondered whether putting off Elsie's rest cure had been the best course of action.

She sat at her writing table and penned a letter to Aleck. Perhaps he would suggest something.

"The children are well. I am trying hard to awaken a love of reading in Elsie and succeeding poorly; in plain words, failing utterly. Elsie doesn't care for anything but company now. She has no resources within herself and no habit of application. She is a dreadful weight on me in consequence. I feel sure that her faults are mostly due to her upbringing, but how to train her into good habits now, I don't know. She is affectionate and thinks she is fond of me, but I doubt it is but surface fondness and I cannot see why she would be really fond of me. It is 'do this, don't do that' all the time, all day long...."[5]

Mabel read her own words. Elsie didn't have the patience for reading. Her nervous disorder prevented her from relaxing; even her sleep was filled with nocturnal wanderings about the house. But understanding didn't help Mabel. She leaned back and closed her eyes thinking of how Elsie had been when she was younger. At three she had developed a game with her father. She used to step onto his shoulders then flip back and somersault to the ground. Mabel had always worried that she would hurt herself, though she never did. Since then she had grown hyperactive—constantly, mindlessly on the move.

The neurologist assured Mabel that the disorder would eventually be cured, still she could not help but feel that if Aleck were around more, Elsie would be easier to handle. She leaned over her letter, and began writing again. "Please think of us, you cannot imagine how much I miss you," she concluded.[6]

CHAPTER SEVENTEEN

Washington, 1888

Aleck descended the winding staircase quickly. At the bottom, he patted the inner breast pocket of his suit to assure himself that the letter was still there. The envelope was long and white, made of fine parchment bearing an impressive gold seal. It was an important letter, an important invitation.

He poked his head into the study—it was empty. He looked in the conservatory—it too was deserted. He wandered into the parlour. Mabel was there, moving through the room like a silent dancer. She was incredibly graceful, he thought as he watched her filling the vases with fresh flowers. The bright yellow crocuses were one of the bounties of an early Washington spring.

She stopped suddenly and looked up. "Oh, how long have you been there?"

"Long enough to know you are the most graceful creature I've ever seen and certainly the most beautiful of women."

She blushed and looked away, wondering how, after so many years of marriage he could still be such a romantic. No matter, it pleased her that he was still full of flattery.

"Do you feel the need for new fashionable clothes?" he asked. Mabel studied his face. He had a twinkle in his eye, and his lips formed an impish smile—a sure sign that he had a secret he was dying to tell her.

"Why?" She demanded sharply. "Aren't my clothes fashionable enough for you?"

She would always play the game so as not to spoil it for him. Aleck's joy was always in the telling.

"Perfectly in fashion, my dear, but surely great ladies can always do with more. Don't you enjoy trying on ravishing hats? Or perhaps you need a pair of fine Italian leather gloves or a collar of Chantilly lace?"

Mabel adjusted the flare on the last flower arrangement and turned away from lip-reading to admire her work. "You're teasing me about something. What is it?"

"I have a wonderful idea! A surprise!"

Mabel crossed the room and stood in front of him. "Are you going to share it with me? Please don't tell me you're leaving again. I hate being alone."

"I know you do. Well, it isn't that kind of surprise—quite."

She scowled. "What do you mean by, 'quite'?"

"I have received an invitation to speak."

"Oh, Aleck! You promised we would leave for Baddeck early this year!"

"This is something very special. I've been invited to London to testify before the Royal Commission on the Education of the Deaf. It's a great honour."

"London! Oh, Aleck, no! You're not going all the way to London?"

"And you are all going with me. What do you think of that?" His large hands circled her tiny waist. He lifted her off the ground as if she were a feather. "I propose we make it a family vacation! You and the girls will go and stay in France with your parents. I will go to testify and meet you later in Paris." He set her down and planted a kiss on her nose.

"But, Aleck, we'll still be apart."

"Not for long. I hardly think they'll need me in London for more than an afternoon—if that!"

"Are you sure?"

"Not sure but reasonably certain. It'll do us all good. Well, my dear, what do you say?"

"Yes." She knew when to agree to Aleck's enthusiasms. After a short pause, she added: "Maybe the trip will help Elsie too."

⁓

"Drat!" Aleck grumbled as he slammed the door to his hotel room. Why didn't anything ever go according to plan? Not only had his testimony before the Royal Commission not ended in an afternoon, it had dragged on for two interminable weeks!

He slumped into a chair and unlaced his shoes. There had been a letter from Mabel for him at the desk. He opened it and read: "I certainly wish I had been there to see although I would also have wished to be invisible. How the gentlemen must have wondered when you brought out document after document in proof of all you said. I hope you looked very neat and nice, had your hair cut and beard trimmed. I wish you would go to the best tailor in London and get yourself a swell suit, and I really wish you would hire a valet temporarily. I don't think you realize even yet the importance of an irreproachable exterior although your neglect nearly cost you a wife. And say what you will, Englishmen of the classes you are now addressing think more of these things than Americans."

He let her letter drop into his lap while he laughed. Here was his American wife telling him, a Scotsman, how the British paid attention to clothes!

He wiped the tears of laughter from his eyes. Oh, how he had needed to laugh. But it hadn't lasted long enough. He felt terrible— ill, and lonely. He read on.

"Please be careful of yourself and don't overwork too much— I can't do without you, as I find every day I want you with me very much and yet I don't want you to shorten your stay in London on that account. Accept all the invitations you get—and meet all the great men you can—I want to hear all about them. I always feel as if you were my second self, and all the interesting people you meet I meet too and enjoy far more than if I really met them. Never mind a little dyspepsia. We will go home to Baddeck and live on bread and milk for the rest of the summer."[1]

Aleck folded her letter and returned it to his pocket. He went to the small writing desk and began his reply. "I wish you were not quite so far away. I want you so much now. I think if you were near me, you would sympathize with me, but far away you cannot realize how much my heart has been wrapped up in my work and how mortified and disgusted with myself I am. I commenced so well and made a great impression but I talked too much and spoilt it all. I feel that my whole testimony whittled down to a tame conclusion. The end is so important. I want to get to the proof of my testimony, especially as the chairman gave me liberty to append to the evidence a brief statement recapitulating the chief points. That will be my chance to end properly. I am as nervous as can be over it. I have worked so hard over the whole matter, you know I have, and I don't want to end in failure. I feel quite ill ... and sick at heart, and I have no one to whom I can turn—I am so miserable and unhappy alone."[2]

He signed the letter, replaced his shoes and pulled himself up to go and mail it. How could these wretched hearings have dragged on for two weeks? He feared that he wasn't doing very well and cursed the slowness of the deliberations.

⁓

Mabel had flown into his arms at the Paris railway station, and she hadn't let go of his hand since. On the spur of the moment, he suggested that they send his bags on to the hotel and spend the rest of the afternoon walking around the city, having coffee in a pastry shops on the Champs Elysées, or along the banks of the Seine, and maybe browsing in the galleries and book shops on the Boulevard du Montparnasse. Mabel hugged him. What a wonderful idea! she agreed.

From the station they took a carriage to the Tuileries garden on the Seine embankment near the Palais du Louvre. They strolled the West Bank to the Hotel de Ville then crossed the river at Notre Dame cathedral, where they found a splendid sidewalk café with a view of both the Grand Palais and the Seine.

"Paris," Mabel commented, "makes much better use of the Seine than London does of the Thames. And aren't the flowers wonderful?"

Aleck agreed on both points. Whereas the Thames separated two areas of London, the Seine meandered through all of Paris. It united the city, rather than separating it. Although the British parliament buildings were majestic, and some of the bridges across the Thames River impressive, the parks and coffee houses along the Seine gave Paris a delightful character that London lacked. London's waterfront was dedicated to commerce, Paris's to people.

"I'm exhausted," Aleck said after a time.

"Did we walk so far?"

"Oh, not from the walking. That felt wonderful. No, I meant from testifying, from all the worry."

She regarded him with concern. For as long as she'd known him, Aleck had always feared failure—and worried about it. Perhaps that drove him to success, she thought, but at what price?

"You look tired too," he observed, studying her face.

"I'm tired of being alone and I'm worried."

"About what?" He covered her gloved hand with his own.

"It's Elsie," Mabel whispered. "Oh, Aleck, she's ever so much worse since we got here. I don't want to send her away for treatments, but I think there's no choice. She's a bundle of nerves, she never stops moving."

Tears filled Mabel's eyes. "I hate the thought of sending her away, and she doesn't want to go."

"I should have been here," he said, feeling guilty.

"You spend more time with other people's children than you do with your own."

Aleck accepted the gentle rebuke. Before they'd left Washington, he'd spent several days with Helen Keller and her father. The child was making remarkable progress. He hadn't spent as much time with Elsie—his own flesh and blood. He was denying his own children his time in order to give it to someone else. What was wrong with him?

They didn't argue often. Mabel believed that arguments never settled anything. "No one ever wins an argument," she once told him. "In the end it just makes both people unhappy." Instead of arguing, she used the more subtle approach of chiding him for his shortcomings. He knew he was being selfish but felt powerless to change. She would have preferred him to remain at home with her and the children and make the world come to him at his convenience. Unfortunately, life didn't work that way he had told her time and again. His work would always be the reason for his existence—family came second. It wasn't the way he had planned it. But that was the way his family life had worked out. It was selfish, egocentric and unacceptable. Did he really have to choose life without his work, or life without Mabel and the children? The alternatives were too grim even to contemplate.

"We'll find a good place for her." he promised.

"I want to go home to Baddeck," she murmured. "We'll send Elsie to that rest home in Philadelphia, and then we'll go home to Baddeck for the rest of the summer."

He squeezed her hand and nodded. It was by far the best plan.

Their carriage bumped along the dirt road between the village of Baddeck and their cottage. As they approached Crescent Grove Cottage—their temporary home until their nearby estate was completed—Aleck sighed, "At last, we're really home." Both of them drank in the scenery they loved so much and relished the fresh cool air of the Nova Scotia summer.

Mabel didn't reply because she had her head turned and had not read his lips. But he knew she felt the same way. Although they lived in Washington and travelled, their real home—their spiritual home—was here in Baddeck.

After their first visit to Baddeck, Aleck had written to Mrs. Dunlop at the Telegraph House requesting her help in finding them a cottage in, or near the town. One of his prerequisites was that it be near a running stream. Mrs. Dunlop turned his request over to Arthur McCurdy, editor of the village newspaper and a local businessman; McCurdy found a small cottage a few miles from the village. The nearest stream flowed through an adjoining property, but the cottage offered a beautiful view and a well-protected beach edged with a stand of fir trees. Aleck bought it immediately and enlarged it by jacking it up on stilts and adding another floor beneath. The villagers were intrigued. They called it "a house on stilts."

At first the cottage had only the barest necessities. Mattresses were stuffed with hay, and fat logs were used as stools. But what a joyful summer! In a storage shed near the privy at the back of the property they discovered an old pump organ and a butter churn in working condition. While Aleck pumped out "Onward Christian Soldiers" on the organ, Mabel and the girls took turns at the churn until the yellow blobs of butter appeared; then they gorged themselves with fresh baked bread slathered with their own butter. The churning was hard work, so Aleck—ever the inventor—solved the problem by devising a windmill to do the churning for them.

That first summer they had found the perfect spot for their permanent home—their spot. In truth, it was not a "spot" but several parcels of adjacent land. The land formed a point known as Red Head.

He tapped Mabel on the shoulder and she turned around. "Do you remember our hike? The day we found the land?"

Mabel nodded.

There was a beautiful waterfall and stream on the land next to theirs. One day, he and Mabel had gotten lost on a hiking expedition. When they broke out of the woods, they found themselves in a clearing at the top of Red Head Mountain. The view was breathtaking. From their perch it seemed as if the whole world lay stretched out beneath them. Surveying the sight, Aleck whispered, "Beinn Bhreagh"—the Gaelic for "beautiful mountain." They stood there for a long while in silence, then, from the valley below, Aleck heard the mournful wail of bagpipes. They learned later that they had been standing on Donald MacAuley's land, and that the keening of the pipes was to mark his funeral.

"How fitting," said Mabel, "that the old master of Red Head was buried at the same moment the new master arrived on the scene."

He told her she had too much romantic imagination, but at that moment he vowed to acquire that land. "We're going to own that property," he promised her. "I'm going to buy it and build a magnificent home here, our home—and we'll call it Beinn Bhreagh."

In the end, it took them eight years to buy the land they wanted. MacAuley's will had divided it among his twelve children. Each year for six successive summer holidays in Baddeck, Aleck negotiated with MacAuley's twelve flint-eyed heirs, buying the land from them one piece at a time. And when finally it belonged to him, he harnessed the waterfall with a waterwheel to operate a generator and produce electricity for their planned estate. Later, that same summer, Aleck's cousin Charlie arrived for a visit. He was touring the region, so the Bells joined him for an exploration of the Bras d'Or Lakes and the Cape Breton coastline.

Before starting to construct the main house, they built a lodge, so that they could hold dinner parties and other social gatherings, which their cottage wouldn't accommodate. Arthur McCurdy became a regular at their home. Aleck soon considered him a true friend. He hired McCurdy as his personal secretary to help him organize his affairs during his time in Baddeck. He also hired Thompson—the young man from Virginia who had sorted through his smoke-blackened library papers—to be his valet. He'd proved so valuable after the fire that he had become one of the family and an invaluable assistant to Mabel when Aleck was away on his endless travels.

"I miss Elsie," Mabel said suddenly. Their daughter was away in Philadelphia under medical care for her condition. "Oh, Aleck, it's such a puzzle. Her constant motion wears me out when she's with me, and I hate it when she isn't."

"So do I," Aleck agreed. "But the doctor is right. She needs this rest. Perhaps when she returns she'll be better."

"I hope so."

"You'll soon be distracted. You have a lot of work to do this summer." After watching Mabel supervise the repairs to their house in Washington he'd had no qualms about letting her supervise the building of their new home in Baddeck, where construction was only possible during the summer. The Baddeck house was to be modelled after their Washington house on Rhode Island Avenue.

"What do you look forward to the most?" Mabel asked.

"My sheep," he said with a mischievous chuckle.

Mabel laughed. "I hope the villagers have forgotten your wicked work of black magic!"

Aleck laughed heartily. Last summer he had been branded a warlock by some of the superstitious residents of the village because of his experiments with his sheep. He had bought the flock to continue his study of genetics. It was an interest he had developed in 1885, when together with the Massachusetts State Board of Health, he began examining the possibility of deafness being an inherited genetic trait. His studies centred in the New England states, whose residents were among the first immigrants to America.

When he bought the land in Baddeck, he reserved an area for raising sheep. He soon decided that he could also use the animals in his experiments with his vacuum jacket. Ever since his infant son, Edward's death, he had been developing a mechanical method of artificial respiration. At first he tested it only on cats, but he switched to sheep because they were more the size of human beings. The day of his success, one of the local children had been with him. A sheep had drowned, then was revived with the jacket. The child spread the word throughout Baddeck that Professor Bell had the power to bring animals back from death. Opinions ranged from black magic to the work of the devil. But, Aleck had noted with humour, none of the workmen building Beinn Bhreagh quit. He paid them too well, and jobs were much too scarce to abandon, even if their employer seemed a bit queer to them.

The carriage halted. Mabel didn't wait to be helped down. "Beinn Bhreagh! We're home!" she said eagerly, and lifting her skirts she ran towards the door.

⁓

Aleck paced back and forth in his Philadelphia office to ease his agitation. Winters in Washington and Philadelphia, summers in Baddeck—time passed so quickly. And although he saw Elsie often since he had moved to Philadelphia to be near her, it didn't seem that she had been institutionalized for a year and a half.

His mind wandered back to the previous summer, the summer of 1890. Baddeck was everything it always was—peaceful, refreshing, a family retreat in the true sense of the words.

Elsie, after nearly a year away, had returned to the family bosom. She loved Beinn Bhreagh, but the stress of the trip and returning home had excited her so much that her enforced rest in Philadelphia, and all the treatment she had undergone were for nothing. Her chorea reappeared, only this time much worse. Her nervous movements seemed to take her over, dominating not only poor Elsie, but every one around her. The child had even confessed to her doctor that she knew she wasn't getting better, and that she felt terribly discouraged.

After a long series of midnight talks, Aleck and Mabel reluctantly decided that he would take Elsie back to Philadelphia for more rest and treatment and remain in Washington to be near her.

They had spirited her away from Baddeck, rowing across the lake to take her directly aboard the SS *Marion* to her stateroom. She was as agitated as he had ever remembered, yet she had no understanding of her illness. She wanted to go out on deck, to be among the other passengers.[3]

When Elsie's condition began improving Aleck and Mabel left her in the care of her doctors and returned to Baddeck. Aleck decided that they would spend Christmas there. Mabel had started a sewing class for the village women, and a drama society flourished during the long winter months. Mabel invited Mary True to come north for the winter and tutor Daisy. She accepted.

For Aleck, it had been a magic winter. Every night, long after everyone else had gone to bed, he sat and played the piano. Doubts and anxiety about his ongoing patent problems spun out of his mind with every tune he played. At the same time, new ideas were born. Gradually, his life settled down again and he returned to Washington in the spring, with renewed purpose and vigour.

Routinely he came to Philadelphia from Washington to be with Elsie. He had felt much encouraged about her health in the past few days. She seemed wonderfully relaxed and in far better spirits than he had seen her in years. He wrote to Mabel in Washington, asking whether he should take Elsie back to Washington with him. Aleck's mother pined over Elsie, since she only had two grandchildren and had not seen her eldest grandchild for more than a year. Mabel's reply had surprised him and seemed overly cautious.

"Please don't take Elsie to Washington with you. I am willing to take more risks with my children for your mother than for anyone else because they are her only grandchildren, but think how long it has taken Elsie to get as well as she is, a whole year and four months, how dreadful it would be for her to have a relapse now. Your mother would not thank you for making her the cause of such a disaster. You think Elsie's perfectly well again. She certainly is well, but she is not established in her good health. If it were anything else, I would not say a word against you taking her, but think of having to pay for it with another year's separation from our child."[4]

Aleck dropped the letter on his desk and sat down. Perhaps she was right, perhaps it was wiser not to take chances. He leaned back and closed his eyes. Yes, he would stay here to be near Elsie until April, then he would return to Beinn Bhreagh for the first breeding season of his special lambs. They had discussed their approaching summer together in a succession of letters, but as the time approached for their spring departure, Mabel insisted on waiting until the summer. Elsie's condition had improved to such an extent that both Aleck and Mabel felt that by summer she could return home. With a clear conscience Aleck left for Beinn Bhreagh alone.

By early summer Elsie was pronounced cured and returned home to Washington. Mabel's thoughts now returned to a continuous stream of written suggestions and instructions for Aleck to keep him busy. "My thoughts are constantly with you at Beinn Bhreagh. I am sure the sheep are safe in your care, but there are so many other things in which I am equally interested: the warehouse, the roads and the workmen's cottages. Why cannot the gardener's cottage go up at the Point? I am most anxious to get the gardens there started as soon a possible. It will only take eighteen months, or at the most two years, to build the house but five years is all too short an allowance for gardens to grow to a real beauty and they will not be begun until the gardener is close at hand.

"Here is the order of importance in my mind: 1. Roads, 2. Warehouse, 3. Gardener's Cottage, 4. Mr. Ellis's cottage, 5. Workmen's cottages, 6. House at the Point. I say roads first because I want them this summer, not wide ones but good narrow ones over which a good strong pony in a cart can go. Then comes the warehouse; Mr. Ellis's cottage does not seem immediately imperative if those two other cottages can be obtained temporarily. However, we must provide decent places for our workmen before we build a big house for ourselves."[5]

⁓

One evening, Mabel was invited to a small gathering at Senator Eugene Hale's home in Washington. The guests were all wives of prominent politicians, scientists, writers, military and naval officers and artists of the day. They met once a week to discuss everything from the latest books to current political events. The women were well-educated with keen incisive minds and diverse interests. Eventually, the group became known as the "Washington Club." Mabel enjoyed herself and was invited to return the following week. The more she reflected on this stimulating gathering of intelligent women, the more she considered the possibility of starting something similar in Baddeck. The local women there were almost continually isolated on their farms. A weekly meeting, a club of sorts, could relieve their boredom and promote the exchange of ideas and opinions.

When she and the girls went to Beinn Bhreagh, she discussed the idea with Aleck, Arthur McCurdy and McCurdy's sister, Georgina. They were all enthusiastic but warned that there were pitfalls to consider. Over the years, Baddeck society had become badly fragmented along political and social lines. The Catholics kept to themselves and the wife of a Conservative couldn't be seen speaking to the wife of a Liberal. Mabel decided that the ladies' club should have no political or religious basis or affiliation. Everyone was free to join, exchange information and meet new friends. The first meeting was held on 10 October 1891. Mabel sent the long boat across the bay to pick up the women. They gave the club an official name, "The Young Ladies' Club of Baddeck."[6] Thirty years later, they would change their name to "The Alexander Graham Bell Club."

If Aleck was worried that Mabel would be lonely in Baddeck, he needn't have. She quickly became good friends with the club's members. "The Young Ladies of Baddeck" were a constant source of entertainment and mental stimulation. She describes one of their evenings for Elsie:

"Yesterday was lovely. The Ladies Club Board came over for a meeting at four o'clock. We talked until five-thirty and then got out our needlework or knitting and gossiped until six, had a jolly dinner and then Papa showed us lantern slides until John came at eight-thirty with the mail and our guests departed and we felt we had a beautiful long evening. I tell you what, there is nothing like real country life when you know how to manage it so that you have real sociability. I have more of this here than I do in Washington."[7]

Socializing was the principal pastime in Baddeck and the Bells were good at it. Each summer they held a wonderful feast and festival called the Harvest Home Celebration. All the villagers and friends from Washington were invited. The result was a grand party, with dancing, eating and merriment that lasted all day and all night. Mabel's cousin, Mary Blatchford, arrived one summer in time for the festival and recorded her impressions.

"The invitations were sent out on Monday to all the men who had been employed on the estate this year to come at two o'clock with their families for games and dancing. There were about fifty men included in the invitation, and their 'families' on this occasion were elastic and took in most of the population within a radius of twenty miles.

"Great preparations were made for receiving our guests and the day was brilliant although rather windy. After breakfast, Mr. McCurdy rowed Mabel and me to Baddeck, about two miles away, to choose the prizes. At the little shop in Baddeck, we had the undivided attention of all hands, including the customers who stood solemnly about in rapt observation.... We chose neckties, suspenders, scarfs, hammers, knives, etc., and came home laden.

"At two o'clock, the people began to file up to the tennis ground, a lovely spot on the mountain slope. I wish you could have seen Mabel, Grace and the children. They were such pictures as one seldom sees outside of European galleries. Mabel so fair and madonna-like with Grace's baby in her arms, Grace with her exquisite piquant face that changes every minute, Elsie and Daisy tall and dark as Gypsies, with magnificent eyes. The games opened with walking on stilts, followed by the throwing of the hammer, putting the shot, potato race, running, etc. Afterward we walked to the 'warehouse,'—why so called I cannot imagine—I should call it an immense two-storey barn. On the ground floor were tables laden with sandwiches of every description and more pies and cakes than I have ever seen. Boilers full of tea and coffee were steaming on the stove and barrels of ginger ale were on tap. The barn was trimmed with vegetables and flowers and was a delight to see. Mrs. Kennan and I sat on the phaeton (carriage) which was warehoused in one corner. Mabel was mounted on the groom's seat behind and there we were served with things to eat and drink. When even the boys could eat no more—and they were all as solemn about their eating as if they were going to be hanged as soon as they were done—we all went up to the loft which had been cleared for dancing. A fiddler was on hand and fiddled steadily. The dancing began at once with four couples who went through what I would call a grand mixture of quadrille, lancers, double shuffle and jig. It was the thing I longed for years to see and was worth the journey here and back.

"Mrs. Kennan, with the courage of her sex ... accepted an invitation to open the dance with a great clumsy looking boy whose shoes alone must have weighed a ton. But, dear me, how he did trip it. His feet went so fast I could not have known whether he had shoes on or not. He shuffled and kicked and pranced and twirled, now and then snatching Mrs. Kennan around the waist and spinning her around in bewildering mazes, then dropping her suddenly, while she smiled and looked pretty, as if she knew all about it and with wonderful agility got out of the way of the other couples.

"One old woman, dancing with a boy young enough to be her grandson, interested me specially. She moved nothing but her feet but they went like lightening. Her face was set like flint, her hands hung straight down and she danced as if her life were at stake. It all seemed more like some religious ritual than something done for amusement. At intervals one of the men would snap his fingers or crash down with one heel but always with the same solemnity, not a smile on a single face or a word exchanged at any time.

"This dance was called the 'Scottish Eights' and was followed by the 'Scottish Fours' and the 'Scottish Twos.' My old woman wiped her face and went in for every dance. When I thanked her, she did not understand a word as she spoke only Gaelic. A man at her side answered for her, 'Oh, she's all right,' from which I gathered he didn't understand much more than she. After a time, the loft got very hot and Gardiner took me home, but I felt that my old woman was still at it, with her set face and hanging arms, like a dancing doll worked by strings."[8]

While Mabel worked to organize the social life of Baddeck, Aleck pursued his relentless quest for knowledge and understanding about life. Why did the wind blow, the earth turn and birds fly? In 1891, he had reached the age of forty-four, in the prime of life, robust health, rich and world famous, a huge bear of a man with the compulsive curiosity and intransigence of a child. People who met him for the first time came away with the impression that a gentleman of such courteous, friendly and gregarious nature must have hundreds of intimate friends. It was a false impression that he cultivated carefully. In reality, Aleck had few friends outside of Mabel and his immediate family. He preferred it that way. Most people bored him, although he was always careful not to offend. Outsiders were kept politely at arm's length.

However, there was one friend with whom he was close—one Samuel Pierpont Langley, from Boston. Langley, who was twelve years older than Aleck, was a self-taught mathematical genius, an astronomer and a physicist. In 1866, at the age of thirty-two, he became professor of mathematics at the U.S. Naval Academy. Later, director of the Allegheny Observatory in Pittsburgh, and still later, secretary of the Smithsonian Institute. He founded the Smithsonian Astrophysical Observatory and invented the bolometer, a sensitive electrical thermometer with which he mapped the invisible infra-red region of the sun's spectrum. A painfully shy bachelor with a gruff exterior, Langley had few close friends—except, of course, for Aleck.

Aleck and Langley shared a common curiosity about flying. How was it possible for a seagull to remain aloft for hours at a time, effortlessly riding the air currents? The notion of man being able to fly, or a machine capable of performing like a bird, was regarded as pure fantasy by theorists. Four centuries earlier, Leonardo da Vinci had written: "There shall be wings. If the accomplishment be not mine then it is for some other." Langley and Aleck had examined several of Da Vinci's sketches for flying machines, one of them a helicopter. Surely modern man could turn Leonardo's vision into a reality.

A year earlier—from his Volta Prize money—Aleck had made a five thousand dollar donation to the Smithsonian Institute. Officially, the money was for the Smithsonian Astrophysical Observatory, but instead was used by Langley, with Aleck's approval, on aeronautical experiments. It was money well spent. In 1891, Langley gave a series of lectures in Washington on his aeronautical experiments. Mabel reported the news: "I wish you were here if only to attend the National Academy meetings and to hear the discussion on Professor Langley's flying machines. Of course the papers treat him more respectfully than they would anyone else, still they cannot resist a sly joke now and again."[9]

Gardiner Hubbard had complained long ago that Aleck never settled down to one thing. Aleck supposed that it was true. He moved restlessly from nature studies to genetics, from medicine to physics and electricity. And now, with Langley's experiments driving him one of his childhood fascinations had again surfaced—the possibility of manned flight.

~

Mabel wore a tight-fitting gold cotton dress with an immaculate white apron. She carried a basket with a few gardening tools and gloves. During late May in Washington, Aleck knew he could always find his wife in the garden, laying out the new flower beds and supervising the planting of the roses. Every winter several died and had to be replaced.

"What do you think—a few more rose bushes over here?" she asked as Aleck approached.

"Wherever you chose to put them, my dear."

"You're no help at all. I hope you'll be more help when I get to Baddeck."

Aleck frowned slightly, "When you get to Baddeck? Aren't we going together?"

Mabel put down her basket and came to him. For the first time he noticed how serious she looked, an expression he knew well. It meant that she had made a decision about something. "I've been thinking," she began.

"You looked troubled. I thought you'd be elated now that Elsie is home.

"I am elated. It's only that I think—well, it might be best if she doesn't return to the familiar quite so suddenly."

"You want us to go to Baddeck earlier?"

Mabel shook her head. "No, I want to take the girls to Europe. I've spoken with Elsie's doctor and now that she is completely back to health, he thinks its a wonderful idea."

"But my dear, I haven't time. I must see to the sheep experiments and to my flight tests. I have papers to write."

"I knew you'd say that. But I'm convinced this trip is a must for Elsie, Aleck. I hate to leave you, I hate being separated, but I know it's the right thing to do."

He looked into her wonderfully determined eyes. She didn't need to tell him that she'd miss him and certainly she knew he'd miss her. Whenever they were apart, they wrote almost every day. Together, they acted as one. If Mabel believed the trip was necessary for Elsie, then it must be. "Take Thompson with you. I'll go to Beinn Bhreagh and wait for you."

Mabel smiled, stood on her tiptoes, and kissed him. "Thank you, darling" she whispered.

———

"To fly, to soar, to ride the currents of the wind...." Like a lad of twelve, Aleck lay in the grass, his eyes fastened above, where a gull dipped and floated, catching a current, and then allowing itself to be lifted, seemingly without effort.

Beside him, Samuel Langley lay back equally fascinated. He was fifty-three, twelve years older than Aleck; nonetheless, they were at this moment two boys of great imagination. They lay on a grassy slope at the rear of Langley's home on the outskirts of Washington. The Ptomac River flowed close by.

"I think flying is my one scientific interest that actually interests me." Aleck told his friend.

"Flying must be some kind of primordial desire. Everyone admits to the fantasy now and again," Langley answered, chuckling.

"It can be more than fantasy," Aleck insisted.

"Yes, and pity the man who proves it. Look at the thanks you've received for the telephone. Lawsuits, hearings, doubters and public ridicule. Our work, yours and mine has to be kept secret, lest others steal it."

"Or laugh at it," Aleck added. It was true—his patent troubles continued. But nonetheless the telephone kept growing in popularity and he grew richer and more famous as a result. All blessings were mixed, of that he was certain.

"I have completed several gliding models, Aleck. One of them flies—at least sometimes."

Aleck turned away from the gull. "Are you going to show me?" he asked, unable to contain his excitement.

Langley pulled himself up to a sitting position. "I was afraid you wouldn't ask."

"As pleasant as lying in the sweet grass discussing flight is, I would rather witness it."

Langley stood. "I planned a demonstration when you said you were coming."

Aleck struggled to his feet, aware that he had put on a little more weight.

He followed Langley into a shed where glider models of all shapes and sizes were scattered about on work tables. "Of course they're small," he said as Aleck ran about like a child in a candy store examining the treasures.

"You've been hiding this light from me under a bushel! Let me see one fly. This is the most exciting thing that has happened to me since Watson said he heard me call him over the wire! I'll have to build some models of my own when I get back to Baddeck! I can't keep out of it!"

Langley grinned. "I never expected you to keep out of it."

Aleck laughed. "Oh, Sam, this will make Mabel happy."

Langley, as fearful of public ridicule and failure as Aleck, allowed no one but Aleck to examine his models. After seeing several of the small, frail craft actually glide and fly, he could barely contain his excitement. "Langley's flying machines; they flew for me today. I shall have to make experiments on my own account in Cape Breton. Can't keep out of it. It will be all UP with us someday!"[10]

A few months later, Aleck began testing crude models of flying machines of his own, searching for the elusive principles of flight. It was a search that would occupy much of his time in one way or another for the rest of his life.

"Faster! Run faster!" Aleck shouted to the enthusiastic boy who had become his legs for the moment.

Across the open field, young Douglas McCurdy, Arthur's son, ran with the kite, then released it. It caught an updraft of wind and soared above the wildflowers that carpeted the field behind Beinn Bhreagh.

Aleck studied it carefully as it rose. It was a new model, one of several he had designed in his workshop—known locally as "the warehouse." Most of the time his kite flying, with young Douglas's assistance, was for scientific purposes. But on a rare day in June, it was an exciting way for two boys— one of whom had a grey beard— to pass the time.

Mabel and the girls were still in Europe. Aleck had returned to Baddeck, eager to begin his own experiments with flight. He began by using kites to study the principles of flight: then he built several flying machine models designed to utilize a steam engine as the power source, but none of them had proved able to lift a flying machine into the air. He soon realized that the engines were much too heavy for the power they developed. But he was getting closer to realizing his latest dream. Only last night he had written optimistically to Mabel,

"Although numerous attempts to fly have been attended with only indifferent success on account of a leaky boiler, I have the feeling that this machine may possibly be the father of a long line of vigorous descendants that will plow the air from Beinn Bhreagh to Washington—and perhaps revolutionize the world. Who can tell? Think of the telephone."[11]

Again his eyes sought the sky and the kite. He was so intent on watching it that he didn't notice Arthur McCurdy coming toward him.

"That one flies well."

Aleck whipped around. "You startled me, I thought I was alone with talking flowers."

McCurdy laughed and pointed towards young Douglas, "My son adores these afternoons."

"Your son adores flight," Aleck replied.

"He says he wants to go to university and study engineering."

"Then he must," Aleck urged. "He is as bright as a new penny. He has a future in science."

"Are you sure?"

"You and I may not live to fly, Arthur, but young Douglas will. I know it."

Arthur nodded. Alexander Graham Bell, the famous man of science, remained a bit of a boy, with the eclectic curiosity of the young.

CHAPTER EIGHTEEN

Beinn Bhreagh, Fall 1894

The autumn leaves bathed the trees in vivid orange, yellows and reds. Against the green firs and the ice-blue lake, the glorious hardwoods were a scene to behold. Autumn's seasonal splendour ranged from Cape Breton south to the Berkshires of Massachusetts and west to the Great Lakes. Whatever the magnificence of the Rockies, the lure of the islands, or the sweet smell of blossoms in the orange groves of California, no part of the continent could rival the northeast in autumn. Frosty mornings and golden days painted the world with vibrant colours, a festival of nature before the white snows of winter.

"They're calling it the "Bell Palace at Baddeck," Mabel told Aleck.

Aleck, dressed in his woollies and tweed jacket, gazed fondly at Beinn Bhreagh Hall, their recently completed home. He supposed that by any standards it was a magnificent structure, and by maritime standards it was indeed a palace.

"You deserve the credit, Mabel. I could never have organized it all."

"Your plans," she reminded him. Together, they had chosen exactly where the windows were to be placed. If one view seemed unsatisfactory, then another was chosen and the plans readjusted. Everyone thought it a very odd way to build a house, but it had worked. The view was perfect from every window in all directions.

"It's what I've always dreamed of," Aleck said, softly. "A house with everything a man could desire, and bounteous nature right outside the doorstep."

The place was huge. It had turrets and balconies, a cedar-shingle roof sprinkled with chimney tops—ten small ones and a large main vent from the living room—and room enough for twenty-six guests as well as their own family and the servants.

"The house is like you," Mabel said, wondering whether Aleck realized how much it reflected his eccentricities—both practical and impractical. His personality seemed to fill every room.

The heart of the house was the study, a book-lined cocoon—a typical overstuffed Victorian library. Beinn Bhreagh Hall was a magnification of his beloved Milton Cottage— the place he had so adored in his youth—and its completion fulfilled his boyhood dreams of creating his own special place amidst the wild beauty of unspoiled nature.

They were returning from an early morning walk, and Aleck seemed relatively calm and undistracted. Mabel knew from long experience how hard it was to get his undivided attention, because his mind moved so quickly from one thing to another.

Seizing the moment, she said firmly, "Aleck, I've decided to take the girls to Europe in the spring."

"But you only just returned from a trip abroad." He raised a bushy brow and looked down at her quizzically.

"That was a pleasure trip. This is strictly for educational purposes. First, I want them to learn French. And naturally they must visit the Tate Gallery, ... spend time some in the British Museum and the Louvre. Besides language classes they ought to take special classes to improve their social graces."

Had he been talking with anyone else, he probably would have made a noncommittal sound, but as Mabel couldn't hear him, his inclination to express mild disdain was thwarted. He either had to object, or approve. "I suppose if you think it's necessary," he said finally.

"I do. I want to keep the girls in Paris for at least a month and let them explore the city and learn its history. I've thought of putting them in the Convent of the Sacred Heart for a few months—as boarders. That would be the fastest way to acquire the language, don't you agree?"

"I suppose," he said absently.

"Will you come?"

Her dark eyes searched his and he looked back at her. At the moment he wanted to pursue flight experiments—they filled his thoughts and held his imagination captive. He wanted to spend all the time he could on them. "I can't come right away," he hedged. "I really think it would be best if you went and I joined you later ... perhaps in a few months."

"We are always separated. ..."

He drew her to him and ran his hand through her dark hair, "We are always together in spirit, my dear."

"I feel I must do this for the girls."

"Then you must do it," he agreed.

⁓

Aleck sat at his desk. The lamp cast shadows in the dimly lit room. "It's like a tomb," he said aloud to no one. Some weeks before, Mabel, Elsie and Daisy, accompanied by Charles Thompson, had left for Europe. His teenage girls were both tall and straight, and dark-haired beauties like their mother. Letters from Mabel came at regular intervals. He plucked the first letter he'd received from her written aboard the ship.

"... People seem to question my right to be the mother of 'those tall girls.' ... Elsie has looked very handsomely and talked right and left in broken French, Italian and English with an ease and composure of manner that amazed me. After all I don't think she will be a wallflower. Daisy is more quiet but she is a dear, thoughtful child and seems to have more heart than I gave her credit for...."[1]

His eyes strayed to her closing lines, "If only I might dare to expect letters from you often, much of the loneliness of exile would be gone. I wish I knew where you were today —Washington or Beinn Bhreagh?"

Two weeks later she had written again with more news about Elsie and Daisy. Her third letter, in response to his, discussed Aleck's favorite topic—manned flight. "I think I understand your experiments even if I don't know the higher mathematics. I think I could explain how you worked out that curve if you left me alone long enough to

digest it in my own way. At last I believe thoroughly in you, Alec dear
... at last you have come up with something that I can understand."[2]

He corresponded with Langley continually. They traded information on their latest thoughts and the results of experiments. Working
with young McCurdy, he reworked, revised and revisited his own
experiments, then dispatched the results for Langley to consider. Yet,
as the summer days grew longer, he missed Mabel more and more.
He wrote and suggested he come to Paris sooner than they had originally planned.

She replied: "I am glad to say the conviction never wavers that as
far as my children's welfare is concerned I did right to come. If I
doubted that I should be horribly homesick. I took the children to the
Louvre this morning and we spent an hour among the naked statues.
Both were vastly edified thereby and somewhat to my horror
improved their knowledge of natural history on a point at which it
has hitherto been deficient. It seems to me there used to be leaves
about and there are none any more. I don't think their absence an
improvement."

He had smiled the first time he had read it, and now he smiled
again. Personally, he'd always thought leaves covering the organs of
statues silly, but supposed their absence had forced Mabel to provide
explanations to their daughters that she'd have preferred to avoid.

He read on to the pertinent point. She didn't seem to think he
should come over earlier than planned.

"Leave them here quietly for another month or two and then come
and take them and show them the wonders of Switzerland. They will
come closer to you than ever before and you will help as you could
in no other way. If you come now, it would be a great delight to have
you with us, but as far as the children learning French is concerned,
we might as well go back to Baddeck if you were here with us. The
only thing to do would be for you and me to go off travelling and
leave the children here alone, which would be a melancholy thing all
around. On the other hand, it is dreadfully hard to have you all alone
at Beinn Bhreagh and be away for so long. But we are in earnest in
the object for which we crossed the ocean, I can't see anything for it
but to continue as we are.

"If you come later, we will have such a good time together that it will pay for your temporary separation now. You will not be harassed with the feeling that you have run away from the Annual Convention of the Teachers of the Deaf and I will not feel that I have needlessly interfered with your flying-machine experiments. Please remember that I am more interested in them than anything you have done for years, and I would feel half my joy in our reunion spoilt if you left them."[3]

He scowled slightly. Mabel wasn't here, but in some way she was making him act responsibly—making him attend the convention and get on with his experiments. The scowl faded and a smile crept across his face. He had married her because he loved her and knew that she would always guide him gently, prodding him in the right direction. She was, of course, quite right as usual. He did have things to do. He would join them in August as they had arranged.

~

Aleck pulled on his trousers, bending over so that his head wouldn't hit the bulkhead of Sam Langley's houseboat. The cabins were large enough, but he was bigger than the average man, and thus the cabin seemed small and confined.

"Peripatetic." Aleck rolled the word off his tongue, deciding it was, in fact, the perfect word to describe his life, since he travelled from place to place and always seemed on the go.

He had joined the family in August as planned and they had all remained in Europe till late fall. Then, as seemed natural, they tired of hotels, strange beds and living out of suitcases. They returned to Washington for a traditional Thanksgiving and Christmas. Daisy and Elsie were sent to boarding school because Mabel wanted them to get into the habit of studying once again, while Aleck resumed his routine of lectures, experiments and business travel. Their whirlwind of travels had not affected Elsie in the least. Her St. Vitus Dance had gone, finally— never to return.

Not that this was a business trip, he thought happily. No, this little excursion to Quantico, Virginia was pure pleasure—with a purpose. And what a purpose! Today, he hoped, might be the first step towards a revolution in transportation.

He buttoned his shirt and pulled on a light jersey. Americans insisted on calling them sweaters, but he was set in his ways. In Scotland, they were jerseys, and it was a name to which he clung. In fact, he always corrected Americans when they used the word "sweater," and sometimes, if he felt they could benefit, he delivered a short lecture on the origin of the garment that proved the validity of its name.

He tied his shoes and then squinting into a tiny tin mirror, casually racked through his beard. No need to primp unnecessarily, since the only person about was Langley. When he had arrived at his friend's houseboat, moored on the Potomac, he had assumed that others from the scientific world would arrive later. He and Langley ate a leisurely lunch on deck, and he'd asked Sam when the others were due to arrive.

Sam had looked shocked. "Aleck, my machines are still imperfect—I couldn't stand the mortification of having them fail in front of a group of sceptical academics and scientists. You're the only one I've invited, because you understand the true potential of flight, and because I trust you."

He had considered Langley's words, then told him he understood. Looking back at his own experience with the telephone, he could only approve of his friend's reticence. Many academics, scientists and members of the press were unthinking and overly harsh critics. They wanted instant success and instant answers to complicated problems. If such were not forthcoming, they became negative. "Nay sayers," he muttered to himself, as he headed for deck.

"Good! You're up!" Sam said enthusiastically. "How did you sleep?"

"Like a baby. Hearing the water lap against the side of the boat lulled me to sleep. Fortunately the bed is longer than the ceiling is high."

Langley gave a rare chuckle. Then, colouring slightly, he confided, "I'm as giddy as a schoolboy."

"So am I, Sam. Let's get on with it, I can hardly wait." Aleck picked up his satchel of photographic equipment. "Documentation is all important," he reminded his colleague, then clambered down the side into a row boat.

"I'll signal you with three waves as soon as I'm set up. Then you launch the aircraft."

"If only it flies," Langley said.

Aleck rowed a few hundred yards, shipped his oars and set up his camera equipment. When all was ready, he signalled with a wave.

Langley started the model aircraft's tiny steam engine. The sound of its whirling propeller drifted across the water. Aleck held his breath as Langley launched the machine off the stern of the houseboat. It dipped momentarily; the nose tilted towards the river then rose to soar effortlessly into a climbing turn in the clear morning sky. Aleck managed to snap one perfect picture as it passed overhead.

"I got it!" he shouted and stood up in the row boat waving his arms excitedly. Langley returned his waves. Both men were laughing triumphantly. Minutes passed as the aircraft climbed higher and higher into the morning sky; then abruptly its motor stopped, and its spiral led slowly into the river. Aleck plucked it to safety, then rowed back to the houseboat as fast as he could.

"This is one of the most memorable days of my life," he said exclaimed jubilantly. "It was like an enormous bird."

"It flew exactly as my mathematical calculations for the design of its airfoil predicted!" said Langley. "It worked!"

"I must change the direction of my own experimentation," Aleck reflected aloud—the ideas now rushing through his mind. "Instead of trying to solve the entire challenge of flight, I think I should work piecemeal on the principles of aeronautics. It seems the central difficulty that has to be overcome is building a large machine that has sufficient wing surface to allow it to fly." After having seen unmanned flight, he was convinced that manned flight could not be far away. However, before there could be manned flight, wing surfaces would have to be increased in size in order to carry the additional weight.

⁓

The rosewood clock on the wall struck one in the morning. Aleck stopped pouring over his papers a moment and waited for what he regarded as "a confounded contraption," to stop its infernal bonging.

Again, he reminded himself to remove the offending clock from his otherwise peaceful workshop.

A smile creased his lips. Some years earlier, in 1880' Mark Twain had attacked the telephone in a sarcastic combat—in fact, Aleck's revolutionary invention continued to be the butt of much of Twain's humour. Aleck went to his bookshelf and took down a volume. From inside its yellowed pages he withdrew three clippings. Although he could never find anything—his notes were a mess, he didn't know nor could he locate anything he'd done yesterday—he somehow knew where he had put these clippings. He unfolded them carefully so as not to tear the brittle paper. The first was from the Christmas edition of *The New York World* with a special note of good wishes from Mark Twain.

Aleck laughed aloud as he read it for the first time in years. He had thought it funny at the time, and he still did. "And I am quite sure, Mr. Twain," he said aloud as he refolded the clippings, "neither you nor I believe in heaven or in hell."

Again, he glanced at the clock. Well, if Mark Twain hates me for inventing the telephone, he thought, then I personally curse the inventor of the clock—most especially the inventor of clocks that strike each hour as a reminder that one's life and precious time are passing.

He rummaged around on his desk—things were such a mess! Where were his notes? The weight of Langley's flying machine had increased by eight times while its wing surface area had only doubled. "Somehow," he muttered, "the ratio of surface area to weight has to be evened out."

He had come back to Baddeck directly from Virginia and for days— or more accurately nights—immersed himself in studying kites and aerodynamics. "Drat! Where are my notes?"

He took up his pen and wrote a note to Arthur McCurdy. "Our work is actually in a chaotic condition. This is entirely my own fault, and I sympathize with you in having to work with such an unsystematic man as myself.... My time does not correspond to any one else's time, and I was never willing to face everyday matters in a proper season."[4]

Aleck stopped thinking about flight. What he needed was a grand plan to reorganize himself and his workshop. As if seized by the demon of good planning, he began making lists of things to be done in order of importance. He would discuss everything with Arthur tomorrow, he decided.

It was late afternoon and Aleck stormed about his workshop, picking up this, and putting that aside. He had slept late because he had stayed up till the first light of dawn. Around noon he had gotten up and gone out with his kites, then returned to the workshop. Arthur McCurdy watched in silence as Aleck rooted through the clutter.

"I had a reorganization plan," Aleck muttered. "I wrote it last night. I made lists—Drat!"

All his searching yielded only the note to Arthur, in which he blamed himself for his extreme disorganization.

"I can't find anything," he muttered.

Arthur stood calmly by watching. It was no surprise to him that his employer's lists of reorganizational priorities had already disappeared into an unknown corner. The man was chronically disorganized, and while McCurdy thought it an incurable condition, he excused it as a side-effect of genius.

"As you can't find your lists, I have a suggestion," he said carefully.

Aleck stopped rummaging and looked up with interest. "Anything," he said, flopping into a chair.

"Rather than lists, I propose a set of principles. I've printed them out and if you can follow them, I'm certain we can straighten things out."

"Principles?"

Arthur nodded and unfolded a large piece of paper on which he had printed his three principles. He proceeded to hang it on the wall. "Now," he said clearing his throat, "in order to get anything done, you must come to the office in some sort of season, and not put off office work until three or four in the afternoon. That's principle number one."

Aleck grimaced and waved his hand for Arthur to continue.

"Don't take letters away from the files of the office and expect me to find them when they are wanted. And finally: don't take unanswered letters away and expect me to find them."

"It seems simple enough."

"It is. Will you try?"

"I will. I promise."

Arthur smiled, knowing that this sudden urge to organize would soon be forgotten. Alexander Graham Bell was quite simply incapable of organizing himself along any specific lines despite the best intentions.

⁓

Mabel sat at her writing desk and surveyed the large pile of reception cards and invitations to tea that had begun coming in the mail shortly after the papers had announced Elsie's coming-out party to be held in two days time.

She had written to Aleck in Baddeck twice now—she shook her head. "If I live to be a hundred I'll never understand you," she said to herself.

"Mrs. Bell?"

Charles Thompson stood in the doorway. His hair was iron grey now. Mabel thought it gave him a distinguished appearance.

"I was just talking to myself, Charles."

"Have you heard from Professor Bell?"

"He's not coming. I'm not surprised."

"He's a busy man."

"We've been married twenty years and I still have trouble understanding him. He works intensely for months, usually by himself, then he spends long periods of time lounging about reading or doing nothing."

"I think he must empty his head creating things, then he has to rest awhile to refill it."

Mabel smiled at this explanation. "That seems to make sense," she allowed. "Still, Elsie's coming-out party is important. I had wanted him here. It's bad enough that Daisy is still in boarding school and won't be on hand. The absence of a sister is one thing, but the absence of a father is unacceptable."

"Plenty of others will be here, Mrs. Bell. We've sent out over 550 invitations."

"I don't suppose they'll all come. Gracious, I don't even know if the house can hold that many."

"We once had five hundred people to a party in the house on 19th Street and it was smaller than this one."

"I suppose you're right. I worry too much. Still, a young lady does only have one coming-out party. I want everything to be perfect."

"I'm sure it will be."

"Thank you for helping me arrange it, Charles."

"I've enjoyed it, ma'am."

Mabel smiled at Charles Thompson. He was one of the family, and she knew he felt the same. Over the years, she had grown to depend on him more and more.

"I just want you to know that I appreciate your help."

"Thank you. I did want to ask you something...."

"What is it?"

"I thought we would serve supper till eleven in the dining room, then clear the tables and make the room ready for dancing—unless of course you would prefer to serve the supper as a buffet."

"No, I think your idea is fine. I like it much better. Much more relaxed."

"I'll get on with the arrangements then."

After Thompson departed, Mabel wrote Daisy to tell her all about the plans for the party. She sighed. It just didn't seem right that Elsie would have her party without Aleck and Daisy there. "But I know you'll be there in spirit," she said, glancing at Aleck's picture. There was no point in trying to reform him at this stage in life. And in any case she was as excited about his experiments into flight as he was, so she could hardly blame him for not wanting to leave Baddeck.

⟳

As large as the house was, it still smelled throughout of fresh flowers. Mabel's hair was brushed out and hung loose almost to her tiny waist. She wore her long white nightdress, and over it a robe. It was late, very late, but she couldn't sleep.

"What a delightful evening," she thought and twirled about in her bedroom. How beautiful Elsie had looked, how perfectly everything had gone. She stopped at her desk and sat down. It was late, but perhaps it would help her sleep if she wrote a note to Daisy. She picked up her pen, and for a moment closed her eyes, recreating the evening's events in her mind's eye to describe to her youngest daughter.

"The party seems to have been a success," she wrote enthusiastically. "Elsie looked very pretty indeed. She had good colour and carried herself well. The poor child confessed that she had not slept much the night before, thinking that she would not get as many flowers as other debutantes—but she got quite a lot. There was one big bouquet of American beauties and lilies of the valley from Papa, which she carried. And another of pink roses from Grandmama. Pink carnations from Uncle Charlie; he really gave her the American beauties but exchanged with Papa as the carnations were all Papa could get and were not as becoming. Grandmama arranged the flowers in the parlor herself. There were at least 450 people in attendance. Dancing began about twelve and continued till two. Elsie was very pleased to be asked for the cotillion at the Bachelor's Ball."[5]

Mabel signed the letter and folded it, placing it in a small blue envelope. She leaned back in satisfaction. Soon Elsie would be courting—and Daisy would certainly not be far behind. Tears filled her eyes—not tears of unhappiness, but tears for the passing years. Where had the time gone? She reached over and picked up the sterling-silver model of the telephone that sat on the corner of her desk. She ran her fingers over it's smooth surface.

"This is perhaps the most historically interesting thing I have," she thought.[6] He'd had the memento made for her with the very first money he earned from his invention. What a wonderful life we have, she reflected. Even separated, they were together. And at Baddeck, life was truly wonderful. They were a close knit family of cousins, aunts and uncles. And one day soon, she thought, there will be grandchildren.

Mabel folded the letter to Daisy and left it on her desk to be posted. She climbed into bed and turned out the light. Tomorrow would bring her one day closer to the summer magic of Baddeck. She sighed with pleasure at the thought and then she slept.

CHAPTER NINETEEN

Baddeck, Summer 1897

"Glad to be home?" Aleck asked as they walked through the woods. It had become a tradition that as soon as they were together at Beinn Bhreagh, they skirted the mountain and walked along the path that paralleled the edge of the cliffs above the Bras d'Or Lakes.

"Never been more glad."

"You say that every year," he said as they plunged out from beneath the northern pine and into the sunlit field.

"I know, and every year it's true. We're going to have a lot of company this year."

"We always have a lot of company."

"You love it," she teased. "You need a large audience when you hold court."

He gave her shoulder a squeeze. "So who are we entertaining this year?"

"Young George Totten is coming up."

"Elsie's would-be-beau?"

"I suppose he is courting her, though I wish he wouldn't."

"I like him. He's a good fellow—kind and gentle and up to anything."

"I like him too," Mabel was quick to answer.

"You can't object to his profession. An architect is an honest creative vocation."

"I don't dislike him and I don't object to his profession."

Aleck stretched out on the grass, "If you don't dislike him and you don't object to his profession, why on earth are you sorry he's courting Elsie?"

Mabel unfolded a lap tartan she had been carrying and spread it out on the ground. She gathered her long skirt around her and sat down next to him. "I'm just concerned, that's all."

"Are you going to confide the nature of your concern?"

"Elsie is young, Aleck."

"Not as young as you were when I fell in love."

"I know, but I can't help worrying. I think she needs to meet more young men before she makes any kind of decision."

Aleck raised his brow and waited for her to continue.

"I mean, she has no standard of comparison."

"Ah! So you have a plan to solve this omission?"

Mabel pressed her lips together and nodded. "I'm going to invite the Grosvenor twins up for a few weeks—while George is here."

Aleck gave hearty laugh. The Grosvenor family were old friends. He and Mabel had been invited down to Amherst College when the Grosvenor boys graduated. Both lads had received the highest academic honours. Their father, a former professor of history at Amherst, had been appointed the editor of the National Geographic publication at Gardiner's insistence. Hubbard had been president of the National Geographic Society since the magazine's inception in 1888. The Society's membership, however, was very small and comprised mainly of scientists and their associates. The magazine's articles were always well written but in the dullest of academic prose. Somehow, it had managed to survive the first few critical years. Then, as the quality of the society's lecturers began to improve, there was a renewed interest in the magazine. Aleck and Gardiner both liked and respected Grosvenor whose two sons just happened to be eligible bachelors.

"You never gave Edwin and Gilbert much thought until we were in Amherst," Aleck reminded her.

"Well, frankly it hadn't occurred to me then."

"What hadn't occurred to you? Matchmaking?"

"I am not matchmaking," she answered, a trifle indignantly. "I simply want Elsie to have some choice, some measure of comparison. Is that so wrong?"

"Not at all."

"But I must say any one of them will make a fine catch."

"Men are not fish," he told her solemnly.

"I know that!"

"Ah, but you want to put them in a bowl so Elsie can see them all swim together."

"You're impossible," she said, turning her head towards the ocean.

Aleck rolled over on his back and looked at the sky. He smiled to himself. Mabel was plotting, no doubt about it.

⁓

The Governor General of Canada, Lord Aberdeen, and his wife together with Premier Murray of Nova Scotia were coming to visit the Bells at Beinn Bhreagh. The weather was frightful.

Sheets of heavy rain swept the landscape. Mabel could barely see the road in front of the house. She stared out the window anxiously.

"Terrible," muttered Mrs. Kennan. "And after all the work the townspeople did decorating Baddeck!"

Mabel glanced at the clock, and shrugged. "It's almost two o'clock. Why aren't they here yet?"

"You're just nervous," Mrs. Kennan said patiently. "Mind you, you've got a right to be nervous. It's not often the Governor General of Canada and the premier of the province come to call at the same time."

"And heaven knows who else," Mabel murmured. No sooner had all the eligible young bachelors departed from Beinn Bhreagh than a steamer bearing the governor general and his entourage had arrived in port.

She had been working feverishly all morning to ready things in time for lunch at one; indeed that was why she had not gone to the reception in town but had sent Aleck. One simply did not have so many people to lunch without preparations. She had instructed the servants to extend the dining-room table to its full length and add another leaf by putting in half of another table. She had prepared settings for thirty. The table itself was a masterpiece, decorated with immense quantities of hydrangea, marigolds and sweet peas. At twelve-thirty, she had to ask Mrs. Kennan to come over and help, so that everything would be ready on time. Now all was prepared and her important guests were late. Worse yet, it was still raining and running rivers of mud lay between the road and the front door.

"Oh, here they come!" Mabel exclaimed, turning away from the window and hurrying for one last look in the mirror. She poked at her hair and smoothed her dress.

The buckboard clattered to a halt at the front door and its occupants, under the shelter of umbrellas, alighted and gingerly made their way across the muck and into the house.

Aleck, Lord and Lady Aberdeen, their daughter, Lady Marjorie and their aide-de-camp, Lt. Keane of the Royal Navy, were all in the buckboard. Premier Murray and the others followed in a collection of carriages. Like a mob of drenched sea birds they streamed through the front door.

Mabel glanced nervously upstairs. Georgia, the maid, stood on the landing to guide the ladies if they wished to refresh themselves; Rose stood at the head of the stairs. Lady Aberdeen looked about expectantly. She saw the two maids but made no move to climb the stairs.

"My wife, Mrs. Bell," Aleck said, introducing Mabel.

Mabel curtsied ever so slightly. These were, after all, Queen Victoria's representatives in the Dominion of Canada.

"Will you see me upstairs?" Lady Aberdeen asked imperiously.

Mabel immediately whirled around and led her guest up to the powder room. "Help yourself to anything you need," she said politely.

"What did you say? I can't understand your accent."

"She said to help yourself to anything you need. She has no accent, Mama."

Mabel looked gratefully at Lady Marjorie. She had understood her, and also seemed able, and indeed willing, to look after herself.

Lady Aberdeen took off her coat, washed up, combed her hair and then swept out of the room as haughtily as she had entered. Mabel followed in her wake.

Lord Aberdeen was a slight, fidgety man, neither as tall nor as big as his wife. Mabel noted his incredible nervousness. He appeared much worse than Elsie had been when she was at the absolute height of her chorea; he moved constantly and talked incessantly about noth-ing in particular.

Mabel tried to be everywhere at once. She turned quickly to Aleck. "You're over an hour late, we're more than ready," she said urgently. "No one seems to understand me, Aleck. Help me get these people lined up properly. You take Lady Aberdeen."

The moment Aleck took Lady Aberdeen's arm, Lord Aberdeen took Mabel's and rushed her into the dining room. Without paying the slightest attention to the prearranged seating arrangements he plopped himself down in a chair.

This was not the way it was supposed to be, Mabel thought. He was not supposed to sit till she sat, but there he was sitting and already talking. She sat too, not knowing what else to do as the confused guests searched the long table for their places.

Mrs. Kennan came in with the premier and sat next to Lord Aberdeen. Mabel felt relieved that the sole responsibility of making conversation with Lord Aberdeen would not rest with her.

After what seemed an interminable time, lunch was served. Premier Murray was a man of very few words. He nodded and answered questions with "yes," or "no," then lapsed into stony silence. Lord Aberdeen, on the other hand, talked continuously—so much that poor Mrs. Kennan had to stop eating and devote herself entirely to the governor general. Across the table, Aleck and Lady Aberdeen and Miss McCurdy appeared to be having a good time, but poor Elsie, seated next to the stiff-backed aide-de-camp, found the handsome young officer to be utterly devoid of conversation. He stared sol-emnly straight ahead. Periodically he would glance at his timepiece. Finally, he interrupted Aberdeen in mid-sentence.

"Excellency, aren't we supposed to be at Gertrude Hall at three?"

"I already told the ladies that you wouldn't be there before three-thirty," Mrs. Kennan interjected. "In any case, even if you're later, people will understand. In fact, the club officers are all here so not to worry."

Lady Aberdeen lifted her brows archly.

The servants had just begun to serve the duck when Mabel ob-served that as soon as Lady Aberdeen had lifted her brows, Lord

Aberdeen stopped eating and became doubly agitated. Suddenly, he stood up and escorted Lady Aberdeen into the hall. When they returned they muttered something about keeping schedules. Mabel strained to understand what was being said, but before she knew it, the whole party seemed to be leaving. And with lunch only half over!

Aleck squeezed her arm, and Mabel turned to face him.

"Don't worry," he said, making sure she could see his lips to read them. "I'll arrange for Lord Aberdeen to remain here with me. You take all the ladies to Gertrude Hall and then come back for tea."[1]

"Didn't they like the lunch?" Mabel asked.

"I'm sure they would have liked it. It would seem that to them schedules are schedules and must be obeyed. They don't understand how life works here."

Mabel shrugged. Lord Aberdeen was fast becoming a nervous wreck while his overbearing wife was impossible to please. "Good," Mabel whispered. "If they liked the place or understood how things worked they might want to come more often. Now that would be a tragedy!"

Aleck winked. "Our paradise will remain unspoiled."

The study of her parent's Washington home was not so homey as theirs, Mabel thought. And tonight it seemed deserted. She felt alone and bewildered. She glanced down at the letter she had been writing.

"I can't see why my father should be ill past recovery now. He is not old as men go nowadays, and he has lived such a healthy life."

She finished the letter to Mrs. Kennan and put it in the envelope. She stood up and walked through the quiet house. Although she had visited a hundred times it never seemed like a home—perhaps because her parents had moved here after she had married and left home. Her first and only home—other than Benn Bhreagh—would always be the house in Cambridge. She stood by the window for a moment watching the cold December rain that seemed to penetrate every joint and bone.

She thought about her father, always such an active man. Lately, he had slowed and was given to shuffling to his library to nap in the great armchair. He had always worked simultaneously on a dozen or more projects, but it had been months since he'd done any of that.

Mabel climbed the stairs to her father's room. She opened the door a crack and looked in. The nurse smiled at her.

"I'll sit with him for a while," Mabel said softly and the nurse nodded and slipped past her, grateful for a break.

Mabel sat down. "Papa," she whispered.

He turned his head toward her, but seemed unable to open his eyes.

"Oh, Papa!" A chill ran right through her. He looked as if he were dying. But wouldn't the nurse have said something? She sat, frozen to her chair, unable to move, unable even to call her mother. He breathed on laboriously and twice he said her name, though he still didn't open his eyes.

The clock ticked on—nearly half an hour passed and the nurse opened the door.

"He's very tired tonight," she said quietly.

"I thought he was dying."

The nurse shook her head, but Mabel knew she wanted to say, "Not yet."

Morning came and Mabel and her sister and mother gathered around the breakfast table.

"He's much stronger this morning," Grace, Mabel's younger sister, announced. "I was in his room early and he was reading."

"Thank heaven," Mrs. Hubbard said, half under her breath.

"Maybe he will get better," Mabel said, although she didn't believe it. But neither could she bring herself to believe that he would die. They ate in near silence, then Mabel took the morning shift. She sat with him for three hours. Most of the time she just held his hand, but sometimes she read to him even though she knew that her articulation was difficult to understand. But if anyone could make out her speech as well as Aleck, it was her father.

Evening had fallen when her mother called them. She didn't say why, she didn't explain how she knew, she just told them to come. "It's nearly time," she whispered, her eyes full of tears.

They gathered round the bed. Her father's hands were folded across his chest and his breathing was heavy, though not laboured. Then, before their eyes, he simply stopped breathing.

Mabel watched—it was as if he had quietly fallen asleep. Then he was gone. Tears ran down Mabel's face. She couldn't help but feel that this was all a dreadful nightmare and that she would wake up and her father would laugh about it. But she knew that would never be.

Her mother wept silently. Her parents had always been so close. What would her mother do now that he wasn't there to hold her hand and read to her by the hour? In her mind she wondered what she would do without Aleck. She knew the answer. She really couldn't live without him.

There were only a selected few guests invited to the elegant annual dinner of the National Geographic Society. Mabel wore black, as did her mother. Both were still in mourning for the passing of Gardiner Hubbard. He had left an emptiness in their lives as well as vacancies at the various organizations he had headed. The one dearest to his heart had been the National Geographic Society.

Aleck had dressed formally—which made it a rare occasion indeed, Mabel thought. Their mutual interest in the National Geographic Society was one of the few enthusiasms that her father and her husband had shared amicably. The two volatile men had such different natures. Aleck did not realize how much, over the years, she and her mother had interceded with her father, while Gardiner never knew that both she and her mother had also been mediators with Aleck. A careful conspiracy had developed over time to keep peace in the family. It had worked.

Mabel looked at her mother, seated at the head of the table. Her black mourning dress looked stark next to the pure white tablecloth ... gracious Gertrude, fighting to hide her grief, forcing herself to maintain a social front. At home it was a different matter—there, she wore an austere black dress with an unnatural white at the throat and sleeves. She would sit for hours in Gardiner's chair trying to readjust her own life and the commitments her husband had made—trying to be brave and bright. But in the morning's glare her eyelids were always swollen and Gypsy, her dead sister's daughter, said she could hear her grandmother sobbing long into the night when no one could see her. Studying her mother's face, Mabel could see how she still struggled to accept that her husband was gone. Mabel, too, found it hard to accept the fact of her father's death.

Gardiner Hubbard had been more than just a husband and a father; he had been a force of nature in all of their lives. Everyone in the room that evening had been affected by him in some way. And where, she wondered, would she have ended up if he had not been the man he was? Her deafness had instigated his important contribution to education and charitable work. He had found Melville Bell, and Aleck—dear sweet Aleck.

She bit her lip. From the beginning, from that moment when, as a small girl, she awoke from her fever into a world of silence, her father had assumed she could lead a perfectly normal life; and he had seen to it that she did.

"How fortunate we are that your husband, Professor Bell, is taking over the National Geographic Society. His presidency will give us great prestige."

"Thank you," Mabel managed. The man who had spoken moved away and for that she was thankful ... one of the academics in the Society that her father had founded. She couldn't remember his name, although she was certain they had been introduced sometime in the past.

She felt her mother's hand on her arm and turned.

"It's good of Aleck to do this—to take over the Society. It meant so much to your father."

"I know," Mabel said. She herself wasn't sure whether she was glad or sorry. One more responsibility meant more meetings—more days, weeks and months away from her. Still, Aleck had only accepted because of her father. The continuation and success of the Society would, in many ways, be the most suitable memorial to Gardiner Hubbard. There were so many things that seemed to conspire to keep Aleck apart from her. And now, the good men of the Society, had in their wisdom nominated him to succeed her father as a Regent of the Smithsonian [2] as well.

Aleck made his way back to the table and sat down next to Mabel. He shook his head, "I've become the master of a sinking ship," he confided.

"The magazine?"

Aleck nodded. "It's seriously in debt and losing subscribers. It needs a full-time editor, and personally, I think it needs photographs to accompany the articles."

"Photographs?" Mabel repeated. It sounded like a novel idea. Certainly it would improve the magazine by making it more interesting. She had always felt that most of the learned articles were far too long and much too dull to interest more than a small, selected readership. Professor Grosvenor had never regarded his tenure as editor of the magazine to be any more than a part-time job. Now, with his retirement, he admitted to Aleck that the magazine needed new blood. Aleck had a sudden thought.

"I could get young Gilbert Grosvenor to give up his teaching job and take over."

Mabel smiled. "That would mean his moving to Washington, wouldn't it?"

Aleck winked. "Yes, it would mean that. I gather you approve … I mean as the official family matchmaker?"

"I can see the advantages."

Aleck didn't react, and she could see that his mind was already at work on plans for the magazine.

"It has limitless possibilities. There are at least thirty million people in this country under the age of twenty-one. We could make it of value to educators, a sort of current text on geography. And of course there could be popular books on geographic subjects."[3]

"Where will you find the time for all this? What about your experiments?"

"I'll have to put my kites away for the time being, perhaps underwrite a salary for young Grosvenor, and go to Washington and straighten the magazine out."

"And what are the goals of this magazine to be?" Mabel asked. She could sense his excitement about a new vision.

"The world and all that is in it!" he replied.

Mabel laughed gently. "Yes, it has no limits," she agreed.

⁓

Daisy looked out over the seventy-two assembled guests, seated eight to a table. The head table, where she sat with the wedding party, stood on a sort of dais and was bedecked with the most flowers. She surveyed a sea of white linen, glittering crystal and sparkling silver with satisfaction. Conversation among the guests was muted by the thick rugs on the floor and the high ceilings. The toasts were over, and impeccable British waiters passed silently around the tables, presenting plates laden with food.

They called it breakfast, but with endless flow of champagne, it seemed more what Americans these days were calling, "brunch"—a combination of a late breakfast and early lunch. She supposed the term had not yet reached England.

Poor mama—she had hoped that only thirty would attend this after-wedding breakfast, but everyday more people who simply "had" to be invited were added to the guest list. Thus, what had begun as a small wedding and breakfast, had grown into a much more elegant affair.

"Quite a bash," Edwin Grosvenor, her new brother-in-law, whispered in her ear.

"Indeed!" Daisy enthusiastically agreed.

"You've been travelling a lot since we last saw each other."

"As always," she smiled.

Two years had passed since grandfather Gardiner's death—two years of trips to and from Washington, Baddeck, boarding school and finally to Japan. Now the whole family was in England for Elsie's wedding.

"But to Japan! Now that is exotic! That's one trip I really envy you."

Daisy laughed. "We were all like giants. Japanese women are so petite. I felt absolutely huge and dreadfully awkward."

"Tell me more."

"Papa was invited to be honoured for his scientific work by the Emperor himself, if you can imagine it."

"Rather like an audience with the Queen."

"Mama said that going to Japan made her realize how famous daddy really is." Daisy giggled. "But oh, Edwin, papa hated dressing up! You know how he hates it! He was summoned to see the

Emperor at ten a.m. and he had to wear formal dress—and I do mean formal!—a silk hat and white gloves and a quite proper morning suit. We called him Daddy-San because he looked so—well, respectable. Everybody is called San in Japanese—Mama-San, Elsie-San, Edwin-San."

"He must have been aghast! A silk hat at ten in the morning?"

"Aghast is the word! He stayed up until four in the morning, and Charles had to get him up and dressed and off to the audience with the Emperor. Afterwards he came right home, took off all his finery and went back to sleep. When he woke up in the afternoon, he asked when his audience with the Emperor was. When Charles told him he'd already had it, daddy grumped that he was glad he wasn't awake."

"He seems wide awake enough now."

"He might have preferred an evening wedding. He's terrible in the morning because he stays up all night working. Mama says she'll never get used to the hours he keeps."

"He's a genius and one has to take that into consideration."[4]

"We do," Daisy replied smiling.

"Well, the wedding has been smashing, and Elsie looked wonderful."

Elsie had indeed made a stunning bride. She carried herself with queenly grace, stateliness and perfect composure. Her white satin and point lace dress was exquisite; she wore a veil and carried a bouquet of lilies of the valley and white heather with streamers falling to the floor.

"She's very much in love," Daisy confided quietly, " ... even though she didn't promise at the altar to obey him."

"She's beautiful and very modern," Edwin smiled. Then he winked at Daisy. "Very soon, my dear sister-in-law, your mama will begin looking for a husband for you."

Daisy shook her head. "I'm going to art school," she said firmly.

"You don't intend to marry?"

She laughed. "Not right away."

He shook his head. "You're another modern miss?"

"Very," Daisy replied firmly.

CHAPTER TWENTY

February 1901

It had turned out to be another grey morning in London, but mercifully milder than the usual depressing February days. Aleck, like most men in London, had dressed in black; his grey beard was trimmed and neat. Mabel too wore black and it made her look small and vulnerable.

"It seems impossible," Aleck muttered. "It seems like only yesterday that I had my audience with her."

"That was twenty-three years ago," Mabel reminded him.

Aleck touched his finger to his lips. "Shh! Don't remind me so exactly of the passing of time."

"I remember," he went on. "I had to set up two or three different lines in order to transmit conversation and music to the royal ears of her majesty. I nearly fell apart when one of the lines broke down— the one to Cowes for the singers. But the ones running through the Queen's Osbourne Cottage worked perfectly."

"That," Mabel said, "is when you committed your *faux pas.*"

Aleck's face reddened. He hated even now to be reminded of it, and he recalled it in excruciating detail. Just as Kate Field—an American performer engaged to sing into the phone for the occasion—was about to begin, her majesty looked the other way. Aleck, so used to touching Mabel in order to get her attention, had reached over and touched the Queen. Alas, no one touched the Queen—not ever! There were murmurs in the room, and headlines in all the British papers.[1]

"You called her, 'humpy, stumpy, dumpy,'" Mabel reminded him.

"I was angered that you weren't invited to attend."

"And I was disappointed. Remember ... I sent to Paris for a dress?"

Aleck patted her hand. "As I told you at the time, you didn't miss that much."

"Well, I should like to have seen her alive," Mabel said, then asked, "Did you read what Henry James wrote?"

"No."

Mabel opened her little black velvet bag and read a newspaper clipping. "'We all feel a bit motherless today. Mysterious little Victoria is dead and fat vulgar Edward is King.' He certainly doesn't like Edward."

"It's hard to replace a legend with a mere mortal. She was the idol of her people—and, of course, the longest reigning monarch in British history."

Mabel nodded in agreement.

"Ah, the procession is starting," Aleck told her, hearing the muffled drumbeat and the clopping of horses' hooves on the pavement.

They had very good seats and Mabel leaned forward not wanting to miss anything. The British certainly were the masters of pomp and ceremony, she thought; and she knew that Queen Victoria's funeral was an occasion like no other. Hundreds of soldiers passed in front of them, slow marching with guns reversed. Hundreds more troops lined the procession. They all stood as still as statues, their heads bared.

Mabel's world was always silent, but she knew that at this moment all of the great multitude around her were silent too. The soldiers passed, followed by the gun carriage and then the King, looking very grave. Behind Edward were the crowned heads and princes of Europe. The Kaiser had to rein in his horse so that the King could stay ahead of him. After them came a brilliant mass of variegated coloured uniforms—the troops of almost every monarch in Europe.[2]

"It's the end of an era," Mabel whispered.

Aleck patted her knee, "And the beginning of a new one."

Daisy met her future husband at one of her father's Wednesday evening receptions for distinguished scientific friends. She and Mabel would prepare the Washington house for these weekly affairs, and Aleck always took time to learn the interests of each guest. During the course of the evening he'd gently try to steer conversation so that everyone had a say.

On this occasion, Gil Grosvenor, who the family called Bert, had brought along his friend, David Grandison Fairchild, who came from a family of brilliant academics. His father had been president of both the Michigan and Kansas state agricultural colleges, his grandfather the founder of another college. David maintained the family interest in agriculture. After earning his master's degree from Kansas State, he'd gone abroad to study various European methods of agriculture. Bert had arranged that he give a National Geographic Society lecture during his brief stopover in Washington and attend the Wednesday night reception. The young man was seated next to Daisy during dinner, and he found her articulate, intelligent and striking. Daisy was equally attracted. The next day, Fairchild cancelled the rest of his trip and began a serious courtship. The love-struck couple were married the following April and lived for a year in the annex of the Bell house, while they built their own home on a large estate in Maryland.

Later that year, while Aleck and Mabel were abroad, they were surprised to learn that David Fairchild was already well known in Europe. Mabel wrote: "Oh Mama dear, I wish you were here with us. Not the least nice thing is to hear about my distinguished son-in-law, David Fairchild. He seems better known abroad than in Washington. Twice people have spoken to Alec of him and his great work, not knowing of his connection with us."[3]

⁓

In 1903, the Wright brothers had successfully flown their first manned aircraft at Kitty Hawk, South Carolina. *The Flyer* (later called the *Kittyhawk*) covered the astonishing distance of three hundred yards. With typical generosity of spirit, Aleck and Sam Langley were delighted by the news. Their success had made Aleck all the more determined to continue his own experiments until he solved what he considered the most serious obstacle to manned flight—lack of stability in the air.

His initial goal had been to build a kite that could carry the weight of a man, then increase the weight by adding a motor. It all took time. *Oionos* was the first of these new kites, followed by a long succession of various shapes and colours. The name meant a bird of omen in Greek, which appealed to Aleck's sense of drama. His next kite, a much stronger version of the first, he named the *Frost King*—in honour of Susan McCurdy's (Arthur McCurdy's daughter) marriage to Walter Frost.

In 1901, Helen Keller—by then a slim and beautifully poised twenty-one-year-old—had come to Beinn Bhreagh to visit. She had helped Aleck with his kites and wrote of the experience. "On one of them I noticed that the strings were of wire, and having had some experience in bead work, I said I thought they would break. Dr. Bell said 'No!' with great confidence, and the kite was sent up. It began to pull and tug, and lo, the wires broke, and off went the great red dragon, and poor Dr. Bell stood looking forlornly after it. After that he asked me if the strings were all right and changed them at once when I answered in the negative. Altogether we had great fun."[4]

Aleck was delighted by the accomplishments of this young woman in the years since Captain Keller had sought his advice. He carefully explained to Helen his various ideas and inventions. She loved his stories and his infectious zest for life. He told her: "One would think I had never done anything worthwhile but the telephone. That is because it is a money-making invention. It is a pity so many people make money the criterion of success. I wish my experiences had resulted in enabling the deaf to speak with less difficulty. That would have made me truly happy."[5] When Keller wrote her autobiography, she described perfectly the effect that Aleck's generosity of spirit had on people. "He makes you feel that if you only had a little more time you, too, might be an inventor."[6]

It wasn't until 1905 that the *Frost King* carried a man into the air. One of the Baddeck girls who helped at the Beinn Bhreagh laboratory, Mayme Morrison Brown, described the excitement.

"The *Frost King* ... that was a beautiful kite. One of the largest. I don't know how many hundred of cells there were in it.... That's the one that picked the man up—Neil MacDermid.... That was a surprise; it really was.... I think Dr. Bell knew it was going that day. They let the guy ropes go! Dr. Bell's father was there lying on a cot—old Melville Bell was a fine old man; he had big whiskers just like Dr. Bell but he didn't have Dr. Bell's keen black eyes—and Melville Grosvenor, he was always with his grandfather when he was a tot of three or four. And I think Dr. Bell and I were standing there too. I had the cameras, anyway. I remember I snapped them in the observation house.... That day there were heavy squalls. A gust of wind comes— maybe from the west—a guy rope slips, and away she goes! Neil went up at least thirty feet hanging from the rope. Oh they said it was more because he was scared to death. It was the end of the world for him. Dr. Bell was quite excited that it had picked him up. Oh, it was perfectly safe. Dr. Bell knew he wasn't going to get hurt—there was nothing to hurt him. But Neil was petrified ... I can hear Dr. Bell yet. He threw up his hands ... he enjoyed it."[7]

The general opinion in Baddeck was that Neil MacDermid's flight had been an accident—that Aleck had meant to release the ropes before MacDermid lifted into the air. In any event, it proved that a lightweight kite could be built strong enough to support the weight of a grown man. The first step of Aleck's aeronautical experiments was completed; the next step would be to install an engine for manned flight.

⌒

Washington, D.C., December 1903

"It's been a wonderful holiday," Mabel said as the maid cleared away the dessert dishes.

There were fifteen guests seated around the big table in the Bell's Washington home. The white tablecloth was still crisp. A few pieces of silver, crystal and fine china remained on the table.

"Yes, a lovely Christmas. But now it's almost New Year's and I'm not at all ready," one of the ladies commented.

"Nor am I," Mabel agreed. "The years are passing much too quickly."

"But you have a fine New Year's gift! A new grandchild in the house."

"Grandson!" Aleck thundered. "Grandson! And not a new one— the first one! The very first one."

"In fact, he's a month old today," Mabel added.

Elsie beamed and Gilbert squeezed her hand. "We hardly get near him," Elsie said.

"The novelty will wear off and in a few years you'll have trouble getting anyone to show an interest," Gilbert warned her.

"I'll always be interested in my grandchildren," Mabel said.

"He's a fine strong lad!" Aleck said fervently "Come to think of it, since he is a month old today, he should be brought down and properly shown off."

"Oh, Papa."

Aleck was on his feet, and before anyone could blink he went bounding up the stairs. He returned with a bundle of baby in his arms and a distraught nurse in his wake, murmuring protests.

"I tried to stop him," she complained. "The child's asleep. He'll wake him up."

"Oh, for heaven's sake woman, it's not the last time someone is going to wake him up."

He turned away from her and held up his grandson. "I present to you, Melville Bell Grosvenor!"

There was a round of applause and the baby blinked open his eyes.

Gilbert stood up. "A toast to Melville Bell Grosvenor!"

"To Melville Bell Grosvenor!" everyone echoed.

Aleck looked at the child, then drew him closer and shouted into his ear, "Baaaa!!" Immediately the baby began screaming.

"Oh, now see what you've done!" the disapproving nurse said irritably.

"See! Perfect hearing!" Aleck proclaimed. "He has perfect hearing!"[8]

Mabel half smiled. Because she and his mother were deaf, he had been investigating hereditary forms of deafness for years. She understood well his extreme satisfaction with his grandson's capacity to hear. Soon they would all be returning to Baddeck, she thought thankfully, where Aleck could get on with his kite experiments and studying aerodynamics.

He was excited about the potential uses of tetrahedrons, the three-dimensional triangles which he'd found worked so well as the basic "building blocks" for his kites. He'd recently written a long article stating that tetrahedrons were: "Applicable to any kind of structure whatever, in which it is desirable to combine the qualities of strength and lightness. Just as we can build houses of all kinds out of bricks, so we can build structures of all sorts out of tetrahedral frames, and the structures can be so formed as to possess the same qualities of strength and lightness which are characteristic of the individual cells."[9]

Early that summer Aleck's father fell ill at Beinn Bhreagh. Throughout the summer Mabel noted, "It is really touching, his concern for Alec. Mrs. Bell says it is the first question of the morning, constantly repeated throughout the day, "Where is Alec? Is he well? When will he come?" And Alec reads to him for hours every evening, or he likes to listen to Alec playing and singing with Mrs. McCurdy." On 7 August 1905, at the age of eighty-six, Alexander Melville Bell died. Mabel wrote that he had passed away quietly, "without struggle" and that he had "held up his hand and then spread it down as he does when a thing is finished, the characteristic elocutionist's gesture, marking the last fluttering breath."[10]

Sam Langley died seven months later in March 1906—in his own mind a failure. Since the initial success on the Potomac River, his experiments had not gone well. His manned-flight machine was tested before the press on 7 October 1903. The event turned into a farce when it " ... slid into the water like a handful of mortar." A second attempt, two months later, was an even worse disaster. The plane, nicknamed Langley's "Buzzard," ended up in shreds when workmen attempted to retrieve it from the river. The resulting press reports effectively snuffed out any prospects of financial backing for more Langley experiments. Aleck believed that it was the humiliation from these two failures that ultimately " ... broke his heart ... [and] contributed materially to the production of the illness that caused his death.... His flying machine never had an opportunity of being fairly tried; the man and his works will permanently endure."[11]

The sky, streaked outrageously in pinks and golds, began to darken as the sun sank from view beyond the purple mountains. Aleck plodded along, walking-stick in one hand, his eyes on the ground, as if studying it.

Mabel walked at his side. She was straight and thin. Her skirt caught the breeze. For some reason, she put him in mind of a Salem clipper knifing through the still water as she seemed to cut through the knee-high grass atop their mountain. Nearby, his flock of sheep grazed lazily in the setting sun.

Finally Aleck came to "his" rock. It overlooked the entire lake. It was smooth to the touch and still comfortably warm to sit on. He stared out, across the lake. Mabel sat beside him.

"You're very pensive today," she finally said.

"Those whom I've long held dear are all dying," he replied finally. "It makes a man consider his own mortality."

"I'm sure you've considered it before."

"First your father, then Langley, now my father."

"There've been marriages and a birth too. You have a grandson who is almost four years old."

"A living memorial to just how fast time passes."

"And now that Daisy's married, I suspect there will be more grandchildren."

"Yes, if the intensity of romance is any indication I shall soon be wading in grandchildren."

"You would adore them!"

He frowned and studied her face.

She knew from his sudden change of expression that he was about to return to his original subject. He was not to be put off with the simple reminder that life had also been added to the their family.

"It's not the dying that holds my thoughts, my dear. It's the men, it's what they missed." Your father and mine were unique men. I know that really successful manned flight will be possible in a few years and that commercial flight can't be far off. How they would have loved to see it! Especially Langley. He really was the first, you know. I saw his model fly. It flew like a bird. Yet his other demonstrations failed."

"But that wasn't manned flight."

"True, the Wright brothers get credit for that ... Langley and I were so excited when we heard the news!"

"Maybe you should turn your experimentation more in the direction of what the Wright brothers are doing."

"Absolutely not!"

Mabel could tell from his lips and facial expression that he had voiced his objections loudly.

"The principal problem for manned flight is lack of stability in the air. The Wright machines are dangerously unstable. I must continue working with kites until I solve the problem."

"We," she said, reminding him she was his partner in the endeavour. Indeed—temporarily at least—everyone in the Baddeck area seemed engaged in kite building.

"We," he corrected. Then he put his arm around her. "Had it not been for you I'd never have thought of using horses to hoist the larger kites aloft."

"Or of fastening the tetrahedral together with sealing wax," she reminded him.

"Sealing wax is now as much a staple in the workshop and laboratory as it is in your kitchen, my dear."

"But there are things I can't do," Mabel said wistfully. Then, as suddenly, her face lit up. "Aleck, you need some young men to help you. We must find you an assistant!"

"You're right, of course. I used to discuss these things with my father and yours. They understood the mechanics but not the specifics. But it is Langley whom I miss most of all. He is the father of aircraft design."

"Mind you," Mabel continued without losing the thrust of her original thought, "even if we do find you an assistant you're not getting rid of me. Flying and all its possibilities fascinate me. I'm in it with you until we succeed."

"Or fail?" Aleck chuckled and hugged her gently. "I know you are." He looked into her face. What a companion he had chosen!

⌒

In the late summer of 1906, Daisy gave birth to Alexander Graham Bell Fairchild (later called Sandy). Mabel wrote to Aleck in Beinn

Bhreagh about the baby's arrival. "It does look like the little picture of our own baby, a regular Bell baby ... no great beauty, but a nice plump, strong, lusty baby, thoroughly satisfactory." The telegram announcing the birth reached Beinn Bhreagh early in the morning. Excitedly, Charles prodded Aleck awake to tell him the news of his grandson. Aleck listened intently while Charles read the telegram aloud. There was a pause, then Aleck looked up and asked, "Yes, but can it fly?" He had been dreaming of his kites.

~

Douglas McCurdy, Arthur's son, walked across the main quadrangle of the University of Toronto on his way to the library. He was dressed in the casual student fashion of the day—tweed knickers, a jersey, an open-necked shirt and a jacket. The young man had practically grown up with the Bells; they had even offered to adopt him when his mother died; but his father had decided against it. Douglas spent his summers at Bein Bhreagh, and the assistance he gave Aleck in building and flying kites had nurtured his interest in engineering, which he was now studying.

"Hey! Wait up!" someone called out.

The open spaces around the university were often used for soccer practice, but today the expanse of green—set amidst buildings patterned after Cambridge and Oxford—was almost empty. Douglas turned to see his classmate, Casey Baldwin, running towards him, his fraternity tie flapping in the wind.

"Hullo, what's up?"

"I want to arrange to do some studying with you. I thought we could quiz each other."

"Sounds good. When?"

"Where are you headed now?"

"To the library. I have to answer a letter."

Casey grinned. "A love letter?"

"No, from Mrs. Bell. She wants me to come to Beinn Bhreagh to work for the summer and to help find an assistant for her husband."

"Her husband?"

McCurdy nodded. "Uncle Aleck—Professor Alexander Graham Bell, the inventor of the telephone."

Casey's eyebrows raised. He was obviously impressed. "Alexander Graham Bell? I had no idea you were related."

Douglas smiled sheepishly. "We're not really, though they once wanted to adopt me. The Bells live near Baddeck. My dad is Professor Bell's secretary.

His classmate looked intrigued. "Tell me more. What does this assistant have to do?"

"Professor Bell is working on flight experiments."

"My God! What an opportunity! To work with the inventor of the telephone! Douglas, look no further. I'm your man. Tell Mrs. Bell that I'll work till I drop."

Douglas looked into his friend's eyes. Casey was one of the brightest students in the engineering class. He was known, as well, for his dry sense of humour, but he seemed deadly serious, and Douglas thought that he might indeed be ideal for the job. "If you're quite sure, I'll write to Mrs. Bell."

"Oh, I'm sure."

"Consider it done," Douglas promised.

"Now then, what about the studying?"

"Sure. Come over to my digs about seven."

Casey veered away. "Tonight," he said, and headed away, walking at breakneck speed.

~

Mabel watched Douglas and Casey wolf down their dinner. They ate as though the act of eating was little more than a waste of precious time. She regarded Douglas as a member of the family, and Aleck adored him as much as she did, but he had developed a special relationship with young Casey Baldwin.

Casey Baldwin was more like Aleck, and he could keep him on track in a way that Douglas never could. They shared the same wry humour and sense of playfulness. At the same time, Casey seemed utterly fascinated with the way Aleck's mind operated—the number of ideas that he had and the dizzying speed with which they came and went. Not least of all, he was inventive and hard working. His attitude was less that of a paid employee than a technical school graduate, studying under Aleck's tutelage, while helping him to direct his ideas along practical lines.

"We're going to build a steel tetrahedron on top of the mountain," Aleck announced.

"Over eighty feet high," Douglas added.

"Won't that require a lot of machinery?" Mabel tried to imagine such a structure.

"He expects to get the whole thing up with just a jackscrew instead of the expensive and complicated machinery that's usually used."[12]

"It's possible because the cells fit together so perfectly," Casey explained.

Mabel smiled. Under other circumstances she would have mentioned the extravagance of building an observation tower, but she knew Aleck had to put his system into practice in order to understand its weak points.

"We're going over to the laboratory now ... well, after dinner," Aleck announced. "I want to look over the model and check the details."

Mabel looked at him in surprise. "You're going to walk?"

"Of course, it's a nice summer evening."

She shrugged and shook her head slowly. "Don't forget, that young Lieutenant Selfridge is arriving tomorrow."

"So he is."

"Who is Lieutenant Selfridge?" Douglas asked.

"An intensely imaginative young artillery officer and a graduate of West Point. He understands the military potential of flying machines. I've invited him to have a look around. I'm rather hoping to get the support of the American military for the development of manned flight."

"Aren't we getting ahead of ourselves?"

"We're only ahead of our experiments. In fact, I'm already looking into building a lighter, but more powerful engine."

Casey grinned, and his eyes twinkled. "We're going to do it! We're going to fly! I can feel it in my bones."

~

"My boys ..." Mabel said aloud to herself as she walked across the open field to where Aleck lay sprawled on his back in the grass, staring at the cloudless sky.

She hugged herself again. As she walked, she reviewed the idea that she wanted to put to him.

Her boys—there were five of them now, counting Aleck, who was both intellectual mentor and a full participant in the youthful joy of experiment and the anticipation of successful flight. Douglas McCurdy—good looking, young and hard working, Casey Baldwin— dedicated, brilliant and yet intensely practical; Lieutenant Thomas Selfridge—dark-haired, round-faced and filled with thoughts of what the future would be like—thoughts fuelled by his own extraordinary imagination. He had now joined them more or less permanently. Aleck had written President Theodore Roosevelt asking for Selfridge's serv- ices as an official military observer. The President had agreed, and Selfridge was given a government salary and ordered to Baddeck to record all observations that he considered to be of military signifi- cance. Mabel smiled to herself as she thought of Thomas. All the boys were polite, but he was the most so.

Motorcycle racer and manufacturer Glenn Curtiss was the fourth member of the group. He was somewhat aloof and reserved, but Mabel felt at ease with him. Moreover, because he had a deaf sister he had become fluent in signing. Of course, Mabel could read his lips and talk to him, but they could also converse rapidly in sign lan- guage. At thirty-four, Curtiss was ten years older than the others ... except Aleck, of course! Mabel smiled to herself at the thought, be- cause her husband seemed, in a way, the youngest of the bunch. Curtiss never involved himself in the horseplay that the others—in- cluding Aleck— engaged in so often. Her boys—all so different from one another—were a wonderful team. She rejoiced in their presence every day. Throughout this new association Aleck had been in per- fect humour. He loved working with them—and they with him.

She reached her husband and for a moment his long, heavy body lying in the grass put her in mind of Swift's Gulliver as he slept after being cast ashore. In such a posture Gulliver had been tethered by the Lilliputians. But there were no Lilliputians to tether Aleck, unless of course it was the small minds of those who could not imagine what he saw in the future.

"Are you asleep?" she asked—although quite sure that he was not, because his mouth was closed. When asleep he snored and snorted, his mouth ajar. In this respect, her deafness served her well. "You ..." the faithful Charles once told her cheerfully, "are surely the only one between here and the village who cannot hear him."

The dark penetrating eyes snapped open, and he smiled and patted the grass next to him.

"My dream has come to me. Sit down and enjoy the summer day."

"You'll never stop working all night and sleeping half the day, will you."

"Never."

"I've come to talk with you—no, I've come to make a proposition."

He rolled his bulk over and leaned on one elbow, supporting his head with his hand. "Oh, this does sound interesting."

"I propose to sell some property in Washington. It's my inheritance, so I can do as I please with the money."

"You can do as you please with all the money."

"This is different. I want to use my money because I want this to be my project."

"I see."

"I have in mind funding a tetrahedral association—like the Volta Association. Its purpose would not be the production of a flying machine, but developing the Tetrahedral system of construction for any commercial use.... The manufacture of flying machines seems to my mind to be only one purpose."

Aleck rubbed his chin thoughtfully. "And who might the members of this association be?"

Mabel laughed. "Well, you, of course, and Douglas, Casey, Thomas and Glenn. I propose to pay each of you one thousand dollars a year. My initial investment would be twenty thousand dollars. That, according to my calculations, would keep the association going for a year and should cover all your expenses. At the end of the year we'll see how much we have accomplished and whether or not to continue."

"It seems more than generous. Are you quite serious?"

"I'm absolutely serious! I want this to succeed. I've been more involved in this than anything you've ever done." She looked down, "And we've been together more too."

"In a way you can't imagine, you've been involved in everything I've ever done, my dear."

"Then I shall say only that I feel more involved."

"Would you agree to dissolve this association after one year if we have accomplished nothing?"

"If you think it best."

Again he ran his fingers through his beard. He had seized on Mabel's idea and was already running with it.

"I think the association's mandate ought to specifically include aerodynamics and getting a man into the air."

"Can it be done so soon?"

"Oh, I think so," Aleck said carefully. An instant later, he thundered, "No, by God, I know so!"

Mabel smiled and touched his face and he in turn kissed her tenderly. "We'll present your idea to the boys tonight." Then he whispered, "the Aerial Experiment Association— that's what we'll call it. The A.E.A.! It has a nice ring to it, doesn't it?"

～

7 November 1907

"Dear Mama, we are having a really good time all by ourselves. The three young fellows here are as nice as they can possibly be, and a hundred times less trouble than girls to entertain. They are out of the house all day and seem perfectly content to remain indoors in the evenings. The only time they have been away has been to attend a Yacht Club meeting. They are so nice to me. I like the Lieutenant ... he is very appreciative of everything one does for him. My boys are all such good friends and yet so different, such jolly boys off duty, all so full of fun and all so earnest when it's time for work.

"We are very much encouraged over the latest experiments. Alec is now ready to abandon flats and aim directly at turning the kite into a man-carrying flying machine. He knows how to send a kite into the air from the water and how to receive it from the air. These are the two things he wanted solved before he would allow anyone to try riding a kite flying-machine."[13]

Mabel reread the letter to her mother. She couldn't remember if she had previously explained that Glenn Curtiss wasn't with them because he had to divide his time between Baddeck and his own business at Hammondsport, New York. Oh, well, if she hadn't mentioned it, her mother would ask in her next letter. Mabel clasped her hands in anticipation. In one month their first trial would take place. The kite had been named *Cygnet*. It consisted of 3,400 red silk-covered tetrahedrons and resembled a fierce red dragon. Tom Selfridge would be making the first flight.

~

December 7 turned out to be a perfect day, a miracle considering that it was winter in Cape Breton. It seemed as if everyone in the district had come out to see the *Cygnet* fly. Mabel looked at it in the distance. It rested on a barge with a tow rope connecting it to the steamer *Blue Hill*. Mabel kept her fingers crossed for Thomas's safety.

Aleck gave the signal, and the vessel began pulling. The tetrahedrons caught the wind, and the giant red dragon rose gracefully into the sky. Aleck jumped up and down like a delighted child and clapped his hands with glee. "It's a success! It's a success!" he shouted.

"Everyone is shouting with happiness," Thomas told her laughing, and Mabel nodded, reading his lips. "So I gather," she said.

Mabel felt her heart soar as the kite floated higher and higher—like a red flame. Then quite suddenly the wind died and it began to descend as gently as a butterfly. But just as it touched down on the water, thick black smoke from the steamer enveloped it.

Aleck ran along the shore, "Cut the line! Cut the line!"

Everyone on shore took up Aleck's cry, but the steamer was too far away for the captain to hear the shouting. Mabel wrung her hands as horrible thoughts flashed through her mind. No one on board the steamer could see the kite, and it seemed Thomas probably couldn't see anything because of the heavy smoke lying between the vessel and the kite. Mabel covered her mouth with her hand. The *Blue Hill* plowed on, dragging the beautiful kite to destruction. Thomas Selfridge was still nowhere in sight.

"Ohhh, no!" Mabel cried out. Aleck, still shouting, ran down the shore. Everyone's eyes were fastened on the water. Then Mabel saw Thomas swimming for shore, and Douglas, a blanket in his arms, quickly waded into the icy water to meet him. Mabel shuddered and heaved a sigh of relief.

"Thank God, you managed to swim free," said Aleck.

More blankets, together with hot drinks, were quickly brought. "I couldn't see," he stuttered. "I didn't know I'd hit the water, so I didn't cut the tow line."

Aleck slapped him on the back. "You're safe, that's what matters, and the experiment was a success even if the kite is lost. We've proven the stability of tetrahedron units for flight."

"As well as Thomas's ability to swim fast in cold water," Casey added.

~

Baddeck, 23 February 1909

Mabel sat in the sleigh, her scarf pulled tight, her hands hidden in a great fur muff. It was a miraculously clear cold day with a blue sky and a weak winter sun. Fourteen months had passed since the *Cygnet* had been destroyed and only five months since poor Tom Selfridge had been killed while flying with Orville Wright. Mabel mourned his loss thinking at the same time of his bravery and his dedication to human flight. Today's flight of the *Silver Dart* would be a kind of memorial by their Aerial Experimental Association to young Tom.

He had conceived the A.E.A.'s first aircraft—*Red Wing*—after conducting an intense study of the Wright patents and a French article on aircraft design published several years earlier. He hadn't even gotten to fly it. He'd been away in Washington when the others had made the difficult decision to fly the *Red Wing* without him. They had temporarily moved their test site from Baddeck to Glenn Curtiss's headquarters in Hammondsport, New York, because of the milder weather. When warm spring winds threatened to melt the ice on the bay there, they knew that if they waited for Tom their winter runway would turn to water. On 12 March 1908, conditions were ideal, so *Red Wing* was prepared for her maiden flight with Casey at the controls. Children were let out of school and the shores of the bay were dotted with townspeople. Douglas swung the propeller. The motor started. Casey, wrapped in a heavy coat, wool scarf and leather gloves, waved to the men holding the wing tips. He opened the throttle. The *Red Wing* rolled along the ice, then ascended gracefully into the air and flew for 319 feet before gliding gently back to earth. It was the first successful public demonstration of manned flight in North America.[14]

Five days later, Casey took *Red Wing* up again. The aircraft rose normally, until a sudden gust of wind tipped it sideways. Casey tried desperately to level the wings by shifting his weight in the cockpit, but that didn't work, and the plane plummeted into the melting snow, losing its wings. For the first time it became apparent why the Wright's machines had not advanced beyond their spectacular inaugural flights of 1903. No one had yet solved the problem of horizontal and lateral stability while airborne. The A.E.A. members went back to their drawing boards.

White Wing, the next aircraft, was designed by Casey Baldwin— they had run out of red cloth and switched to white for the wing coverings. Drawing on experience from the *Red Wing,* Casey incor- porated several improvements into its successor. A tricycle landing gear was added, and additional cockpit controls, which allowed the pilot to adjust the movement of the wingtips for increased stability. The *White Wing* was finished in late May, and each of them had a chance to fly it. Curtiss covered the longest distance with a flight of one thousand feet. Although technically a more stable design than the *Red Wing,* the second machine met the same fate on 23 May. The group remained optimistic. *Red Wing*'s success had earned the A.E.A. the position of honour at an Aero Club of America banquet, where Aleck insisted repeatedly that he had nothing to do with any of the association's aeronautical developments.

Glenn Curtiss's *June Bug* was the third aircraft, and it was a con- siderable improvement over the previous two. Baldwin had calcu- lated that the escape of air through the thin porous wing fabric while the aircraft was in flight caused a forty per cent loss of lift from the wings. A thicker material—such as canvas—might reduce the air loss, but would also be much heavier. Would the increased weight be offset by the higher wing performance? No one knew for sure. They discussed the problem for several days.

During one of her visits to the shop, Mabel suggested painting the existing fabric with a light mixture of linseed oil to seal the material. The idea worked beautifully and led eventually to the "doping" of all aircraft fabric.[15]

June Bug flew—appropriately—in June. Nearly all of the stability problems had been solved. Curtiss remained airborne for an amazing one kilometre, the minimum distance required to claim the Scientific American Trophy. He repeated the feat on 4 July, in front of official judges, this time flying much farther than the required distance. Daisy and David Fairchild witnessed the flight. Daisy wrote to her parents at Beinn Bhreagh.

"In spite of all I have read and heard, and all the photographs I have seen, the actual sight of a man flying past me through the air was thrilling to a degree that I can't express. We all lost our heads. David shouted and I cried, and everybody cheered and clapped and engines hooted.... The banks were crowded with spectators, but the flight on the 4th for the Trophy was not as well attended as the one on the 5th, as the weather was so uncertain. It showered and blew all day until about six o'clock, when it cleared and ideal flying conditions prevailed. Before that, much of the time was taken up with measuring the course. No very pleasant task through a wet meadow, plowed potato patch and swamps. David started off immaculate in his white clothes and came back a sorry sight.

"At the first flight, I was at the corner of the vineyard nearest the road with Douglas, and David was at the starting line. The machine rose beautifully and flew by us, but didn't quite make the kilometer. It was flying pretty high and Mr. Curtiss wanted to bring it down but she didn't answer her controls quickly, and when he got her down, he couldn't get her up again. Nothing was hurt, and all hands towed her back to the starting point. For the second flight, David, Mrs. Curtiss and I, chose our stand on the old log at the far side of the potato patch.

"The first flight raised excitement to the boiling point, and as Mr. Curtiss flew over the red flag that marked the finish and away on towards the trees, I don't think any of us quite knew what we were doing. One lady was so absorbed as not to hear the coming train and was struck by the engine and had two ribs broken."[16]

David Fairchild sensed the historical and future implications of the day when, many years later, he wrote: "That brief afternoon at Hammondsport had changed my vision of the world as it was to be. There was no longer the shadow of doubt in my mind that the sky would be full of aeroplanes, and that the time would come when people would travel through the air faster and more safely than they did on the surface of the earth."[17]

Tom Selfridge had been called back to Washington early in August to help organize the Aeronautical Board of the U.S. Army. A few weeks after his return to the capital, he was ordered to Fort Myer, Virginia, to assist and judge in a series of flight tests with Orville Wright. Selfridge was ecstatic. On the morning of 17 September 1908, Tom, with Orville Wright at the controls, took off before a group of military officers and government officials, and crashed. Orville Wright was seriously injured. Tom Selfridge died later in the day from his injuries. He became history's first aircraft fatality. When Aleck and Casey Baldwin heard the news they left Baddeck immediately for Washington. The next day, after composing herself, Mabel wrote to Aleck.

"I can't get over Tom being taken. I simply can't realize it—it doesn't seem possible. Isn't it heartbreaking? Yet, it is better for him than to die as poor Langley did [of a broken heart]. He was so happy to the very end. I know he would have said he was having the time of his life, although he must have realized his danger; those last seconds he would still hope to escape and he had no time for unavailing regrets. I miss the thought of him so much. Nobody ever did so many little things for me as he. Others have loved me more, of course, but he just saw the little things, pushing up my chair to the table or bringing a screen to shut off drafts, all so quietly and unobtrusively that no one noticed. I am so sorry for you dear, in this breaking of our beautiful Association. But it was beautiful and the memory of it will endure.

"Bell, Curtiss, Baldwin, McCurdy and Selfridge—it was indeed a 'Brilliant coterie' as one paper has said.... Give my love to them all and let's hold tight together, all the tighter for the one that is gone. Casey called me the 'little mother of us all' and so I want to be. I love all our boys and there can't be any others just the same."[18]

Casey Baldwin had been helping Aleck at Beinn Bhreagh to prepare a successor to the demolished *Cygnet* while the other A.E.A. members were in Hammondsport building the fourth aircraft—based upon Douglas McCurdy's design. Douglas suggested using a more powerful engine and incorporating better wing-tip controls for stability. The others agreed. And instead of using linseed oil for the wing fabric, they selected a rubberized compound normally reserved for sealing balloon cloth. When this substance was applied to the wing covers they turned a bright silver hue, so Douglas named his aircraft the *Silver Dart*.

There was some doubt that the *Silver Dart* would be ready in time to meet the Association's year-end deadline for winding up its affairs. Mabel offered ten thousand dollars of funding for another six months. It was gratefully accepted. The *Silver Dart* was completed and shipped to Baddeck, then reassembled. An advance announcement brought a dozen reporters and photographers hurrying in from the Halifax papers. Most of the homes, schools and businesses throughout the district shut down, as everyone headed out to the bay to see the first manned flight of an aircraft in the British Empire.

Mabel, journal in hand, prepared to record the historic occasion. It was, she thought, just perfect. All of Baddeck was out in sleighs and sleds and skates. A collage of children wore long colourful scarves and bulky snowsuits. Fires burned and people huddled round them, roasting potatoes. The air smelled of winter and burning wood.

The *Silver Dart,* glistening in the sun, took flight, and Mabel, her hands over her eyes to block the sun, followed it through the sky. It was a beautiful flight, then the craft sailed downward on a light wind and landed across the bay.

Lines from Tennyson ran though her thoughts:

"For I dipped into the future, far as human eye could see,
Saw the vision of the world, and all the wonder that would be;

Saw the heavens fill with commerce, argosies of magic sails,
Pilots of the purple twilight, dropping down with costly bale."

She wasn't certain what the last lines meant, but surely in the first part of his vision, Tennyson had imagined flight. And now, she thought with satisfaction, it had come to fruition; and she, who lived her years in silence, was a real part of what she felt would be the wonderful world of this new century.

She wrote to Daisy, "We all pleaded hard with Papa for another flight but he was firm. It was the first flight of an airship in Canada and he would take no chance of disaster to spoil this first success. All Baddeck was out in sleighs or on skates. We had to wait two hours and … whiled away the time with horse races up and down the smooth hard ice. Can you realize people dashing up and down feeling perfectly secure with only a foot or so of ice between them and forty feet of water? I just love Baddeck these glorious winter days— you poor Southerners know nothing of their exhilaration."[19]

Aleck agreed to a second flight the following day, and Mabel continued with her report. "It was really a wonderful flight Douglas made this morning. He started about 100 yards from the boathouse out on the bay, and flew across toward Kennan's boathouse and thence toward the lighthouse, making a glorious sweep and came back past Beinn Bhreagh shore, passing close to me purposely as I said I hadn't really seen yesterday's flight—swept out of sight on the tongue of land which forms the entrance to the harbor—way up the bay. Unfortunately he miscalculated the space there for making the return curve and he was obliged to make a bad landing to avoid trees. In the air six minutes—a beautiful sight."[20]

Mabel returned to Washington to see her mother. As the date approached for dissolving the A.E.A., she longed for news about what Aleck had planned. It was obvious that there was still much more work to be done.

Chapter Twenty-One

April 1910

The water's of Bras d'Or Lake shimmered under the full moon and lapped to shore in low, soft, white-fringed waves that caressed the rocks rather than breaking against them. Mabel walked beside Casey Baldwin, who idly prodded the ground with a crooked walking stick. They walked in silence, because it was too dark for her to read his lips.

Mabel smiled to herself. When she'd been younger, she had relished taking Aleck out on long walks in the dark. On such occasions he was compelled to listen to her and she felt it was one of the few ways she could get him to listen. Her mind came quickly back to the present when, ahead of them on the beach, they saw the remnants of *Baddeck No. 2*. It hardly resembled its original self—rather, it looked like a ghost machine, or perhaps the discarded toy of some giant's child, tossed aside to disintegrate on the cold grey rocks. Just seeing it brought back all that had happened since its glory days. Success and betrayal—or at least she felt betrayed since she had placed so much faith in Glenn Curtiss.

Aleck had proposed to turn the A.E.A. into a joint-stock company, set up for the purpose of developing flying machines. He had wanted Glenn Curtiss to manage the firm since he had the most business experience. They had all been excited at the prospect, until they learned that Curtiss had, without informing any of them, founded the Herring-Curtiss Company in order to build his own flying machines. Aleck had been absolutely flabbergasted. He sent Curtiss a telegram asking him to explain fully concerning his arrangements with Herring and how they would affect his relations with the A.E.A.

But Curtiss consolidated his corporate position before replying, and his answer was not what one would have hoped for from a loyal co-worker. He had written: "I found Mr. Herring quite anxious to close the deal with me and I finally made him an offer, a little better than his original proposition. Mr. Herring showed me a great deal, and I would not be at all surprised if his patents, backed by a strong company, would pretty well control the use of the Gyroscope in sustaining automatic equilibrium. This seems to be about the only road to success in securing automating stability in an aeroplane.

"If the deal goes through, I will be the manager of the company and everything will go on just as it has, except that we will have Mr. Herring's devices on the machines which we may build. By the way, that reminds me, I have accepted an order from the Aeronautical Society for an aeroplane to be delivered in the spring at Morris Park, N.Y., I did this on my own responsibility, with the idea that if the consolidation was made with Herring, it would be turned over to the new company, or if a commercial organization succeeded the A.E.A. the order could be turned over to them. If neither of these materialized the Curtiss company would endeavour to fill the order itself."

Aleck had asked Curtiss to return to Baddeck at the end of March, but he did not come. Thus, on the evening of 31 March, the A.E.A. dissolved itself after graciously thanking Mabel for her support.

The goal of the A.E.A. had been to produce aircraft for the U.S. and Canadian Governments; when the association dissolved itself, Curtiss used the knowledge he had gained at Baddeck in his partnership with Herring. They were faced with two choices: sue Curtiss, or form another aircraft production company. Aleck would not sue, so he financed Casey and Douglas to form the Canadian Aerodrome Company.

The Canadian Club in Ottawa invited Aleck to speak on the A.E.A.'s accomplishments. The guests included Sir Wilfred Laurier, Prime Minister of Canada, members of his cabinet and Earl Grey, the governor general. Aleck wrote a less than enthusiastic description of the affair to Mabel. He had become weary of these formal occasions. Mabel gave his ego a massage with a cheerful reply.

"Of course you found the Ottawa trip fatiguing but what an experience! How delightful to move a large audience of worthwhile men to enthusiasm! This is one of the things you can do as few men can and you must enjoy the doing of it."[1]

While in Ottawa, Aleck had been asked to demonstrate his flying machines to an assessment group for evaluation, so work immediately began on two new, improved biplanes—*Baddeck No.1* and *Baddeck No. 2*. The new planes and the *Silver Dart* were shipped to Camp Petawawa, the military base outside of Ottawa. Contrary to Aleck's request, the test site chosen was filled with knolls and dips, which created a number of optical illusions that made it totally unsuitable for a test. Nonetheless, Casey and Douglas decided to proceed.

The day was clear, and Douglas took the *Silver Dart* up on five successive flights before a crowd of military and government officials. On his fifth flight, blinded by the sun, he dropped too low. The plane's wheels nicked the top of a sandy knoll and the aircraft nose-dived into the ground and disintegrated. Miraculously, Douglas escaped unhurt, but the aircraft was beyond repair, and even worse damage was done to Canadian Aerodrome Company's reputation.

After some discussion, a second demonstration was arranged the following week using *Baddeck No. 1*. Unhappily, ignition problems cut short the first flight on takeoff. The plane was badly damaged. The government officials returned to Ottawa smirking and claiming that while flying machines were interesting toys—when they worked— they could see no military value in their use.

Mabel and Aleck had huddled and finally defined the problem. Mabel reported to Daisy: "The *Toronto Star* telegraphed to know what Father had to say about the *Baddeck No. 1* failure. He replied it was one of the finest aerodromes ever built but that a novel device never before employed was used on it and possibly it was not properly adjusted.

"Father and I have concluded that the curved front control was the cause of the accident. It, having greater lifting power than the plane surface to which Douglas is accustomed, would cause the machine to rise with dangerous rapidity in front and not having as great descending power, would not act as effectively as the old one. So it would be impossible for Douglas to check the backward tilt."[2]

Still, for a time, hope surfaced. Although the government had been unimpressed, the governor general, Earl Grey, was intrigued, and he asked if he could visit Baddeck later in the fall for a demonstration. Just before the vice-regal visit, tragedy struck. Gertrude Hubbard was killed in a car accident in Washington when another vehicle smashed into the rear of her Peerless automobile, causing it to smash into a pole. She and her chauffeur were rushed to hospital, but only the driver survived.

Mabel was heartbroken. She and Aleck hurried to Washington, leaving Casey and his wife to meet the governor general. After the funeral, Mabel insisted that Aleck return to Beinn Bhreagh while she and her sister Grace sorted through their mother's home and personal effects. The home and everything in it resurrected the ghosts of her mother, father and sisters. She described her feelings to Aleck in a letter.

"Nobody was as proud of me as she was, nobody else ever made the most of any bright little thing I ever did or said. It is growing more and more strange to have to do without that underlying sense of her love and of pride in me which has lain deep down at the bottom of my heart and comforted me in my moments of deepest depression. 'Mama would see, mama would care,' and it didn't matter that she really neither knew nor cared, I had but to tell her to get all the sympathy and understanding I wanted."[3]

As a result of the governor general's visit, the Canadian Government agreed to a second evaluation of the Bell flying machine. The flight was a great success, but despite all the excitement and enthusiasm, the government decided that the aviation industry would have to develop to the point of commercial viability on its own. Without government contracts, the Canadian Aerodrome Company fizzled out and the once beauteous *Baddeck No. 2* was left to the elements.

Mabel stopped walking. She slowly approached the remains of *Baddeck No. 2* and touched them almost tenderly.

"I can't stand seeing it here, night after night," she said to Casey. She looked up at him imploringly, and he nodded his head, turning so that his face was silhouetted in the moonlight and she could see his lips.

"It deserves a decent burial."

"Build a fire!" Mabel suddenly ordered.

Casey didn't hesitate. He gathered together some small dry sticks and set them alight. They nurtured the little fire until it had caught and was blazing brightly. Mabel pressed her lips together tightly. "Torch it," she said evenly.

He smiled at her and lifting a flaming torch from the fire walked to the plane. "Are you sure?"

"I'm sure," Mabel answered. The flames lapped the skeleton and then caught with a crackle. A bright swath of light lit the night. Casey returned to her side and they stood watching as the biplane roared into flaming glory.

"It's better this way," she said softly, " ... better."

The Bells and the Baldwins decided to take the ultimate vacation in 1910—a trip around the world. But by the following spring Mabel had grown weary of wandering and longed again for the comfort and relaxation of Beinn Bhreagh. She wrote to Elsie, "I wish we could come straight home to you, but Papa and Casey want to stay for the Aviation Meet at Monaco on April 11th, to have an opportunity of examining the motors and probably investing in one with which to make another attempt to fly his own machine. [Cygnet II] I do not feel I have the right to stand in their way and it is exactly the spur they need before beginning work again. I also think that perhaps a few days rest on the Riviera is what we all need. You see I lost a lot of strength in India and even the week we had in Mentone did not quite set me up again, although it worked wonders."[4]

While in Italy, Aleck and Casey had taken a ride in the impressive Forlanini hydrofoil boat. After talking to the designers and picking and sketching a variety of design ideas, they could hardly wait to get home to try duplicating this relatively new invention. Work began on their version of a hydrofoil in Beinn Bhreagh in the late summer of 1911, using plans prepared by Casey. They called it a hydrodrome—

half boat, half plane. It resembled a mutated flying machine on pontoons. Aleck once again refused to accept any credit for the work.

As far back as 1908, Casey had been so upset by this cavalier attitude that he told Mabel he could no longer work with Aleck unless he agreed to take credit for the results. Mabel pleaded with her husband to be reasonable, and Aleck agreed. But her pleas had gone in one ear and out the other, for in the next issue of the *A.E.A. Bulletin,* he wrote a lengthy article accrediting the latest aircraft developments solely to Casey. Mabel was livid and wrote to Daisy and David Fairchild promptly in the hope of reaching Aleck from another angle.

"Daddysan[5] makes me mad, he will pile credit on other people vicariously. I am perfectly devoted to Casey as you know, and most certainly want him to have all the credit he deserves, and that is a lot. But Father is working on the *Dhonnas Beag*[6] (HD–1), too, and no step is made without him. It is not fair for Father to report in the Bulletin that 'Mr. Baldwin proposes to do so and so,' just as if Casey were moving entirely independent of him, which he certainly is not.... My point is that this work is conjointly Daddysan's and Casey's— while from what Daddysan has written, one would think is was Casey's solely and absolutely.

"Father did the same thing about the Hammondsport aerodromes. The *Red Wing, White Wing, June Bug* and the *Silver Dart* were all the collective product of all the A.E.A. associates working as an Association.... So that while the *White Wing* was approved by Casey, the *June Bug* by Curtiss, the *Silver Dart* by Douglas, as a matter of fact they are all the work of the whole Association including Daddysan, and Daddysan's work certainly was quite as important in the original features as any, to say the least.

"I am writing all this to you and David on purpose, because this is history and I want it to go on record—so please keep this letter. I might appeal to Casey to correct Papa's report, but I don't want to do that because it would only make him uncomfortable and might make him hesitate to go on. There was never anyone more regardless of self in these matters than Casey. He simply wants to get things done and he wants to push them through with all his might, regardless of whose the idea originally was. If it appeals to his judgment, he will work at it and will never lift a finger if some other fellow claims credit for the idea. I am the only selfish person in the trinity, but I like to have things fair. I want Casey given every credit for independent ideas and for the energy in carrying it out and pushing it to completion. Many of the engineering details are of his sole devising. Father expressed it correctly in the beginning, 'he turned over this branch of the problem,' that is right—but this does not mean that he himself had not thought it all out in gross.... He is the author and inventor of many devices—but Father has helped him with valuable suggestions also—so that the work is not solely Casey's. That's all."[7]

The *Dhonnas Beag* was originally designed to become one of the A.E.A. aerodromes. A second hydrofoil, the *Query*, was subsequently built; however, only a few water tests had been conducted on the new machine before the Bells and Baldwins left on their world tour. After their return, the *Dhonnas Beag* was rebuilt into the *Hydrodrome 1* (HD–1) based on what they'd learned about the Italian hydrofoils. It was tested—unsuccessfully—on Baddock Bay until the water froze.

Throughout the winter of 1911–12 Casey and Aleck tinkered constantly with the machine, taking it apart, then redesigning, rebuilding and finally renaming it, HD–2. They tested it throughout the summer and fall. Operational results were wildly inconsistent, although it eventually reached a top speed of fifty miles per hour before breaking in half.[8]

Aleck came up with a novel idea for a hydrofoil sailboat. Casey, an experienced sailor, pointed out gently that even the fastest sailboats were unable to reach the speed required for a hydrofoil to lift its hull from the water. Aleck remained undaunted, insisting that with a few adjustments and the addition of horizontal sails, the idea would work. Casey humoured him and worked on the sailboat idea while continuing trials on the HD–3, their latest hydrodrome. Although better than its predecessors, it was still not good enough. When the Prince of Monaco sailed into Baddeck on a visit, an official demonstration of the HD–3 turned into another public-relations disaster: the craft suddenly went belly up due to a structural flaw.

⌐

People flooded the tennis grounds on the side of the mountain. The games, which had started an hour before, were going full tilt. Men and boys walked on stilts, threw the hammer, took part in putting the shot, potato racing and three-legged races. The ground floor of the "warehouse," was filled with tables, each laden with sandwiches, pies and cakes and boilers full of tea and coffee. Later, old and young alike would join in for the dancing. This was the Bell's annual Harvest Home Festival and nearly everyone within a radius of twenty miles attended.[9]

"I missed this most of all," Mabel told Elsie. "Travelling is all well and good, but living out of suitcases and eating out all the time gets to be a bit of a bore."

"You could have come home sooner."

"The moment Aleck saw that Forlanini hydrofoil boat, it was love at first sight."

"He and Casey have been trying to duplicate the design ever since they got back," Elsie laughed. "The only time he stops is to tell stories to the grandchildren."

"You know Daddysan." Mabel shrugged.

"Do I hear my name being taken in vain?" Aleck thundered up to them. The Baldwins followed in his wake.

"Where's young Melville?" Aleck demanded.

Mabel pointed into the distance, and Aleck bellowed for his grandson, now a strapping lad of eleven. The boy turned, and galloped towards them.

"Can't you see the three legged-race is about to begin? Aren't you going to be my partner?"

Melville nodded enthusiastically, and the two hurried off towards where the racers were assembling.

Mabel frowned. "He's getting too old for three-legged races."

"He's quite fit," Casey insisted.

Mabel just shook her head. "Sometimes I wonder what to do with him."

They laughed, knowing exactly what she meant.

Casey grinned. "I will never, if I live to be a hundred, forget the midnight swim."

Mabel's face flushed. "I should like very much to forget it."

The incident recalled, that so embarrassed her, was indeed one of Aleck's most notorious escapades. Over time, it had become almost legendary. Aleck had decided to go for a swim in the buff. He had stripped down and floated off peacefully in the cool water, paddling like a great grampus. When he finally waded ashore he couldn't find his clothes, so, covering his privates, he ran to the house and called to his growing family of grandchildren to help him. They threw a sheet from the window which he wrapped around his bulk as best he could. Thereupon he marched through the living room—looking for all the world like a conquering Caesar—and into the midst of a Ladies' Club meeting, which Mabel hastily adjourned.

"Daddysan enjoys himself here. He's not like this in Washington."

"True," Casey agreed. It was clear that here, in Baddeck, Aleck was at ease. He was the Laird of the Manor, and the townspeople treated him as such.

"I know Aleck always talks about developing things and he always insists that with a few adjustments the hydrofoils will work perfectly, but I do wish they would. You and he have been tinkering with them for nearly three years now, on and off."

Casey grinned, "We do keep busy, though."

"It's just as well," Elsie added. "Being hidden away with your experiments is good. Everyday the world is getting to be an uglier place."

"You're talking about Europe," Casey surmised.

"Of course, Europe. Everyone says there's going to be war."

Mabel looked at their faces. She hated the thought of war. "Let's go join the others," she said, propelling Casey on her arm. "The race is about to begin, and we wouldn't want to miss Aleck and Melville winning?"

"Will they win?" Elsie asked.

"They always do," Mabel answered briskly. Then she whispered, "I think they all let him win, you know."

⁓

Aleck's study, was, as always, comfortably cluttered. The desk and every other available surface were covered with papers. Aleck sunk happily into the depths of the big plush chair, his long legs extended so that his slippered feet rested on the footstool. As comfortable as his body felt, his thoughts were anything but comfortable. He reread the newspaper. His expression reflected his dismay. War had broken out in Europe, and while Canada was involved as a member of the British Commonwealth, the United States, of which he was a citizen, remained neutral. He pondered a course of action. With a great heave, he left the warmth of the chair, pulled himself to his feet and padded to the foot of the stairs. Casey had stayed overnight because they had worked late.

"Casey, are you up?"

Casey appeared at the top of the stairs, fully dressed and looking wide awake.

"Gone are the days when I can look so chipper after a late night," he said, puffing on his giant cigar.

"You don't look ready to work Aleck ... I thought I'd take a walk."

"I want to talk," Aleck said.

Casey followed him into the study. "This war business in Europe..."

"What about it?" Casey inquired.

"I'm uncomfortable," Aleck confided. "The hydrofoil has potential military uses. Canada is part of the war, but I'm an American, and my country is neutral. It wouldn't be right for me to continue to experiment now."

"What about the workers?"

"Oh, they can keep their jobs. They can build pleasure boats for the local market—for awhile at least."

"And if America is drawn into it?"

"Then we'll try for a government contract."

"I hate giving it all up," Casey admitted.

Aleck turned away and looked out the window. "Honour is as important as success," he replied. He turned back to Casey, "Mind you, if the Americans get into it, we'll have the business opportunity of a lifetime."

⁓

That summer, after reading Robinson Crusoe, Aleck and young Melville set off into the woods of Beinn Bhreagh. They planned to spend a few days, just as Crusoe and his faithful companion Friday had done. But the forest floor was still wet from recent rains, making it impossible to start a fire or build a shelter. The adventurers returned to Beinn Bhreagh after dark. Mabel laughed as they entered the house. Aleck snorted, "Well, Robinson Crusoe was lucky. His island was tropical." As a consolation for their misadventure, they spent the night roughing it on board the houseboat.[10]

Mabel may have been jealous of the amount of attention Aleck lavished on their grandson, but Bert and Elsie appreciated it. Bert expressed his gratitude for their taking care of Melville during the summer. "The first child is always horribly handicapped by the ignorance of the parents. I have tried to make it up to Melville, but realize how lamentably I failed ... especially in those early days."

Aleck and Mabel both had very progressive ideas about education and went to great lengths to provide their grandchildren with the best education possible. Early in 1912, Mabel made a trip to Tarrytown, New York, to confer with teachers Roberta Fletcher and Ann E. George. Both women had been studying a revolutionary new teaching method created by Dr. Maria Montessori in Rome. The Montessori system allowed children to pursue their own interests—learning without realizing it. Results were often socially unacceptable, yet there was no doubt that Montessori-educated children were able to acquire basic knowledge much faster than their peers who attended schools where conventional education methods were practised. At Mabel's invitation, Fletcher spent that summer teaching their grandchildren at Beinn Bhreagh, then accompanied the family to Washington in the fall, where she opened a Montessori school in an annex of the Bell's home. Twenty-three children—mostly friends of the Bells, Fairchilds and Grosvenors—were enrolled. The results were so successful that the following April a Montessori Educational Association was established in the capital, with Mabel as its president. She bought a house for the school and in 1914 Dr. Montessori visited, while on a lecture tour. The controversial educator gave Mabel her unqualified support for founding Montessori schools throughout the United States.

But enthusiasm for the new teaching method was short-lived. Most supporters were either wealthy, or elitist parents with progressive ideas. Local school-board officials across the nation remained unconvinced. Professor William Kilpatrick—an influential educator—criticized the method in his book, the *Montessori System Examined*. In the face of official rejection, the Montessori system's popularity in America faded away. Aleck and Mabel, however, remained committed, and Mabel eventually became the sole financial support for Americans to train as Montessori teachers in Rome. As the war progressed it became impractical to continue overseas training, and when Montessori-trained teachers found that there was no demand for their skills, they drifted back to the regular school system. Disheartened, Mabel closed her little school in 1919.

Aleck became increasingly preoccupied with educating his grandchildren. Often he would set up experiments at Beinn Bhreagh for the children, presenting ideas for them to think about and try out for themselves.

"He would adjust our glasses of water and they would be at different levels and then we would put our finger in the water and go around and around the top of the glass and he would show us the difference of the vibrations. We would think it was magic, but it was a form of teaching us.... He would place a candle with a glass upside down and you would see it burn until all the oxygen had gone.... He would put a piece of paper in the milk bottle and drop a match in it and put an egg on top and watch the flame burn and it would suck the hard boiled egg into the bottle."[11]

A mixture of magic and science filled the grandchildren's visits to Beinn Bhreagh. When they arrived at Baddeck they were be taken across the bay by motorboat. Mabel waited for them at the dock and accompanied them by carriage to the main house, where a hot breakfast was waiting. Mornings were set aside for quiet time, as their grandfather maintained his lifetime habit of late nights at work and late mornings asleep. As the summer progressed, Mabel had problems getting all of the children downstairs in time for their 8:30 A.M. breakfast. "So grandma introduced a system of fines and rewards. They had those big [English] pennies and if we were on time we got a penny and if we weren't we had to pay a penny.... We arranged it so that we came out even in the end. Except Sandy. He often got away with it. He would have a good excuse and he wouldn't be fined."[12]

The grandchildren understood and observed absolute silence while their grandfather was asleep in his verandah bed. Mabel herded the children outside to play where they could hear his snores from the garden. The children's sleeping quarters were situated directly above the verandah. "At night when they talked in bed, we would hear grandma say something and then absolute silence and then she would question him again and there would still be silence. We figured out that he was spelling out his answers to her with his hands in the dark." During the day he would " ... drive down on that white horse they had, Champ, and then he would get out and put the rein over the dashboard [of the carriage] and clap his hands. Champ would go back to the stable by himself."[13] While Aleck worked at the laboratory, Mabel joined the rest of the family for lunch and then retired to her office to take care of correspondence and finances.

There were two rules at the dinner table: no one sat unless he or she had brought some interesting news to share, and they must always look at their grandmother whenever they spoke. It was never explained that they had to look at grandma " ... so she can read your lips, or because she is deaf ... you just always looked at Grandma when you spoke to her."[14] At mealtimes, when soup was served, Aleck used a straw. "He felt it was utterly ridiculous to sink his moustache into a cup of tea [or soup].... So he had a series of glass tubes, short ones for a cup and long ones that bent, like you see now in hospitals for drinking out of a tall glass. He sucked the contents into his mouth, rather than put his mouth down into the liquid.... He was very proud of his moustache and used to ask us to feel it. See! he'd say. How soft it is? When we were very young he'd let us pull his beard and then make funny faces with each tug."[15]

From the moment they were old enough to understand, the grandchildren were taught to respect their grandparents. Aleck was especially careful to see that they treated Mabel with the proper respect. On one occasion a group of grandchildren had gone down to the warehouse after supper to play "I Spy." Darkness fell, and before they knew, it was an hour past the time they had promised to return. Hurrying back towards the house, they had to go through a graveyard; images of goblins and ghostly apparitions filled their minds as they passed the moonlit headstones. Suddenly, a giant cloaked figure appeared holding a glowing lantern. The children froze in their tracks. "Are you all there?" It was Aleck. Like Moses, he led them back to the house and delivered them Mabel. "Here is your grandmother," and he closed the door and went back to his study. The children apologized to Mabel.

Aleck teased the children, the servants, relatives—and of course Mabel—incessantly. "When we were very little, he would ask us constantly, 'What is heavier, a pound of lead or a pound of feathers?' And of course we would say a pound of lead. And it wasn't until you finally realized they were both the same weight that he would admit that you were no longer a baby. He did this often, asking questions.... When we gave the wrong answer everybody would laugh. It was always embarrassing but Grampy thought it was great fun."[16]

Aleck had more than his share of eccentric phobias and notions. No one was allowed to call a sweater a sweater. It was a jersey, because ladies did not sweat, they glowed. Gentlemen perspired. Only labourers sweated—and they never wore jerseys. He held to the ancient superstition that moonlight could induce madness, and he would cite the Latin word luna, for moon, as being from the same root word as lunacy. Full moons were the most dangerous times of the month. When the moon was full and everyone in the house was asleep, he crept into the bedrooms, rearranging blankets and curtains so that the beam of the full moon would not fall upon any family members.

One fall, the children went to a great effort to organize a small orchestra at the Bell's Washington home. Admission was one cent. Barbara Fairchild, Alexander Graham Bell Fairchild's younger sister, asked Mabel if she would come to hear their music. "I went up to the morning room and she was sitting there and I said, 'Grandma we are having a concert. Will you come and hear us?' She looked at me ... 'Thank you dear, but have you forgotten, I can't hear'... She was like that, because to us there was no reality to her deafness."[17]

The hydrofoils enchanted the children. When young Barbara asked if they might all have a ride in the machine, Aleck replied: "My grandfather had two sides to him. One side was very good to all his granddaughters and the other side was ... that girls couldn't do what boys did.' So when the hydrofoil left the wharf it carried my brother and he crowed about it because I wasn't allowed to go. My grandfather said, 'Girls do not ride in experimental craft. You stay here with me.' But Casey had heard what he said, and after Grampy left, he told me, 'You come with me,' and I had a ride on the hydrofoil.'"[18]

As the war dragged on and changed, so too did the landscape around Beinn Bhreagh. When the United States finally entered the conflict in March 1917, Aleck pursued his idea of building small boats for the government. He was awarded a contract for fourteen boats, to be ready within one hundred days for delivery F.O.B to Halifax. "We are hewing down cherished trees, destroying the best-loved beauty spots on Beinn Bhreagh and erecting in their place huge ugly sheds just in the hope that we may be allowed to build ships for the U.S. Government. We don't even know we will be allowed to do it, but Daddysan's orders are that no time is to be lost in waiting."[19]

"It *was* a big gamble," Casey stated. "But I knew from the beginning that we could do a quality job as cheap as any, except possibly the biggest firms."

"It was always ... a question of time," Aleck said. Many townsfolk were employed in the construction, but only so many people could profitably work on one boat at a time. In the end, they out did themselves, finishing the contract ten days ahead of schedule. The occasion demanded a celebration.

"Our guests are arriving," said Casey, hearing the voices at the front door. They had invited thirty-eight to dinner. Most were laboratory staff, but there were some visitors from the city as well. "I think they'll all be very impressed with the table settings," Casey told Mabel, " ... especially the 'city magnets.' "

Mabel nodded. Casey always called businessmen from the city, 'city magnets.' She had arranged the place settings herself. There were little name cards and allied flags, with a tiny English and American flag at each place setting. On the cards were pictures of the little vessels built at Beinn Bhreagh.

At eleven-thirty, the dishes from the last course were taken away. "Music!" Aleck declared.

Aleck, dressed in what Mabel called his Santa Claus best—a white waistcoat trimmed in velvet—sat down at the piano and began with a long prelude to "God Save the King." He was in fine spirits, because they'd fulfilled the naval contract so successfully. Mabel knew that his voice boomed throughout the room, but often she wondered what it really sounded like. She knew from the reactions of others—and from the way he opened his mouth—when he was too loud. His happiness pleased Mabel.

Completing the first contract fuelled hopes for more work. In the spring of 1918, they offered to build three submarine chasers for the government and optimistically began to clear more land. But this time the government wasn't interested. A telegram from Elsie's husband, Bert, confirmed the terrible disappointment.

"The Government regrets that it cannot place an order for any boats for such late delivery as specified in your telegram. Conditions have materially changed during the past several days and no further orders are now being placed for these boats. Exceedingly regret outcome of this affair."[20]

For the second time in four years the government had rejected the idea of hydrodromes for military service. Aleck was heartbroken. Government backing was critical to finance the next hydrodrome, the HD-4. Mabel soothed his feelings and offered to back the project herself. Aleck accepted. Two 350-horsepower Liberty engines were borrowed from the United States Navy Department and work began.

~

10 December 1917

"No matter what, it feels better to have tried to help."

Mabel's hair was unusually unkempt. Strands had escaped her ordinarily tight bun and in spite of the cold weather, they clung to the perspiration on her brow.

"You shouldn't have come down to the docks, Mrs. Bell," Casey said.

"I wanted to come. I wanted to see that everything was loaded properly."

"You know I'll see to that."

"I can't believe what's happened, I can't even imagine the devastation." She rubbed her hands against her winter coat in agitation. She felt helpless, though she knew she had done all she could. "I wish I could come with you," she finally said.

Casey shook his head. "You know they've asked people to stay away if they're not absolutely needed. Everyone who goes to Halifax is one more person to house and to feed."

She nodded. It was true enough that only essential personnel were wanted.

"No one could do more than you have already done," Casey said as he touched her shoulder.

"I just keep thinking of all those poor homeless children, and in this cold. It's terrible, all the hurt ... " Her eyes filled with tears and Casey hugged her.

"I think we're ready," he said.

"I'll see to it that the ladies keep working. We'll send more."

What they had already done, Casey knew, was a minor miracle, achieved mainly through the strength of Mabel Bell's will.

"Do what you can," she said, looking up at him imploringly. "Remember, you are working for all of us. You're our representative."

Casey gave her another hug and then turned and climbed aboard the ship. It was loaded with blankets, food and timber. He had twelve workmen with him and heaven knew how much clothing—all assembled in record time by Mabel's sewing club. By all reports, the need was unimaginable. Casey watched as the anchor lifted and the vessel drifted from the dock. The ships moved off slowly, and gradually the figure of Mabel Bell grew smaller and smaller, till she was lost from view and he went below deck.

⟿

On the morning of 6 December they had all just sat down to lunch. The table was set informally, and Casey and Aleck were still in their work clothes. Casey remembered the smell of the fresh bread and the taste of the hot split-pea soup—the perfect meal for a cold winter's day. Suddenly there had been a rumbling sound, and all the windows in Beinn Bhreagh had shaken. They had stopped talking at once.

"Was that an earthquake?" one of the children asked.

"They only have those in California," another replied.

"No, they have them everywhere!" yet another argued.

"They had the biggest one in the world in New Madrid, Missouri in ... 1811. It made the Mississippi run backwards!"

"Did not!"

"Did too! Anyway, earthquakes can happen anywhere, can't they Grandpa?"

All eyes had turned to Aleck.

"It wasn't an earthquake," he said flatly. I don't know what it was, but I'm sure it was a disaster."

It was hours before the news came over the telegraph wires. Aleck had been right. It was one of the greatest man-made disasters of all time, causing monumental devastation. In Halifax Harbour one hundred and seventy-seven miles to the west, the *Imo*—a Belgian relief ship from the United States—had collided with the *Mont Blanc,* a French ammunition vessel carrying explosives. The *Mont Blanc* had caught fire and blew up minutes later. It flattened the north end of Halifax, destroying one-fifth of the city in an instant.

Miraculously, passengers on the Halifax-Dartmouth ferry, travelling a few hundred yards from the explosion were spared, but the force of the blast was said to have displaced the water in the harbour so that the bottom was visible to those on the ferry. Somehow the little craft managed to ride out the resulting tidal wave that smashed through hundreds of warehouses and wharves.

Over a thousand were known to have died in the explosion, countless thousands were homeless and more were dying every day from their wounds and exposure. Shortly after the cataclysm, a winter storm buried the city under ice and snow, making the emergency operations more difficult—and more urgent. Every day there were more homeless as damaged buildings were declared unsafe for occupancy.

Mabel and the ladies of Baddeck started working into the night making winter clothing. She organized the first boatload of relief supplies and enlisted Casey and twelve workmen from Baddeck to go and help in any way they could.

"The war," she told him tearfully, "has come in an unexpected way to the peaceful faraway capital of Nova Scotia."

Mabel's determined response to the disaster reminded Casey that she had a will of iron to match her compassionate heart.

⌐

After several weeks of helping to rebuild the city, Casey returned to Beinn Bhreagh to continue work on the HD–4. When it was finished, the craft resembled a sixty-foot-long grey cigar on pontoons. Hydrofoils were installed on either side of the hull, with a third one at the bow. Two propellers—without motors to drive them—were mounted above the port and starboard hydrofoils. Finally, late in July 1918, nearly a year after construction had started, the U.S. Navy shipped two motors to Baddeck. Unfortunately, they were 250-horsepower, instead of the 350-horsepower that had been promised. Still, they were better than nothing. Official trials began, and in the early weeks of 1919—two months after the war ended—Aleck reported to the U.S. Navy office in Washington that his hydrodrome had reached the impressive speed of fifty-four miles per hour but could go no faster without the larger engines that had been promised. His report managed to pry two 350-horsepower engines out of the department, and speed trials were resumed in July.

On 9 September, 1919, the HD-4 set an official world record of 70.86 miles per hour on water. Despite the success and enthusiastic news coverage of the event, neither the U. S., Canadian British Governments were interested. The hydrodrome was a marvel ahead of its time, but the war to end all wars had ended. There was no money available for what was considered to be an instrument of war. When this depressing realization sank in, the HD-4 was abandoned on the shores of Beinn Bhreagh. The only two bright spots from the venture were the world record for marine speed and a patent on their idea, issued on 28 March 1922.

⁓

Over the years Aleck had tried to teach Casey Baldwin some business sense, reasoning that the best way was to give him more responsibility in the hydrodrome venture. Unfortunately, every commercial attempt with the hydrodromes seemed doomed to failure. Although this wasn't Casey's fault, other family members found it hard to understand why such a wonderful invention was a commercial flop. They suspected Baldwin of incompetence. David Fairchild wrote to his in-laws, thoroughly criticizing Casey's track record in business. He even compared him, unfavourably, to Glenn Curtiss, who, he said, had much better business sense. It was a pity, he felt, that Aleck had been unable to find someone as good as Curtiss for a business partner. Mabel jumped to Casey's defence. In an uncharacteristic, scathing denunciation she wrote:

"I feel sure from the tone of some of your recent letters to Daddysan and me that you really know very little about Mr. Curtiss's relations to the old Aerial Experiment Association, that I feel I want to tell you something about them and the reasons why we cannot give him either respect or friendship. I would not feel so concerned about your evident appreciation of him as a successful man who has made aeroplanes and millions while we others have dropped out, did it not also involve deprecation of others, which does them injustice. This hurts me dreadfully.

"The Aerial Experiment Association was a great, a marvellous success yet very few know this; fewer still the magnitude of that success. It accomplished what it set out to do—evolve a practical type of flying machine—a type so remarkably perfect that all progress since has lain in details adapting it to the various uses to which it has been put. A.E.A. machines not only won the Scientific American Prize in 1908, and the International prize in France the next year, but they are the only type of biplanes successfully flying today. This is the type with which the wonderful aerial biplane battles have been fought over the battlefields of the Great War. French, English, German, Italian—all are typical Aerial Experiment Association machines.

"This is because the Aerial Experiment associates were the first of all men to discover, describe and apply the fundamental principles underlying all really practical biplane construction. The Wrights did not. Their type, as well as all others, have been discarded for ours. Curtiss, who knew every secret of the A.E.A., tried to find other methods and failed utterly. He changed a few unessential details but his claim of having got around our principles had no more justification than would an assertion that putting the Bell Receiver in a slightly different holder made it no longer the Bell Receiver. Those biplanes you saw flying overhead and thought of as Curtiss biplanes are not really Curtiss biplanes at all, they are Baldwin biplanes constructed on A.E.A. principles, just as are every other biplane now flying. The world does not know this—but Curtiss does, and it is due to him that the world does not.

"The other associates were mere enthusiastic boys, totally inexperienced in business, absolutely trustful of him. They were full of eagerness, fresh from college, but with no definite plans or prospects. None of them, or Mr. Bell either, could have conceived that Curtiss was already scheming to betray them all in such a way as to make it practically impossible for them to reap their fair share of their mutual labours. After the Association dissolved, Casey and Douglas were thrown out of work. The machines they had helped to create were sufficiently perfected. To go on tinkering with them would have been a waste of money. Patents had been applied for, but until they were granted, there was scant hope of their getting a hearing from ordinary businessmen.

"Very different was Glenn Curtiss's position. The close of the Association found him in sole possession of its workshop which had been especially equipped for the making of aeroplanes; with men trained to the work and all the expensive, unprofitable, but absolutely necessary, preliminary experimental work done, and without cost to himself, and by a trained mechanical engineer, whose services he could never alone have obtained. No other firm in the country, except perhaps the Wrights, was in such a favourable position to grasp the great opportunity to inaugurate a new business with immense possibilities.

"He owed his introduction to the A.E.A. to his own energy and enterprise in having the fastest and lightest going motor then known in America. But the equipping of his shop, the training of his men and the doing of the experimental work he owed to my money, Dr. Bell's brains, and those of the other associates—all unobtainable otherwise. Curtiss himself had contributed little of value, apart from the fitting of his motor, to the development of the aeroplanes. Indeed it was not he, but Herring, who designed the camouflaged A.E.A. machine in which he later won the International Prize.

"Casey departed with us. Douglas, helped once more by Mr. Bell, struggled alone for awhile but discredited by Curtiss accomplished nothing and finally was glad to accept a position with Curtiss as a pilot—a position that acknowledged in no way his former equality with Curtiss. Well, the years passed. Curtiss, having squeezed Herring dry, tried to throw him off also, but is now defendant in a suit Herring has brought with good chance of winning. By various means—

wrecking one of his companies for instance, so that the Wrights could not collect on his infringement of their royalties—royalties which he would not have had to pay, had he stood squarely on our patents—Curtiss has amassed millions, and the rest of us have had to accept—almost as a gratuity—a few thousands and stock in a questionable company; and to share this little with Curtiss too!...

"In 1917 as in 1878, men who could invent things people wanted were opposed by men, strong and unscrupulous, who knew better how to sell them. The vital difference was Gardiner G. Hubbard. But for him, Mr. Bell probably would have been put off with a few thousands. Had a man like Mr. Hubbard, a born promoter—developer would be the truer word—been on our side in 1917, things might have been different now. Certainly he would not have yielded without a struggle as was done. Glenn Curtiss stands before the public, a conspicuous figure, a millionaire, a successful man, who has developed a wonderful new industry. Casey Baldwin does not. Mr. Bell's name is rarely mentioned with aviation. Now, once again Graham Bell and Casey Baldwin have something to offer the world.

"As you say, just now the wonder of flying a hundred or two hundred miles in the air and of crossing the Atlantic in an air machine, appeals more to the imagination than just skimming the surface of the water at a paltry seventy or eighty miles an hour, but even these amazing feats will pall as they become the commonplaces of every day and the water highway will resume interest. So the question I am asking today is: 'Must the experience of the A.E.A. be repeated, or is there any way by which some honour and pecuniary reward may be assured to those who have rightfully earned them?' ...What I am looking for is someone who is willing to be the leader of a forlorn hope, for this is about the size of our job. Nevertheless, it is a big undertaking, worth a big man's best efforts and full of big possibilities. Nothing less in fact than the attempt to revolutionize our age-long methods of water travel. Where shall I find him? I feel I have set myself a job on the face of it as absurd as the mouse's offer to help the lion. But she succeeded! Any suggestions thankfully received."[21]

David and Daisy, though now better informed on the history of Curtiss and Baldwin, were unable to help. Casey turned to his brother-in-law, Colonel John F. Lash, a Toronto lawyer. They planned to join forces with Italian developer, Forlanini, and three Americans—Dr. Peter Cooper-Hewitt, W. M. Meacham and L. E. Meacham—all of whom held various patents crucial to the hydrofoil. The group gained control of the Forlanini and Cooper-Hewitt patents and arranged a solid agreement with the Meachams; however, nothing of a commercial nature materialized. Colonel Lash became president of Bell-Baldwin Hydrodromes Limited, but he lacked the Yankee persistence and foresight of Gardiner Hubbard that had ensured the telephone's success. Despite its world-record speeds and obvious potential, the hydrodrome was doomed as an idea ahead of its time. Fifty years later, it would experience a rebirth when the Canadian naval hydrofoil, *Bras d'Or,* achieved the technological triumph and international acceptance that Aleck and Casey had predicted.

EPILOGUE

Baddeck, 31 July 1922

The night sky glowed with what seemed like billions of stars, and a huge yellow moon hung in the sky. Aleck lay on his verandah bed, bundled in blankets, his eyes half closed. Mabel sat next to him, holding his big bear paw of a hand in hers. Her thoughts moved through the years, fastening now and again on a scene or a conversation.

Two years ago they had returned to Edinburgh. Aleck had said it would be their last trip, but she hadn't listened. "We'll come again and again," she had told him. He hadn't argued, but he had known.

And how upset he had been with his boyhood home, the home that had remained frozen only in his mind. The grassy fields of his youth had been paved over, and the old buildings had been torn down.

Worse, most of those he had known were dead. He found, at last, one old school chum from the Royal High School and the two of them had spent a day chuckling over boyhood pranks and adventures. "The world has spun past us," Aleck had muttered. "The end of our road is over the horizon."

The trip had depressed both of them. But as they were about to leave, they were summoned back and Aleck was presented to his old high school as its most famous old boy. Immediately thereafter had come official recognition from the City of Edinburgh, complete with pomp and circumstance. With tears in his eyes, Aleck accepted the silver casket of the Freedom of the City of Edinburgh, then told the audience, "I have received many honours in the course of my life, but none that has so touched my heart as this gift of the freedom of my native city."

The next day, Mabel recalled, the newspapers proclaimed that not even the city's association with Sir Walter Scott had brought it as much pride and honour as had Alexander Graham Bell.

She smiled faintly at the thought of his pleasure and remembered that he had been more or less asleep when presented with a similar award from the Emperor of Japan. His recognition by Edinburgh had been followed by many more honours, as though the world knew his end was approaching. No one, Mabel thought, realized how very much those honours meant to him.

For a few moments she closed her eyes, realizing that she too was tired. Dreams flooded over her—disjointed dreams of Aleck telling stories to the grandchildren who delighted at his imitation of bears and sheep, and who sat transfixed by his tales. Images of Beinn Bhreagh filled her thoughts. It had become a huge, family summer resort and its summers past washed over her like the incoming tide.

"Are you awake, Mama?"

Mabel's eyes snapped open. Daisy was there, with David Fairchild, her husband, standing behind her. They had arrived a few days ago, and to her relief taken over the household and helped to provide an around-the-clock watch over Aleck who appeared to be fading by the moment.

"Yes, I was just thinking, maybe half dreaming."

"Do you want David to sit with Daddysan for awhile?"

Mabel shook her head. "No, I want to stay for a bit. I'll call if I want someone to take over."

They both nodded and Daisy bent over and kissed her father's forehead.

The day before, David had entered the library to find Aleck bundled in blankets and reading a book. He beckoned David to come in and sit with him awhile. They discussed his illness. David inquired whether the source of the problem might be "electrical." Aleck was too tired to consider the possibility. "Je ne sais pas, monsieur. Je ne sais pas," he replied.

Later, he dictated a memo to Catherine MacKenzie. "I want to say that ... Mrs. Bell and I have both had a very happy life together and we couldn't have had better daughters than Elsie and Daisy, or better sons-in-law than Bert and David and we couldn't have had finer grand-children.... We want to stand by Casey as he has stood by us ... want to look upon Casey and his wife Kathleen as sort of children." He sighed and sank back into his pillows. That evening the night sky glowed with a billion stars and a huge yellow moon.

Mabel gave an involuntary shudder and inhaled deeply. The fragrance of flowers from her garden outside filled the verandah. How Aleck loved the smell of her flowers. His breathing became slower and laboured. Midnight passed. She sat with him, holding his hand, feeling his life slipping away. He made a strange gurgling sound. She leaned forward apprehensively. His breathing stopped. His eyes were closed.

"Don't leave me ... Aleck, don't leave me," she whispered urgently.

His bright black eyes opened for a moment. He looked at her with a gentle smile and squeezed her hand. Then she felt his fingers relax, as his spirit took flight.

"Oh, Aleck," she said as the tears began streaming down her face. A terrible emptiness enveloped her in spite of her Daisy and David. She felt lonely and somehow mutilated, as though an appendage had been cut off.

"You promised," she whispered. "You promised not to leave."

"Come, Mama. It's all right."

She felt Daisy's hand on her shoulder and knew that her child was calling her back—I won't be long, she thought silently. We belong together.

Mabel cabled to Bert and Elsie the following morning, "Father died peacefully today. Only within a few days did we realize any danger." Daisy knew how badly her sister and Bert must have felt about not being there when their mother needed them most—and in missing the funeral. She wrote her sister a detailed account of their father's passing.

"One could not wish for a more beautiful ending. He was in the porch with the fresh air about him and it was a beautiful moonlight night and not cold.... I don't think you need fear that Mother will break down.... It makes you cry to see her. She goes on just as usual—makes all the motions—laughs and talks but you never forget for a moment that the heart of everything has gone out of her life forever. She isn't wearing mourning clothes.... Up here, it has seemed so natural and so beautiful an ending. There was no crepe on the door—no drawn blinds—the children played about and ran up and down stairs—there was no feeling at all that death was terrible.

The men in the laboratory made the coffin out of good rugged pine and forged the iron handles. It was lined with aeroplane linen. The children made a pall of green, entirely covered with balsam fir. They cut the branches very short.... If you had seen them fitting it over the coffin themselves and doing it so sweetly and seriously, so glad there was something they too could do for Grampy, you would be thankful for them that death can never seem a thing to fear.

"The only flowers on the coffin were from the American Tel and Tel Company. The wreath must have been chosen by someone 'with tenderness and imagination,' Mother feels. It was made of laurel, sheaves of wheat and pink roses, and Mother feels they were chosen—'the laurel for victory, the wheat for the gathered harvest and the roses for gentleness and sweetness.'

"Mother stepped forward and stood alone with her arm resting on the coffin, bare-headed and in white with a soft white scarf around her neck while the Rev. John MacKinnon read a few verses from the 90th Psalm—just the beautiful ones, skipping the others. Miss Jean MacDonald sang "Where Grew a Bonnie Briar Bush" and then played Mendelssohn's funeral march as they carried him out....

"There were a great many people there. The grave was blasted out of the rock and lined with fir boughs—and there was a steel vault—in case mother feels later she wants father to go back to America. On the right the American flag and on the left the British were at half-mast on short poles. Miss MacDonald sang the verses and we all joined in singing the chorus of "Bringing in the Sheaves." Mother watched Miss MacDonald's face and joined in.... Miss MacDonald's voice is beautiful and she sang so that every word was understood. She sang right to Mother. The music of it is as beautiful as the words and as she sang, we looked over the beautiful stretch of water and hills and sky and it was gray and misty as Father loved it best.... The coffin was lowered into the grave. "Lord, now let thou thy servant depart in peace. May the peace of God that passeth all understanding be with you and remain with you always, amen."[1]

On the day of the funeral, 4 August, at 6:25 P. M., all across North America telephone services paused for one minute. The flags in front of every building belonging to the Bell Telephone System were lowered to half-mast. Then the ceaseless heartbeat of global communications resumed.

In the months that followed, Mabel was constantly tired; nevertheless, she made preparations to continue all of Aleck's unfinished work with the help of Casey Baldwin and signed a ten-year contract with him for $10,000 per annum. Projects such as Sheepville, a new water condenser and further development on the HD-4 were to be carried on.

In late September the principal of the Clarke School for the Deaf offered her Aleck's position on the Board of Trustees and she accepted. Earlier, she had written to Bert that she felt it important that family members stay involved in the Clarke School, because it had been Aleck's proudest achievement.[2]

Her health began to fail noticeably in November. Elsie wrote to Bert, "Mama is not well. She has no appetite and her food disturbs her when she eats it. Her symptoms are somewhat like Papa's. Please consult Dr. Foot and let me know. We cannot allow this condition to run on as Papa's did."[3]

Elsie took Mabel to Washington in December to see the doctor. The diagnosis was cancer. She was given six weeks. Daisy took her mother home and put her to bed. Late one evening in December Mabel remarked to her daughter, "Wasn't I clever not to get ill until Daddysan didn't need me any more."[4]

She missed Aleck terribly. On 1 January she wrote to Bert, expressing her concerns about his biography. "You must see that the biography does not picture Father as a perfect man. He was a very clever man and a good man, but he had his faults, just like every other human being. And I loved him for his faults."[5] She died two days later.

One year to the day after Aleck's simple funeral, they buried her, as she had wished, alongside her husband on the summit of Beinn Bhreagh. The Rev. John MacKinnon scheduled a small family service at precisely five o'clock, the time when Mabel had always met Aleck at his laboratory and walked home with him hand in hand. There was no sadness. The day was clear and beautiful. Occasional rainbows of wildflowers splashed the surrounding hills. Once again the Rev. MacKinnon intoned, "Lord, now let thy servants depart in peace."

Tears streamed down Daisy's face as she clenched David's hand. Everyone was there—Casey, and Douglas, faithful Charles Thompson and all the grandchildren. The day warm and clear, with only a slight breeze moving the leaves. As they paused before the grave atop the summit of Beinn Bhreagh, Daisy's eyes strayed to the profusion of wild flowers in the meadow, then to her father's headstone. She pressed her lips together as her mother's small coffin was lowered into the grave.

It was suddenly silent, as silent as she could ever remember—but only for a moment. A breeze broke through the trees and the tall grass, and the leaves whispered audibly as though her father were greeting her mother, as though the sound had enveloped the silence for all eternity.

"In death as in life," Daisy whispered.

⁓

It has been conservatively estimated that over one and a half billion people on earth owe their livelihood and well being—at least in part—to the genius of Alexander Graham Bell.

Halifax, Nova Scotia
30 June 1995

⁓

351

ENDNOTES

Chapter 1

1 *Beinn Bhreagh Recorder* XXIV.
2 Bell vs Murray 1833, Scottish court record office.
3 Ibid.
4 D. Bell letter 13 Sept. 1837
5 Ibid.
6 From a letter to his mother and sister Elizabeth, 22 Sept. 1838.
7 *Beinn Bhreagh Recorder* XXV, p. 86.
8 *Beinn Bhreagh Recorder.*
9 Ibid, "Delirious from Scarlet Fever."
10 Ibid, "Stealing a postage stamp and telling a lie."
11 Ibid, Vol 9, poetry selections by young A. G. B.
12 Ibid, Vol 5, "My First Invention."
13 Ibid, Vol 5, "Juvenile Research."
14 Ibid, Vol 5, "Moral Education in Childhood."
15 Ibid.
16 Shaw, G. B., *Pygmalion*. (first Published 1916, London) Penguin Books Ltd. Harmondsworth, England, Published in 1957.
17 *Beinn Bhreagh Recorder*, "Life with my Grandfather" from dictated notes of 1906, p 49.
18 Ibid, p. 73, 1903.
19 Ibid.
20 Ibid, p. 70.
21 A rubbery substance derived from the sap of the genera Palaquim and Payena rubber trees.

Chapter 3

1 Alexander Bell to Alexander Melville Bell, 1864.
2 A. Ellis to Melville Bell, 29 Aug. 1864; *London Morning Star*, 31 Aug. 1864.

Chapter 4

1 Journals of Mabel Hubbard, Vol 103
2 *Beinn Bhreagh Recorder*, "Recollections of Mary True." Vol. 214. p. 56.
3 Over a million in today's dollars.
4 *Conquest of Solitude* by Robert Bruce, p. 86.
5 Journals of Mabel Hubbard, Vol 103.

6 Mabel's letters to her mother, Vol 77.

7 Journals of Mabel Hubbard, Vol 103.

8 Mabel's letter to her mother, Vol 77.

9 Journals of Mabel Hubbard, Vol 103.

10 Journals of Mabel Hubbard, Vol 104.

11 Ibid, Vol 104.

12 Ibid.

Chapter 5

1 *Conquest of Solitude* , p. 43.

2 Eliza Bell to Aleck, 13 Jan. 1866.

3 Alexander Ellis to Aleck, 32 March 1865.

4 Aleck to Mrs. A. Acklone, 7 Sept. 1906.

5 A. Ellis to S. Haldeman, 16 July 1866.

6 Aleck to Eliza and Melville, 9 June 1867.

7 Aleck to parents, 11 June 1867.

8 "Scribbling Diary," 1867.

9 A. Scott to Melville Bell, 12 Oct. 1903 and to Mabel Bell, 26 March 1918.

10 No relation to the Wm. Murry who caused the Alexander Bell divorce in 1828.

11 Eliza Bell to Aleck, 1 June 1867.

12 *Beinn Bhreagh Recorder,* "Teaching a Dog to Talk," pp. 100–101 from notes dictated in 1900, pp. 55.

13 Ibid.

14 Biographical material extracted from Aleck's journal, 21 May 1868, Vol. 126.

15 Aleck to Melville Bell, 29 Sept. 1868.

16 Eliza Bell to Melville, 8 Aug., 30 Sept. 1868.

17 Melville Bell to Eliza, 23 Aug. 1869.

18 First Prime Minister of Canada.

19 Developed international standard time.

20 Eliza to Melville, 16 Sept. 1868.

21 Melville Bell Jr. to Aleck, 1 April 1870.

22 Aleck to Mabel Bell, 26 Sept. 1875.

23 Marie Ecclestone to Aleck 2 July 1870.

24 Aleck to Eliza and Melville, 30 June 1875.

Chapter 6

1 About $30,000 in current purchasing power.

2 Alexander Graham Bell to his parents, 16 April 1871.

3 Ibid.

Chapter 7

1 Journals of Mabel Hubbard, Vol 103.
2 Aleck to his parents, 1872.
3 Journals of Mabel Hubbard, Jan. 1873.
4 Ibid.
5 Letters of Mabel to her mother, Vol. 78.

Chapter 8

1 Daughters of the celebrated American poet and close friends of the Hubbard family.
2 Gertrude to Gardiner Hubbard, 14 Feb. 1874.
3 Aleck to his parents, 8 March 1874.

Chapter 9

1 Mabel's Journal, 6 Jan. 1879.

Chapter 10

1 Mabel Hubbard to Gertrude, 2 August 1875.

Chapter 11

1 Mabel to Aleck, 16 Feb. 1876.
2 Aleck to Mabel, 17 Feb. 1876.
3 Aleck to Melville Bell, 7 March 1876.
4 *Boston Transcript,* 31 May 1876.
5 Aleck to Mabel, 6 April 1877.
6 Aleck to Miss Fuller, 25 June 1877.
7 Mabel to Gertrude Hubbard, July 1877.
8 Mabel to Melville Bell, 30 July 1877.

Chapter 12

1 Aleck to Eliza Bell, Aug. 1877.
2 Mabel wrote Aleck's name as "Alec" in her correspondence.
3 Mabel to Gertrude Hubbard, 11 Aug. 1877.
4 Ibid, 15 Aug. 1877.
5 Ibid, 27 Sept. 1877.
6 Ibid.
7 Ibid, 8 Oct. 1877.

8 Ibid, 10 Nov. 1877.

9 Ibid.

10 Ibid, 27 Nov. 1877.

11 Ibid, 21 Nov. 1877.

12 Ibid, 11 Dec. 1877.

13 Ibid.

14 Ibid, 26 Dec. 1877.

15 Ibid.

16 Ibid.

17 Ibid, 4 Jan. 1878.

18 Ibid.

19 Ibid, 9 Jan. 1878.

20 Ibid, 12 Jan. 1878.

21 Ibid, 26 Feb. 1879.

22 Aleck to Gertrude Hubbard, 21 Feb. 1878.

23 Gertrude Hubbard to Gardiner Hubbard, 17 April 1878.

24 Mabel to Gertrude Hubbard, 10 May 1878.

25 Aleck to Mabel, 5 Sept. 1878.

Chapter 13

1 Mabel to Aleck, 21 Aug. 1878.

2 Aleck to Mabel, 21 Aug. 1878.

3 Aleck to Mabel, 9 Sept. 1878.

4 Mabel to Gertrude Hubbard, 15 Nov. 1878.

5 Aleck to Mabel, Nov. 1878.

6 Aleck to Mabel, March 1879.

7 Mabel Bell Journal, March 1879.

8 Mabel to Aleck, 9 March 1879.

9 Aleck to Mabel, 12 March 1879.

10 Mabel Bell Journal, March 1879.

11 Ibid, 12 Aug. 1879.

12 Ibid, March 1879.

13 Ibid, 14 Feb. 1879.

14 Ibid, 23 Feb. 1879.

15 Ibid, 12 Feb. 1879.

16 Aleck to Mabel, March 1879.

17 Aleck to Mabel 11 Jan. 1879.

18 Mabel to Aleck, 9 March 1879.

19 Aleck to Thomas Edison, 25 May 1879.

Chapter 14

1 Mabel Bell Journal, 26 March 1879.

2 Mabel Bell to Eliza Bell, 14 Dec. 1879.

3 Ibid, 20 Jan. 1880.

4 Ibid, 20 Feb. 1880.

5 Mabel Bell to Gertrude Hubbard, 5 July 1880.

6 Mabel to Aleck, 19 June 1880.

7 Mabel to Gertrude Hubbard, 24 June 1881.

8 Ibid, 5 July 1881.

9 Mabel to Eliza Bell, 17 July 1881.

10 Mabel to Aleck, 16 July 1881.

11 Aleck to Mabel, 26 July 1881.

12 Mabel to Aleck, 24 July 1881.

13 Mabel to Aleck 1 Aug. 1881.

14 Aleck to Mabel, 19 Sept. 1881.

15 Mabel and Aleck to Eliza Bell, 28 Sept. 1881.

Chapter 15

1 Victorian custom dictated that a woman use the prefix of her husband's Christian name.

2 Mabel to Gertrude Hubbard, 9 April 1882.

3 *Science* magazine, June 1882.

4 S. Scudder to J. L. LeConte, 19 Nov. 1882.

5 American Association for the Advancement of Science.

6 Mabel Bell Journal, Feb. 1884.

7 Ibid, Oct. 1884.

8 Ibid, 14 Nov. 1884.

9 Mabel Bell Journal, Sept. 1885.

Chapter 16

1 Mabel Bell's Journal, 25 Oct. 1885.

2 Ibid, 19 Nov. 1885.

3 Mabel to Eliza Bell, 17 July 1881.

4 Helen Keller, *The Story of My Life,* 1902.

5 Mabel Bell Journal, 30 June 1887.

6 Mabel to Aleck, 18 June 1888.

Chapter 17

1 Mabel to Aleck, 18 June 1888.

2 Aleck to Mabel, 29 June 1888.
3 Mabel Bell to Gertrude Hubbard, 17 Sept. 1890.
4 Mabel to Aleck, 18 Jan. 1891.
5 Mabel to Aleck, 29 April 1891.
6 It still exists and is the oldest ladies' club in Canada.
7 Mabel to Elsie Bell, Nov. 1891.
8 Mary Blatchford letters, *Beinn Bhreagh Recorder,* Vol. 23.
9 Mabel to Aleck, 21 April 1891.
10 Aleck to Mabel, 15 June 1891.
11 Aleck to Mabel, 23 July 1895.

Chapter 18

1 Mabel to Aleck, 12 May 1895.
2 Ibid, 25 May 1895.
3 Mabel to Aleck, 2 June 1895.
4 Aleck to A. McCurdy, 13 Dec. 1896.
5 Mabel to Daisy Bell, Dec. 1896.
6 A statement made by Mabel Bell, June 1922, when she felt the model should be held at the Smithsonian Institute for safe keeping.

Chapter 19

1 Mabel to Daisy Bell, Oct. 1897.
2 Mabel to Mrs. Kennan, 22 Jan. 1898.
3 Aleck to various publishers, 16 Aug. 1899.
4 Mabel to Gertrude Hubbard, 15 Nov. 1898.

Chapter 20

1 Mabel to Gertrude Hubbard, 9 Jan. 1878.
2 Mabel to Elsie Grosvenor, 11 Feb. 1901.
3 Mabel to Gertrude Hubbard, Aug. 1905.
4 Helen Keller, *The Story of My Life,* 1902.
5 Ibid. Speculation remains that the idea for the telephone began as an instrument to help the deaf, Mabel in particular. Bell never confirmed this fact.
6 Ibid.
7 Recollections of Mayme Morrison Brown, *Genius at Work,* Nimbus Publishing, Halifax.
8 *Beinn Bhreagh Recorder,* "Life with Grandfather Grosvenor," 17 Sept. 1910.
9 Bell, "Tetrahedral Principle," pp. 231–248.

10 Mabel to Elsie, 9 Aug. 1905.

11 From the eulogy given by Aleck at Langley's funeral.

12 Mabel to Daisy Fairchild, undated, 1906.

13 Mabel to Gertrude Hubbard, 7 Nov. 1907.

14 Experimental flights by the Wright brothers had always been conducted in the greatest secrecy while they attempted to try and correct a variety of stability problems in the design of their flying machines.

15 A process that is still used today on the fabric-covered aircraft surfaces.

16 Daisy Fairchild to Mabel, July 1908.

17 David Fairchild, *The World Was My Garden,* p. 344, New York Charles Scribner's & Sons Ltd., 1945.

18 Mabel to Aleck, 17 Sept. 1908.

19 Mabel to Daisy Fairchild, 23 Feb. 1909.

20 Ibid, 24 Feb. 1909.

Chapter 21

1 Mabel to Aleck, April 1909.

2 Mabel to Daisy Fairchild, Aug. 1909.

3 Mabel to Aleck, 8 Nov. 1909.

4 Mabel to Elsie Grosvenor, 17 March 1911.

5 Mabel to Daisy and David Fairchild, 1 Sept. 1908. The family occasionally attached "san" to his name after their visit to Japan.

6 Gaelic words for "Little Devil."

7 Mabel to Daisy and David Fairchild, 1 Sept. 1908.

8 Probably due to engine vibration causing structural fatigue, a phenomena unknown in 1912.

9 *Beinn Bhreagh Recorder,* Mary Blatchford letters, Vol. 23.

10 Grosvenor, "Life With Grandfather."

11 Recollections of Mrs. Barbara Muller (Fairchild) given to author, Sept. 1984.

12 Ibid.

13 Recollections of Dr. Mabel Grosvenor, given to author, Sept. 1984.

14 Recollections of Mrs. Gertrude Cayley, given to author, Sept. 1984.

15 Ibid.

16 Recollections of Mrs. Carol Myers, given to author, Sept. 1984.

17 Recollections of Mrs. Barbara Muller, given to author, Sept. 1984.

18 Ibid.

19 Mabel to Daisy Fairchild, 24 June. 1917.

20 Home Notes, Vol. 106.

21 Mabel to David Fairchild, Apr. 1919.

Epilogue

1 Daisy Fairchild to Elsie Grosvenor, 6 Aug. 1922.
2 Her wishes were observed and a family member has been on the board ever since.
3 Elsie Grosvenor to Bert Grosvenor, 5 Nov. 1922.
4 Recollections of Daisy Fairchild.
5 Memorandum, G. Grosvenor, 1 Jan. 1923.

BIBLIOGRAPHY

Primary Unpublished Sources

Dr. Mabel Grosvenor
Dr. Alexander Graham Bell Fairchild
Mrs. Gertrude Cayley
Mrs. Carol Myers
Mrs. Barbara Muller
Polly Dobson
Additional source material provided by Lilias Toward Q.C., Halifax, Nova Scotia

Published Sources

Alexander Graham Bell Museum, Baddeck, Nova Scotia.
AT & T, Historical collection.
Beinn Bhreagh Recorder, mimeographed periodical issued on an irregular basis between 1909 and 1923 by A. G. Bell.
Bell, Alexander Melville, *Visible Speech: The Science of Universal Alphabetics*, London, 1867.
Bell Telephone Collection, Montreal.
Bruce, Robert V. *BELL: Alexander Graham Bell and the Conquest of Solitude*, Little, Brown and Company, Boston, 1973.
Eber, Dorothy Harley, *Genius At Work*, Nimbus Publishing, Halifax, 1993.
Fairchild, David, "Alexander Graham Bell: Some Characters of His Greatness," *Journal of Heredity* XIII, 1923.
———. *The World was My Garden*, New York, 1939.
Grosvenor, Lilian, "My Grandfather Bell," *The New Yorker*, 11 November 1950.
Parks Canada.
Public Archives of Canada.
Public Archives of Nova Scotia—PANS.
The Bell Homestead, Brantford, Ontario.
The Bell Institute, Baddeck, Nova Scotia.
The *Halifax Herald* archives.
The National Geographic Society.
The *Toronto Globe* archives, *The Globe and Mail*, Toronto, Ontario.
The United States Library of Congress.
Toward, Lilias M., *Mabel Bell: Alexander's Silent Partner*. Methuen, Toronto, 1984.
Watson, Thomas A., *Exploring Life*, New York, 1926.
Wisconsin Phonological Institute, *Improvement of the Wisconsin System of Education for Deaf Mutes*, Milwaukee, 1894.